Marketing Handbook

For The Design & Construction Professional

Society for Marketing Professional Services

BNi. Building News

BNi. Building News

Editor-In-Chief
William D. Mahoney, P.E.

Graphic/Technical Services
Eric Mahoney
Guillermo Chavez-Zavala
Rod A. Yabut

Cover Design
Robert O. Wright

BNi PUBLICATIONS, INC.

LOS ANGELES
10801 National Blvd., Ste.100
Los Angeles, CA 90064

ANAHEIM
1612 S. Clementine St.
Anaheim, CA 92802

NEW ENGLAND
PO BOX 14527
East Providence, RI 02914

WASHINGTON,D.C.
502 Maple Ave. West
Vienna, VA 22180

1-800-873-6397

ISBN 1-55701-369-1

Table of Contents

Authors

Carol A. Adey, FSMPS
President
Adey Associates

Randy Anagnostis, FSMPS
President
Anagnostis Associates Inc.

Bruce A. Babiarz, APR
Director of Marketing
Ghafari Associates Inc.

George Biderman, FSMPS
Director of Business Development
Fru-Con Construction Corp.

Dana L. Birkes, CPSM

Lois E. Boemer, FSMPS
Principal
BA Communications

Edward Bond Jr., FSMPS
CEO
Bond Bros. Inc.

Joan Capelin, FSMPS
President
Capelin Communications Inc.

C. Ronald Capps
Managing Director and Partner
The Beck Group

Jane Cohn, FSMPS
Principal
Jane Cohn Public Relations

John Coyne, FSMPS, APR
President
Coyne Associates, Marketing and
    Public Relations Associates

Charles C. Crevo, Ph.D., FSMPS
Senior Associate
Louis Berger & Associates Inc.

Susan R. Daylor, FSMPS
Principal
Mariposa Consulting

Rose M. Dela Vega
Vice President
RTKL Associates Inc.

Kenneth G. Diehl Jr., P.E.
Vice President of Marketing and
    Business Development
Smith Seckman Reid Inc.

Ellen Flynn-Heapes, FSMPS
President
SPARKS: The Center for Strategic Planning

Rena Frankle, CPSM
Principal
Reichman Frankle Inc.

Rolf Fuessler, APR
President
Fuessler Group Inc.

Ron W. Garikes, FSMPS
Senior Vice President
Karlsberger

Barry R. Gaston
Business Development Manager
Harley Ellis

Ford Harding
President
Harding & Co.

Betty Hearn, FSMPS
Business Development Manager
Carlson

Richard T. Hewlett, Esq.
Butzel Long P.C.

Graham K. Hill, P.E.
President and CEO
Tomlin Inc.

J. Michael Huget, Esq.
Butzel Long P.C.

Ellen Jackson

Brian J. Lewis, P.E.
Principal
The Brian J. Lewis Co.

Dianne Ludman Frank, FSMPS
Principal
Dianne Ludman Frank Public Relations

Julie G. Luers, FSMPS
Director of Marketing
TSP

Sheryl B. Maibach, FSMPS
Vice President
Barton Malow Co.

Laurin McCracken, AIA, MCRS, FSMPS
Chief Executive Officer
Global Design Alliance

Trude Noble
Vice President and Marketing Manager
Wade-Trim

Amy Ostigny, CPSM

Dennis A. Paoletti, CPSM, FAIA
President
Paoletti Associates Inc.

Craig Park, FSMPS
Vice President, Integrated Solutions
Intellisys Group Inc.

Randle Pollock, FSMPS
Regional Director
Carlson

Lisbeth Quebe, FSMPS
Vice President of Marketing
RTKL Associates Inc.

J. Rossi
Vice President
HLM Design

Janet S. Sanders, Ph.D., CPSM
Clayton Consulting Group

Dennis B. Schultz, Esq.
Butzel Long P.C.

Wendy Sherrill
Marketing Coordinator
Wade-Trim

Bonnie Sloan, FSMPS
Principal
The Learning Curve

Thomas E. Smith Jr., AICP, FSMPS
President
BonTerra Consulting

Julie S. Stanton, CPSM
Marketing and Communications Consultant

Randolph W. Tucker, P.E.
Senior Vice President
The RJA Group Inc.

Philip F. Valence, FSMPS
President
Blackridge Ltd.

Jean R. Valence, FSMPS
Vice President
Blackridge Ltd.

Sandra J. Werthman
Vice President of Marketing
Kitchell Contractors Inc.

Karen W. Winters, FSMPS
Associate and Director of Marketing and
    Administration
King & King, Architects

Nadine R. Yates, CPSM
Principal
N.R. Yates and Associates

Reviewers

Phil E. Bannan, CPSM
Director, Business Development
Gillan & Hartmann Inc.

Karleen Belmont, CPSM
President
KB Consultants

Mary Findlen, FSMPS
Corporate Communications
URS Greiner Woodward Clyde

Kay C. Godwin, CPSM
Principal
Marketing Avenues

Renee M. Godwin, CPSM
Corporate Marketing Manager
W&H Pacific

Sue Gonsior
Marketing Manager
Ellerbe Becket

Jeanne L. Harwin, CPSM
Director
Sverdrup Civil Inc.

Peter J. Kienle, CPSM
Director of Marketing/Business Development
Moody/Nolan Ltd.

Linda M. Koch, CPSM
Director of Marketing
BSC Group Inc.

Michael F. Lehnhoff, P.E., CPSM
Vice President
EDM Incorporated

Julie A. Olson, CPSM
Director of Project Services
ARCHITECTS Barrentine.Bates.Lee AIA

Dennis Schrag, Ed.D., CPSM
Corporate Marketing Manager
The Stanley Group

Nancy D. Sullivan, CPSM
Manager, Marketing and Communications
Symmes Maini & McKee Associates

Introduction

Laurin McCracken, AIA, MCRS, FSMPS

The Society for Marketing Professional Services (SMPS) was chartered more than 25 years ago to serve the needs of individuals who market architectural, engineering, interior design, construction, and related services that create the built environment. Through its formation and growth, SMPS created the profession of professional services marketing. Today, marketing is an integral part of almost all the services that design and build the environment in which we live, work, and play.

Over the years, SMPS has helped create and identify the leaders in this profession. It is those leaders who were called upon to revise and expand the *Handbook for Marketing Professional Services*. The original handbook was created to fill a gap that existed in the literature of marketing. While much has been written about product marketing, little has been written about services marketing and even less about marketing services for the built environment.

The original handbook was edited by Ellen Jackson Biancanello. Ellen worked with the SMPS staff to identify the "experts" in many of the facets that make up services marketing. She then prodded and cajoled us to write chapters that were folded together to create the first edition.

When SMPS created its Certified Professional Services Marketer Program, the lack of published material in this special area of marketing again became apparent. Even the books that many of us had used as our basic texts — those by Weld Coxe and Jerry Jones, as well as the original edition of the *Handbook for Marketing Professional Services* — had gone out of print. There was a clear need for an updated, broad-based book covering the many aspects of professional services marketing.

The SMPS Foundation decided the creation of this new handbook edition was in keeping with its mission of education, research, and scholarship in support of the members of SMPS. The Foundation trustees, aided by the able stewardship of Lisa Jenkins, were glad to lead this effort. Sheryl Maibach, FSMPS, Foundation president, set ambitious goals in terms of the schedule and quality for this publication. We, the trustees of the Foundation, are pleased to report that this edition lives up to — and exceeds — those goals.

Many of the original authors, including me, have updated their material and much has been added. The original book had 44 chapters. The book you are holding has eight additional chapters. Many of these new chapters are reflective of how much more mature and complex the process of marketing professional services has become.

SMPS National and the SMPS Foundation Board would like to thank the 50 authors who contributed to this publication. We also would like to thank those who worked unselfishly as reviewers and coordinators in the effort to make this handbook readable and press-ready. Our collective goal has been to create a handbook that will become the indispensable publication for those involved in marketing professional services for the built environment. We hope this edition will become a well-worn volume on the bookshelves of the many individuals who market professional services around the world.

We welcome your comments and suggestions. These will help us make future editions of this handbook even better.

Washington, DC
November 1999

Society for Marketing Professional Services
99 Canal Center Plaza #250
Alexandria, VA 22314
800-292-7677
www.smps.org

Part 1:
Planning

1.1 Marketing Research: The Road to Profits

Bruce A. Babiarz, APR
Director of Marketing
Ghafari Associates Inc.

Preface

This chapter is geared toward the majority of firms that make up the built environment — the mid-sized and small companies. While larger companies may also glean a few things from this chapter, it is the author's fervent hope that the larger players in the industry have already incorporated market research and the broader role of marketing into their firms. If marketing and market research are not the driving forces in your company, it's not too late to make a priority change that should be driven from the top down and bottom up!

— **Bruce Babiarz**

"Thinking is the hardest work there is, which is probably the reason why so few engage in it."

— **Henry Ford**

I think it entirely apropos that a book published by the Society for Marketing Professional Services (SMPS) about marketing should start with a chapter about market research. Accordingly, it seems appropriate to lead this chapter with the profound words of one of the greatest thinkers, inventors and, yes, "researchers" of the 20th century: Henry Ford.

The driving forces in the automobile industry at the turn of the century and now are not too much different from those in the built environment today. There is intense competition with a host of quality companies competing for a piece of the existing market share with seemingly few looking at ways to expand the market or enter into new markets. By using proven research methodologies and monitoring marketplace trends, smart, cutting-edge A/E/C firms can leap ahead of their competitors into more profitable work while letting their competitors slug it out in long bid processes for limited margins.

The strong firms in the year 2000 and beyond will embrace research and create new and more lucrative ways of delivering their services to current and new markets. These successful firms will "market" rather than "sell" their professional services to clients and markets they may have never served in the past. What will these forward-thinking firms do differently than their competitors? They will use the latest technologies to see where markets are going rather than where they have been, and they will make marketing and market research as important as any other discipline within their firm. The dinosaurs — those that sell by looking through their rearview mirror — will shrink, be acquired or die.

As a consultant to numerous professional services firms in the past 20 years, I believe the A/E/C industry is the least progressive of the "truly professional" firms that include accountants, lawyers, medical practices and other licensed professions. The upside? Imagine the innovation waiting to happen! I predict a watershed coming in the whole industry. Some firms will sweep out in front, others will go by the wayside. The choice of your firm's direction is really up to you!

Before we get into the heart of research, let's talk for a moment about what your clients want in general. Virtually all clients want a good quality facility as fast as the schedule will allow (and often sooner) and they want it at the lowest price possible. Some clients or prospects may place a higher priority on the schedule, others will focus on cost. Do you really know what your prospect's hot buttons are? What revs their engine? You can find out by conducting primary research and by talking to them in broad terms about expectations. Starting with a current project is a great way to obtain this first-hand information. Please read the chapter about debriefing clients. I would strongly suggest you "pre-brief" clients and customers to learn more about their unique wants and needs before they have a project of any kind. Isn't that what a project manager should be doing? Ideally yes, but few project managers are trained in marketing. The vast majority wants to focus only on the technical aspects of the project.

Henry Ford offered Model T's in any color you wanted — as long as it was black. But the marketplace changed and people not only wanted different colors, they wanted cars to go faster, and market-driven companies soon began offering other features as well. Is your firm holding the line by offering any color you want as long as it's black or are you giving clients what they want? Are you offering services they may not realize they want or need yet? That's the hardest work to do and very few A/E/C firms make the time to do it. Right now we're all too busy getting projects done. Research, innovation, foresight and customer service are placed on the back burner for some time in the future.

Ford discovered that inventing the world's first production assembly line and producing high-quality cars at low cost, faster than anyone, WAS NOT ENOUGH!! How could that be? Think about it. Before long other companies had assembly lines, they offered cars in different colors, and competition became fierce. Are you at the top of your field right now because you produce the highest quality product, quickly and at low cost? That won't be enough to compete effectively in the year 2000 and beyond. In my opinion, the majority of firms have made little effort differentiating themselves from competitors and have miles to go before meeting or anticipating client needs.

(Change, get over it. Embrace it. Better yet, lead it.)

In some cases, speed to the marketplace is more important than cost. For example, one of the major car companies wants to build a facility or assembly plant in an emerging market to capture the growth in car sales in that market. The faster the facility can be delivered and put into production the greater the opportunity to secure market share and establish its brand. Money can be replaced, lost time cannot. Have you helped a client bring its facility into production faster?

There are many outstanding firms in the environmental testing, architectural-engineering and construction fields in the United States and within the cities that make up the local community-based marketplace. Why should a prospective client hire your firm? For some of you, the following pages will be a review of basics, for others a primer on the work you have to do to stay competitive.

Marketing 101

Marketing is everything a firm does to create awareness and demand for its services. Market research is a critical element to defining where you are in the marketplace, who your customers are and what they want, and who your competitors are. What differentiates your firm so that a client would choose you over a competitor? Marketing includes the corporate brochure, segment brochures, fliers and direct mail pieces that keep your name in front of clients and prospects. Marketing includes the database and tracking systems and literally all aspects of the company that involve image and perception in the marketplace. Marketing is the key to success in any organization and should be driven from the top down and the bottom up. Everyone in the firm, regardless of title or position, from the CEO to the receptionist, is a marketer.

Sales 101

Sales is closing the deal, the specific project or program. It's the signing of a contract, the exchange of money for services. Everything up to that point is marketing. It's the difference between winning the new assembly plant and winning a long-term relationship with an automaker. Selling is transactional; marketing is ongoing. You can have the best sales force in the world but if they are selling "buggy whips" instead of leather-covered steering wheels and "interior systems" you won't have any customers.

"Knowledge is power," wrote Sir Francis Bacon. "Imagination is more powerful than knowledge," countered Albert Einstein. Use creativity to create new markets instead of bidding over an existing slice of pie. Henry Ford imagined the gasoline-powered car and created one. Orville and Wilbur Wright turned bicycle parts into flying machines. Where is imagination in the A/E/C industry? Who is offering cutting-edge concepts and highly innovative solutions to client needs?

In the mid-1980s I attended a meeting of the Automotive Press Association at which the chairman of Dana Corp., a global automotive supplier, spoke. Woody Morcott addressed the automotive media on his company's growth plans. He had charts and graphs on the projected growth in consumer demand for pickup trucks and something called sport utility vehicles (SUVs). Morcott explained that, based on the research, his company was gearing up its production capacities to meet this future demand projected over the next decade. The research he cited turned out to be a little inaccurate — future demand was greater than projected and the company sold billions of dollars worth of parts to automakers producing pickup trucks and SUVs. At the time the research was conducted SUVs were not even a blip on the chart of vehicle sales.

So what does this have to do with research in the A/E/C industry? As retired hockey legend Wayne Gretzky said: "Skate to where the puck is going, not where it's been." Are you skating to where the A/E/C market is going or where it's been?

Research is "a systematic investigation in a field of knowledge, to discover facts or principles." Or the "systematic gathering of information for the purpose of describing and understanding situations as a basis for testing informed assumptions."

Simply stated, research is:

- A method of analyzing what has been
- A method of analyzing what is now
- A method of projecting knowledge and imagination to determine what might be, a basis for "testing informed assumptions."

It's the key to getting ready and we know what Henry Ford said about that — it's the key to success. How many of us get ready? As a man who is guilty of "not asking for directions," I reluctantly use this cliché to illustrate that it is better to have a plan, goals and objectives (destination and directions) than it is to simply start driving. I have observed so many firms in our industry driving on the road to the future without maps, business plans or research on their destinations. Because they have profit-producing companies, good reputations and a good product, they think the marketplace — and clients — will always be at their doorstep. These firms better wake up and smell the gas or they'll become the Packard Motor Car Co. of the A/E/C industry.

The RMM Factor — Rearview Mirror Marketing — is already happening in our industry. Many firms were asleep at the drafting table when CADD roared past them. How many have embraced the world wide web, Internet and 3-D graphic animations for virtual reality tours of projects? Driving your business while ignoring what's coming can cause a Really Wicked Crash (RWC) that could severely limit your growth and profitability or even prove fatal. The number of A/E firms is already shrinking — like margins — in the United States, and construction firms can't find the skilled workers they need to produce the work. The human resource requirement has not been a priority so little thought has been given to this area. (Remember, thinking is the hardest work there is.)

The RMM Factor in driving your business is analogous to driving a car. How much time do you spend looking in your rearview mirror? Don't you spend the majority of your time looking through the windshield? You may take advantage of new technologies (or old ones like maps) that help you look forward and focus such as heads-up displays on the windshield or infrared radar that enhances vision at night. You may even have a dash-mounted Global Positioning System (GPS) so you know exactly where you are and have a map at your fingertips for where you want to go. If you're a smart driver, you check the rearview mirror periodically to understand what's immediately behind you and around you to avoid accidents when you're changing lanes, turning or slowing down. Otherwise, you look forward to what's coming and prepare yourself to handle any changes that would impede you from arriving at your destination.

It has been my experience that most professional service firms do not look forward through the windshield and do not have clearly defined "destinations" or goals for the business. In short, they drive until they arrive at places they think they want to do business, or clients flag them down and hire them based on a referral, reputation or geographic location. Some firms have prospered by taking advantage of what comes their way. To those firms ignorance is bliss. They have no way of knowing or quantifying opportunities lost.

Smart firms look through the rearview mirror by conducting research on who their customers and competitors are, why projects were won and lost and what resources were required to win a project or break into a market segment. They focus by market segment and by each customer and conduct thorough research and think about what it took to make success a reality. Like a good auto racing team or other sports team, they replay the videotape of the race event on a VCR and study what went right, what went wrong, as well as opportunities and threats that came up during the race. Think of your marketing director or vice president as the car driver, your CEO as the owner and the rest of the organization as the pit crew. If you don't have a professional marketer in the front seat, preferably at the wheel, chances are you're not taking advantage of all the business opportunities your firm could enjoy. (In marketing parlance this methodology is called a SWOTs analysis of strengths, weaknesses, opportunities and threats.)

Smarter firms do that research and analysis, then do it again through the "windshield" instead of the "rearview mirror." Each market segment must be well-defined and researched. Secondary research is thoroughly conducted before embarking on primary research with key target prospects to determine where they are now (snapshot within the marketplace) and where they are going.

"Anyone not doing market research is a fool."

— Tom Peters, management guru

Peters was quick to add that anyone who relies entirely on market research is also a fool. I couldn't agree more. You have to know your business and know all the variables that impact your business, use research in combination with a lot of thoughtful reflection and analysis and do a "gut check" of where you want to go with your business.

"Getting ready is the secret of success."

— Henry Ford

What Is Research Anyway?

Marketing Research: "Is a function that links the marketer to consumers and the public through information. It is used to identify and define marketing opportunities ... problems ... evaluate actions ... monitor performance ... improve the marketing process."

— *Principles of Marketing,* Philip Kotler and Gary Armstrong

Research is the single most important factor in "getting ready for success." Firms that want to grow in revenues and remain viable must conduct research by whatever name you call it. (I once had a CEO forbid me to use the word research. He said, "We're not a research company, we're architects and engineers. Leave that to the drug companies and other industries that need research. I don't want you spending any time on that.") I used to conduct research nevertheless and present results to this same CEO who valued the information. We had a 90 percent or better likelihood of winning a project that was well-researched than one in which no research was conducted.

Research is not just for statisticians, drug companies, laboratories or universities. Research can have a profoundly dramatic, positive impact on your A/E/C firm in identifying customer needs and wants, new market segments and better ways of doing business.

Primary Research

This is original research you conduct yourself or hire an outside firm to do, such as a survey of clients in a specific market. You decide what questions will be asked and the format of the survey (telephone, mail, e-mail, etc.). You also decide (hopefully with professional guidance) how the survey will be done, when it will be done and to whom you will send it. Because it is original research it is almost always more expensive and time consuming than conducting secondary research. Correspondingly, such research is usually more valuable since it is proprietary — it's yours and no one else has this information. Primary research is critically important to your firm's success. How do you measure how well you are doing in serving existing clients?

Every firm I know has a supercomputer they don't use to its full potential: the human brain. I've found direct observation to be a powerful primary research tool. For example, as I waited in line in a relatively new parking lot in downtown Detroit, I heard the sound of a drill. A soil testing truck was set up on its hydraulic legs and was drilling through the blacktop. Given the size of the drill and the existing parking lot, it didn't take a rocket scientist or even a technical professional to deduce that the parking lot I was waiting to exit would soon be the first floor of a new skyscraper or parking deck in Detroit. No request for proposals (RFPs) had been issued, no contractor had been asked to bid on the job. Simple observation yielded a solid lead. The parking lot happens to be located next to the One Woodward Building developed by Hines Interests.

The pros and cons of primary research:

Pros	Cons
First-hand reliability	Costly (excepting direct observation methods)
Proprietary information	Time consuming
Focused	Requires experience/skills
Market- or issue-specific	Requires outside consultant
Potentially image building	

Secondary Research

This is research that already exists. It's been done by someone or some institution for a specific purpose and may be directly relevant to your needs. It's easy to obtain, generally reliable and extremely cost-effective. The public library is the best source I know of for secondary research. The Internet and world wide web are also outstanding sources. Say you want to find a list of the top 500 design and construction firms in the United States. The best place to look is in trade publications such as McGraw-Hill's *Engineering News-Record* magazine. You can then check local publications in your market like Crain's *Detroit Business,* which publishes a "Book of Lists" on the leading companies in virtually all sectors including architects, engineers and contractors. By looking at these two publications you have identified the largest players (competitors) nationally and in your local market.

There are seemingly endless sources of secondary research. Think about which tools make the most sense for your marketplace. I've listed a few sources later in this article.

The pros and cons of secondary research:

Pros	Cons
Cost-effective	Not case-specific
Readily available	Too general
Already done	Potentially flawed data
Focused	Too much data
Market- or issue-specific	Variables have changed since the research was done

Qualitative Research

Basically this is research used to determine a meaning behind an action or to discover an attitude or behavioral information on a corporate culture or individual. Why are you a Republican or Democrat? The methodology to get at these underlying and important aspects could come through an in-person interview asking open-ended questions. You're meeting the new prospect. Who have they used in the past and why? What's gone right, what's gone wrong? How do they prefer working with an A/E/C firm? This methodology can help you get to the heart of the issues of concern to your client or prospect.

Quantitative Research

If you don't feel comfortable doing statistical analysis or quantifying data, hire a professional firm or enlist the aid of a marketing professional from a local college or university. An example of quantitative research is McGraw-Hill analyzing the number of design/build projects in 1999 and conducting surveys to determine the growth potential of this delivery method in 2000, 2001, etc. Based on the surveys they can project a growth trend of the design/build delivery method with reasonable accuracy.

Research Process and Methodologies
(or How Do I Find Out What I Need to Know?)

It's a good starting point to determine what you're looking for and to be open to possibilities because you'll never know when they will arise. And good marketers can create new markets for existing services.

Define your market sectors. A market sector or segment is a group of buyers or clients with common wants and needs. Determine which market segments have the best growth potential. Can you effectively service and promote your company to this sector? Can you make a profit doing it and is there repeat business?

Start with a snapshot of your firm. Who are you and what do you do well now? What do you aspire to do and what resources will you require to get there?

Research Process

- Identify and state the issue. Example: we want to expand our geographic presence or move into a new market segment.
- Identify research goals.
- Determine information requirements.
- Determine research method.
- Decide on research sample (e.g., top five competitors in terms of revenues).
- Determine what to ask.
- Construct a questionnaire.
- Test the questionnaire and modify.
- Conduct interviews.
- Document results of interviews in writing.
- Write a report on the research project results. Think, reflect and analyze before you write it.

Research Methods

- Written surveys. (Mail or e-mail. Do you have a survey on your web site? Why not?)
- Phone interviews.
- Face-to-face interviews.
- Focus groups.
- Benchmarking studies.
- SMPS National cited an example of "reverse seminars" — bringing your clients in to speak to the firm or discipline about their needs, goals and objectives.

Items and Issues to Address in Research

Hit rates: The total market is the projects you won plus the projects you lost. This will show your competitiveness within a self-defined portion of the market or market segment.

Sales: Go to your accounting department and find out where your revenues are coming from. Who are your top clients ranked by revenues? What services are they buying (by type)? If you notice a lot of sales or revenues by a specific project type, that could be indicative of a trend or increased market demand.

Market share: Total sales within the market (by size and geography). This is a highly authoritative measure that can rank you as the No. 1 or No. 5 player in a given market. Clients and prospects want to go with a proven winner. There is a high correlation between market share and long-term profitability, which can spark debate between ego and hard data.

Market share can give you position within a segment but it doesn't tell you qualitative information such as current attitudes about your firm or the sustainability of the service type. Low market share can be related to your market coverage, competitive factors or a changing market.

Customer satisfaction: The client's overall rating of their experience with the company, its product and service. This is critically important information that a lot of firms don't bother tracking. You can do it fairly easily and cost effectively by client debriefings from the time of winning a project, at the 60 percent delivery point and at project close-out. This can be done by questionnaires, in-person interviews or other survey methods. Do you routinely ask clients for reference letters? Do you ask them for written referrals? If not, you may be missing opportunities to build your marketing arsenal and an "enthusiastic supporter" of your business and reputation.

Client satisfaction is more important than market share information in my opinion for the following reasons:

- It's key to the success of the company.
- It's a critical factor to competitive advantage.
- Satisfaction is used by clients to make choices (I liked the service, let's use them again).
- It can reduce concerns about fees and schedule.

Meta Studies show that 65 percent of customers leave a service supplier because they don't like the way they are treated. Some firms don't know about client dissatisfaction because the client quietly goes elsewhere.

It costs seven times as much to earn a new client versus retaining an existing one. Lesson: Take care of existing clients and preempt complaints through excellent service and routine feedback and communication. Leading companies are easy to do business with.

We touched earlier on the commodity of A/E/C services and gasoline. Mobil Oil Corp. conducted extensive market research to find out what its customers and prospects really wanted. They conducted focus groups, in person and written surveys, facilitated brainstorming sessions and even benchmarked a professional car racing team and pit crews. Why? Because they realized people want to get their gas and get out as fast as possible. Sometimes, they may want a cup of coffee or a quart of milk as well. One of the questions they posed was what can we do to provide the ultimate service to our customers and get them gassed up faster than any other gasoline vendor?

Mobil's research became a Harvard Business School case study. The research resulted in the "speed pass" where a little chip attached to your keychain automatically bills your credit card. No fumbling in your purse or wallet; a wave of the little magic wand and gas is pumped as fast as possible and you're on your way.

The Mobil speed passes are "free." Yes, there is a cost to them but where are you going to buy ALL of your gas? That's right, they've just virtually guaranteed repeat customers until they give them a reason to leave or someone builds a faster gas pump.

What's the "speed pass" in your A/E/C customer service and retention plan? Think about it! Research it and act on it before your competitor does. Why should I choose your firm? What differentiates you from everyone else?

How Do We Utilize Research to Track Trends Through the Windshield?

Let me start by giving you a real-life example. As an avid car buff, I've attended the North American International Auto Show (NAIAS) in Detroit for many years. They hold a black-tie charity preview to open the show each January and raise millions of dollars for great causes in the city. The car show is used by automakers to exhibit their latest models and court media from around the world. (More than 4,000 credentialed journalists attended the Detroit show last year.) At the 1998 show, Volkswagen used Detroit to introduce the new "Beetle."

Volkswagen spent millions of dollars on the two-story exhibit. It was such a smash success that people waited in lines for hours to see a new car! After marveling at this phenomenon, I started doing more research on Volkswagen's marketing plans for the car by reading *Automotive News*, *Adweek* and other industry publications. They had an aggressive TV, radio, magazine, newspaper, direct mail and web site campaign to sell the bug. The introduction at the auto show was just the start of an international sensation.

After conducting primary and secondary research, I put on my thinking cap. Isn't this still Detroit — home of the Big Three (before Daimler)? How could General Motors and Ford Motor Co. — two of the largest corporations in the world — let a foreign car maker upstage them in their own backyard? It happened. I seriously doubted they would let it happen again.

I started making calls to the marketing people at GM and Ford since research showed Chrysler already invested in a substantial display and that the exhibits have a two- to- three-year lifecycle. By investigating and conducting research on a limited basis that winter and early spring, I discovered that Ford was planning a major display — larger than any ever previously done in North America. I started contacting the exhibit company that serves Ford and we discussed their business plans and major forthcoming projects. We discussed the Beetle exhibit but the Ford issue was top secret. I simply stated the capabilities of my firm and said to keep us in mind if they did a major display that required assistance from a full-service A/E firm. As the design concept began to unfold, the "display" included a theater to seat 350 people and a bridge nearly the length of a football field that would eventually require 250 tons of structural steel to hold cars and thousands of people visiting the site.

By positioning ourselves correctly we won the project without a formal presentation, without a formal proposal and without bidding against another firm. In addition, we positioned ourselves with the NAIAS to inspect other major displays at substantial fees. The benefit of breaking into this "new" market was six-figure fees for structural engineering and the experience of having done engineering for the largest automotive exhibit in the United States. That's an example of marketing through the windshield at a cost of 30 to 40 total hours of research, internal and external communication and business development over a three-month period. At the time of this writing the firm was pursuing another major exhibit and related "spin-off" work.

By conducting traditional research on markets you are interested in pursuing, you can reasonably predict where the market is going. By using solid research, deductive reasoning, logic and good communication skills you can win projects and create whole new "pies" of business for your firm.

Where's the Pit Stop for Good Industry Information (Sources)?

Industry associations are a good starting point for information. When it comes to competitors, you can research firms through the American Institute of Architects (AIA) or professional building and engineering societies.

Construction Online McGraw-Hill offers the following sources of information for the industry:

- Construction Information Group is a preeminent source of project news, product information, industry analysis and editorial coverage for design and construction professionals. Its powerful brands include F.W. Dodge, Sweet's Group, *Engineering News-Record* and *Architectural Record*. *Architectural Record Online* is the leading journal for architects, engineers and other building design professionals.
- CAP Online provides comprehensive computer applications for the contract furniture industry.
- *Design-Build* is the official publication of the Design-Build Institute of America, serving design builders and owners in the worldwide, non-residential construction marketplace.
- ENR Online (*Engineering News-Record*) is the weekly news magazine covering the business and technical news of the construction industry.
- F.W. Dodge Online provides building project leads, plans and specifications and construction market analysis services in both print and electronic formats.
- The F.W. Dodge Regional Publications' portfolio of local and regional publications provides current and advance construction news and bid information to the construction community.
- MAG Online (Market Analysis Group) provides historical and forecast information, market demand indicators and custom market studies for the construction, real estate and financial industries.
- Sweet's Online is the construction industry's primary product information source.

Other great sources include:

- Industry publications.
- General publications (*Business Week*, *Fortune*, *Forbes* are great publications to see where markets are going and where money is being invested).
- Corporate annual reports (Learn about geographic market goals and capital investment plans).
- Dun & Bradstreet (Learn about competitors and prospective client's financial standing, employees, locations and ownership quickly and cost-effectively).
- Dow Jones News.
- Hoover Reports.
- Internet search engines. The volume of information available on the Internet is growing in geometric proportions. The good news is most of it is current information. There is a lot of historical information that isn't on the web because it simply costs too much money to dig it out of the archives and put it there.

I'm online multiple times every day and find the information avenues fascinating and highly useful. A potential negative is what makes the Internet so great in the first place: too much data.

How do you quickly and efficiently find the relevant information you're looking for? A basic rule of thumb is to stick with known and reputable sources of information. Always use multiple sources, then take the time to think about the issue.

Another limitation of the Internet is its impersonality. It's a universe of data. Meeting with people, clients, prospects, secretaries and seeing physical places gives you a much more well-rounded picture and a whole lot of insights that are unattainable electronically. For example, a small company may present itself as a global giant on their web pages. The reality and reliability may be something entirely different. When it comes to the Internet, researcher be wary.

- Web sites of companies or institutions are great ways of finding out background information and getting a glimpse of corporate cultures.
- Government agencies and departments. Aside from libraries, it's amazing the kind of information you can obtain from your local city and county clerk's offices, ranging from zoning requirements to the mortgage balance of a business or person you may be doing business with. Familiarize yourself with what's available from public entities. It's generally reliable and cheap information. Copying costs and your time are the biggest expenses. If you're looking for sensitive information, you may need to file a Freedom of Information Act or (FOIA) request. You can find out about filing FOIA requests at the library or from your local newspaper or the National Society of Professional Journalists.

Hire Third Parties

Research is important. If you're not going to invest the time and effort to do it right, hire someone who will. I have seen quite a number of business plans, strategic plans, market analyses and trend forecasts become "shelf" documents. Sources for third-party research include:

- Marketing departments of major colleges and universities.
- National "Big Five" accounting firms. (Check out Arthur Andersen's web site. They even offer industry-specific information tracking systems right on the web — customized to your specific requirements.)
- Local or national public relations and marketing firms. There are professionals out there who can conduct primary or secondary research for you much faster and more professionally than you could in-house.
- Polling companies. A random stratified sampling of a prospective market sector can provide you with a tremendous amount of valuable information, quickly, reliably and cost-effectively.

What Are My Competitors Doing? Should I Care?

Keeping a close eye on your competitors is simply good business. In this world they may be a lot more than your competitor — they may be your short-term, long-term or segment-specific partners. The more you know about your competitors, the more business intelligence you have to deal with them. I know a senior veteran architect who refuses to pay any attention to competitors. His philosophy is that a firm should take care of its own business, not spend any time on the competition. Why wouldn't you take advantage of business intelligence that can be easily gathered and monitored? If you were marching into battle, wouldn't you want to know everything about your enemy's strengths and weaknesses? Of course you would.

At the very least you want to know who your competitors are, what segments they serve, what marketing tactics they use and how they are organized. Smart firms also look down the list and track the fast-growing, aggressive A/E/C firm. They may be doing something differently that warrants study. They may be worth acquiring or they may take on too much and need your assistance on larger projects.

There is a trend toward consolidation in the A/E/C industry. It's a good idea to keep an eye on the national and global players who are in your market. What are they doing and will they be acquiring a competitor or perhaps your firm?

Market Segment Research

The days of the generalist firm are over. You can specialize in a lot of areas but you cannot be a jack of all trades in a global marketplace. Facility types and all the peripheral issues have become so complex that a firm must specialize in certain areas in order to be considered for a project. Unless a firm is focused on its core business services it will be fragmented. By focusing on what your firm does well, you can factor in the training, growth requirements, market sector growth and delivery patterns. By really focusing on your key clients and service type you cannot only build a solid base of experience and expertise in a particular project type but also lead innovations in that market sector and make your business more profitable and fun.

Your market sectors could cover one or many of the following service areas:

- K-12 schools.
- Higher education.
- Health care (hospitals or medical office buildings).
- Corporate offices (new or renovation).
- Research and development and lab centers.
- Call centers.
- Heavy industrial manufacturing.
- Light industrial manufacturing.
- Transportation systems.
- Municipal governments.
- Computer software companies.
- Fast-growing businesses.

The simple beauty of establishing market segments is the ability to research them and quantify what the total "market" potential is within a specific geographic area. For example, you could target the 150 top system suppliers to the automotive industry in Detroit. Can you find out who they are, who the key decision-makers are and how they buy your services? Absolutely. Then you are armed with knowledge, and knowledge is power.

Researching Clients and Prospects: The Fundamentals

Learn as much about the industry as well as the specific business within that broader industry. If it is a publicly traded company, obtain its annual report, talk to investment analysts and talk to key vendors and suppliers to the company. Review the organization's web site and links to industries or associations. Who are the major shareholders and who are the opinion leaders that influence the management decision-makers? Understand what their core business is and main products or services. What are their growth patterns and plans? Who do they use for A/E/C suppliers? Why?

Once you've done your research on the company, it's time to shift your focus to key influential decision-makers with respect to your company's service or product offering. If it's a publicly traded company these people and organization charts are easy to obtain. For privately held firms, conduct research through Dun & Bradstreet, Dow Jones, Thompson's Registrar, Hoover's or other companies that track business financials and statistics.

From Dun & Bradstreet, for example, you can find out a company's financial history, ownership, stock plans, key clients, incorporation date, acquisition dates and a host of other valuable information including key managers and executives.

You want to know everything you can, both professionally and personally, about the people who may be your long-term client. You can never have too much information about individual clients or prospects. A small kernel of information can make the difference between success and failure. But make sure your information arsenal is accessible and easy to update. Use the information to help establish common ground between you and the individual and your respective organizations. If the client likes to play golf, play golf.

Aside from conducting formal research on someone through press clipping services or data bases, inviting prospects to lunch or breakfast is a great way to break the ice and introduce your firm. Offer to pick them up at their office and make the visit as stress-free as possible. Make observations about what they wear and how their office is furnished and decorated. Are there multiple pictures of prized possessions on the wall? Is there a college degree or degrees on the wall? Is that information valuable? You bet. You'll get a better feel for what makes that individual tick.

During this breakfast or lunch you want to start with casual conversation and ask a lot of open-ended questions. My rule of thumb is to talk 20 percent of the time and listen 80 percent. Listening skills are critically important and highly underrated. In the A/E/C business, like most other businesses, technical professionals and executives have a hard time sublimating their egos for the benefit of the client, the relationship and the business.

The Trend Toward A/E/C Industry Consolidation and Niche Specialists

There is a big shakeout coming in the A/E/C industry in the next few years. Are you ready for the changes that will be coming at you faster than an Indy car on Memorial Day weekend? The industry faces consolidation, the end of a record peacetime economic expansion cycle, radically new ways of communication and productivity through technology, not to mention globalization and increasing demands from customers for more "turnkey" services so they can stay focused on their core business. Hold on to your mouse pads because the changes will be coming faster than you can surf a web site.

I also think the new millennium will see a quantum leap in the design/construction industry. I believe there will be new technologies and processes that will radically change the way facilities come into being. Who will be the next Henry Ford of the built environment? I'm certain she is out there and I predict the revolution will occur within the next decade. The firms that are systematically conducting market research will be prepared and lead the business revolution in the A/E/C industry. Those that do not conduct market research will likely go the way of the old carmakers and become footnotes to history. The future is of your making.

What Tom Peters said in the mid-'90s will hold true through the ages: "Change or die." If you don't conduct continuous market research, you risk losing your market. Whether you do research in-house or hire outside consultants to conduct research for you, take charge in leading the change!

Bruce A. Babiarz, APR

- Babiarz has more than 15 years of experience in marketing, sales, media and public relations and a decade of experience in the built environment. His experience is in corporate marketing, business development planning and execution, market research data base development, strategic planning and multimedia communications.

- Previously, Babiarz served as a journalist, editor and business development executive with an international media organization. He knows firsthand where to find information and how to develop sources of information for targeted subjects. He brings this unique perspective to the built environment industry.

- As director of marketing for Ghafari Associates Inc., he led the firm's efforts to:
  ⇒ Create the first web site for a Michigan-based A/E firm in 1995.
  ⇒ Utilize the Internet and online services for research.
  ⇒ Utilize CD-ROMs for data storage and retrieval.
  ⇒ Create a marketing department data base and online information system.
  ⇒ Assist the firm in a major diversification effort.
  ⇒ Submit six winning design award entries.
  ⇒ Produce dozens of articles on the firm in local and national publications.
  ⇒ Write and produce all marketing materials used by the firm.

Acknowledgment

Special thanks to Susan Prater Scott who authored the original chapter on marketing research for the first edition of *The Handbook for Marketing Professional Services.*

1.2 Strategic Planning and Marketing Business Planning

Sandra J. Werthman
Vice President of Marketing
Kitchell Contractors

Julie S. Stanton
Marketing and Communications Consultant

We all know individuals who seem to have a clear sense of their own identity and direction in life. They know who they are and where they are going and they inevitably have a plan for how to reach their goals. Then there are those who seem to wander aimlessly, chasing the latest fashion trend, the latest pot of gold and wonder why they never get what they want, *if* they have even figured out what *that* is!

Companies are much the same. We can all identify firms with strong, positive identities in the marketplace, the ones that seem to know just what they want and how to achieve it. Look closer at these firms and invariably you will see a strong commitment to strategic planning and/or marketing planning.

In simple terms, a strategic plan is a three- to five-year road map for a firm, and the marketing business plan is a one-year increment of that plan. These plans represent the consensus of management about a firm's current and future identity, relationship to its markets and clients, and its potential. At best, these plans create a culture and image that distinguish the firm's people, services, performance and products. How ironic that building and design firms almost always start their new projects with a "plan," but many times, they do not create and follow a plan for their own businesses.

The Strategic Planning Process
A Hallmark of Successful Firms

Strategic planning is both a visionary and practical management tool. It defines what a firm wants to be and where it wants to go in the future, as well as how it is going to get there. It is also an ongoing process. Strategic planning allows a firm to step back from day-to-day pressures, consider new and future requirements of doing business, and maintain a competitive edge. As a valuable guide for the future, it lays a solid foundation upon which all other actions of the firm will be based, providing the firm with a systematic approach to enhanced communication, focus, self-awareness, trust and cohesion.

Sounds like the next best thing since sliced bread! As a hallmark of most successful firms, maybe it is. Many consider it to be top management's most important task. As a marketing professional, your involvement is critical, so it is important to know what can and should be accomplished, since it will be the basis for all subsequent marketing efforts.

Strategic planning has two major components: 1) the initial planning sessions, yielding a planning document; and, 2) more importantly, implementation of the plan over a few or several years, through the accomplishment of milestones and goals.

Strategic planning processes are as unique as the companies applying them. While the overall process, including research, decision-making and implementation will probably take several months, the core planning team's most active involvement can be anything from a one-day session to several meetings over the course of weeks. Participation may consist of a few, some or all members of the firm. Regardless of logistics, the backbone of successful planning can be summed up in a five-step process (as illustrated in Figure 1):

1. Internal and external research and analysis.
2. Collective decision-making.
3. Organizational engineering and communication.
4. Implementation.
5. Evaluation/results.

Figure 1
Strategic Planning Model

Strategic Planning Model

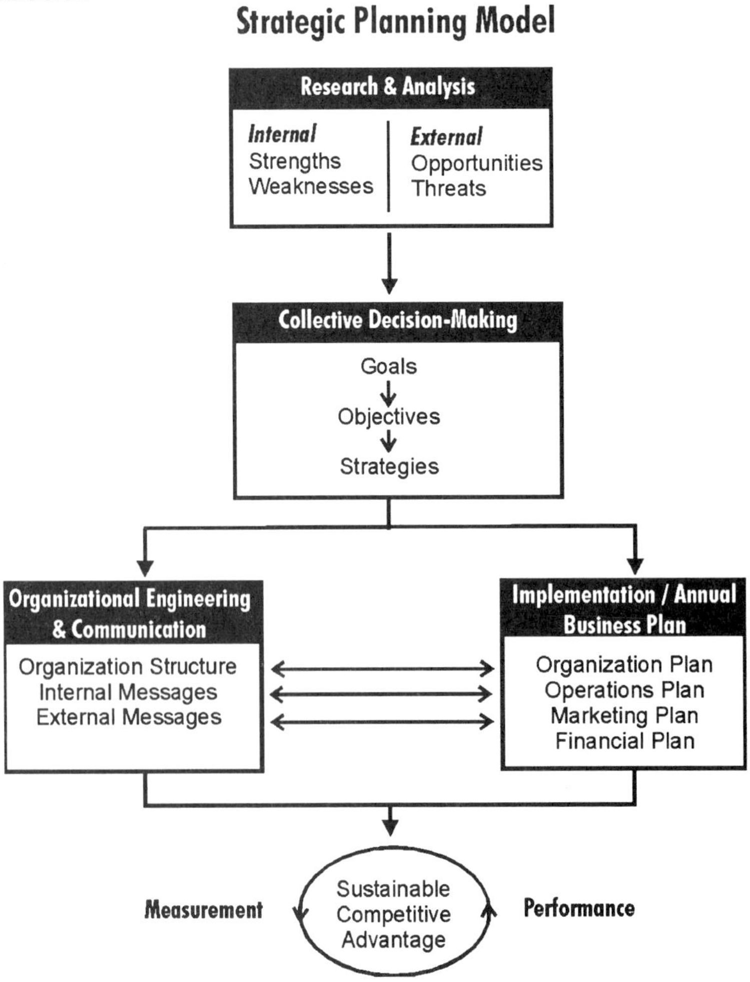

Internal and External Research and Analysis
Getting a Clear Picture

The research and analysis phase provides you with a clear picture of the marketplace and your firm's position in it. Interviews, surveys, audits, and primary and secondary market research, as described in the chapter about market research, can provide a view of the firm's current market position, challenges to that position, and opportunities for future growth and development.

The familiar SWOT (strengths, weaknesses, opportunities and threats) assessment is a good tool to use for organizing your information:

- **Strengths** and **weaknesses** focus internally. You will gather perceptions of your firm's capabilities, expertise, performance and image in various markets from your staff, client and consultants/affiliates.

- **Opportunities** identify external factors, determined by analyzing broad-based social, demographic, cultural and economic trends for marketing and business implications, as well as specific possibilities presented by client/market requirements.

- **Threats** look at the external environment in terms of your market position in relation to your competitors and any negative effects of industry, social, demographic, cultural and economic trends.

The SWOT items with most importance to the firm's future become the basis for the decision-making process. The information should be gathered from both internal and external sources for presentation at the planning session. In fact, having a SWOT brainstorming session with your staff can yield unexpectedly insightful information as well as get everyone who will be involved in the strategic planning on board early. As the natural facilitator of this session, the marketer's position in the subsequent strategic planning sessions is bolstered.

The Decision-Making Phase
Developing Consensus on the Firm's Direction and Initiatives

At this point, the firm's core management gathers to digest and analyze the research, identify relevant issues, develop consensus on a direction and initiatives, and set goals.

Two basic strategy generators for the group's discussion are: (1) How do we make the most of the firm's strengths and opportunities? and (2) How do we neutralize our weaknesses and threats? Additionally, to avoid a "business as usual" attitude, identify emerging business practices and the possible responses for the firm.

From these ideas, identify goals and prioritize them. Once priorities are set, consider the operational, organizational, marketing and financial perspectives of each one.

In the course of this process, you will determine target markets: those areas where the firm's interests and capabilities match up with opportunity and demand. For each target market, set achievable goals that address the specific market position the firm wants to achieve and outline strategies for pursuing work.

Even at the strategic level, define all of the firm's target markets as specifically as possible. Agree upon project types, size, geographic locations, target clients, contract types, fee goals and other criteria that will become the official "criteria for pursuing work." (The annual marketing plan will determine annual sales targets and specific strategies for project/client pursuit.)

One of the biggest challenges that many firms face is simply creating consensus on a direction(s). Consensus is essential to progress and worth spending the time to reach in order to prevent future roadblocks. Start with wide-ranging input from clients, staff and affiliated business partners, then develop agreement on SWOT items. Also beware of taking on too many initiatives. If the firm gets spread too thin, the danger arises of not having enough energy and focus to see things through.

Organizational Engineering and Communication
Aligning Resources with the Firm's New Directions

Once you select strategic directions, the firm must be organized to fulfill its mission and goals. New job roles and responsibilities may emerge, and one or more business units may need to be reorganized. This process should minimize short-term fixes and focus on achieving long-term value creation and future growth.

The success of the initiatives depends on how they are communicated to the rest of the firm. Use a variety of methods to communicate ideas and the status of the implementation. Build enthusiasm, understanding and motivation by delivering consistent messages in every internal forum: company meetings, in-house newsletters, in-house e-mail messaging, posters/displays, printed pocket cards, etc. These activities help translate the plan's goals into a shared vision that galvanizes the firm to action. Some firms have a company-wide meeting (one for each location, if multiple offices), conducted by the CEO, to kick off the implementation phase, featuring a reception or box lunch format that promotes a positive, even celebratory atmosphere.

External communication is equally important since the firm is positioning itself in an active marketplace. A variety of communication and public relations functions, as detailed in subsequent chapters of this book, allows the firm to transmit new messages about its capabilities and business objectives to appropriate external audiences.

Implementation
Translating Broad Corporate Goals into Day-to-Day Actions

By now, a champion and implementation team should be in place for each strategic initiative. This person or group will go on to develop and refine an action plan, including goals, objectives and tactics for implementation. Some of their challenges include maintaining the buy-in of the management team, avoiding over-analysis and resisting impatience. Again, communication and the flexibility to make adjustments will help ensure success.

On a daily basis, the firm's leadership should be verifying that strategic initiatives are in action. On the marketing level, this means that all marketing, business development, sales, public relations and communications are focused on strategic objectives, target markets and the priorities of the firm. For example, making a sale may not be important, in and of itself, unless it advances the firm's strategic goals.

Evaluation/Results
Leading to Sustainable Competitive Advantages

When the strategic goals are set, corresponding measurements to mark progress should be established as well. Benchmarks might include volume, profit, sales ratios, key clients and other performance indicators. Measure progress monthly, quarterly and annually. By continually using measurement to adjust and improve performance, the firm can turn strategies into actions and ultimately into sustainable competitive advantages, that is, differentiated benefits of doing business with your firm that cannot be matched by other firms. Regular measurement is particularly useful in helping the firm determine whether progress is being made toward its goals. If the current course is not working, then corrective actions may be needed. However, make those corrections cautiously. Quick fixes are not the way to implement long-term strategies.

Communication remains a critical element. Positive discussions throughout the firm help to promote the benefits of change. As progress occurs, it should be recognized, celebrated, and become a foundation for ongoing change and improvement.

Marketing Business Planning
A One-Year Increment of the Strategic Plan

A good strategic planning process will include a definition of the scope and goals of a firm's marketing efforts. The annual business plan, with a marketing component, outlines in detail the firm's strategic objectives for one year.

Market-Segment Analysis

On an annual basis, evaluate each market segment for its potential based on:

- **Experience and performance record:** Isolate and evaluate relevant statistics for each market segment such as number of projects completed, billings, profitability, hit rate and repeat clients.

- **Market trends:** From the market research, project the volume for the market segment and where it falls on the life cycle curve. Is the market just beginning to boom, at its peak or ready to decline? (See Figure 2)

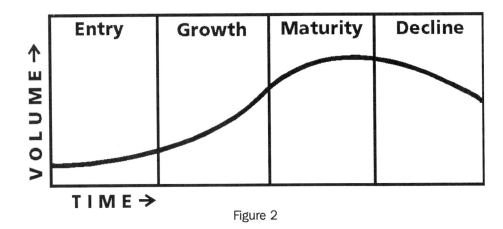

Figure 2

- **Client analysis:** Who is the buyer? It may not be the client/user (e.g., a developer is developing a build-to-suit office building for a corporation). What specific benefits do they need/want? What is driving the project?

- **Competition analysis:** Determine which other firms do work in this market segment and how your firm compares in terms of experience, project delivery methods, pricing, project size, etc.

- **Networking/Affiliation Requirements:** Identify other types of firms involved in the market. For example, an architectural firm would research and gather information from the engineers, contractors, lenders and business consultants typically involved in the market segment and with major clients.

The Marketing Plan: Action + Focus = Results

The information from the market-segment analysis can then be refined into a marketing plan, in which specific, measurable goals are set for market penetration. Overall marketing goals for the firm and specific goals for each target market are identified. Each goal is supported by strategies and action items. For each goal and/or strategy, include the name of the responsible person, milestone dates and the resources the firm is allocating toward that goal (e.g., financial, human resource, materials). Sufficiently define strategies and action items so that they are measurable and universally understood.

For example, if the annual marketing plan goal is to book $2 million in fees in the hospitality market sector, one strategy could be to increase repeat work to generate $1 million in fees. The corresponding action plan strategies could include:

- Performing project feedback surveys for completed work, with 100 percent client satisfaction.
- Developing individual client development plans for the firm's three largest hospitality clients.
- Selling ongoing service agreements with all hospitality clients.

For firms with several markets, it is useful to create a matrix formulating key marketing criteria, goals and strategies into a marketing plan overview. This highly condensed format shows the year's strategic objectives, provides a firm-wide marketing overview of goals and expertise, and is easily understood throughout the firm.

Marketing Plan Overview

	Hotels & Resorts	Office (LA office)	Industrial	Military Housing	Public Bid
Mkt Leader/ Marketer	Sam Davis / Bill Day	Jim Rhen / Sue Niva	Stan Werth / Carol Kent	Larry F / Bill Day	Brian W (Est.)
Geographic target	Southwestern U.S. Mexico Hawaii	LA area only	Western US	International, focus on Latin America	Arizona only
Project / Building Type	Mid-range hotels Luxury hotels Resorts	Mid- and high-rise Developer Corporate	Semiconductor Manufacturing Large warehouse Robotics	Pre-engineered base housing (2000 units min.)	High schools City projects State projects No federal
Minimum - Maximum Size	$5 - 40 M	$15 - 100 M	$2 - 40 M local $10 M min. out-of- state	$20 - 50 M	$12 - 80 M
Sales Goals: Volume Fees	$30 M $0.9 M	$40 M $1.2 M	$50 M $2.0 M	$20 M $1.0 M	$25 M $0.75 M
Target clients					
Key messages					
Identified projects					
Key Relationships					

As with the strategic plan, it is advisable to establish measures for all elements of the marketing plan and evaluate progress monthly and quarterly. As implementation progresses, strategies will be proven effective or ineffective, and adjustments will be necessary. Major failures or changes in strategy require a new start of the entire strategic process. Minor setbacks and changes may only require adjustment to the annual marketing plan.

New Markets and Start-Ups

Strategic planning often yields major new undertakings for the firm in the form of new geographic locations and offices, mergers and acquisitions, and start-ups of new businesses. These strategic initiatives have greater potential risks and rewards than the day-to-day established business of the firm. They require substantial, ongoing research and feedback to ascertain market response to the new offerings. From this input, the implementation team must adjust continually until it finds the right mix of strategy, services, staffing and clients to move from a start-up operation to sustainability. These ventures will require greater flexibility, innovation and resource allocation than the firm's core business. Consider such strategies as hiring new expertise, associating with a leading firm in that market, and using existing clients to take you into new markets. It seems that firms in our industry almost always underestimate the time and money required to make a new venture successful. Marketers need to be analytical about these efforts in terms of costs and staffing.

Summary

The strategic and marketing planning processes are key management tools to create a sound organizational foundation. What makes planning effective and successful? Test it against four essential elements of good management:

- **Consensus:** Have you established a dynamic team environment within your firm that shares the vision and goals?
- **Clarity:** Is the firm's mission clearly understood internally and externally and is it reflected in the planning goals?
- **Control:** Do you have the ability to generate and manage the firm's outcomes and make adjustments as needed?
- **Consistency:** Do the work product, image and actions by the entire firm have a similar look and feel?

An ongoing commitment to strategic and marketing planning will not solve all your problems or guarantee that you will never embark on a faulty initiative. However, a dedicated planning effort will make life at your firm more fulfilling and more productive. With everyone's energies focused on a few, well-thought-out objectives, it is much more likely that you will reach those goals important to the continued and future success of your company.

Sandra J. Werthman

- Sandy Werthman is vice president of marketing for Kitchell Contractors, a Phoenix-based commercial general contractor and construction manager. Since 1989 she has overseen the firm's strategic planning, sales efforts and business development activities and has been involved in the start-up of five new business ventures for Kitchell: a New Mexico subsidiary (1993), Custom Home company (1994), Nevada regional office (1994), a new service division (1999) and the consolidation of its hospital practice as Kitchell Health Care (1999).
- Previously she held marketing positions for three large architecture and engineering firms in Arizona and New York and holds a bachelor's degree from the University of Colorado.
- In the late 1970s, she was a founding member of SMPS Upstate New York Chapter and has served the Arizona Chapter as chair of numerous committees.

Julie S. Stanton

- Julie Stanton has provided marketing and communications consulting services to the design and construction industry since 1996. She is also a development officer for Arizona State University.
- Previously, she held marketing positions with the firms of Smith, Hinchman & Grylls, OWP&P, and Skidmore, Owings & Merrill.
- She holds a bachelor's degree from the University of Illinois.
- She is certified by SMPS as a Senior Marketing Professional, was one of the founders of the Chicago Chapter of SMPS, has held numerous officer and chair positions in the Arizona Chapter of SMPS and established a Program Committee for national SMPS.

For the last two years, Werthman and Stanton have jointly developed and taught marketing workshops for design and construction professionals in the Phoenix area, sponsored by the Arizona Builders Alliance and endorsed by the Central Arizona Chapter of the American Institute of Architects.

Acknowledgment

Special thanks to Karen Kerruish Roper who authored the original chapter on strategic and marketing business planning for the first edition of *The Handbook for Marketing Professional Services.*

1.3 Market-Driven Versus Client-Driven Marketing

Karen W. Winters, FSMPS
Associate and Director of Marketing & Administration
King & King, Architects

Overview

The pursuit of new business will take varied paths for professional services firms as they attempt to differentiate themselves from each other. The path taken depends on firm philosophy and many other variables — the demands of the marketplace, levels of expertise, economic conditions, research, planning, knowing the right people and being in the right place at the right time.

Prior to the 1970s, when firms secured new business almost exclusively through repeat business and referrals, it didn't matter which path you took. Most firms were generalists, dabbling in any market that offered opportunity. Today is another matter. Competition is fierce, even in an economic boom when work is abundant. Our industry is changing so dramatically that firms must focus or develop a niche. They must know what they are good at, what opportunities are available and which of the many paths available is best for them. They must anticipate what lies around the next curve, be willing to switch to the fast lane and be ready to forge a new road.

"Do not follow where the path may lead, instead go where there is no path and leave a trail."

—Anonymous

Two alternate paths — market-driven marketing and client-driven marketing — are the topic of this chapter. Market-driven marketing consists of pursuing a group of clients with similar or specific building-type needs, such as hospitals or schools. To carry this concept even further, firms are successfully developing niches within a market segment, and pursuing a more specialized segment focus, such as children's hospitals. (More detailed information on niche marketing can be found in the chapter by Ellen Flynn-Heapes, "The Niche Strategy.") Market-driven marketing is widely accepted throughout the design and construction industry, and is a common practice among many firms.

In contrast, client-driven marketing focuses on pursuing specific clients, such as Kodak or Disney, and meeting whatever needs they might have, e.g., high-technology manufacturing, corporate offices, resort hotels, theatres, museums. Client-driven marketing is practiced by fewer firms, and will therefore be contrasted to market-driven marketing, and described in greater depth.

The complexity is that these two paths are not mutually exclusive. For simplicity's sake, however, let's examine each of these paths separately.

Market-Driven Marketing

A market-driven firm can respond best by developing strategic goals and a structure to meet the specialized needs of a building type and specialized staff to respond to those needs. The firm can respond to one market segment; develop a specialty niche within a market, such as forensic laboratories within the criminal justice market; or focus on several market segments that are similar — or very different, such as commercial waterfront buildings and religious buildings. The important element is that the market segment or building type drives what the firm provides. Research and a firm's knowledge base are focused on information about the market segment and trends that impact it, which allow them to easily transition from one client to another.

As an example, it is much easier for a firm to sell its expertise to a prospective client, such as a hospital, if it has a depth of experience in health care design and its proposed staff can demonstrate the same. This allows the firm to not only talk the client's language, but demonstrate they have walked the path before. The perceived benefit to the client might be in terms of a better design because the firm understands how a hospital functions, a shorter schedule or lower costs because of the firm's experience.

As today's clients "right-size" and seek non-traditional approaches to getting a project off the ground, the design firm may be pulled into new arenas. It might mean new alliances for delivery, partnering with non-design firms or helping the client with funding sources.

Client-Driven Marketing

A client-driven A/E/C firm is just that, focused on its clients — their businesses, their decision-making processes, their bottom lines, etc. — and is structured to meet the needs of its individual clients. What is important is getting inside the client's head and becoming part of the corporate entity, understanding its specific needs, and where it is going — its goals and objectives. For some clients this might result in a production-oriented, high-volume building program, such as what might be required for McDonald's or The Limited. For other clients it might mean incorporating non-traditional services and staff in their firm's offerings, such as demographers, research analysts or strategic planners. And for others, it might mean you become the equivalent of an in-house design team, doing whatever is needed to meet the client's facility needs.

Client-driven firms tend to be very, very selective with whom they work. They target "annuity clients," or clients who have a continuous stream of work and opportunities. Design-oriented, client-driven firms may select only a few distinguished clients with whom they fit culturally, and with whom they want to establish a long-term relationship to design and develop highly visible projects.

Client-driven firms that work on high-volume production and fast turnaround, on the other hand, don't necessarily care what they design, or where they design it, as long as there is a high volume of projects over an extended period of time. The client is the expert or specialist in the building type, while the client-driven design firm uses the depth of experience of its staff to provide a good service mix. The focus for the design firm and the added value for the client are production, turnaround, knowledge of the client's organization and facilities, and lower costs.

A case study, which highlights a client-driven relationship and marketing focus, is my firm's response to an existing client of more than 20 years. As this large, high-volume client looked toward streamlining its planning and design process, it became apparent to us that the client was leaning toward hiring one firm (or consortium of firms) instead of outsourcing to the more than 20 firms on its preferred provider list. Prior to the request for proposal (RFP) being issued, my firm aligned with two other design firms to pursue this client. Together we spent more than six months doing one-to-one focused research within various levels of the client organization, gathering and synthesizing information. The relationships and the information were powerful, and our strategy was on target for this large organization that was trying to "break away" from its traditional way of doing business. One of the advantages to our team was our familiarity with the organization, and a prime factor was strengthening a relationship with the key decision-maker and understanding his and the client's motivation for wanting to implement change. We went to the depth of setting up a separate corporate entity to provide sole-source design services devoted exclusively to this client's needs and this was what clinched it! As the saying goes, "The proof is in the pudding." We saved them 10 percent in consulting fees our first year of operation, and are on target to do the same this year. Together we were able to significantly shorten the turnaround time from conception to occupation, which had a crucial impact on end-users and revenue generation for the client. By becoming an integral part of the client organization, our firm, and more important, the client, has a greater stake in making the relationship work.

Regardless of the client base, client-driven firms know they have to be very selective in pursuing clients that meet their criteria of success. The research process to gather in-depth information to pre-qualify clients can be quite lengthy — three to six months — and tends to be more qualitative in nature. They seek clients that fit their corporate culture and goals, whether that's high-design or some other value that is important to the design firm. Qualitative research is important, as firms seek to find clients that meet their criteria for a long-term relationship. These criteria might include: business philosophy; a minimum number of projects in the client's portfolio, e.g., 10; a minimum amount of time for these projects to span, e.g., five years; sustained volume of work; number of buildings or sites; or a minimum dollar value, e.g., $100 million total. The marketing costs per client are usually high; however, firm success might be measured in terms of securing one or two "very select" annuity clients a year.

One-to-one marketing often is a key element of client-driven marketing, as it focuses on creating a learning relationship between the A/E/C staff and the client, so that the marketing (and ultimately the service) response can be individually customized to that client. Client-driven relationships often provide better opportunities to be aware of the issues so design firms can determine what the client needs next, and then make proposals to provide it. It places A/E/C firms at a better vantage point to take the initiative, in contrast to simply responding to needs the client has identified. By unearthing needs early, firms can decide whether to add "non-design" integrated services to their service mix, form an alliance to meet the client's needs or respond in some other creative way.

Market-driven firms that seek to either change to a client-driven orientation or provide a mix of focus typically transition over time as they begin to add services and/or capture more of the client's design business. Getting to the client very, very early in a project's development also offers opportunities for the design firm to expand its services to a client that is ripe for either outsourcing to one firm or limiting the number of resource firms.

The matrix that follows differentiates some of the distinct marketing approaches for each type of firm.

Marketing Approach by A/E/C Firms	Market-Driven Firms	Client-Driven Firms
Staff	Knowledge base is focused in target market(s): allows staff to become specialists in its market arena.	Understanding the client and its goals is important. Fosters staff to become part of client's corporate culture and to be a team player.
Research	Focused on tracking market trends, changes and outside forces, such as regulations, foreign competition, etc., that affect the market. Research is ongoing but becomes easy as knowledge base grows.	Focused on client's business; what is important to the company, to different levels of individuals within the client organization, and external forces which impact that client's business. Research *very* extensive; usually qualitative; some similarities by client type, but often unique. Knowledge base unique.
Determining Client Viability	Limited research needed on specific clients. As long as they do business in the specialized market, market information is easily transferable.	In-depth research needed on each client to determine viability and culture "fit."
Networking with the Client	Access to clients often facilitated through trade associations and other organizations focused on issues of the target market.	Unless marketing similar client types, access and networking opportunities are often new and unique to each client.
Database	Basic client information; depth of market information.	Extensive client information, including market information.
Penetration	Market penetration can be achieved with a streamlined approach using tailored services.	Client penetration best achieved through relationships, customized research and specialized approach.
Marketing Costs	Opportunities for cost savings with base approach, tweaked for client. Volume of clients unrestricted.	Specialized one-to-one approach to each client creates high marketing costs. Volume of clients often focused on targeted few.
Value Pricing	Opportunities to sell specialization, quality and service (value) instead of price.	Opportunities to sell relationships, continuity, volume, speed and service (value) instead of price.
Value Delivery	New alliances and structures of delivery may be important (e.g., financial advisor, design-build, turnkey).	Knowledge of the organization and how it operates, speed and production turnaround may be important.
Value Services	Knowledge of the market segment allows transferable services and easy transition from one client to another.	Knowledge of the client facilitates identification of what services the client needs next.

Summary

In reality the differences between a market-driven firm and a client-driven firm often are in sequencing and customization of marketing and service activities. A market-driven firm wants and needs to know how the client functions — its vision, goals and objectives — in order to create designs that meet the client's needs. It probably won't know the client as intimately as a client-driven firm, but it will know enough about a specific client to transfer experiences from the market and the other clients it services. Conversely, a client-driven firm needs to know about the marketplace in which their client functions — the competition and the trends — in order to create designs that meet their client's needs. A client-driven firm may not know as much about the market trends as a market-driven firm, unless it has several clients in the same market segment, but it will probably know it better from the client's perspective.

The structure of the marketing approach, service offerings and firm focus are all a matter of perspective and choice. As a firm, you need to look strategically at your strengths, weaknesses, opportunities and threats. More importantly, you should determine which clients or markets you have a passion for! That decision will help determine your approach.

Bibliography

Beckwith, Harry. "The Adapter's Edge." *Selling the Invisible, A Field Guide to Modern Marketing,* Warner Books, Inc., 1997, 47-50.

—. "The First Rule of Marketing Planning." *Selling the Invisible, A Field Guide to Modern Marketing,* Warner Books, Inc., 1997, 18.

—. "What Color Is Your Company's Parachute?" *Selling the Invisible, A Field Guide to Modern Marketing,* Warner Books, Inc., 1997, 38-40.

Dempsey, John G., Ph.D., P.E., and Gretchen Wesenberg, R.A., NCARB. "The Design Partner." *Facilities Manager*, Association of Higher Education Facilities Officers (April 1998): 25-26.

Flynn-Heapes, Ellen. "Strategic Planning." *Architecture* (Feb. 1994): 105-109.

Kerruish, Karen. "The Marketing Plan." *SMPS Core Series.* SMPS (1991).

Kogan, Raymond. "Market Research: Intelligence For Your Firm's Future." SMPS (1996).

Lea, Bruce. "Creative Strategy Derives from Market Segmentation" *The Marketing Plan: Supplement.* SMPS Publication.

MacLachan, Douglas L. "Marketing Research, What It Is and Isn't." *SMPS Marketer*, Special Edition.

Peppers, Don, Martha Rogers, Ph.D., and Bob Dorf. *The One to One Fieldbook.* Doubleday, 1999.

Tuttle, Donald J., and Carla D. Thompson. "Flying with Eagles: An Interview with Gerry Gerron, Founder and Principal, G2 Architecture." *SMPS Marketer* (Feb. 1999): 4-7, 16-17.

Karen W. Winters, FSMPS

- Karen Winters is an associate and director of marketing and administration at King & King, Architects (Syracuse, N.Y.), where she has key marketing and management responsibilities.
- She is a Fellow of the Society for Marketing Professional Services.
- She is a Certified Professional Services Marketer.
- Fifteen years of direct marketing experience and 14 years as an SMPS member have provided her with a comprehensive exposure to marketing professional services.
- SMPS National Certification Commission, 1998-present.
- SMPS National Board of Directors, Northeast Regional Director, 1993-95.
- SMPS Presidents Leadership Symposium, 1991 and 1992.
- SMPS Upstate New York Chapter, past president, president, vice president, program director, 1987-91.
- SMPS National Committee chair, Member & Chapter Services, 1990-92.
- SMPS National Marketing Plan Task Force, 1991.
- SMPS National Education & Program Committee, 1988-90.
- SMPS National Conference – 12 years.

1.4 Clear Company Direction: The Deciding Factor in Business Success

Ellen Flynn-Heapes, FSMPS
President
SPARKS: The Center for Strategic Planning

The most critical success factor in marketing is this: *working with a firm that is clear about who they are and what they want to become.* How many talented marketers do you know who have failed because their firms just couldn't decide on a clear direction? Chasing everything is a high-stakes gamble at best, but more often it's a losing proposition for everyone.

The research is in. Large and small, **experts** will lead the millennium. The only questions are, "What will you be an expert in?" and "How will you choose to *lead* the market?"

For any marketer or marketing program to be successful, company leaders must have answers to these questions. The answers come in the form of a well-chosen identity, a consciously conceived business design and a profit model that works.

Any firm can go along with conventional growth and diversification tactics, but as Lee Iacocca said, "My biggest mistake with Chrysler was to diversify beyond our expertise." Jack Welch, chairman of GE and the most distinguished leader in business today, said, "We released half of our staff and businesses, and we became No. 1 or No. 2 in each of our markets." Focused spin-offs in industry have reached record numbers in the last three years, and they're doing *better* than their parent companies.[1]

Well-focused firms just plain do better. They build a marketplace leadership position, and as a result, gain the choicest clients, fees and talent. By riveting their attention on what they do best, they push their expertise. And expertise is the key factor in establishing a strong bargaining position in the market.

Nobody's pigeon-holed. Instead, staff members delight in seeking mastery. Their work is challenging, and their businesses make meaningful contributions to the world.

To create marketplace leadership, company leaders must be the *executive designers* of their firm's distinctive enterprise. They must treat this responsibility with all the care and passion that they bring to their projects.

What's Your Frustration?

Truly, it's difficult to design yourself. It's hard to think strategically into a vague future. And it takes a lot of gumption to keep focused and stand for something.

Like the doctor, we begin the discussion of company direction with the question: "Where does it hurt?" This is how we find the energy points for forward motion. What frustrates people in our industry the most? Here is the list of major headaches:

1. Competing on price.
2. Unreasonable client expectations in schedule and budget.
3. Not making the profit we deserve.
4. Not getting and keeping talented people.
5. Lack of leadership and leadership transition.

Most of these problems stem from a lack of clear direction in the company. *The Sparks Framework* is a technology we've developed over the years to help firms create a clear, compelling direction, build consensus and operate at a very high level of performance.

The Sparks Framework: A Cast of Characters

At its core, *The Sparks Framework* helps firms choose to be great. It offers a simple yet breakthrough concept:

You must become *MASTERFUL* at something — a building type, a client type, a niche, a locale, a process — something that you build to a high level of worth. Only then are you in a position to truly create value — sustainable value in the face of tough competition.

In their planning, many firms still default to hackneyed mission statements and vague wishes to be "the premier firm in (blank), providing excellence in service and quality, and meeting or exceeding the client's expectations." In other words, company leaders plod along as nice guys doing good work, but are unable to stand for something special in which to excel. They desperately need a detailed road map of their possible choices — a clear way to decide their best direction, choose the right investments and build their firm for the future.

We studied (and tried) many models for creating strategy, but our favorite was the framework created by Benjamin Tregoe and John W. Zimmerman in *Top Management Strategy: What It Is and How to Make It Work*.[2] The authors outlined nine specific driving forces that form the heart of differing corporations. We were also inspired by the personality structures of Swiss psychologist Carl Jung's six *Heroic Characters*.[3] And we were impressed with the Coxe Group's construct of idea, service and delivery firms overlaid with practice-based versus business-based values.[4]

Ultimately we developed our own six character types for the design professions. They are:

- The Einsteins
- The Niche Experts
- The Market Partners
- The Community Leaders
- The Orchestrators
- The Builders

In *The Sparks Framework,* each character has a personality. When you get to know them, you can say, "An Einstein would never do *this*," or "Of course they did *that* — they're an Orchestrator." In fact, each character is a full portrait that includes: (1) the underlying driving forces and core values that comprise its *identity*, (2) a scaffold of best practices that comprise its *operating model* and (3) an optimizing *profit model*.

See if you can find your firm among the following types. Is it steadfastly seated in one of the profiles? Is it a well-designed hybrid of two *characters*? Or is it straddling the fence across the board — a little of this, a little of that?

Type 1: The Einstein

Einstein firms are built around the generation of original ideas and new technologies. In architecture, they are the high-profile design firms with original styles or philosophies. In engineering, they're the Ph.D.s with strong research and development functions. The firm often works with research grants or endowments, and staff members love to experiment as well as teach and publish. Renowned French designer Renzo Piano even hosts an online design workshop for those interested in the design experience.[5]

Other examples are Norman Foster, Frank Gehry, Michel Virlogeux, Santiago Calatrava and Buckminster Fuller. Einsteins are known for a distinctive set of original ideas, and can apply them across building types and across the world geographically. Their philosophy, however, is singularly focused.

Type 2: The Niche Expert

Niche Experts are dedicated to a specific project-type or service-type within a broader market. They watch the experiments of the Einsteins, and adapt them to create state-of-the-art work. They frequently team through a network of other firms to provide full services for a given project, and are often national or international in scope.

HOK Sport is a project-type nicher. Besides its highly successful focus on sports facilities, it enjoys a unique, uncompromised reputation relative to its parent company, HOK. It benefits from a separate, descriptive name, a separate location and separate management.

Duany Plater-Zyberk is a service-type nicher focusing on "new urbanism" master planning. Andres Duany and Elizabeth Plater-Zyberk have built a marketplace powerhouse commanding some of the highest fees in the profession.

Wiss Janney Elstner is known for its building technology forensic work; Cini-Little is known for food service; Rolf Jensen leads the market in fire protection; Kroll Schiff & Associates excels in security; Stone Engineering holds the niche in tourist railroads; Walter P. Moore is expert in sports and convention center structures; and Allan Greenberg specializes in neoclassical architecture. Some firms make niches in an ethnic background, such as Douglas Cardinal of American Indian descent. Large or small, the difference is that Nichers are specialists.

Type 3: The Market Partner

Market Partners lead in one or a few major markets such as health care, higher education, the food and beverage industry or transportation. Montgomery Watson and CDM, for example, are committed to the water/waste water market. Shepley Bulfinch Richardson and Abbott is a Market Partner committed to the academic/health care market. ADP Marshall is committed to the microelectronics/research and development/lab market.

Market Partners are strong advocates for their clients and the client industry, often leading lobbying efforts and crusading at client trade meetings. They enjoy a number of patrons with whom they share the same goals and values, creating a base of personal friendships. Market Partners typically serve multiple segments within their industry, and benefit from offering a broad range of services to support their chosen market (and keep them coming back for more).

Another characteristic practice of the Market Partner is to incorporate former client-side staffers into the firm. Ai, an architecture, engineering and interior design firm focused on the corporate market, gains legitimacy from Rusty Meadows' AT&T background. General Sverdrup used his client-side experience in building McArthur's airfields in the Pacific and his experience building the Missouri Highway Department's roads and bridges to leverage his transportation-based engineering enterprise. Many firms keyed to the federal markets have former employees of the targeted agencies in high-level marketing and project management positions. This represents real commitment to the market of choice.

Type 4: Community Leaders

Community Leaders aim for a leadership role in their town's action. They sink deep roots into the community, developing close relationships on both a social and political level. They seek the premier local project work, which ranges across the board in size and type, including public buildings, police and fire stations, recreation centers, schools, shelters, public works and other municipal facilities. For those projects requiring significant technical knowledge, they team with a network of Niche Experts around the country.

Many design professionals begin with a small, local practice. The difference, however, between being a high-performing Community Leader and an under-performing generalist, is that Community Leaders are so woven into the fabric of the community that they open doors that are closed to outsiders. They can expedite decision-making by virtue of their professional and personal relationships in the community.

One of the best examples of a Community Leader is Carde Ten Architects in Santa Monica, Calif. Focused on community projects, the firm scouts opportunities for funding, arranges real estate opportunities and organizes the entire project for the *potential* client. This packaging process takes them out of the realm of competition and fee-for-time. Besides their healthy design fee, they also take part in the development and construction management fees.

Community Leaders invest heavily in their local networks. Freidl Bohm, president of NBBJ, established his infrastructure in Columbus, Ohio, with YPO, local board involvement and ownership in a successful chain of restaurants in town. Jack Kinstlinger of KCI Technologies is one of the few engineers participating in Maryland economic development. Harvey Gantt served as mayor of Charlotte, N.C., again illustrating a depth of commitment to the community.

Type 5: The Orchestrator

Orchestrators focus on outstanding project management, bringing their skills to bear on large, complex projects, including the best design/build jobs. Emphasis is on speed, coordination and control. Many Orchestrators are known for their PM/CM expertise.

Bechtel, Fluor-Daniel and the engineer/contractors are classic Orchestrators. The leading program managers, such as Heery International, 3D-International and CRS Constructors are Orchestrators.

In some A/E circles, practitioners bemoan the fact that the big accounting firms, including Ernst & Young and Andersen Consulting, are moving into our industry. In fact, they are taking advantage of a high-demand Orchestrator role. You won't see them active in the other archetype configurations.

Askew Nixon Ferguson Architects is an example of a smaller firm operating as an Orchestrator. Early in its history, ANFA started out working for Federal Express, by definition a speed and logistics-oriented client. They developed a culture to match, full of high-energy people concerned with project management. Today they are still working for Federal Express, but have added casinos, another fast-paced project type.

Privatization is the realm of the Orchestrator. Because Orchestrators know their work, know their process, and enjoy time and cost challenges, they are effective with these financial/technical behemoths. Of all the character types, this is where we find the most MBAs.

Type 6: The Builder

Builders have the real cost advantage, focusing on prototypes, site adaptations and multi-site project rollouts for retail stores, HMOs, branch banks, service stations, telecommunications towers, U.S. Job Corps centers and mass government office space.

Volume rollouts, a fast and inexpensive way for client organizations to expand into multiple geographic markets, save the costs of individually developed and designed units. Tulsa-based BSW International is a leader here, specializing in "multiple facility building programs" for clients such as Wal-Mart, Circuit City and Marriott. BSW is unabashedly dedicated to improving their clients' financial success, and even casts itself as a real estate development services company that offers program management, real estate and site development services as well as design and construction. The firm has been featured in the *Wall Street*

Journal, Business Week, Inc, and *Fortune* as a thriving example not only in design, but also as a leader among American service firms.

Black and Veatch is another top Builder. A major engineering/construction firm, it has a production center base in Kansas City where staff executes the work in an extremely efficient manner. This allows them to dominate many markets, to reap the benefits of high volume and to extend themselves internationally at a lower risk than those who struggle to produce a consistently reliable work product.

Interestingly, Builders have been successful with total quality management, unlike other firms in the profession that view speed and cost leadership as unprofessional. Because Builders are such an integral part of their client's financial success, they move very quickly. And if you're committed to beating the budget and schedule, you need a serious program that assures quality — just like their clients have.

The Sparks Principles

The Sparks Framework is based on three major principles:

1. Each of the six characters has a bold, clear identity driven by internal goals and values, and matched to complementary client groups.
2. Each of the six characters has a cohesive, integrated business design — a scaffold of best practices that comprise its operating model.
3. Each of the six characters has a specific profit model that optimizes its financial performance. (Please refer to the bibliography for *The Sparks Framework: a Handbook of Value-Creating Strategies*, in which we address the profit models.)

Principle 1: Bold, Clear Identity

Any meaningful discussion of corporate direction begins with the question of identity. This is especially true for organizations in the knowledge industry, with no tangible product until after the fact.

Can you answer the following questions? What are the firm's most deeply held values? What are its driving forces? How is it distinctive? How is it expert? What is its greatest value to the client? What does it hope to accomplish in the next 20 years?

It's not easy to uncover and articulate the unique ingredients that make up the essence of a firm. In fact, in strategy retreats, when we ask top leaders about their purpose, many tell the familiar story of how they were taken aside early by the firm's founder, the "old man," and told to shed their schoolboy idealism. "The reason we're in business, son, is to make money." I learned this catechism myself in business school. Question: "What is the purpose of business?" Answer: "To maximize shareholder wealth."

Certainly creating wealth is a good thing, but like King Midas, if you haven't got your values and purpose right first, you can run into trouble. According to management guru Peter Drucker, this is especially critical today. Since the best and most dedicated people are ultimately volunteers, they have many lucrative opportunities from which to choose. They have multiple job offers, and pick a firm because it's doing something that they consider important. Companies need to have a clear understanding of their identity in order to attract, motivate and retain outstanding people. This goes *double* for attracting the best clients.

"Tell us about your firm" is a question that frequently meets with the following set of answers. We were established in 1909/1949/1979. We have 30/300/3000 people and 3/7/15 offices. We have this (laundry list) of services, and work in a wide variety (laundry list) of project types. Next in the formula is how great their service and quality is.

In an effort to hedge our bets, we look and act neutral. Ted Kennedy, chairman of BE&K, mega-engineer/constructor and one of *Fortune* magazine's top 100 companies to work for, said, "We have not done well differentiating ourselves from each other. If we don't stop acting like pork bellies, we're in for big trouble."

When clients perceive that they're buying a pork belly, they select on price. If they're a government agency, they select on qualifications (but ask for your overhead rates in advance).

"Understand my problems and deliver to my needs efficiently," owners tell us over and over again. In our research, 96 percent of owners we interview want the expert, the firm that knows what it's doing. Visualize a bulging muscle and make it your secret logo.

Many of the larger firms know that cross-selling services is tough; the fact is that clients today do not want a wide variety of project types. They only want to hear about how you relate to their problem. And they don't care about one-stop shopping, unless the package gets their current job done most efficiently.

A representative from Smith Kline said recently, "Please tell us how you're different. We want to hire you. But we can't if you won't tell us how you're the best. Give us real reasons! Give us *meat*!"

The Source of Identity: The Driving Force

Although many firms operate expediently and reactively, most have a favorite place that they live — or at least aspire to. They have an array of values, but a single special one reigns supreme. The firm's supreme business value is called its driving force, and if we can capture it, we're on our way to building the right business model.

For example, the driving force of the Orchestrator is a love of the logistics chess game. Project management, they believe, is the greatest challenge in the world, and the most worthwhile endeavor of all. They consider themselves an "elite cadre" — a SWAT team. As applied to their business design, we would see a very well-organized and planned firm, corporate in feel. Its top staff members are the best PMs. They have formal training curricula, and they make their highest profit on the most complex projects. All staff members understand what's really important.

Specific driving forces characterize each of the types in *The Sparks Framework*. They are shared, gut-level beliefs about what's most essential to accomplish together. More than any cultural value, such as integrity, collaboration and "fun," agreement upon these driving forces influences the success of the firm. Conflicts on this pivotal point can also destroy the firm.

The following driving forces are associated with each character:

Character	Distinctive Driving Force
Einstein	Cutting-Edge Innovation
Niche Expert	Perfecting the Specialty
Market Partner	Customer Partnership
Community Leader	Community Connectivity
Orchestrator	Project Management Challenge
Builder	Cost/Quality Challenge

When probing for the deepest elements of identity, we encounter a common fearful protest: "You have to be flexible!" "You can't survive without having all these abilities!" "You have to keep looking for new opportunities!"

In fact, flexibility, openness and responsiveness to clients are *always* required. But reactivity at a firm's core is predictive of the company that loses its way.

Every firm must have a solid baseline of quality, efficiency, creativity, flexibility, openness and client service in its work. The key is to keep your eye on where your real distinctive value is, and build strength. The essential position is NOT how can we respond well, *but how can we lead well.*

Driving forces tend to be "discovered" rather than invented.

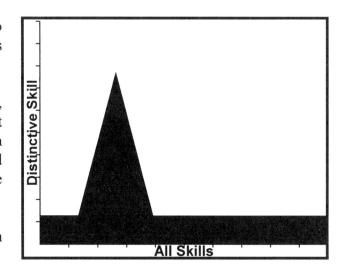

Through exercises and models, firms can learn what's been driving them to date. Most likely, a hidden structure that either facilitates or presents obstacles to the full expression of the driver can be ferreted out. And if we can discover these structures, we can discover the driving forces that have been surreptitiously operating. Then we can work with them.

Rather than seeking simple discovery and refinement, some firms go well beyond to revolutionize things with a brand new driving force. Sienna Architecture, a mid-sized firm in Portland, Ore., is a good example. Over the course of several years, and through a well-designed strategic planning process, the firm's owners successfully moved from a cost/quality-driven firm to a cutting-edge design leader in the Pacific Northwest.

When you decide to make a stand on your driving force, you'll foster certain values and weed out others, using care and patience. You'll fine-tune your entire business model, including staffing, marketing, project systems and perhaps your ownership structure. Once this model is in focus and consensus is built, you almost can't help but bring the more powerful vision into reality. It becomes so clear.

Driving Forces and the Hidden Client Agenda

The beauty of an identity is that it acts like a magnet to attract a group of clients seeking your kind of expertise. In other words, certain client groupings have typical agendas for which they need certain kinds of firms. Rarely do clients go outside their unspoken agendas, and if they do, they tend *not* to recognize value.

It's tricky to determine what the client views as most valuable; in fact some don't consciously know themselves. Sure they want and need everything it takes to do their project. But certain aspects will be more critical than others. Needless to say, it's wise to spend time on this question and get real answers. Go beyond the first blush of what the client tells you. Push beyond the shorthand cliches: *be faster*, *be cheaper* and *give us good service*. Question if these are the most highly charged client needs, or if they're just the outside layer of the onion. Whatever your chosen client values most highly — and you find worthwhile challenges — make your firm the ultimate expert in it.

Here are the essential linkages from driver to typical hidden agenda, by character.

Character	Driving Force	Hidden Client Agenda
Einstein	*Innovation*	*Needs to fulfill need for prestige, improved image*
Niche Expert	*Cutting-edge Method*	*Needs to overcome risky, adverse conditions*
Market Partner	*Customer Partnership*	*Needs to augment client's own skills, as full-services "partner*
Community Leader	*Community Contribution*	*Needs facilitation through community gatekeepers*
Orchestrator	*Project Management Challenge*	*Needs to control project complexity*
Builder	*Cost/Quality Challenge*	*Needs to deliver the product, optimizing the budget*

Driving Forces and the Sacred Technology

Very specific technologies (defined here as methodologies for doing things rather than computer technologies) characterize each of the types in *The Sparks Framework*. These are the true centers of excellence for which the firm is valued in the marketplace. They are links on the overall project value-chain, and it's a rare customer that considers them all equally valuable.

Ask yourself this question: Are you so busy getting the work in and out that you neglect to nurture the more difficult and risky technology that makes you special? When the firm's driving force is clear, and its leaders understand what's most valuable to its clients, then its Sacred Technology also becomes clear.

Character Type	Driving Force	Hidden Client Agenda	Sacred Technology
Einstein	Innovation	Needs to fulfill need for prestige, improved image	Generating brand new ideas and technologies
Niche Expert	Cutting-edge Method	Needs to overcome risky, adverse conditions	Transferring new knowledge to the target niche
Market Partner	Customer Partnership	Needs to augment client's own skills, as full-services "partner"	Expanding ways to help the sector-specific client
Community Leader	Community Connectivity	Needs facilitation through community gatekeepers	Nurturing the network of relationships with local leaders
Orchestrator	Project Management Challenge	Needs to control project complexity	Pushing sophisticated logistics control on large projects
Builder	Cost/Quality Challenge	Needs to deliver the product, optimizing the budget	Advancing brilliant new production technologies

The Exclamation Point of Identity: The Name

In our strategy courses we play a game called "Design a Great Firm." As part of the exercise, the firm has to have a ... name. *Never* have we said it can't be the principals' names, yet never has a group voluntarily selected personal names. Perhaps the selection of a descriptive name is a subtle design mechanism to keep the firm on focus?

We get lots of exciting new ventures designed (and sometimes actually started!). For example:

- *"Global Eagle"* is a golf clubhouse and resort community design firm, operating internationally.
- *"Zeitgeist"* is a high-tech project management/construction management firm.
- *"ZipZap"* dominates the world of speedy retail rollouts.
- *"Atlantatude"* is a design atelier with a unique southern-style influence.
- *"Design for Healthcare"* provides lifecycle services for hospital clients in the Midwest.
- *"Life Critical"* is a cutting-edge designer of emergency rooms and trauma centers.
- *"U.P. Community Design"* is part of every major project in the Upper Peninsula of Michigan, and is built on community participation.
- *"AirMax"* does design/build airport projects throughout the country.

In general, using the founders' names leaves room for un-strategic shenanigans: perceptual confusion and survivalist reactivity that can kill success. "Buyers want a shortcut," says Ed Razek, president of marketing and creative services for The Limited Inc. "They have too many choices and not enough time. There's too much stimulation. They want it made easy, explicit, and predictable."

Most firms entertaining branding now are hoping that their existing company name will do the trick and they can avoid a big statement about anything specific. Some dip their toe in, keeping the standard name and perhaps adding another, e.g., KPS Justice or Baker/Environmental. By the way, research shows that initials distance the client from the firm. They may be convenient legally, but they're a weak compromise from a marketing standpoint. Most customers prefer a "product/promise" name or even a personal name to initials.

Principle 2: Business Design — The Web of Strategy and Structure

Curiously, many design firms are themselves not designed. They simply do their clients' bidding and react to whatever is needed at the time. Some firms inadvertently build a business design that is dysfunctional, with lots of structural obstacles in the way of success. Perhaps you know a firm that wanted to build deep community relationships, but the leaders were introverted technical folks. Some firms want to build their project management expertise, but have a chronic fear of becoming "paper pushers." Some want to master a specialty service, but feel they must be *flexible*.

Beyond choosing the firm's identity, the next essential element is a conscious design of the business such that it can play at its peak. When a firm is "playing the game well," it's using a scaffold of practices that are both cohesive and aligned. Things aren't in conflict; they're in *flow*.

Although we can't see what's supporting this desired state, the firm is working with a very specific web of internal strategies and structures that comprise an understood operating model or business design. In a healthy situation, they encourage the desired behaviors and inhibit the undesired behaviors, on a fairly effortless basis. Business designs are largely intangible, reflecting culture, aspiration and even policy — and they are powerful shapers of behavior.

Strategic planning, if done correctly, is the process that helps the firm think through its business design and make deliberate refinements. Some people think the end result of strategic planning is a sequential list of tasks to be implemented, but a list is ineffectual compared with business design.

The Scaffold of Business Design

In *The Sparks Framework*, each of the six characters relies on a distinct business design. And each business design is organized into three distinct strands that form the structural elements of the design. The three strands are in fact primary strategic systems that operate in every firm.

1. **Getting Work:** Markets and Marketing.
2. **Doing Work:** Projects and People.
3. **Organizing Work:** Money and Leadership.

Broadly speaking, we can use a continuum to array these strategies and activities, ranging from the Einsteins and Nichers at one end, and the Orchestrators and Builders at the other. A macro view only, the following chart illustrates the range of these basic practices.

For example, when the characters at the left seek higher visibility, they increase their writing, teaching and speaking. When the characters at the right seek higher visibility, they benefit more from exhibits, direct mail and advertising. When the characters at the left seek to improve their work, they try more experimentation and collaboration, while their colleagues at the right focus on greater utilization and productivity. When the characters at the left seek to track their performance, they look for design-related statistics, while their colleagues at the right aim for budget and schedule statistics.

	Einsteins	Niche Experts	Market Partners	Community Leaders	Orchestrators	Builders
Getting Work	Writing, Teaching and Speaking ⟵⟶ Exhibits, Direct Mail, Advertising					
Doing Work	Experiment and Collaboration ⟵⟶ High Utilization and Productivity					
Organizing Work	Design Performance & Statistics ⟵⟶ Budget and Schedule Statistics					

In application, we set strategy not only in the broad systems but also the subsystems. The basic subsystems of most firms are listed below.

Getting Work: Markets and Marketing

What Is the Firm Known for?
- Sales Message
- Promotional Strategy
- Geographical Reach
- Best Fees

Doing Work: Projects and People

What Are the Firm's Targets?
- Deep Expertise
- Staff Mix
- Project Management
- Learning

Organizing Work: Money and Leadership

How Does the Firm Organize for Business?
- Ownership
- Investments
- Offices
- Information Systems

Our graphic models (see Einstein example on the next page) initially assist in teaching individuals and groups about company design. In strategic planning, where the designs are crafted to the specific organization, the graphic models improve strategic clarity as well as communication of the ideas to all stakeholders in the firm.

Note that each triangle corner of the business design model refers to one of the system strands; the boxes refer to the linked subsystems.

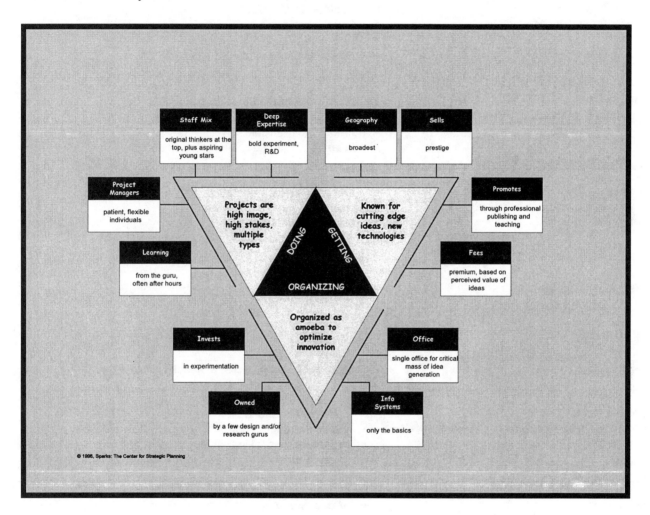

The following business designs are based on extensive research and practical experience with successful design firms throughout the country. Our findings show that these organizations are most successful when their strategies are aligned with one model, rather than a blend of various models.

That being said, most firms find themselves practicing under several models. We see hybrids, for example, of Market Partners using a Niche strategy, Orchestrators using a Community Leader strategy, etc. However, the best choice is to be firmly anchored in one character type, and then cross-fertilize in a deliberately designed way.

Business Design 1:
The Einsteins

Client Agenda	Needs prestige, improved image
Client Value	Cutting-edge ideas or technologies

Getting Work *Known for cutting-edge ideas*	• *Geography*: Broadest • *Sells*: Prestige • *Promotes*: Teaching/ publishing • *Fees*: Premium, perceived value of ideas
Doing Work *High-image, high-stakes, multiple types*	• *Deep expertise*: Bold experiment, R&D • *Staff*: Original thinkers, aspiring stars • *PM*: Patient, flexible • *Learning*: From guru, often after hours
Organizing Work *Organized as an amoeba to optimize innovation*	• *Invests*: In experimentation • *Owned*: Main or a few gurus • *Info Systems*: Basics • *Office*: Single, critical mass of ideas

Business Design 2:
The Niche Experts

Client Agenda	Needs to overcome project risk, adverse conditions
Client Value	Unsurpassed leadership in a specific area

Getting Work *Known for deep expertise in project or service specialty*	• *Geography*: Broadest • *Sells*: Rare knowledge • *Promotes*: Speaking/writing to client groups • *Fees*: Premium, documented results
Doing Work *Complex or high-risk requiring, singular type*	• *Deep expertise*: Latest approaches • *Staff*: Specialists at top, dedicated youngsters and stabilizers in middle • *PM*: Dedicated specialists who can also handle the realities of the management process • *Learning*: Juniors initiate mentoring
Organizing Work *Organized around specialists to optimize advancement of the niche*	• *Invests*: New applications, depth of network • *Owned*: Distinguished experts • *Info Systems*: Benefit statistics • *Office*: Single for critical mass, alliances

Business Design 3:
The Market Partners

Client Agenda	Needs a trusted partner, augment skills
Client Value	Service depth within a market area

Getting Work *Known for broad experience within an industry*	▪ **Geography**: Regional or national ▪ **Sells**: Market dedication, experience, access ▪ **Promotes**: Industry connections, trend letters ▪ **Fees**: Improved with patron clients
Doing Work *Range of types within one or few markets*	▪ **Deep expertise**: Industry operations, people ▪ **Staff**: Stable array of professionals, some from within client industry ▪ **PM**: Well-organized, experienced in market ▪ **Learning**: Conventions, informal mentors
Organizing Work *Organized as practice groups to optimize market expertise*	▪ **Invests**: Bench depth, like-firm acquisitions ▪ **Owned**: Known market players, select techs ▪ **Info Systems**: Stats by market, repeat clients ▪ **Office**: Select regional offices

Business Design 4:
The Community Leaders

Client Agenda	Needs access and service
Client Value	Mutual commitment to community

Getting Work *Known for contribution to the community*	▪ **Geography**: Community-based ▪ **Sells**: Access, service, connectedness ▪ **Promotes**: Community events, PR, network ▪ **Fees**: Improved when "wired in"
Doing Work *Range of types, moderate complexity*	▪ **Deep expertise**: Local relationships, issues ▪ **Staff**: Multi-discipline groups ▪ **PM**: Combined PM/discipline chiefs; if large firm has strong work-sharing process ▪ **Learning**: Networking locally, professionally
Organizing Work *Organized around local leaders to optimize connectivity*	▪ **Invests**: Local visibility, niche partners, new offices ▪ **Owned**: Broad group, may be ESOP ▪ **Info Systems**: Performance by local office ▪ **Office**: One or multi, for local access

Business Design 5:
The Orchestrators

Client Agenda	Needs logistical control
Client Value	Skilled PM for larger, complex projects

Getting Work *Known for great project management, organizational skills*	▪ *Geography*: Regional or national ▪ *Sells*: Speed, process control ▪ *Promotes*: Through business press ▪ *Fees*: Premium fees for PM/CM
Doing Work *Highly complex logistically, larger scale, often design/build*	▪ *Deep expertise*: In PM ▪ *Staff:* Senior and jr. PMs, MBAs ▪ *PM*: Top PM systems, tools, resources ▪ *Learning*: Formal training curriculum
Organizing Work *Organized around PMs to optimize systems and technologies*	▪ *Invests*: Elite corps of PMs, local firm alliances ▪ *Owned*: Current or former PMs, corporate ▪ *Info Systems*: Project-level statistics ▪ *Office*: Corp HQ plus satellites, PMs travel

Business Design 6:
The Builders

Client Agenda	Needs product delivered, budget optimized
Client Value	Cost, quality and consistency

Getting Work *Known for quality work at a low cost*	▪ *Geography*: Regional base, broad site alliances ▪ *Sells*: Best quality for price, consistency ▪ *Promotes*: Direct mail, ads, sales reps ▪ *Fees*: Bid work, clever efficiencies
Doing Work *Mostly prototype/site adaptations*	▪ *Deep expertise*: In replication efficiencies ▪ *Staff:* Jr. professionals and techs ▪ *PM*: Accountability, standard procedures ▪ *Learning*: Formal training classes
Organizing Work *Organized around production teams to optimize efficiency*	▪ *Invests*: Production capacity, technology ▪ *Owned*: One or few entrepreneurs, may be family-owned ▪ *Info Systems*: Production unit costs ▪ *Office*: Production center, field offices

A Challenge

We challenge you to look at a fresh reality: *the age of the expert.*

- Devote your firm to what you do best.
- Seize the necessary resources to fund your business design.
- Assert leadership of your market.

As Tom Peters says, "There is no excuse for not being great!"

Endnotes

[1] David Sadtler, et al., *Break-Up: How Companies Use Spin-offs to Gain Focus and Grow Strong* (The Free Press, 1997).

[2] Benjamin Tregoe, and John W. Zimmerman, *Top Management Strategy: What It Is and How to Make It Work* (Touchstone/Simon & Schuster, 1980).

[3] Carol S. Pearson, *The Hero Within: Six Characters We Live By,* (Harper, 1998).

[4] The Coxe Group, *Success Strategies for Design Professionals* (McGraw-Hill, 1987).

[5] See **www.RPWF.org**.

Bibliography

Flynn-Heapes, Ellen. *Creating Wealth: Principles and Practices for Design Firms.* SPARKS: The Center for Strategic Planning (1999).

—. *The Sparks Framework: A Handbook of Value-Creation Strategies.* SPARKS: The Center for Strategic Planning (2000).

—. "Strategic Planning." *Design Professionals' Handbook of Business and Law.* John Wiley & Sons, 1993.

—. "Ten Bold Strategies for the New Millennium." *SMPS Marketer* (April 1999).

—. "Values," "How to Get Strategic," "The Guts of Competitive Strategy." *Strategic Planning: Preparing Your Firm for Success in the Future,* PSMJ Resources (1997).

Ellen Flynn-Heapes, FSMPS

- Ellen Flynn-Heapes is president, SPARKS: The Center for Strategic Planning, Alexandria, Va.
- Flynn-Heapes is a nationally recognized authority on competitive and organizational strategy for the design and construction professions.
- She was the first management consultant in the country to specialize in strategic planning for firms in the industry, and over the years has earned considerable praise for both her pioneering work and her continued innovations.
- SPARKS clients include design and construction firms throughout the United States as well as government agencies and corporations related to the built environment.
- With an MBA and as a 25-year veteran in the A/E/C industry, Flynn-Heapes grounded her career with HOK and later Skidmore Owings and Merrill. Today, she coaches company leaders on how to design their desired futures, and build the strongest, most successful organizations possible.
- She conducts seminars around the country, and lectures to both academic and professional groups, including AIA, ACEC and SMPS.
- She is a Fellow of the Society for Marketing Professional Services, and served four years on its national board of directors.

www.ForSparks.com
Ellen@ForSparks.com

Reprinted with permission from The Sparks Environment: A Handbook of Value-Creation Strategies, by Ellen Flynn-Heapes, SPARKS: The Center for Strategic Planning, 2001.

1.5 The Niche Strategy: A Stronger Way to Compete

Ellen Flynn-Heapes, FSMPS
President
SPARKS: The Center for Strategic Planning

In recent years, the niche strategy has become the single-most popular competitive strategy outside of traditional practice. This wasn't always so.

In 1986, fresh out of business school, I wrote an article for the *SMPS Newsletter* entitled "The Virtues of a Specialized Practice." A few people liked the article, but more than a few sent hate mail. Specialization, or niching as we call it now, is one of the basic strategies in industry, but it was considered radical in the design and construction world at that time. The conventional wisdom was "diversify and build volume," which is still the only strategy many firms ever consider.

When the construction market reached its trough in the early 1990s, a significant part of our industry was completely out of luck. Clients could pick and choose as they pleased from a nice, low-cost menu. Firms bemoaned fee competition, and all wrung their hands over bidding. A few did very well, however: those that kept a focused eye on what they did very well, and for whom.

The more focused you are, the better position you are in to see what the client will need next. Then you can *create* the trend by developing it before anyone else does. Diversified generalists, by contrast, have blurred vision. They do not understand anything well enough to be in front of the curve and *lead the market* (which is where the goodies are).

Today, things are even more competitive. Virtually any client can get the *world's* best expert in an instant. And why go to an all-things-to-all-people-and-master-of-none when you can easily assemble a team of the best?

In our globally linked world, with tremendously expanded options, clients select only what they want from the huge array of choices. An (anonymous) representative from the Corps of Engineers Medical Group confided to us recently that the organization hires only the "*real* experts in hospitals." If an architect or engineer doesn't have "a ton of hospital experience," he said, "no amount of relationship, service or price will help. These days there are so many A/Es to choose from, you can just go down to the corner — and flag one down!"

What Exactly Is a Niche?

Niche Basics

Those firms that are thriving, says Tom Peters in *Thriving on Chaos*, increasingly share common traits. "Most pronounced is the emergence of the specialist producer of high value-added goods or services — the niche creator — which is either a stand-alone firm or a downsized, more entrepreneurial unit of a big firm," says Peters.[1]

The ideal niche is a small segment of a broader market in which demand is high and supply is low: the very definition of value. How small a piece of the market qualifies as a niche? As small as it takes to reach this high-value state.

In Chapter 1.4 we discussed *The Sparks Framework,* which outlines six basic configurations for building a firm's expertise. From a broad-brush perspective, each of the six could be considered a way to specialize. However, the Niche Expert has a very specific business design, and tends to focus on one of the following four formats:

1. The *project-type niche,* in which the firm focuses on such project types as academic library buildings, corporate airports or embassies.

2. The *service-type niche,* in which the firm specializes in such services as acoustics, fire protection or programming.

3. The *client-type niche,* in which the firm targets a small segment of an overall client type, such as consumer goods manufacturers, small municipalities or the Mennonite community.

4. The *theme niche,* in which the firm offers a substantive quality or feature such as sustainable design, visioning and consensus-building, or MBE/WBE.

For more perspective on niches, consider health care construction. By itself, health care is a broad market, not a niche. Health care niches might include women's centers, children's hospitals, heart centers and life-care facilities. They can be further refined into such micro-niches as inner city life-care facilities, specialty children's clinics or women-owned professional women's health centers.

Why Niche?

Research shows that well-differentiated, focused firms are much more profitable than generalists. Michael Porter's famous U-curve (see Figure 1) indicates that both nichers and production firms yield higher returns on investment (ROI) than those with a generalist approach. In fact, we have found that the left or specialist side of the curve can reach profit levels up to 50 percent and beyond, while the low-cost, high-volume producer can reach up to 20 percent. The generalist trough on the curve speaks for itself.

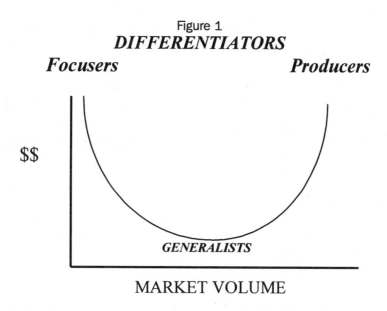

Figure 1
DIFFERENTIATORS
Focusers   *Producers*

Michael Porter's U-Curve model illustrates the greater returns on investment enjoyed by both niche firms and production firms over generalists, by virtue of their respective types of efficiency. (Reprinted by permission of the Free Press, and imprint of Simon & Schuster from Competitive Strategy: Techniques for Analyzing Industries and Competitors by Michael E. Porter. Copyright 1980 by The Free Press.)

Getting to Know the Niche Experts

HOK Sport is a *project-type nicher*. Besides its focus on sports facilities, it enjoys a unique, uncompromised reputation relative to its parent company, HOK. It benefits from a separate, descriptive name, a separate location and separate management. What's even more interesting is that it has micro-niches: NHL/NBA arenas, collegiate and minor league arenas, Olympic arenas, major league ballparks, training ballparks, collegiate ballparks, minor league ballparks, NFL stadiums, collegiate stadiums, rugby/soccer stadiums and university recreation centers. The market recognizes HOK Sport internationally. Few other design firms can boast a cover story in *USA Today*!

HOK Sport is particularly strong because it holds the "first there" position in the market, which almost guarantees a dominant place. Clients are willing to pay a premium for this expertise because they perceive that their return will be higher and/or their risk will be lower.

Duany Plater-Zyberk is a *service-type niche expert* focusing on "new urbanism" master planning. Andres Duany and Elizabeth Plater-Zyberk have built a marketplace powerhouse commanding some of the highest fees in the profession. Sherry Plaster Carter, *Engineering News Record's* 1996 Award of Excellence Winner, runs Carter & Carter, a service-type niche practice specializing in crime prevention through environmental design (CPTED). This technology is used to deter criminals by attracting citizens to public, educational and commercial venues.

Certainly many firms were given life by *client-type niching* of the most classical type: the military niche. In our industry, this ranges from the high-tech Weidlinger Associates through the "beltway bandits," SAIC, PSI and others. At the other end of the spectrum is the mid-market residential client, the subject of Sarah Suzanka's best seller and practice-builder, *The Not So Big House: a Blueprint for the Way We Really Live*.

The Croxton Collaborative and William McDonough are both *theme-type nichers*, with strong leadership positions in the design of environmentally sustainable "green" design.

Some firms use a hybrid strategy, using niches as a natural extension of their market-focused practice. For example, Karlsberger Companies, a health care leader, has a niche in children's hospitals. Hayes, Seay, Mattern & Mattern holds the niche in watershed management. WTW in Pittsburgh is a niche leader in student unions. Ricci & Associates deepens its corrections practice with a niche in juvenile detention centers. Small or large, they are all Niche Experts.

How Niche Firms Operate and Grow

Each of the characters in *The Sparks Framework* has a distinct business design that expresses its philosophy of optimal operations. Think of the business design as a scaffold of strategies, structures and systems that support the firm's ability to generate value.

The underlying business design of the Niche Expert is guided by the following specific principles:

- They aim to own the market in their chosen specialty, often operating nationally or internationally.
- They frequently collaborate with other members of a team, alliance or network.
- Their client's agenda is to overcome problem conditions (technically or politically) on complex, risky projects.
- Their value is in providing the best knowledge available about the problem.
- Their essential technology is to seek and apply new information and research to increase their performance.
- They frequently turn away work that another firm is better suited to accomplishing.

The following diagram is the basic Niche Expert business design. Note that the business design is organized into three distinct strands that form the structural elements of the design. These are:

1. **Getting Work:** Markets and Marketing.
2. **Doing Work:** Projects and People.
3. **Organizing Work:** Money and Leadership.

The three strands are in fact primary strategic systems that operate in every firm. And each archetype has characteristic strategies and activities that operate within the three systems. (Please refer to Chapter 1.4 to compare the Niche Expert with other business designs.)

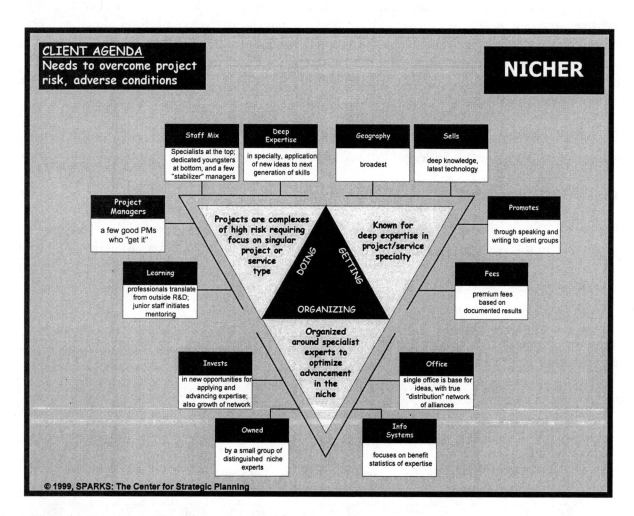

Graphic depiction of the business design for the Niche Expert.

If your firm aspires to be a Niche Expert, consider any of the above areas in which you're not fully operating to be strong potential opportunities for growth.

How to Niche

Tapping into the Passionate Interest

All the trend data and market research statistics in the world pale by comparison to someone with a passionate interest. To select the right niche, begin by seeking out people who are excited about something they're doing and want to push it further. Sparks fly when your passionate interest is the wellspring of your expertise. And when this interest is shared, you release a vibrancy that unites the firm and energizes it. You can't help but attract great clients and great staff.

Several years ago, we conducted a set of 12 market-specific focus groups for one of our clients in order to help find the very best possible focus match. The firm narrowed the possibilities down to schools, libraries and restaurants, none of which caused much excitement. Finally I said to the president, "Bob, I want to give you a personal observation. Here's what you love: You love to play golf. In fact, you love it much better than this conventional design practice." "Hmm," he said. "Do you think we could make a specialty around that?"

So we put together a plan and program to make it happen. The excitement played out beautifully: He now has a national golf course clubhouse design firm that has projects from Seattle to Stowe, VT.

Selecting a Niche and Building Group Consensus

Another client of ours is a strong force in education but wanted to move into a higher leverage Niche Expert position. In this case, we had the passionate champion, but we also had a problem: The firm had *too many* passionate champions. When considering a niche choice (between good and better) we conduct a value analysis to facilitate decision-making. The process goes like this:

1. Begin by brainstorming the possibilities.
2. Identify the criteria that the niche must satisfy.
3. Assign weights to each criterion.
4. Go through each option and assign a value, using a scale of 1 to 5.
5. Tally up your score and debate the outcome and its implications.

Just to validate, we sometimes give participants a "wild card" of several votes just for subjective desire. This can confirm the vote or open the discussion again. Either way, value analysis is an excellent process for thinking through this important decision. Here is an example format:

POSSIBLE CHOICES (vote on scale of 1 to 5 then multiply by weight)	Current experience x3	Design oppt'y x2	Ease of acquiring staff x1	Sub-total	Wild card 1 each +10	TOTAL
Performing Arts	45	50	5	100	10	110
Science/Labs*	60	40	10	110	30	140
Private/Charter	45	35	10	90	10	100
Urban	20	25	25	70	0	70
Computer or Technology	10	35	25	70	0	70
Sports	3	35	10	48	0	48

*The winning niche for this firm was Science/Labs.

Know Your Demographics

When shopping for niches, make sure you have a firm grasp of demographics. Yes, taxation, regulations, economics and technological advances have a strong influence on the market, but keep in mind that the baby boom generation has doubled or tripled the value of every real estate market they've passed through in their life cycle.

For example, the peak pre-school bulge of 1960 and the subsequent school-building boom was followed, as predicted, by a higher-education boom. Twenty years later, the office boom of the 1980s was fueled by consumer need and served by all those kids entering the market as office workers.

What is the next demographic boom? To begin to understand where demand will come from, ask yourself three demographic questions:

1. What are the largest age groups and what are their compositions?
2. What issues and needs do they tend to be preoccupied with most?
3. What groups have money, and in what areas are they spending?

A population's greatest earning power normally lies in the 45- to 54-year-old age group, and the leading-edge Baby Boomers were born in 1946. This group's tendencies are to spend on recreational and personal investment activities. They are 38 percent more likely to own a second home than the rest of the population. Notice also that between the years 2000 and 2010 a major shift in assets to this generation will occur through inheritances, making this the wealthiest generation ever to live in the United States.

But the largest group right now in terms of numbers is 32- to 36-year-olds. What are they doing? Raising families. In fact, 60 percent of all Baby Boom households contain children. Youth and family activities are the key, and again, recreational activities come out strongly. This generation of children is expected to exceed the Baby Boom generation in size.

Three Trends to Watch

Three broad trends are seen coming from the baby boom: one toward enrichment/education, one toward recreation/entertainment and one toward recreation/personal investment. Several markets will come out on top, and niches abound in each.

Niche 1: Recreation/Entertainment

Plan on plenty of new and renovated sports facilities, including stadiums at the municipal and college levels, community athletic facilities and private clubs skyrocketing in popularity. Commercial ventures such as Dave and Busters are flourishing, as are casinos. The flow of money is enormous, as serious fans, alumni, couples and families seek the thrill of the game.

Lots of cities are looking for gaming opportunities to raise money for public use. One of the most dramatic examples is riverboat gambling along the Mississippi River. Dubuque, Iowa, for example, a town of 65,000 people, will get more than two million visitors this year. Planning and spin-off facilities are in great demand and low supply.

Futurist Faith Popcorn in *The Popcorn Report*[2] predicts an explosion of festival marketplaces, the kind that Rouse Development made famous like Fanueil Hall in Boston and HarborPlace in Baltimore. Note also that Benjamin Thompson, architect for many of the landmark marketplace projects, received the Gold Medal from the American Institute of Architects. Main Street development will also experience a resurgence, as vibrant places where people want to see and be seen. President Clinton and Vice President Gore have made "livable cities" an important agenda item with real funding.

Niche 2: Enrichment/Education

Certainly a record number of schools are being built to accommodate children of Boomers. Schools are a huge market, but again, a broad market, not a niche. One can look for niches within the market, or one can look beyond to other enrichment and educational opportunities for adults as well as children.

John Naisbitt in *Megatrends 2000*[3] says that the arts will eventually overtake sports as the number one entertainment business. Museums are gaining steam at a surprising rate, even for the most modest and obscure of collections. Aquariums have been strong for the past few years and will continue to require expansion and renovation. Performing arts centers are in demand, as are facilities for "participative history" (colonial parks such as Claude Moore and heritage parks that preserve urban villages such as Lowell, Mass.).

Although religious facilities cannot rightly be classified as recreation, they can certainly be called enrichment. As Baby Boomers raising children seek to reconnect with their roots, look for a resurgence of interest in religion translating into new churches and additions, retreat centers, schools and facilities for seniors. If religion is your niche, add a fund-raising component to your service mix.

Don't forget educational components within the traditional markets: corporate training facilities, adult education facilities, auditoriums and so on. Even as our technological era gathers steam, we can never replace group experiences.

Niche 3: Second Home/Recreational Property

Look for second homes and vacation properties to come on strong as families first vacation and then decide to invest in an asset for future sale or retirement. Demand will be hot for site engineering, marinas, golf courses, outlet malls and civic facilities over the next few years.

Seaside, an upscale planned development outside Panama City, Fla., is a prime example. Intended originally to offer a variety of large, medium and small-scaled homes, the property values have shot up so dramatically that only the larger houses make financial sense. It's particularly encouraging that a big part of Seaside's success is its architectural design.

In the not-too-distant future, we'll see life-care facilities as an integral part of these second home developments.

Other Observations

Equity Participation

Firms with the capacity to offer upstream economic support and services will be stronger players in any marketplace than their competitors. This may seem like a stretch for conservative professionals, but true niche experts know their business very, very well. They are masters of their domain, and are highly focused on all dimensions of the economy that affect their work and their clients such that equity participation in their projects is fully in the realm of possibility.

In *"How to Get Rich in America"*[4] author Edward O. Welles cites Palo Alto's Lunar Design, an industrial design firm that has forsaken the fee-for-services treadmill. Lunar now structures part or all of its design fees to include equity in its client's firm. Although it experiences some short-term risks and trade-offs, its increased profitability has allowed it benefits only dreamed of by most professionals.

At the least, firms gain considerable leverage if they can participate in their projects beyond traditional services. If not equity, then consider grant-writing, fund-raising and public process/public relations assistance. Begin to create alliances with development consultants that may eventually become part of your package.

What If the Market Dries Up?

We're almost always asked this question. The reality is that very few niches really extinguish completely. Instead, they migrate to other parts of the country or the world. Take high-rise office buildings, for example. They didn't die out; they simply moved to the Pacific Rim. Corporate offices weakened in the mid-'80s, and the new service of facilities management grew. Oil prices rose, and we created a new area of study in sustainable design. Firms with their eyes on the ball now have more, not less, to offer the client.

To resist market cycles, some firms develop two to three counter-cyclical niches rather than place all their eggs in one basket. One simple technique is to provide the same basic services in public and private sector settings, for example high-end single family housing and congregate care housing. As a nicher, don't forget your position of strength across a wide geography: The world is your oyster.

Keep the Faith and Innovate

Some of the most celebrated niche experts are secretly dying to get into other markets. Although they've achieved a high degree of mastery, they've done better than their peers financially and they're highly respected by their clients, they somehow still feel the lure of the paradigm to "get bigger and diversify."

The best antidote to this thinking is to renew a commitment to innovation. It's nobler in the long run to make a real contribution to the world by pushing the state of the art to the next level of performance than to indulge short-sighted fears of being pigeon-holed. In truth, firms that rivet their attention on some area of expertise, liberate resources to build strength and soundly reject marginal temptations are the firms that do best.

Keep the Faith and Spin-Out New Ventures

When you have a successful niche practice, protect it from the forces of "diversification." Many niche ventures are undermined through fear, boredom, believing the Fortune 500 hype or just plain lack of discipline.

If a new idea is truly compelling, consider spinning it out instead of diluting the successful niche practice. The success rate is quite high for spin-outs. Keep the original firm intact while letting the creative urge express itself in a new venture. Bill Gross, author of "The New Math of Ownership,"[5] outlines how he struggled with this issue and was very well-rewarded by bucking the conventional expansion measures.

Askew Nixon Ferguson Architects in Memphis finds the spin-out strategy very effective, and in fact is working on its third such venture. Says Lee Askew, "If we made these new ideas into company divisions, they would wither and die. Spun out, the development team gets charged up over 'their baby.' They have their own name, their own identity, and a high percent of equity. Ideally, we aim for a 25 percent (us) and 75 percent (them) split. They think big, and they grow into their vision quickly. Their two spun-out entities, On-Line FM and CM Plus, have reaped rewards for the firm."

Another example is Jung/Brannen that spun-off Archibus, the top-selling facilities management software, in 1982. Set free to sink or swim, the firm built an enviable position as "best in class" of CAFM and has more than 50,000 users managing more than 16 billion square feet of space.

Endnotes

[1] Tom Peters, *Thriving on Chaos* (Alfred Knopf Inc., 1987).

[2] Faith Popcorn, *The Popcorn Report on the Future* (Doubleday, 1991).

[3] John Naisbitt and Patricia Aburdene, *Megatrends 2000* (William Morrow and Co. Inc., 1990).

[4] Edward O. Welles, "How to Get Rich in America," *Inc. Magazine* (April 1999).

[5] Bill Gross, "The New Math of Ownership," *Inc. Magazine* (Nov.-Dec. 1998).

Bibliography

"Carving a Niche in the '90s." *Architecture* (May 1992).

Flynn-Heapes, Ellen. *Creating Wealth: Principles and Practices for Design Firms.* SPARKS: The Center for Strategic Planning (1999).

— . "The Demographics of Demand: How to Select Strong Future Markets." *SMPS Marketer* (Feb. 1994).

— . *The Sparks Framework: A Handbook of Value-Creation Strategies.* SPARKS: The Center for Strategic Planning (2000).

— . "The Virtues of a Specialized Practice." *SMPS News* (April 1986).

Linneman, Robert, and John L. Stanton, Jr. *Making Niche Marketing Work: How to Grow Bigger by Acting Smaller.* McGraw-Hill (1991).

Ellen Flynn-Heapes, FSMPS

- Ellen Flynn-Heapes is president of SPARKS: The Center for Strategic Planning, Alexandria, Va.
- Flynn-Heapes is a nationally recognized authority on competitive and organizational strategy for the design and construction professions.
- She was the first management consultant in the country to specialize in strategic planning for firms in the industry, and over the years has earned considerable praise for both her pioneering work and her continued innovations.
- SPARKS clients include design and construction firms throughout the United States as well as government agencies and corporations related to the built environment.
- With an MBA and as a 25-year veteran in the A/E/C industry, Flynn-Heapes grounded her career with HOK and later Skidmore Owings and Merrill. Today, she coaches company leaders on how to design their desired futures, and build the strongest, most successful organizations possible.
- She conducts seminars around the country and lectures to both academic and professional groups, including AIA, ACEC and SMPS.
- She is a Fellow of the Society for Marketing Professional Services and served four years on its national board of directors.

www.ForSparks.com
Ellen@ForSparks.com

Reprinted with permissions from The Sparks Environment: A Handbook of Value-Creation Strategies, by Ellen Flynn-Heapes, SPARKS: The Center for Strategic Planning, 2001.

1.6 International Marketing

Randolph W. Tucker, P.E.
Senior Vice President
The RJA Group Inc.
Senior Vice President – International Development
Rolf Jensen & Associates Inc.

Overview

With the globalization of world economies, it is the rare professional services firm that does not have a stake in the international marketplace. Quantum leaps in communications (most notably the Internet and cellular telephone technology) have provided the ability to serve client and project needs on a timely basis throughout the world. Trade agreements are opening new markets to trading partners. And, one of the strongest drivers for U.S.-based firms, multinational firms are looking for the latest in building design and technology for their facilities no matter where in the world the facility may be located.

The fundamentals of international marketing for the professional services firm vary little from marketing domestic services. Key elements include:

- Identifying the unique benefits your firm has to offer.
- Determining where there is a need for the services you offer.
- Identifying potential clients in the target markets.
- Developing name recognition in the target markets.
- Building relationships.
- Selling your services.

Other chapters in this handbook deal with these topics in some detail. This chapter offers guidance in the application of these principles to the international marketplace. The specific topics this chapter will cover are:

- Defining the international marketplace for your firm.
- Developing an international strategy.
- Understanding local culture and custom.
- Building international relationships.
- Finding international opportunities.

Defining the International Marketplace

Going global does not necessarily mean doing work outside the United States. Your firm can become global by working with international clients in your own backyard. Many international owners and developers are finding that the United States offers better development opportunities and return on investment than in their home country. As such, your international practice may be targeted at meeting the needs of these owners and developers for their U.S. projects.

Many of your current clients may also have international operations. Serving their global needs can be an extension of the domestic services you currently provide.

Of course, the true plunge into the international scene is developing international project work with international-based clients. Although starting your global focus directly at this level may prove to be costly, getting to this level through your current clients and networks may prove to be far easier than it may first appear.

Because of the various ways to define the international marketplace, it is important that your firm adopt an international focus and understanding. The relationship you develop with a client next door may result in a project with one of that client's suppliers from the other side of the world. Also keep in mind: If you can't meet your client's global needs, how much longer do you believe you will retain that client's domestic work?

Developing an International Strategy

In order to enter any new market, one needs to develop a strategy. The strategy you develop for the international marketplace follows many of the same steps you would follow if you were entering any new geographic market:

- Assess internal capabilities that can provide a competitive advantage.
- Evaluate the market needs for these capabilities in other countries.
- Determine how these capabilities can be promoted in the marketplace.
- Establish strategic positioning for the target market(s).
- Develop strategies to overcome challenges to market entry.

Capabilities Assessment

Assessment of internal capabilities is something that successful firms do regularly. For the international marketplace, a similar assessment should be conducted, but with a view to how these capabilities can be delivered globally. What problem-solving skills can you offer? Have you developed a project management system that can deliver a better result faster, cheaper and with higher quality? Can you quantify the skills you have compared to the competition? Are the skills you have identified able to be delivered anywhere in the world? If so, how?

Market Needs

Following your assessment of what your unique skills are, you need to see how these capabilities match the markets you wish to pursue. The key to the assessment of these considerations for global opportunities is to understand what others in the marketplace currently offer, how professional services are delivered, and what the clients expect and need. Often you will find that, although you have a distinct technical edge over your domestic competition, the global clients may not understand the differentiation of skills you offer because no one currently provides the service in their country. In such cases, expect that, although you may have great long-term market potential, it will likely take considerable time to educate the market about the benefits you bring to the table. Always remember to view your skills and the market needs through the eyes of the client, considering the culture, customs and sophistication of the market.

Promotional Strategy

Promotional decisions for market entry will need to cover a vast array of options depending on the resources you have available to commit to the market. These decisions will also be contingent on how you have defined your "international marketplace." If you are using the "going global by staying home" approach, your promotional needs (as well as costs) may be significantly less than the full plunge of the "global project/global client" approach. Strategically, a firm may adopt an approach that starts small (single country, single client type) and expands as successes are achieved. Regardless of the strategic mix, the promotional decisions will need to address issues of name recognition, image and critical skills offered that can be understood by the target market. This understanding must transcend language barriers, cultures and customs. The promotional mantra must be to limit, as much as possible, the "buzz words," technical jargon and American idioms that can (and most likely will) be misunderstood by the target audience.

Market Positioning

Positioning decisions in the market can make or break your global initiative. Just because you provide "full service" capabilities to your domestic clients does not necessarily mean you can (or should) offer them globally. Consider offering only a portion of your overall services while linking with an in-country service provider, thereby positioning yourself as a specialty consultant whose unique capability is offered by a "domestic" service provider. You may wish to offer design consultation and have a local firm do production (which in many cases may be required by law). Although you may have a broad-based domestic practice, you may choose to work only in one building type in a particular market due to your critical skills edge over what is currently offered in that market. Remember: However you choose to position yourself, be sure that you have adequately researched both your capabilities and the market's perception of the need (and value) of the service before spending too much time and money on promotional efforts.

Challenges to Market Entry

While many challenges to market entry can appear to be obvious, others are not. Several key challenges to international market entry include:

- Local expectations in building design and construction.
- Local competition.
- Desire for foreign technology.
- Regulatory environment.

Local expectations in the building and design industry in developing countries may often be lower than what you may be used to in your domestic practice. When you first visit a construction site in a developing country, you often recoil at the way a job site looks and is run. It is not uncommon to see workers without shoes or hard hats leaning over the side of a high-rise building that has no protection against falls. You may also wonder how a steel frame building more than eight stories tall can be built without a construction crane on the site. However, buildings do seem to get built. You must understand these differences and be sure that your technical approach considers them. Lacking this appreciation will likely result in a bad experience and limited prospects for future work. Finding a way to deliver the quality level your client expects from you in this challenging market will build the long-term relationship you are striving to achieve.

Never underestimate the local competition. Architects and engineers in developing parts of the world are performing some outstanding design. Don't expect that you are going to enter their market and be successful just because you have a unique skill or that you are an "internationally known expert." They may actually share such skills and expertise. As a strategic consideration, it may be wise to identify such good local firms and form an alliance rather than attempting to compete head-to-head.

Another challenge to market entry is foreign technology. This issue is a two-edged sword. On the one hand, a client may inform you that foreign (U.S.) technology is wanted. As such, you are pleased to design the latest and greatest systems for installation in its project. Unfortunately, such technology may not be able to be used due to government limitations on imports. Additionally, there may not be sufficiently skilled labor to install the systems. Lastly, due to lack of maintenance (and often no in-country factory support), the equipment may not function shortly after the building has been completed. Before touting your ability to design the latest technology as a reason why a client should retain your services, be sure it can be delivered, installed and maintained in that country.

The regulatory environment may also create a challenge to market entry. You should become fully conversant with laws for professional practice and business practice, including registrations, limitations on service offering and taxes. Fee structures in some countries are controlled (and limited) by government regulation. Taxes may be imposed on professional services conducted in-country. In many cases, there are limitations on the amount of cash that can be taken out of the country. In some developing parts of the world, hard currency is so difficult to come by that the owner may want to pay you in a commodity (such as pig iron or vodka) rather than cash.

Another regulatory issue is that of codes and standards. Even developing countries today have become quite progressive in their development and application of building and product codes and standards. As such, one should not expect to prepare building designs in accordance with U.S. codes and standards and gain local acceptance. Be sure that your project design team understands the local requirements of design and materials to prevent embarrassment to you and your client during the regulatory review process.

Closing Comments on Your International Strategy

The key difference in international marketplace strategy is dealing with not only geographic distance in your assessments, but language, culture and customs differences. These key elements must be carefully considered in each strategic decision. For instance, even though you may have a project delivery capability that offers a competitive advantage in the United States, can you deliver this same capability in Mandarin? And even if you can, will a Chinese client understand the value and benefit to them as well as your U.S. client does?

Although there are many critical considerations that one must evaluate in forming an international strategy, here are a few pointers from experience.

Don't:
- Target a country strictly because the citizens speak a language you understand.
- Target a country just because it's easy to reach by air.
- Expect the political climate in a developing country (or any country) to be predictable.

Do:
- Be sure the target client type in a target country has the ability to pay your fees.
- Carefully check the licensing requirements, business fees and taxes.
- Have an exit strategy.

The Importance of Understanding Local Culture and Custom

The need to understand the local societal expectations and culture cannot be overstressed. Cultural gaffs and blunders litter the trail for those unprepared for the local market. To minimize making these blunders, training and understanding the culture and customs of the countries you plan to work in are a must. Even if you are doing only domestic work with a foreign client, learn their culture and customs.

There are many ways you can achieve a reasonable level of cultural awareness. The easiest is to get a good travel guidebook about the country. These guides typically provide information about the history, art, culture, economy, religion and philosophy. Another source is a series of books titled "Culture Shock," which provide a guide to customs and etiquette in many of the major countries around the world (including the United States). Many colleges and universities offer courses in culture and customs of various countries through their anthropology departments and adult education programs. Regardless of the source, develop a cultural awareness and put it to use. Showing you have an appreciation for the country, its heritage and culture will go a long way in demonstrating you have an honest interest in developing a meaningful business relationship.

If lacking a guide to local customs and culture, remember: You are a guest in their country. Behave as you would in the company of someone you greatly respect and admire. Follow the lead of the locals. Don't complain or criticize. Always be aware of yourself: Your actions and body language will speak loudly in any language. And finally, and probably most important, your hosts are going to form an opinion of you, your company and your country by your attitude and actions toward them and their country.

Building International Relationships

Regardless of what you may have heard, realize that in the international marketplace it is imperative that you spend time developing personal relationships. In Latin cultures, you may find prospective clients won't discuss details of doing business together until your third or fourth meeting. In many Asian countries, you may be warmly received and discuss business from the first meeting, yet no actual business is transacted even after several subsequent visits. In each case, you are experiencing the courtship period of that particular culture. Your prospective client is finding out how serious you are about building the personal relationship that is necessary in their culture to form a business relationship. In order to build these relationships, you must have patience and a real desire to get to know the client.

International relationships must be built not only with your prospective clients. You will need to create a network of relationships with related firms, government officials and others in the business community. Depending on your strategic approach to a particular market, you may choose to develop business alliances with local firms. Some of the key steps in the process of developing a business alliance include:

- Establish criteria for the type of alliance you need.
- Identify and evaluate prospective partners.
- Create realistic expectations.
- Determine the form of agreement that best suits the alliance.
- Nurture the alliance.

Alliance Criteria

In forming an alliance, you need to consider why you want or need the alliance and how the alliance fits in your long-term market strategy. Should the alliance be a firm that offers similar services or one that provides complementary services? Do you want or need the alliance to have local political connections or would such connections be viewed as a liability? How do you and your alliance plan to deliver services together? Will the alliance be a partnership, a joint venture or a sub-consultant relationship? What registrations do you and your alliance need? Are there certain business connections or relationships you don't want your alliance to have? Answering these and other questions you deem necessary to meet your objectives will help in targeting the alliance partner(s) you need.

Identifying and Evaluating Prospective Partners

Your knowledge of the local market will be your guide to where to find prospective alliance partners. If you already have experience in the market, you may be aware of the players that may be considered. If not, local professional societies may offer a starting point. Remember: The key to a successful alliance is that both parties perceive they will receive value from the association that they may not otherwise gain on their own. For instance, you may find a local service provider (competitor) that, due to limited size or specific expertise, may be unable to develop a desired relationship with a local client. Your specific abilities may be what that firm needs to serve that particular client's needs. Conversely, the relationship you form with a firm in one country may help both firms pursue work together in the United States or a third country.

Do you want, or need, an alliance partner with political connections? Although political connections may be advantageous, be sure to understand local politics well enough to know when they may be detrimental. Political connections could range from being good friends with the local building official to being a relative of a head of state. Regardless, identify the type of political connection you believe you need, verify the accuracy of the relationship that you are told exists, and make an informed decision on whether the relationship is consistent with your needs in the market.

If there are particular professional or company registrations necessary to practice in the market, be sure the alliance partner you select has the requisite ones. In some countries you may find that having an alliance partner with appropriate registration will relieve you of also gaining such registration. Additionally, depending on local requirements (or that of your insurance carrier), verify what professional liability and business insurance they carry.

In your evaluation of prospective partners you may also want to know what other business connections they have. Are there any types of businesses with which you do not want your alliance partner associated? Do you want an exclusive alliance with your partner in a particular country or region? Do you, or your potential alliance, have other agreements that would preclude you from forming an alliance?

Once you have screened the potential alliance partners and made a selection, you may wish to try a "trial" association before forming a more binding, long-term agreement. Although this will offer both of you a chance to see how an alliance could work, be careful how you suggest and structure such a trial period. Depending on the culture, it may be taken as a lack of trust between the firms and can result only in failure. On the other hand, such a trial could well save both firms from committing to an uncomfortable, unsuccessful alliance.

Expectations

Part of the success of international business alliances comes from each party having a clear understanding of expectations. The expectations must be realistic with each party committed to their participation in the alliance. In a typical alliance, you may expect your partner to provide support in such things as business development, local information and staffing, and continuous communication on prospect and project activities. For your part, your alliance may expect support from you in business development activities, responsiveness in provision of needed information, staff availability for client needs, and continuous communication. Regardless, be sure you both have an understanding of what each party will be expected to provide throughout the course of the alliance.

Forms of Agreement

Forms of agreement will vary depending on your international positioning strategy, local law and market exit strategy. Typical forms of agreement include letter agreement, memorandum of understanding, joint venture or ownership. As with any binding contract document, you should have an attorney well-versed in international law review your agreement before signing.

Care and Nurturing

No alliance will survive and flourish without care and nurturing. For your international alliance to be successful you will need to work hard on communication. Keep your alliance informed about what you are doing not only in their country, but also in all areas of your practice. If you have a newsletter or send direct mail pieces to clients, include your alliance(s) in the mailings. Periodically contact your alliance, if for no other reason than to see how they are doing. Make them feel a part of your regular business activities.

In all your dealings with your alliance, be fair. Be sure they are receiving value from the relationship. In project work, be sure they get full credit for their efforts and let them know when they have done good work.

Always appreciate the cultural differences between your firm and your alliance. If practical, conduct some type of employee sharing. The better your staff and that of the alliance know each other, the better the business relationship will be.

Continue to strive for mutual profitability in the alliance. If both parties cannot show a sustained profit from the alliance, the alliance will not survive.

Finding International Opportunities

There are many ways of finding international business opportunities. Beyond the methods you currently use domestically, sources for finding international opportunities essentially fall into three basic areas: government, current clients and the Internet.

From the government side, the single best source is the U.S. Department of Commerce. The U.S. Export Assistance Center of the Department of Commerce provides a wealth of information and many services to those looking for export opportunities. Some of the more commonly used services include briefings, conferences, exhibitions, matchmaker events and trade delegations. They have an enormous amount of basic data on most regions of the world with respect to the construction market and trading opportunities. In addition, the embassies regularly send information on project leads to the Washington, D.C., office, which in turn makes it available to the professional services community.

A specific "client introduction" service offered by the U.S. Department of Commerce is the Gold Key program in which meetings are arranged with targeted potential clients in major cities around the world. The meetings are arranged by foreign service nationals in the local consulate office who know their country, the customs, the industry and the decision-makers. The service offers a cost-effective means of introduction to potential clients.

Governmental sources for finding international opportunities in your backyard include your local and state economic development groups. These groups typically know what international firms are interested in relocating to the neighborhood long before any announcements are made.

A source of international project opportunities often overlooked is your current domestic client base. Even though they may not have international operations themselves, your domestic clients often are aware of global building plans of their suppliers and business associates. An introduction from a satisfied client to one of their associates can be key in the development of the business relationship you want to cultivate.

Finally, one can find vast stores of information and opportunities through the Internet. It is the rare company today that does not have a web site. Mining these sites provides contact names, information about companies' long-range development plans and other information to aid in targeting clients as well as finding actual project opportunities. Additionally, many foreign governments and development banks (such as the Asian Development Bank and the World Bank) post project opportunities on their web sites.

Randolph W. Tucker, P.E.

- Randolph W. Tucker, P.E., is senior vice president of The RJA Group Inc. and senior vice president – international development for Rolf Jensen & Associates Inc., the fire protection engineering and security subsidiary of The RJA Group Inc. The RJA Group Inc. provides creative solutions for its clients' fire safety and security challenges through consulting engineering, construction management and knowledge transfer subsidiaries. The group has offices located throughout the United States and business alliances in more than 20 countries.
- Tucker has more than 25 years' experience in the practice of fire protection engineering.
- He has a bachelor's degree in fire protection engineering from the Illinois Institute of Technology and a master's degree in marketing and management policy from Northwestern University.
- His current responsibilities with The RJA Group Inc. include operations for the Atlanta, Houston and Orlando offices of Rolf Jensen & Associates Inc. and the development of international alliances and projects. His consulting engineering project experience includes commercial, institutional, industrial and transportation projects throughout the United States and in more than 30 countries around the world.
- Tucker is a past president of the Houston SMPS Chapter, has served on several National SMPS committees and is a National SMPS past president.
- He has lectured on fire protection engineering and business development topics around the world.

1.7 The Marketing Budget

Lisbeth Quebe, FSMPS
Vice President of Marketing
RTKL Associates Inc.

The marketing budget is an integral part of a planning continuum. It is part of the marketing plan, which is part of an annual business plan, which in turn is completed to support the strategic vision of your firm. When you begin to prepare the marketing budget, you should already have a marketing plan (or a draft of one) in place. Your budget can then be developed to price the implementation of your marketing plan.

The marketing budget is a very important piece of the marketing plan. By forcing you to put a dollar amount to each activity outlined in the marketing plan, the marketing budget commits you to action. It tells you if you can afford the time and money allocation required to meet your firm's marketing goals. It ultimately tells you if your goals are realistic.

Before you undertake the budget itself, you need to consider the structure of your firm. Like the plan, the budget must support a unique organization as it relates to the number of offices, market sectors or services within your firm. You may want to create one plan and one budget for the firm as a whole. This is certainly the way to go in smaller firms. You may want to create a plan and budget for each office or each market sector within the firm. For large multi-office diversified firms, you may want a sophisticated budget matrix, in which you plan and budget for each market sector within each office. The latter is the most involved, but it imparts the optimum degree of accountability and control in multiple-office, multiple-market scenarios.

In addition to direct marketing costs — those associating with selling work — you should consider indirect marketing costs as a part of your budget. Indirect costs are the hardest to define, as just about everything in the office, from the pictures on the wall to the skills of the receptionist, can be construed as marketing. I include marketing management, market research, market planning and public relations activities in indirect marketing. I also include collateral materials such as photography, the general brochure system and database systems. Firms with multiple offices sometimes support these costs on a firm-wide basis with a corporate budget, since all offices and market sectors use them.

Just as marketing plans fail if they are written by one person, so will budgets, and not just because marketers are rarely given unlimited access to the firm's bank account. Principals and key staff must have input into the budgeting process if the budget is to be either realistic or respected. If there is no buy-in, the budget will be ignored. The level of participation will vary, as will the individual interests of the participants. An individual responsible for sales in a particular market will advocate a larger expenditure, while an individual responsible for profits is invariably a proponent of frugality.

Because the budget supports the business plan, it is accomplished on an annual basis and tied to the firm's fiscal year. Since the budget should be reviewed by a number of people with varying agendas, you should allow sufficient time for preparation, comment and amendment.

The first time you prepare a budget, it seems a daunting task. Over time, as you get to know the marketing habits of your particular cast of characters, and the costs to accomplish certain tasks, it gets easier. First, you choose your approach. There are three basic methodologies for creating a marketing budget: the projection method, the percentage method and the goal-based method.

The projection method, also referred to as the comparison method, relies on using prior year costs for development of the upcoming year's budget. This means doing some digging, especially if your firm has not captured marketing costs in any organized fashion. You need to determine what has been spent year-to-date on marketing labor and expenses. If the data isn't available, make your best guess (you have to start somewhere). Next, project the final year-end costs. If you're nine months through the fiscal year, take a line item, divide it by nine and then multiply it by 12. The challenging step — the one that takes some thought — is to decide if that item will stay the same, increase or decrease in the upcoming year. Add the line items, and you have your budget.

This projection methodology works best if you have a stable, established marketing effort that doesn't vary much from year to year. The method is flawed because it does not consider the goals of this year's marketing plan or the conditions of the market. It is more of an arithmetical exercise than a dynamic marketing tool.

The next method is the percentage method. Also called the top-down method, it simply allocates a set percentage of the firm's total operating revenues to marketing. That percentage will generally range between 5 to 15 percent, although some firms report costs as low as 3 percent and as high as 18 percent. The accepted average, as we approach the year 2000, is probably between 7 to 9 percent, but then, what firm is average?

Anyway, you have historical cost data that will give you an idea of the percent of net revenue spent on marketing in past years. If no such data exists, you may seek information on firms of comparable size, services, markets and geographical locations from a number of sources. SMPS publishes a salary and expense survey every few years that yields this information. *Professional Services Management Journal's* Financial Statistics Survey provides this information on a yearly basis. Zweig White Associates produces a very comprehensive marketing survey on an annual basis. Other organizations, such as the American Institute of Architects, gather similar statistics. You will quickly see that there is a broad spectrum of percentages from which to choose, due to limited available information and a great diversity in the way firms track marketing costs.

The percentage method fails for the same reasons that the projection method does. It does not consider market conditions and the individual marketing plan of the firm. By spending what others are spending, you may disregard your firm's specific needs.

Now for my preferred method: goal-based budgeting. This technique, the "bottom-up" method, assigns costs to each item in your marketing plan. This methodology allows you to base your budgeting on the year's business plan revenue goals and marketing plan implementation tasks. Although more time-consuming to set up initially, it is by far the most accurate and manageable budgeting methodology.

With a detailed marketing plan, you will be able to estimate the funding required to complete any identified task. Once you have priced what you want to accomplish, you can test this number against available dollars. If you can't afford the marketing program identified in your plan, you can cut specific items intelligently. Thus, planning continues throughout the budgeting process.

Goal-based budgeting is the best way to develop a credible budget. For a triple insurance policy, however, use all three methods. Start from the bottom to cost out your plan. Compare your numbers to those of the prior year as a historical check. Finally, compare your numbers to industry averages as a sanity check.

Now for the budgeted items themselves — to put it in the simplest of terms, I call it "staff" and "stuff." CPAs call it "labor" and "expenses."

It is highly likely that the majority of your marketing costs will be related to personnel. Sometimes the reason that marketing costs appear low in surveys is that firms don't include labor costs (mainly principals' time) in their accounting. This is (in my humble opinion) obviously ridiculous, as principals' time is one of the most significant costs of marketing. It is important to make an honest estimate of the time *everyone* in the firm will devote to marketing. The easiest way to accomplish this is by taking a percentage of an individual's available time. This should be done for all of the individuals who have a key role to play in marketing. Once you have made an estimate of the hours that an individual will devote to marketing, you can assign an hourly rate and determine the associated labor cost.

Be sure to consider the time spent in all marketing and sales activities. Direct sales activities include cold or "warm" calling, courtship, preparation of statements of qualification and proposals, presentations and interviews, debriefing and negotiation. Indirect marketing activities include marketing management, market research, planning and budgeting, and public relations. You will probably find that labor, or "staff" costs, will account for anywhere from 50 to 70 percent of your marketing budget.

As I mentioned earlier, the items firms categorize as marketing expenses vary widely. Some firms track every paper clip; some do not care to deal with such minutiae. Again, you'll have to use some judgment, given the preferences of your principals and your own ability to deal with the paperwork. Some of the main categories of items to consider include: supplies; telephone and facsimiles; dues, subscriptions; reproduction (especially printing of brochures or brochure components); seminars and conventions; travel and meals (including entertainment); consultants, awards and exhibits; web page; special events; contributions; and occupancy and equipment. Your "stuff" costs are likely to be between 30 and 50 percent of your budget.

Firms have struggled to arrive at a "correct" allocation of revenue for marketing activities ever since marketing became an accepted line item on the professional services firm's financial statement. Average costs of marketing have been surveyed in one form or another since the 1970s. As we approach the millennium, typical marketing costs are running around 6 to 11 percent of net revenues (excluding consultants and reimbursable expenses), with the accepted average at about 7 to 9 percent. In smaller firms, the percentage can run as high as 18 percent. There seems to be a fairly widespread feeling, however, that the ceiling for marketing costs is around 15 percent. The key is that the percentage must be acceptable for your firm *that year*. You must consider the effect of marketing costs on the year's bottom line, as well as your investment in the future. I always calculate the costs as a percentage of revenue (to see if the marketing program is affordable) and as a percentage of sales (to see if we are spending enough to meet our goals).

If your marketing budget is supporting a new effort (a new sector or a new location), in the first year you may spend as much as $1 for every $5 you bring in (20 percent). This should tail down significantly as you become more effective in the market, and by the time you are at pace, some three to five years later (depending on the market) you should see something more like 5 to 8 percent for a mature market. This allows you to invest in more markets, or sub-markets. You must look at markets over time. In "fast-burn" markets, such as corporate interiors, you can expect to be at speed faster than in the "slow burners," such as health care architecture. The ultimate test of your investment is in comparing what you have spent (your marketing costs) to what you have gained (your sales revenues) over time (generally a three-year period at minimum). If you are getting a good return on your investment, then your money has been well spent. If not, consider another market, or correct what is lacking in your attack.

Once the marketing budget is completed and approved, it must be integrated into the firm's business plan. At minimum, this is as two line items: marketing labor and marketing expense. If the firm has more than one office, it is likely that these line items will appear in the budget for each office, and in a consolidated statement. From a macro perspective, marketing costs can be tracked against budget each month when the Income and Expense Statements are issued. If you have used the percentage method to arrive at your budget, this is the only tracking tool available, as detail does not exist.

If you are to monitor specific marketing expenditures, you will need more detail. This is the best way to track budgets that have been put in place using the projection method or the goal-based method because you can determine the specific costs of specific activities. It's also the best way to track a matrix budgeting structure, in which you are tracking separate sectors within an office. The easiest way to do this is to assign job numbers to the marketing efforts that you have budgeted, and to track costs just as you would on a project. By simply assigning a job number to the sector within the office, you can capture the costs to market, say, the health care sector in the Chicago market. You can tell exactly how much it cost to produce a direct mail piece or mount an exhibit. And over time, you can determine how much you have invested in the market and how much (the total fee sales) that investment has generated. By tracking by job number, you take advantage of the financial management systems already in place in your firm. Staff members will record marketing time on their time sheets just as they will project time, and expenses will be captured as bills are received. You will simply review the expenditures, much like your project managers do for their design or construction projects.

In 1998, only about half of surveyed design firms were preparing marketing budgets. The firms that are not preparing them are probably disposing of 5 to 15 percent of their revenues without a plan for doing so. Marketing is expensive; how this chunk of money is used should be well thought out. The exercise of preparing a marketing budget involves verification of marketing planning. It allows realistic testing of plan goals, from an affordability standpoint and from a results-oriented view. Ultimately, the results that stem from the total marketing expenditure measure its true success, and only if you can identify what you spent and what you got, can you determine how you're really doing.

Bibliography

Zweig White & Associates, Inc. "Chapter 9: Marketing Expenditures." *Marketing Survey of Architecture, Engineering, Planning and Environmental Consulting Firms.* 1998, 277-302.

Simpson, Scott. "The Cost of Sales." *Design Intelligence* (Oct. 10, 1996): 1.

"Your Marketing Budget." *AEMJ* (June 1996): 3.

"Marketing Tools/Budgets." *AEMJ* (Nov. 1995): 7.

Coxe, Weld. "The Marketing Budget." *Marketing Architectural and Engineering Services.* New York: Van Nostrand Reinhold Company, Inc., 1993.

"Marketing Costs." *PSMJ* (March 1995): 5.

Coyne, John. "The Marketing Plan." *A/E Marketing Journal* (Aug. 1986): 3.

"Is Marketing Payback Real?" *A/E Marketing Journal* (July 1990): 7.

Jones, Gerre. "Getting Organized." *How to Market Professional Design Services.* New York: McGraw-Hill, 1983.

Kerruish, Karen L. "Plan for Success: The Marketing Budget." SMPS *Marketer* 15 (Oct. 1990): 3.

Lentz, Kay. "Is Marketing Cost Effective?" *A/E Marketing Journal* (July 1990): 3.

"The Marketing Budget." *A/E Marketing Journal* (Nov. 1986): 5.

"Marketing Cost." *A/E Marketing Journal* (Jan. 1987): 7.

1992 Marketing Salary & Expense Survey. Alexandria, VA: SMPS, 1992.

Spaulding, Margaret, and William D'Elia. *Advanced Marketing Techniques for Architecture and Engineering Firms.* New York: McGraw Hill, 1989.

Stasiowski, Frank. "Marketing Costs." *PSMJ Financial Statistics Survey.* Boston: Practice Management Associates, Ltd., 1991.

"Your Marketing Budget." *A/E Marketing Journal* (Jan. 1988): 4.

Lisbeth Quebe, FSMPS

- Lisbeth Quebe is vice president of marketing for RTKL Associates Inc., a 700-person architecture /engineering /planning / interior design firm that practices internationally. She has spent her 29-year career in the practice of architecture, and has focused on A/E marketing since 1978.
- Quebe is a member of SMPS, Professional Services Management Association, Urban Land Institute and the Chicago Chapter of the American Institute of Architects.
- She is a founding member of the Chicago SMPS chapter and served as chapter vice president from 1982 to 1985. Her national SMPS involvement includes chairing the Marketing Achievement Award Committee from 1988 to 1991 and serving as national treasurer from 1990 to 1992. She was elected a Fellow of SMPS and was awarded its coveted top honor, the Marketing Achievement Award, in 1995.
- She is a frequent speaker on marketing planning and budgeting for both SMPS and the AIA, and is a guest speaker on marketing at the University of Illinois School of Architecture.

1.8 The Use of Technology in Marketing:
Providing Coordinated Marketing Efforts and Communication Links Across Departments, Disciplines and Operations

Craig Park, FSMPS
Vice President, Integrated Solutions
Intellisys Group Inc.

Contemporary information technology systems offer the building industry professional services enterprise a wealth of tools that can help support the marketing of the firm's services. From simple contact management software to sophisticated relational databases in sales and marketing automation systems, these technology tools can be customized to meet the specific goals of each business. Used effectively, information technology provides real-time data on potential and existing clients, allowing for increased return on invested time and money.

Combining these hand-held, desktop and enterprise marketing systems with the power of Internet, intranet and extranet, communication technology allows for cross-discipline and cross-enterprise collaboration in marketing and project efforts. Utilizing in-person, telecommunications and web-based technologies can increase the effectiveness of marketing presentations.

Moore's Law — from Gordon Moore, founder of Intel — says that computing power doubles every 18 months while the cost of computation drops 30 percent a year. Metcalf's Law — from Bob Metcalf, founder of network technology pioneers 3Com — postulates that the value of a network to any organization grows by the square of the number of users. In the last decade we have witnessed this combination of rapidly increasing, affordable computing power and bandwidth and their impact on the competitive factors in the building industry market. The growth and acceptance of information technology as a viable tool by customers and competitors alike, virtually ensures that the logarithmic rate of change brought on by the information age will have a profound, and technologically focused, impact on the marketing of the professional services firm in the next millennium.

Potential Marketing Technology

There are a wide variety of technologies that can improve and enhance the marketing effort. For the most part, these technologies have been developed as general marketing solutions and will by necessity be adapted to meet the specific needs of companies practicing in the built environment. The most common of these technologies is the database, and the bulk of this chapter will focus on marketing database development and applications. The relational information database systems are the basis for all other technology applications in marketing.

Databases come in the form of simple contact management software or sales/marketing automation tools. This technology falls into the category of customer relationship management. More full-featured, relational database software can be customized to meet specific corporate information goals. Systems customized for the A/E/C industry provide a pre-defined toolkit for storing and retrieving historic data (e.g., resumes, project profiles, 254/255 forms) that can be used in preparing marketing collateral and proposal responses. The simplicity and ease of use of personal digital assistants allow this database information to travel with the business development staff for rapid access to important client and historic information.

The explosion of the Internet has opened the door to new marketing technologies that range from e-mail to e-commerce. Business communications that until just a few years ago relied on phone, mail and fax, now routinely depend on electronic information exchange to meet market demands. That has had a significant impact on the technology infrastructure a professional services business will need to compete. As increasing telecommunication bandwidth becomes available (through broadband and high-speed data transmission services), it will be both possible and necessary to provide real-time access to corporate information by both collaborators and customers.

Thus a corporate intranet can offer shared information about firm history, clients, projects and personnel to principals, project managers as well as marketing and business development personnel. Taken further, an extranet allows for collaborative data sharing and project execution between the prime contracted firm and all of the sub-contract design, consulting, engineering and contracting disciplines necessary to pursue, acquire and deliver new projects (including the customer).

Qualifications and proposal presentation is another area where technology can aid the marketing effort. Increasingly, clients rely on strategic and tactical electronic presentations to demonstrate value of their own services to their own customers. They expect the same from their service providers.

Digital cameras provide a simple method to capture images of projects and personnel for use in technology-based presentations. Software-based presentation tools combined with high-resolution projection systems allow for high-impact, person-to-person demonstrations that illustrate the firm's capabilities, experience and approach. Further, software-based presentations, complete with audio and video, can be stored on CD-ROM or DVD-ROM for duplication and distribution in the form of an interactive electronic brochure.

Audio conferencing, videoconferencing and Internet-based meetings are other mediums for the distribution of your message. They can simplify access to distant or international clients and work effectively for both pre-sale and post-sale coordination, reducing travel and expenses.

Regis McKenna, a marketing guru formerly with Apple Computer, said, "At a time where the gap between need or desire and fulfillment is approaching zero — where any physical distance equals only a microsecond in lapsed connection time — the forces of the market will increasingly demand a real-time response from you and your firm." Using technology, you will afford the customer the ability to determine what, when and how much they will buy. Using technology, your client will shop, compare and negotiate. Using technology, you and your client will work collaboratively and strategically to customize your service offerings to meet the specific requirements of each project.

Getting Started

Technology can support and enhance any A/E/C firm's effectiveness. Freeing time and extending resources are two excellent reasons for integrating technology within an organization. Determining the appropriate technology application requires an assessment process and a methodology for the creation, implementation and eventual planned use of the technology. Purchasing any technology for technology's sake is a recipe for disaster. Assessing current and future needs, and developing a clear purpose for the technology is the best way to avoid this obstacle. The phases of assessment are similar to the strategic planning process that most businesses use effectively, and one in which the marketing organization is generally a primary participant.

Begin by researching existing conditions. What hardware and software is currently in place? Do the original vendors continue to support the systems? Are the systems contemporary with other systems in use in the business? Can the existing systems expand to include input from outside collaborators (e.g., consultants, engineers, suppliers, clients)? Establish clear goals. What is the "vision" or aspiration of the business for the technology? What purpose will it serve? What processes will it improve?

Conduct a needs assessment. Assessment is a tool design that engineering service providers typically use in measuring the effectiveness of their clients' practices, using the feedback for future planning and building accountability into the system. This same approach can be applied to marketing technology. There are four things that can be done to effectively build more accountability for the technology implementation into the organization:

- Develop consensus on expected outcomes with all primary users
- Encourage continuous improvement and regularly measure improvements
- Ensure that all staff (from marketing to principals) participate in the assessment process
- Take diversity into account; do not mandate one-solution for all, but allow for multiple solutions to reach the same goals

Performing an in-depth analysis of the firm's marketing technology needs should be part of a larger technology program evaluation effort. The lesson learned from past technology-implementation efforts is that a technology needs assessment is more effective when the analysis is based on business goals and available resources. Available resources include not only existing hardware and software, but also the capacity to acquire funds for infrastructure building to provide ongoing professional development programs for those who will be using the new technology. Ask questions such as:

⊠ How many members of the staff have access to the marketing database?
  - What kinds of projects do they pursue?
  - Are their clients or potential clients using collaborative technologies (e.g., project-specific Internet sites, electronic requests for proposals [RFPs])?
  - Do they share their personal database with the firm's?
⊠ What customer descriptive data is or should be included in the database?
  - Demographics, psychographics, firm-specific data?
  - Transactional categorizations or summary customer data?

- Strategic customer value (growth potential, per customer)?
- What outside data is overlaid on the customer database?

⊠ How is new or updated information input into the database now?
- Who has authority to enter new information?
- What internal and external systems automatically feed information into it?
- Who oversees and supervises the processes?

⊠ What interconnectivity exists that can support distribution of the database?
- Do we have the appropriate Local Area Network (LAN) and Wide Area Network (WAN) systems?
- Do the company's network, servers, routers, firewalls, etc., support the needs of distributed secure data?

⊠ What supporting technology is available to utilize/manipulate the information in the database?
- Presentation software?
- Digital cameras, scanners, CD-ROM recorders, etc.?
- Company web site?
- Digital projectors?
- Audio or videoconference systems?

How a firm does business will determine the kind of information to be tracked. A large firm with multiple national or multinational offices will need a much more robust system than a small, boutique design firm. Both will benefit from applying technology appropriately. Final decisions should be made based on goals and resources, and the determination of the extent to which technology will be incorporated into the operations of the business.

Once it has been determined what technologies will best support the marketing effort, the next step is implementation. Determine whether in-house resources are available (and capable) or if an outside system integrator should be used. Don't underestimate the time involved. As much or more time as went into planning is often required in implementing the technology. Speak with several vendors that handle competing products. This analysis gives the broadest range of options available for the integration of the plan. The vendor should be experienced in the type of technology system integration planned for the business application. Obtain references. They should also have adequate support staff should something go wrong.

Keep in mind that any technology system will need to grow with the business. Computers and peripherals should be upgradable and not already obsolete when they are installed. Software should be upgradable, allowing for growth. Including network capabilities and multi-user licenses will allow for increasing the number of people who can utilize a technology-based system as the business grows.

Simple personal information managers (e.g., ACT!, Goldmine, Maximizer, Outlook, Notes) or more robust sales automation tool sets (e.g., Pivotal, Siebel Systems, MarketForce) can be used to catalog and retrieve client and project-specific data. Relational database software (e.g., Access, FileMaker Pro, Approach) is designed to be completely customized to each business's information storage and retrieval requirements. Building industry-specific solutions (e.g., RFP, AE Award, PDM - Architect/ Engineer/ Contractor) are pre-designed to provide the typical fields and data required by A/E/C firms. After evaluating the options, the selection of the database engine should meet the demands of the company now and be able to expand into the future.

To ensure success, a marketing information system needs the support and approval of both management and user groups. Without management support, the system will fail due to lack of credibility. Without user support, the system will fail from lack of relevant, accurate data. During the technology development phase or when evaluating commercial hardware or software, it is essential to solicit involvement and feedback from both of these groups.

Analyzing and Utilizing the Data

In today's competitive business environment firms need to do more faster and better in finding and qualifying new clients, analyzing and researching markets, calculating and monitoring success, and defining new opportunities. It has been shown in many "go, no go" analyses, that the best new clients will always closely resemble your best existing clients. Using technology to "mine" the database of characteristics (e.g., industry, size, location) of your existing client base can help identify the demographics of potential new customers. A computerized marketing information system provides flexible, selective retrieval of data, regular activity reports, accessibility to firm-wide marketing information and an accurate basis for relating marketing efforts to marketing results. Cataloging a firm's project history and comparing the client demographics in the successful projects (i.e., projects that were profitable) can help identify the types of clients your firm should (or should not) pursue.

The combination of information technology and marketing information come together in a marketing database. Identifying the best targets and sizing the market opportunity are areas of marketing where technology can be a great benefit. Information is the key element that gives any firm a leg up on the competition. Learning as much as possible about a prospective client can make the difference. Insights into the client's perspective of its real needs for a project are often that which differentiates the winning firm from the rest of the short list. In profiling both existing and potential new clients, some questions to ask might include:

- What are their principal lines of business?
- How big are they?
- Where are they located geographically?
- Who are their competitors?
- What is their history of building?
- Do they own or lease their properties?
- What is their history of capital expenditure for buildings?
- Does their current market growth support the need for more building?
- Do they have internal resources for designing, engineering or managing projects?

The questions developed will vary depending on whether your firm is in architecture, engineering or construction; whether you take a primary role in the building development process or whether your firm is a consultant.

The advantage of a thorough profile is the potential for useful data reduction. The key is the development of an information base that includes the mass of potential clients that can be filtered down to specific target groups. That data set can be further refined to specific postal codes to help define regional and local marketing efforts. With sufficient input data, the dimension of information can be focused to the smallest imaginable level, the individual who can be traced by name and address.

Thus it is the technology that provides the means to move from generalization to the specific and identifiable. Another aspect of the profile is the type of information used. Generally it is research data combined with larger demographic trends. It can include changes in economic conditions or societal and behavioral attitudes. Which industries are growing? What business types are expanding or consolidating? As the technology becomes more sophisticated, we gain tools that assist in forecasting future opportunities.

From a practical standpoint, gathering data should include as much consistency as possible. A single record (the information about a person, company or project) is only as good as the individual fields of specific data about that record (e.g., first name, last name, title, address, phone). Since so much of professional services marketing is person-to-person, it becomes imperative to ensure the completeness of all fields of the database. This applies equally to the personal information or contact management software as it does to an enterprise-wide relational database that includes information on project history, costs and schedule. This type of marketing technology allows you to keep detailed information on thousands of records from company name down to individual contacts, what they purchased, when and why. For prospects, you can track where you met them, what their interest level is, and when and how to contact them next.

Potential prospect lists can be obtained through a variety of list-brokerage services, hard research (i.e., the library) and digital research on the web (e.g., Hoover's, Dun & Bradstreet, Standard & Poors, American Business Information/InfoUSA). Prioritizing these lists into useful data is where a well-designed marketing technology system will prove its worth. Qualifying leads is a process of comparison.

Matching the service provider's strengths and offerings and its existing client database demographics with the prospect list's characteristics yields the best matches and establishes the priority for the firm's marketing efforts. At this point you can create customized communication pieces that are tailored to the immediate and long-term requirements of each qualified prospect. This information, in turn, can be used by the front-line, business-development personnel making sales calls that are more effective and more memorable.

Prioritizing the marketing effort with technology helps avoid the "shotgun" approach to blanket marketing every possible customer with generic information. Accurate and useful data can help prioritize the firm's "reactive" response to the qualifications or proposal request you did not anticipate. And it can focus the firm on "proactive" marketing and selling to the customers most likely to buy your services.

Once a database of existing and potential customers is created, the profile information can be used to identify and qualify potential prospects. One of the great advantages of technology-based marketing is the ability to personalize the offer to the target market. The marketing effort is much more effective when comparative analysis is utilized. By closely matching the services offered to the needs of the potential clients with similar demographics to other, existing clients, the firm's marketing effectiveness can be improved.

Reaching the target audience in the A/E/C industry is a combination of determining the best sequence of contacts to communicate the message. From producing and delivering appropriate collateral information that is specific to their project requirements, to direct presentation of qualifications and solutions, the focus of the prospect effort is to develop new business. Introducing your firm to the client can come as a result of relationships with other service providers in the industry, but is more proactive when your database is setting the strategic direction to the potential clients you want as customers.

Whether using direct mail or one-to-one business development, the marketing database technology can assist by providing quantifiable response rate metrics. It can be used to both classify where the best opportunities are found, and analyze the data to determine the best return on investment.

Measuring and Profiting

By defining the profile and prospect-tracking fields, database technology systems also provide flexibility in tracking business development effectiveness at various levels. The data can be sorted to provide information such as:

- Are projects coming from new clients, repeat clients or additional services?
- How much service has been committed and how much is actually under contract?
- How many new service opportunity initiatives have been identified?
- What kinds of facilities and services are clients buying?
- What has each marketing effort cost in terms of labor and expenses?
- What is our hit rate from prospect to proposal? Proposal to short list? Short list to award?

Technology is a tool not only for tracking information on leads and business development performance, but also for supporting the marketing function by storing and organizing data on firm resources and past project histories. The amount of information and detail required in proposal requests is increasing as both new and existing clients search for ways to differentiate between professional services firms.

Project history data fields should contain information on project costs (estimated and actual and number of change orders), schedule information, square footages, special features of the facility, project team, consultants or associate firms, and client references. Special firm resources and services and staff resumes should also be stored in the marketing information system.

No technology system has value unless it provides a means for measuring response and results. By profiling responders, measuring project profitability and calculating the return on investment, the information technology system can provide the necessary analysis for building a profit model that can be replicated again and again. Graphic depiction of data helps communicate results. Exporting the data to a spread sheet program or graphing software can graph any information that can be quantified, such as budget and project size. This information, in turn, can be used to evaluate current and existing markets and determine the barriers to entry into new and evolving markets where your firm may want to pursue opportunities.

Communicating and Publicizing

The new technology paradigm of "information everywhere" requires that you constantly and consistently strive to keep your firm's data accessible and current. Without currency, the data has limited or even potentially damaging value. Therefore, one of the top priorities in any technology implementation needs to be maintenance. Leverage the data in ways that will benefit your customer. Share your successes, publicize your services and demonstrate your qualifications as the source for their solutions. Technology can be used to poll and survey customers, keep personnel and position data up-to-date, and foster strategic collaboration to meet mutual goals. Handheld personal digital assistants (e.g., Palm III/IV/VII and similar Windows CE-based units from Philips, Casio, NEC and Sharp) can be used to carry vital information with each member of the business development staff.

The world wide web and the Internet offer the marketing professional new forums for publicizing your firm's efforts. A corporate web presence has become a de facto requirement of doing business in the contemporary market (covered in more detail later in this book). Major web-based outlets such as PRNewswire and BusinessWire provide venues for a targeted electronic publicity campaign with press releases to the millions of people who currently have access to the Internet.

"Webcasts" (i.e., web-based broadcasts) that utilize streaming audio and video to provide real-time press conferences are becoming more popular. This technology allows the firm to make a virtual presentation that can combine full-motion video, still images, and 3-D software "walkthroughs" to both clients and the public.

Using ubiquitous e-mail provides a medium for creating an electronic newsletter that you can send to subscribers. Sent out weekly, bi-weekly or monthly, this is a great way to promote your company and services, and you can also offer interesting information about your industry.

CD-ROM and DVD-ROM technology has become an effective delivery tool for multimedia, electronic brochures. Combining traditional firm history, service and qualifications with images, audio and video, this technology is on the forefront of interactive marketing. Presentation software (e.g., PowerPoint, Director, Astound, Freelance) provides the platform to build these presentations.

New tools for presenting using multimedia and information technology are quickly becoming cost effective and reliable. Advances in digital imaging technology have created a new breed of high-resolution and high-brightness cameras, scanners and projection systems (e.g., Epson, Canon, Hewlett-Packard, Compaq, In Focus, Sharp, NEC, Sony, Proxima), replacing older, optical technologies like overhead transparencies and 35mm slides, with direct computer image display. These lightweight and small devices can be hooked to a laptop or desktop computer for capturing and presenting marketing summaries, project photos, CAD drawings and other collateral data. In fixed installations, these imaging systems can be combined with access to video, sound and the corporate network or Internet for enhanced presentation capabilities.

One of the challenges of expanding business into new geographies is the travel associated with both securing and producing the work. Audio conferencing systems (e.g., Polycom, Lucent, Gentner) have improved dramatically, allowing for small and large group meetings in multiple locations to communicate with a high degree of intelligibility. Audio conference bridge services (e.g., AT&T, Sprint, Gentner, Meeting Place) simplify connecting multiple sites by providing pre-arranged, operator-assisted group meeting sites, accessed via toll-free, call-in phone numbers.

With the advent of faster data distribution through integrated switched digital networks (ISDN), digital subscriber lines (DSL) and broadband cable network access (e.g., @Home and @Work from TCI/AT&T), net-based conferencing (e.g., NetMeeting) and videoconferencing (e.g., PictureTel, Polycom, Sony) are increasingly being used for long-distance, face-to-face communication. These systems offer the ability to communicate voice, video and data (including "whiteboard" annotation of documents and drawings) between two or more sites anywhere in the world.

The Next Step

Information technology permeates all aspects of business — from automated systems and empowered teams — as today's organizations come to grips with the dynamics of a truly global, 24-hour market for their products and services. In a "market-facing enterprise," all relationships and functions are enhanced through technology, as the focus moves from inside the company to its network of suppliers, customers and partners.

There is a virtually endless list of ways that you can effectively use technology to boost your marketing skills and your company's professional image. Information data systems provide a look at your current and potential clients. The world wide web provides a resource for data gathering and competitive analysis. Electronic mail can be used for sending newsletters, marketing messages and creating electronic public relations campaigns. The Internet can be a forum for online interaction with your staff, your vendors, your peers and your clients (and potential clients). Conventional print collateral can be replaced with an interactive CD-ROM, DVD-ROM or web site. High-resolution, high-brightness computer projectors replace 35mm slides and darkened presentation rooms. Videoconferencing can provide a medium for communicating with long-distance or international customers. And, e-commerce looms as the future of transactional and service contracting.

Effective use of technology in marketing is a process of planning, implementation, training, measurement and updating. No one system will meet the needs of every professional services business. Each system will need the vision and support of the firm's principals and marketing staff. The effort can be challenging. The results can be the difference in long-term success or evolutionary extinction.

To be successful in professional services marketing today demands understanding of a vast body of information about prospective and current clients *and* their businesses. Market intelligence is critical to any firm trying to secure and perform work that creates and retains clients. Increased competition requires a greater number of leads and prospects to attain or maintain desired market share. With the demand for more and better information, computer-mediated marketing information technology becomes a necessary tool to organize, retrieve, analyze, communicate and present the data that will lead to new and profitable business.

Author's Note: The products and services listed in this chapter are provided for example and reference only. The author and SMPS neither make nor imply any specific recommendation for these products and companies. Similarly, there are many products and services that are not listed. Failure to list these is inadvertent and implies no prejudicial judgment of their quality or applicability to your technology requirements.

Links to Product and Company References

Access (www.microsoft.com)

ACT! (www.symantec.com)

AE Award (www.infomax-corp.com)

American Business Information/InfoUSA (www.abii.com; www.infousa.com)

Apple Computer (www.apple.com)

Approach (www.lotus.com)

Astound (www.astoundinc.com)

@Home/@Work (www.tci.net; www.att.net)

BusinessWire (www.businesswire.com)

Canon (www.canon.com)

Casio (www.casio.com)

Compaq (www.compaq.com)

Director (www.macromedia.com)

Dun & Bradstreet (www.dnb.com)

Epson (www.epson.com)

Filemaker Pro (www.filemaker.com)

Freelance (www.lotus.com)

Gentner (www.gentner.com)

Goldmine (www.goldminesw.com)

Hewlett-Packard (www.hp.com)

Hoover's (www.hoovers.com)

In Focus (www.infocus.com)

Intel (www.intel.com)

Lucent (www.lucent.com)

MarketForce (www.marketforce.com)

Maximizer (www.maximizer.com)

Meeting Place (www.latitude.com)

NEC (www.nec.com)

NetMeeting (www.microsoft.com)

Notes (www.lotus.com)

Outlook (www.microsoft.com)

Palm Computing (www.palmpilot.com)

Philips (www.philips.com)

PictureTel (www.picturetel.com)

Pivotal (www.pivotal.com)

Polycom (www.polycom.com)

PowerPoint (www.microsoft.com)

PRNewswire (www.prnewswire.com)

Proxima (www.proxima.com)

RFP (www.rfpsoftware.com)

Sharp (www.sharp.com)

Siebel Systems (www.siebel.com)

Sony (www.sony.com)

Sprint (www.sprint.com)

Standard & Poors (www.standardandpoors.com)

3Com (www.3Com.com)

Windows CE (www.microsoft.com)

Recommended Reading

Kalakota, Ravi M., and Andrew B. Whinston. *Electronic Commerce: A Manager's Guide*. Reading, MA: Addison-Wesley, 1997.

McKenna, Regis. *Real Time: Preparing for the Age of the Never Satisfied Customer*. Boston: Harvard Business School Press, 1997.

Papows, Jeff. *Enterprise.com: Market Leadership in the Information Age*. Reading, MA: Perseus Books, 1998.

Postma, Paul. *The New Marketing Era: Marketing to the Imagination in a Technology-Driven World*. New York: McGraw Hill, 1999.

Rodin, Robert. *Free, Perfect & Now: Connecting to the Three Insatiable Customer Demands*. New York: Simon & Schuster, 1999.

Craig Park, FSMPS

- Craig Park, a Fellow of the Society for Marketing Professional Services, is a marketing professional with nearly 30 years' experience in professional services, consulting engineering and systems integration firms. His experience includes business development, marketing management and the development of promotional marketing materials.
- Park is vice president of integrated solutions at Intellisys Group (**www.intellisysgroup.com**), engineered design/builders of multimedia communication systems. He is responsible for the firm's corporate design and national business development activities.
- Park received his bachelor's degree in architecture from California State Polytechnic University, San Luis Obispo.
- He currently serves as Fellows Delegate to the national board of directors of the Society for Marketing Professional Services (SMPS), and is past president of the San Francisco/Bay Area chapter.
- Park has presented programs on technology and marketing to SMPS, the American Institute of Architects (AIA), the International Institute of Interior Designers (IIDA), the Institute of Business Designers (IBD) and the International Facilities Management Association (IFMA).
- Park has published more than 50 articles on technology and marketing, and writes a regular column, "On Virtuality," focusing on improving business processes for the multimedia integration industry's magazine, *Systems Contractor News* (**www.systemscontractor.com**).
- Park can be reached by phone at (415) 472-0930, by fax at (415) 472-0934, by e-mail at **craig@craigpark.com**, by contact at **www.craigpark.com**, or by videoconference at SPIDs (415) 472-0930/34.

Acknowledgment

I want to acknowledge the fine original article on this subject prepared by Julie Luers, FSMPS, for the first edition of this book. It helped form the outline for my writing and I have tried to include much of her original information herein.

1.9 Marketing Implementation Planning: Striving for Marketing Wellness

Susan R. Daylor, FSMPS
Principal
Mariposa Consulting

In most firms, marketing is intended to support sales or business development. Once a marketing strategy has been developed and a marketing plan has been written, it is important to develop a structure for managing and executing the firm's entire marketing program. The first step to effective marketing implementation is building a knowledgeable, reliable team. Team members can be comprised of marketing staff, technical staff, principals, project managers and/or consultants. The key to the marketing team's success lies in its ability to communicate effectively, both among team members and with others.

There are two components to the marketing effort — the reactive mode and the self-initiated mode. The reactive mode accounts for all the proposal, presentation and other deadline-driven needs that arise under the prospective client's control. Marketing departments must and should react to these opportunities. But due to the oftentimes sporadic nature of these opportunities, they often infringe on what we plan to do — the self-initiated component, those programs identified in a firm's marketing plan, including market research, image studies, direct mail and the like. What results is a vicious circle of playing catch-up.

There are ways, however, to better implement the marketing effort to allow the two functions to coexist without chaos. The following is a suggested prescription for a healthy renewal of your firm's marketing implementation.

Diagnose Your Program

Your marketing program begins with your marketing plan. The marketing plan is the firm's road map for developing and maintaining its clients. Think of it not only as a guide for senior staff, but also as an aid in facilitating your job as a marketing manager. Use the plan not only to focus your marketing strategy, but also as a management tool, a guide for scheduling and a navigational aid. Revise it, boost it and talk about it. If you do this as a group, either within the marketing department or by incorporating the technical staff, you will be team building. As the team generates discussion, you'll be surprised how many new, creative ideas come up. Volunteers often emerge as well. Take the team concept further. Establish monthly or weekly team meetings to review current projects and programs.

In addition to including goals and objectives, strategies, action items and time frames, the marketing plan should also designate who will be responsible for undertaking the various activities. It's a good idea to make sure the marketing plan gets executed by a balanced work force — marketing staff, technical staff, principals, project managers and consultants. That way you are building a structure in which a cross section of people becomes enrolled in the marketing of your firm. The plan's authors and executors should meet at least quarterly to measure your accomplishments, identify remaining tasks to be done and to modify the plan in accordance with market cycles. Further capitalize on this meeting opportunity by reviewing your firm's overall goals and discussing emerging new markets and strategies to develop those markets. Post the plan or keep it visible via internal e-mail to communicate your accomplishments and to serve as a reminder of what needs to be done.

Step back and look at your marketing effort objectively. Look to see where redundancies occur. For example, are two people managing the execution of proposals? Ask yourself, what should we be doing that we can't seem to ever get to? Re-examine marketing roles, giving thought to who is good at doing what. Don't forget the technical staff — how are they currently participating in the marketing effort? Is it working? What more could they be doing? Do they need marketing training? Are your marketing costs in check? Are there areas in which you can derive cost savings? Write down all the problem areas so you don't overlook anything. Develop an organized structure and make way for change. Such an analysis is a good start in creating an internal marketing plan — a plan to help you and your department better promote your roles, responsibilities and accomplishments to the entire firm.

Strive for a Healthy Lifestyle

Make sure your marketing staff is knowledgeable. Principals, prospective clients and clients expect marketers to know about a firm's experience. Does your marketing staff know which of the firm's projects are successful and why, in terms of design, management, profitability and strong references? The marketing director should expose marketing coordinators to tangible projects, helping them to build project (and firm) knowledge beyond the fundamental record photos and descriptive facts. Visit job sites, attend building dedications and openings, and shadow a designer or construction administrator on the job. Try giving your staff members a pop quiz to test their knowledge. Once the knowledge builds, link their knowledge with future marketing initiatives. For example, if you know that design/build senior living facilities is a profitable building type in which clients see you excel, and the market demand is strong, chances are you'd want to grow in that direction. Encourage your staff to develop ideas to penetrate that market. The more you and your staff know about your firm and the markets it serves, the greater the interest and motivation levels on the part of the staff.

Think about how the marketing staff does its job. Examine the effectiveness of systems used to maintain project information, lead reports, consultants' material, mailing lists, graphics, collateral, boilerplate material and prior proposals. Are you automating as much as you can? Develop a database to manage your project information. Many firms are structuring the database so that marketing and technical staff can access it. Opening up your treasure trove of project information to project managers helps in gathering up-to-date, accurate project information, and saves you future scrambling. If developing a database in-house is not feasible, consider hiring a student to devise or revise your databases. Computer scan the project photos used most often. Doing so will enable easy retrieval for use in brochures, proposals and presentations. Create an index for quick identification and retrieval of consultants' material. Categorize your mailing lists to reflect your various market segments. Indicate on mailing lists who received what when. Keep track of client feedback on brochures and mailers. Use that feedback in future internal and external marketing programs.

Seek out time-savers. If your firm uses PowerPoint for presentations, develop routine or standard sections, such as firm background, experience and schedule formats to reduce ensuing preparation time. If you do a lot of in-house board presentations, advance order standard "firm background" boards. Develop different "firm background" boards for your various markets. Whether computerized or in file drawers, organize your photo library to reflect your markets. For example, if you specialize in educational facilities, categorize your slides and photos according to building components — libraries, athletic facilities and so on. This type of organization will allow you to retrieve needed images quickly and help identify inventory needs. When teaming with other firms, transfer information via e-mail or disks.

Standardize systems. Systems can range from marketing reports to presentation graphics. Once the standards are set, communicate to all staff their existence, how they're organized and how they can be accessed. Try not to allow reinvention of the wheel.

Negotiate costs with vendors and partners. You can usually get cost breaks on quantity orders of photography, printing or color laser copies. When teaming with other firms for proposals, photography, exhibits and awards, make sure you share the costs.

Marketing managers need to challenge marketing staff members. Ask them to assess and tackle one area of deficiency. Challenge them to come up with a proposed solution for change. They'll get excited and so will you.

After generating a mammoth proposal, don't just throw it in the drawer and forget about it. Go through it and use the new information to update your marketing records. That way you'll always have current records. Then circulate that proposal among staff members — keep them updated, not only on current work but work you are pursuing. This is also a great way to market your hard work internally.

Lastly, give yourself a break from the daily fast pace. How can you do that? Advance planning *can* avoid burnout. For example, determine all the awards programs you plan to pursue for the year. Schedule them in a calendar. Order photos in advance to save rush charges and headaches. Enlist the technical staff to assist in drawings early, preferably as part of a project's phases. The sooner things get started, the more breathing room in the end. Another way to lessen the pace is to vary activities. Instead of gluing yourself to the keyboard for eight hours straight, take a walk through the office and ask staff members to share their projects with you. You'll not only get your break, but you'll get educated and engage staff in the marketing effort at the same time.

Exercise Your Power

Believe it or not, marketers do wield considerable power within firms. Marketing usually maintains a direct link to the firm's senior echelon. Marketing is the first phase of a project. Marketing knows where the next hot building type will be. Marketing is where technical staff turns to learn about the firm's experience. Marketing departments need to market marketing internally so that marketing becomes everybody's business. But in order to earn your power, you need to demonstrate your value to your firm. Marketers need to increase collaboration effectiveness with the firm's sellers, and they need to ensure that the entire marketing department knows the firm and the markets it serves.

We've all heard stories about how difficult it is to get principals and project managers to follow up on their marketing calls and assignments. This is because they are not held accountable. One way to organize the process and elicit principals' follow-through, is to utilize a networked computer tracking and reminder system, such as Lotus Notes or ACT. Another vehicle is to set up an intranet web site that collects data and gives up-to-the-minute status reports on leads and other marketing opportunities. To keep web sites lively and refreshed, augment marketing reports with marketing tips, industry trends and news items. In other words, give information to get response. Marketers need to manage these programs, but instead of marketers being the ones hounding the principals, the computer becomes the nag, and the marketer becomes the orchestrator, the information resource. Such a program creates peer pressure for principals to act. It becomes a vehicle to reinforce senior management's commitment to marketing. It builds a basis for principals' marketing efforts to become part of their performance evaluations. Finally, it serves to promote marketing internally, elevating the importance of marketing in the firm's overall management structure.

Managing and supervising the activities of your marketing and support staff is an important component to running an effective marketing department. Constant communication is essential. Your employees need to know their roles and responsibilities, as they pertain to the marketing plan, to the day-to-day operation of the department and to the deadline-driven activities, such as proposals, presentations and awards programs. Don't assume your staff will know how to set priorities. Marketing directors need to train their staff to differentiate between a crisis, an urgent project and something that can wait. Moody/Nolan, Ltd., architects/engineers of Columbus, Ohio, calls the priority-setting process "triage," a term borrowed from the medical profession to handle urgent tasks that need immediate help first.

Seek Good Nutrition

Build upon your knowledge. Always be on the lookout for better ways of doing things. Read general business magazines and look for ideas on how companies in other industries address various marketing challenges. Try to apply these scenarios to your firm. Read publications in your own professions, such as *Architectural Record, Engineering News Record*, and *Building Design and Construction*. Keeping abreast of current projects is certainly a benefit, but don't neglect the business departments and features in these publications. They can be very insightful when it comes to doing business (marketing) better. Reading trade press relevant to your markets is also very helpful, particularly to learn about industry growth patterns and new legislative measures that may affect your market and how you communicate to it. Sign up for free publications that often come with software installations, such as *FileMaker Pro Advisor* magazine. Though such publications may have technical leanings, scanning these publications can give you ideas for improving your management systems development.

Consider starting a small lead exchange group with key leaders in the A/E/C industry. If you select strong people to be among participants, they themselves will be the draw for other leaders to attend meetings. Discussions can begin with leads, but more often than not, conversations will steer toward new markets and savvy clients. For these groups to be successful, care should be taken in selecting non-competing participants, and each person must be prepared to bring information, insights and a willingness to share ideas.

Mentoring and training are musts in this business. Consider developing a marketing in-house training program for your project managers, led by you, your marketing staff, an industry consultant, or a combination thereof. One firm that has developed an extremely successful training program is Haley & Aldrich, geotechnical engineers in Cambridge, Mass. Entitled "Technical Experience and Marketing Skills Exchange," the one-and-a-half-day program involves a cross section of senior staff. Topics range from developing client relationships to personal goal setting. Through this type of internal marketing, the marketing department generates newfound excitement and participation among the technical staff, and the technical staff learns more about the firm's strengths and marketing how-to's, which they can put to use in their own marketing pursuits — a win-win victory.

Keep the Family Healthy

As stated above, an efficient, successful marketing program is based on good communication. Meet with your principals at least twice a month to apprise them of your lead generation, marketing strategies, promotional work, proposals, presentations and other marketing activities. They want to hear about results, not how you plan to develop new systems to do your job better. Show them how the results of one marketing program led to project opportunities or opened up another market for you. Always give them new, exciting information, and you can all look forward to a strong marketing exchange.

If no structure exists in your firm for regular communication with project managers and technical staff, create one. Consider organizing a marketing forum. Invite project teams to present their current projects. Organize a guest speaker series, inviting current clients or industry specialists to educate staff on market trends or industry profiles. For example, TRO/The Ritchie Organization, of Newton, Mass., initiated a health care educational forum, and invited guest speakers (clients and prospective clients) to discuss the business of health care — operations and cost containment, financing mechanisms and hospital strategic planning. Principals, project architects and the marketing staff participated, resulting in a stronger knowledge base about the health care industry beyond building projects. This knowledge helped the technical staff to better communicate with its clients through all phases of projects, and the marketing department became more aware of the factors influencing the rationale behind future projects.

What about branch offices? Because branch offices are remote, many firms adopt an out-of-sight, out-of-mind mentality about them. (That goes for headquarters to branch A, vice versa, and branch A to branch B.) Here are some suggestions for improving marketing management for both the home and branch offices.

If you're the parent:

- Share the corporate vision with all offices.
- Ask each branch office to develop a marketing plan around the corporate plan.
- Communicate plans and ideas frequently — set scheduled conference calls using agendas.
- Ask that branch offices keep you informed and up to date on marketing activities.
- Encourage new ideas to be brought forward.
- Share resources — people, materials, systems.
- Assist in strategies for new client development.

- Visit the branch offices frequently.
- Invite staff from the branch offices to your office.
- Schedule visits around SMPS meetings to familiarize yourself with regional networks.

If you're one of the offspring:

- Communicate frequently with each office.
- Ask questions about strategic direction.
- Don't be afraid to generate new ideas.
- Learn the corporate systems.
- Share regional trends with other offices.
- Introduce your network to other offices — either by phone or meeting.
- Invite staff from the parent office to your office.

Get Regular Checkups

Overhauling a marketing effort does not constitute a one-shot deal. You need to constantly monitor progress through both formal and informal communication. Share your successes with other firms and in exchange, ask what works well for them. Remember that the most effective marketing efforts are those stemming from a strong team mindset. Continue to challenge yourself to be a good team leader and a good team member. You'll be on the road to recovery!

Bibliography

Edgerly, Cathy. Cathy Edgerly Consulting, 1999.

Hankinson, Bill. "Changing Attitudes Toward Marketing." SMPS *Marketer* (Aug. 1991).

Hochberg, Hugh. "Unplugged: The Marketing Profession From the Principals' Perspective." *SMPS Marketer* (April 1997).

Kienle, MBA, SMP, Peter. Moody/Nolan, Ltd., 1999.

Practice Management Associates, Ltd. "Streamlining Your Marketing Operations." *A/E Marketing Journal* (May 1993).

TRO/The Ritchie Organization, 1997.

Wheeler, Sylvia J. Haley & Aldrich, 1992.

Susan R. Daylor, FSMPS

- Susan R. Daylor, FSMPS, is principal and owner of Mariposa Consulting, a market positioning consulting firm. Located in Newton, Mass., Mariposa provides strategic market planning, market research, public relations and communications services to firms within the built environment.
- Formerly vice president, marketing of TRO/The Ritchie Organization, Daylor has more than 20 years' experience in marketing professional services. Prior to joining TRO, Daylor was associated with Payette Associates in Boston.

Accomplishments:

- SMPS Fellow.
- SMPS Boston Past President, 1990-91.
- SMPS Boston Board of Directors, 1985-92.
- SMPS Boston Achievement Award for Outstanding Professional Contribution, 1993.
- SMPS National Marketing Communications Awards, First Place, Special Market Brochure, 1994.
- SMPS Boston Communications Awards, First Place, Public Relations Campaign, 1995.
- SMPS Boston Communications Awards, Second Place, Special Market Brochure, 1994.
- SMPS Alabama Marketing Awards, Best of Show, Direct Mail Campaign, 1993.
- SMPS Alabama Marketing Awards, First Place, Direct Mail, 1993.
- SMPS Boston Marketing Awards Program, Second Place, Direct Mail Campaign, 1990.
- Speaker, Harvard University Graduate School of Design, Career Options in the Design Professions, 1993.
- SMPS Boston, Marketing Fundamentals Course Instructor, 1999, 1994, 1993.
- Boston College School of Management, Speaker, "Marketing Career Opportunities," 1992.
- Boston College School of Management, Panelist, "Marketing Professional Services," 1991.
- Build Boston, Speaker, "Using Publicity to Build Business," 1993.
- Build Boston, Speaker, "How and Why Designers are Selected ... or Forgotten," 1989.
- Author, SMPS *The Handbook for Marketing Professional Services*, "Keeping the Marketing Effort Alive, Well and Prosperous," 1994.

1.10 Quality/ISO 9000 as a Marketing Tool

Carol A. Adey, FSMPS
President
Adey Associates

Graham K. Hill, P.E.
President and CEO
Tomlin Inc.

Quality's Relevance to Client Concerns/Expectations

Does your proposal address the real concern of the client? Can the client trust that your firm will protect and enhance their assets? How does your firm validate its ability to deliver superb customer care every time *as well as* the technical expertise needed for a project? How is your firm's excellence described and how are the distinctive features promoted? Can your firm validate its ability to meet cost, time and quality?

New clients are concerned about how an untried relationship will work. Existing clients will need assurance that care and attention will continue over the life of a relationship — not just project by project. But today, superb technical qualifications and a strong technical track record will *not* separate your proposal from other equally well-qualified competitors. Something more is needed!

Research indicates that clients are more likely to make a choice about a design firm when some fundamental and emotional concerns have been answered. For example:

- The firm's track record for customer care, diligence and consistency in managing time, cost and quality
- How well the firm has genuinely implemented sound management methods to run the business
- The methods used to protect the client, through control of the project requirements, resources, time, budgets, and errors.

This is *Quality*.

This chapter will:
- Provide an overview of Quality/ISO 9000
- Discuss its' relevance to professional service firms
- Explain why Quality/ISO 9000 offers direct benefits.

We will present an example of how a Quality/ISO 9000 firm might respond to the frequently asked question in an RFP "describe your firm's quality management system."

What or Who Is ISO?

ISO comes from a Greek word that means equal — as in Isosceles triangle, Isobars, etc. The word ISO, when linked to ISO 9000 is used to signify equal acceptance of standards around the world — the creation of a level playing field about reliability and improvement in service.

The number 9000 was set aside for the family (or series) of standards that specifically apply to the implementation of Quality Systems. Hence the ISO 9000 standard (more about the different members of the ISO 9000 family later in this chapter). The ISO organization has issued other standards that are accepted internationally — the ISO 10000 series (Auditing), ISO 14000 series (Environmental Management) and so on. These will not be covered here.

The organization that publishes these international standards is officially known as "The International Organization for Standards" — or IOS — a confusing similarity.

In summary, ISO 9000 states that clients are better assured of getting what they expect when a firm adheres to the management, operations and administrative practices described below.

Management leads in providing the following:

- Objectives, goals and the approach to quality within the business are clearly expressed
- Responsibilities are clear
- Company plans are clearly understood at all levels within the firm
- Plans are effectively implemented, well tracked, reported and reviewed
- Plans are aligned with client needs
- A common structured process for fixing problems and making improvements exists
- The firm relies on factual, objective data and trends regarding performance

Operations are routinely benchmarked and tested to see that:

- Best practices and expectations are clearly defined for all personnel — across the complete "customer relationship cycle"
- A complete customer relationship cycle would include initial contact, proposal development, contract definition, project/scope definitions, project control, review and release of project deliverables, delivery, project closeout, support, performance evaluation, customer satisfaction.

Administration: Support structures for administrative processes are equally well designed. These will cover:

- Document and data management, purchasing (especially of sub-consultant services)
- Archiving/records
- The training/professional development of employees.

A professional services firm can use Quality/ISO 9000 as a way to:

- Stand above the competition
- Construct distinctive proposals based upon excellence
- Remove hidden, emotional or perceived client concerns about a firm's ability to deliver exceptional service
- Raise customer confidence based on clearly validated quality performance
- Create operational methods that meet budget, schedule and deliver exceptional customer service, time after time
- Build lasting relationships with clients
- Create operational methods that have the potential to raise productivity and lower operational costs.

The Changing Marketplace in Quality & ISO 9000

Industry

Industrial clients have developed a strong history of quality. They have learned to run their businesses more effectively and what to expect from other businesses that work with them. Their vision of mutual and peer-based relationships has made them highly selective about whom they chose to work and grow with.

Industry has set higher demands about what constitutes good service based upon their own experience and ability to change the norms of performance. They want to work and grow only with those who share the same values for constantly learning and being the best. For many years industrial companies have been the leaders in ISO 9000 application. They do not want to partner with those closed to the notion of change or improvement. They do not want to partner with those that say ISO 9000 or quality is only a manufacturing issue.

Industrial clients increasingly demand equality in perspective from their suppliers regarding quality. They have worked on quality/ISO 9000 with their primary (or first-level) suppliers who provide raw materials or components to their own products. They are now shifting their attention and demands to the second-level suppliers — the professional service firms.

Government

When it comes to managing tax dollars, state authorities have also seen the benefit of demanding ISO 9000 style performance from supplier firms. Pennsylvania DOT (PennDOT), Maryland DOT, New Jersey DOT, New York DOT, California DOT and Massachusetts DOT are among those either demanding or giving notice of ISO 9000 requirements from their consultants.

Government departments, such as GSA Property Management Division, use ISO 9000 themselves and expect similar performance from their design consultants.

Global activity now makes ISO 9000 a minimum requirement for RFP's in Europe, Australia and the Southeast Asian Countries. Canada, Mexico and other Latin American countries are also leaders in ISO 9000 application for design consultants. The United States lags many of these nations in the use of quality or ISO 9000.

Commercial market place clients are becoming savvy about quality and the specific benefits of ISO 9000, but lag behind the industrial market place. Few individual commercial clients have embraced ISO 9000 as a model. Their time will come.

Health, education and local government groups have not, as of yet, adopted ISO 9000 as an operational need — primarily from a lack of resources, rather than a lack of knowledge or desire.

Because of the risk of being accused of trade restriction, no U.S.-based client will actually mandate ISO 9000 as a requirement for continued business. Most "requests" from clients are expressed as a preference for the supplier to have a "quality program" or to be ISO 9000 registered. This lack of a clear mandate can be misunderstood as lack of client interest. However stated, the implication is still there — ***listen to your client's needs***.

As a strategic goal, a firm can decide to anticipate client requests for equality in perspective with regard to quality and be among the group of leaders — or the firm can decide to resist until actual loss of clientele and competitor gains become all too clear.

The implementation of ISO 9000 ***may*** gain a firm some new clients or market activity. However, the lack of ISO 9000 or a strong quality program will eventually lead to a loss of clients and contracts. In this context, ISO 9000 is similar to the implementation of CADD or EDI technologies during the late '80's early '90's.

It is important to note that liability insurance organizations provide discounts to professional design consulting firms registered to ISO 9000. Some membership organizations provide funds directly to firms to aid ISO 9000 registration.

As of early 1999, the number of ISO 9000 Registered A/E/C firms still remained small. However certain factors should be taken into account in looking at the numbers. In the last 18 months the fastest rate of growth in ISO 9000 registrations has been among service organizations, including design and engineering businesses. These businesses lead the current drive in ISO 9000 registrations.

An analysis of the "Top 500" engineering/design firms and the activity growth in ISO 9000 registrations indicates this growth is coming from small-mid size firms (100 to 400 employees).

What is the plan in your firm for ISO 9000?

Case Illustration: "Why Quality Is Important in Our Marketplace"

A prestigious institution engaged a respected architecture practice (with an equally impressive history) to design and oversee the construction of a major public building. The building won awards for its design.

All of the important dignitaries attended the opening award ceremony. The building met the basic functional specifications of the design criteria. However, client input regarding design aspects was consistently ignored or overruled by the architects and the project was late and over budget. The building worked — the quality of the relationship did not.

Outcome: The client has vowed never to use the architect again for any of their projects and retells this story, with delight, often and vigorously.

How Is Quality in a Design Firm Identified?

A quality design firm consciously ensures that all aspects of a client project flow faultlessly through each phase of work and at *a consistent level within each unit and among all personnel.* Quality is about taking as much pride and care over the management of a project and the client's relationship as in the technical excellence of the design. Quality is about meeting both the firm's goals for excellence and profit *as well as* the client's expectations for care and delivery of a desired solution.

A quality firm knows how well:

- Client needs have been understood and written down
- Project criteria have been defined and communicated
- Work plans have been prepared
- Team integration occurs at firm and client levels
- Scope or design changes are managed
- A project is proceeding against plan
- Design reviews find and eliminate errors and omissions
- Final design meets client goals
- Project follow-up and close-out is practiced
- Personnel use the best methods for delivering superb service.

"Knows" means that the firm routinely checks and collects information about its project management performance and can validate its performance.

"Knows", means that the firm can provide clients with track record data and qualifications about its project management performance. These will be testimonials and predictions about a firm's reliability in meeting time, cost and quality expectations.

"Knows", means that the firm has a clear assessment on how well personnel understand the best practices and utilize them consistently.

How to Address Quality/Performance in a Proposal/Response

Quality Policy

A quality policy states where the firm is now, *not* where it intends (or hopes) to be. The integrity of any policy statement is entirely dependent on the ability of the firm to validate its claims through proven examples supported by solid historical data.

A Quality Policy Example

Customer focus forms the basis of our actions. This is demonstrated in the way we:
  a) *Satisfy customer expectations through designs and professional services that conform to client specifications,*
  b) *Continually review our performance through objective data regarding both our processes and result measures. These also help drive our opportunities for improvement.*
We achieve our customer focus through a Quality Management System that utilizes standardized management practices with the following features:

  1. *Routine business planning, clearly set strategies, goals and objectives communicated and assigned for action within the firm.*
  2. *Employees know what is expected of them regarding Quality, are trained in standardized tools and methodologies and know how they relate to each other in taking responsibility for their own work.*
  3. *Clear expectations, quality information and job standards are communicated, via controlled means, to those involved in our project teams, both for client work and our own improvement teams.*
  4. *Consistent processes and capable employees are in place so that work is performed in a quality manner.*
  5. *Errors revealed in our work, or indicated by records, are investigated for root cause to prevent recurrence.*

Management considers these principles to be of such importance to our business that a member of our executive management team has been appointed as Quality Manager. The assignment includes a responsibility to ensure that all employees are aware of and understand these principles, and that the Quality Management System continues to work effectively.

The ISO 9000 FAMILY

The ISO 9000 series of standards contain different documents within the family — *Standards* used to assess a company and *Guidelines* to help guide selection and implementation. Common practice has created a language where firms often say they are pursuing ISO 9000 or are ISO 9000 Registered. In truth they will obtain a certificate for just the specific standard from within the family used to assess their quality management.

The series (or family) contains the following documents.

1 - Guideline on Selection:

ISO 9000   This is used to help a firm chose which standard applies to their business. As this is only a guidance document, a firm cannot be registered to ISO 9000. A company is registered either to ISO 9001, ISO 9002 or ISO 9003.

2 - Applicable Standards:

ISO 9001   The standard for a business that has a design, production, inspection and service capability. This is the definitive standard for design/consulting firms. It contains 20 elements (criteria) that outline required good practice for the management of quality. A/E/C design, consulting firms would use this standard.

ISO 9002   The standard for a business that has production, inspection and service capability. This is the definitive standard for manufacturing firms — which do not offer design service but manufacture a product others have designed. This contains 19 elements. ISO 9002 would also apply to a pure construction firm.

ISO 9003   The standard for a business that has inspection and service capability. This was the definitive standard for distributors and warehouse companies. It is rarely used these days. This contains only 11 elements.

3 - Guideline on Implementation:

ISO 9004   Guidelines that expand on the descriptions within the standards that aid understanding on best practices. It covers different types of businesses within its eight sections.

Design Practice (A&E) and the Fit with ISO 9001

Many firms have stringently followed the layout and structure of ISO 9001 in designing their quality manual. This is not required nor recommended by the authors. It is better that the ISO 9001 elements be arranged to reflect the normal way of doing business for the firm. No firm need be "bent out of shape" to suit this external standard.

Existing elements within the standards covering benchmarking, strategic planning, continuous improvement and customer satisfaction are currently being revised and strengthened.

The different elements (or requirements) of ISO 9001 and their fit with a design practice can best be shown through the following diagrams.

Basic Work Processes

This diagram shows a typical model for an A&E design practice and the flow of key events involved in performing project activities for an owner or client. The events include the *Contract* stage (Proposal and Contract Setting), the actual *Project Control (Design)* activity followed by the delivery of *Contract Documents* (Drawings), leading to *Construction Administration* (C/A).

In this section of the chapter, this model will be used to show the fit between A&E design activities and the requirements of ISO 9001. At each stage the A&E activities will be indicated first, followed by the relevant ISO 9001 requirement.

For ISO 9001 each of the requirements *must* be addressed and in place. Typically, gap analysis audits show that firms perform most of the required activities but have poor formal procedures defining their methods.

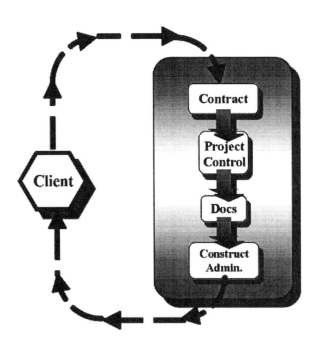

As you proceed, you may wish to perform a mental assessment of the extent to which your firm already has these in place — and as a result make an early and broad estimate about how much work may be involved in achieving ISO 9001 compliance.

The 20 Elements of ISO 9001

4.1 Management responsibility
4.2 Quality system
4.3 Contract review
4.4 Design control
4.5 Document & data control
4.6 Purchasing
4.7 Customer supplied product
4.8 Product ID & traceability
4.9 Process control
4.10 Inspection & testing

4.11 Control of inspection, measuring and test equipment
4.12 Inspection & test status
4.13 Control of nonconforming product
4.14 Corrective and preventive action
4.15 Handling, storage, packaging, preservation & delivery.
4.16 Control of quality records
4.17 Internal quality audits
4.18 Training
4.19 Servicing
4.20 Statistical techniques

Note: For an A/E/C firm the elements 4.9, 4.10, 4.12, 4.13 and 4.19 can be covered within element 4.4 Design control and can therefore be excused from full documentation.

Stage 1 - Basic Business Model

This diagram shows the key A/E/C events with descriptors shown in **bold font**. The ISO 9001 associated elements are shown in *italic font*.

ISO 9001 requires that each of the processes listed in the diagrams be defined in documents available to all personnel.

Documents can be in the form of traditional text based procedures, flow charts, drawings, forms, video tapes, etc., or any combination of the above. Any media can be used to capture and document the designated process.

Documents in the company manual may be arranged to follow the sequence set by ISO 9000 or to follow the sequence set by the normal flow of business.

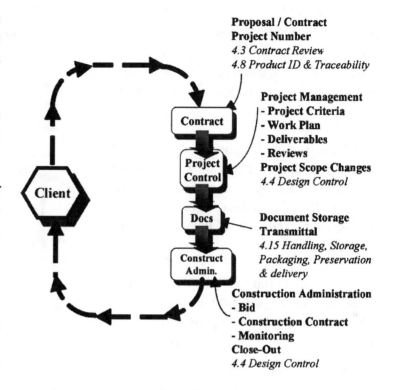

Proposal / Contract
Project Number
4.3 Contract Review
4.8 Product ID & Traceability

Project Management
- Project Criteria
- Work Plan
- Deliverables
- Reviews
Project Scope Changes
4.4 Design Control

Document Storage
Transmittal
4.15 Handling, Storage, Packaging, Preservation & delivery

Construction Administration
- Bid
- Construction Contract
- Monitoring
Close-Out
4.4 Design Control

Stage 2 - Administrative Procedures and Sub-Contracting Added

ISO 9001 requires clear descriptions of the firm's policies and procedures for: a) guiding personnel in the performance of their work; b) providing training to employees and c) for archiving project records.

Additionally, the firm needs to describe how it supervises the work of sub-contractors hired directly by the firm (e.g., consultants, suppliers, reprographics, temporary labor) and how purchases of materials or goods are handled.

There is also a need to show how owner supplied information (data, prior drawings, etc.) are protected and made secure while in the firm's care.

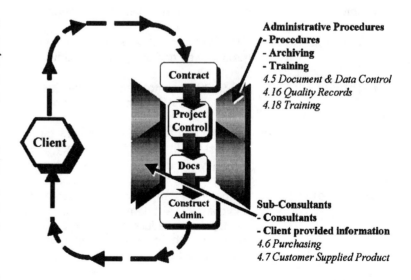

Administrative Procedures
- Procedures
- Archiving
- Training
4.5 Document & Data Control
4.16 Quality Records
4.18 Training

Sub-Consultants
- Consultants
- Client provided information
4.6 Purchasing
4.7 Customer Supplied Product

Stage 3 - Adding the Management Components

The firm should have a clear organizational structure, stated company policies with objectives and someone responsible for quality. The management team should perform routine reviews of the business to test its effectiveness.

Additionally, management should have established indicators and measures for the key parts of their business and for customer satisfaction. To collect data for these reviews, there should be planned internal audits of effectiveness.

Finally it is required that firms have a formal process in place to identify and take action on problems and opportunities for improvement. The process should be accessible to employees and include sub-contractor performance and customer complaints.

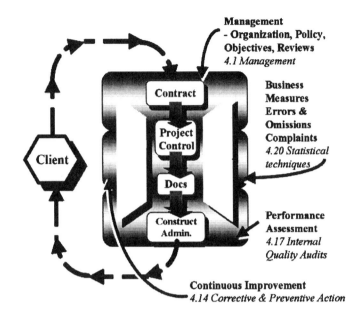

Note: Five elements of ISO 9001 are applicable to manufacturing. As such they are not *directly applicable* to an A&E design practice and can be excused from direct action. Those five have not been included in this article.

Summary: Benefits to Quality/ISO 9001 Implementation

Efficiency ISO 9000 can manage the allocation of time and skill in a planned, structured manner.

Effectiveness ISO 9000 can deliver significant improvements in the use of time and how work is managed (productivity) and bring about positive changes in work habits.

Creativity ISO 9000 does not hamper creativity. It does help to reduce wasted time. Improvements in the management of time mean less time on production and more time for creativity.

Cost/Profit Profile Systematic methods implemented through ISO 9000 can be used to create larger margins in the cost/profit profile. Consistency and speed are among the keys — plus a "right first time" mentality (accuracy). This is project management *par excellence*.

Scope Definition Scope drift is an enemy to the design consulting firm. ISO 9000 processes can clarify, define and control client demands. Nurturing the client includes proactively managing scope definition. ISO 9000 can reduce scope "drift" through strong, clear, proactive management of the client at the start of the project and during each of the project design phases. This is customer service *par excellence*.

Consistency ISO 9000 methods ensure that all employees work from a common model of efficiency and effectiveness in project management. New employees are brought "on board" more quickly.

Benefits to Marketing

- Customer relations improved
- Clear agreements about expectations (fewer changes)
- Increased reliability (in budget, on time)
- Recognition (firm "benchmarked")
- Improved qualifications to bid
- Broader market coverage

Benefits to Operations

- Commonly understood best practices
- Focus on project management effectiveness
- Reduction in project design re-work
- Enlarged resource capacity (throughput)
- Data-based management
- Less variability in techniques
- Reduced project overruns (time & cost)

ISO 9000 is:

About

- Developing "best practices" in the business
- Leadership and energy
- Simplicity and guidance
- Quality management by everyone
- Staying with what you do best
- Improving the business
- Shaping ISO 9000 to suit your business

Not About

- Controlling innovation or creativity
- Abandoning individuality
- Regimentation or repetitiveness
- Paperwork, paperwork, paperwork
- Quality engineering
- Changing the business to suit ISO 9000

Resources

ISO Central Secretariat
Case postale 56
CH-1211 Geneve 20
Switzerland
Tel: 41 22 749 01 11
Fax: 41 22 733 34 30

American National Standards Institute
11 West 42nd Street
13th Floor
New York, NY 10036

American Society for Quality (ASQ)
300 West Wisconsin Avenue
Milwaukee, WI 53202
Tel: (800) 248-1946
www.asq.org

Internet Resources

International Organization of Standards: All the ISO standards and information from the international body are available from this site. American Society for Quality (ASQC): the largest quality organization in the U.S. with chapters all over the country.
http://www.mastercontrol.com/links.htm

CFITS Standards Document Library: Standards organized by the different publishing bodies. Updated regularly by SDL-Webmaster for ANSI (American National Standards Institute) .
http://www.library.itsi.disa.mil/by_org.html

Carol A. Adey, FSMPS

Carol A. Adey, FSMPS, is President of Adey Associates, a Medford, MA-based consulting firm that supports the organizational and business development activities of A/E/C firms. A former national secretary/treasurer of SMPS, she was project manager for ISO implementation at the first design firm in New England to receive certification.

Graham K. Hill, P.E.

Graham K. Hill is an international consultant with more than 30 years experience in business improvement, quality, and ISO 9001. He specializes in simple, speedy, and cost-effective ISO implementation solutions to the A/E/C community. In North America he has assisted Case Corporation, Erdman Anthony & Associates, Gannett Fleming, Henschel Company, Lucket & Farley, Modern Engineering, Parkin Associates, Shepley Bullfinch & Richardson, Symmes Maini & McKee Associates, Tenneco Corporation, and United Technologies with design and design consulting issues. He was a practicing design engineer for 15 years prior to becoming a consultant. His business, Tomlin Inc., is located in Falmouth, MA.

Part 2:
Sales & Business Development

2.1 Sales and Business Development

Kenneth G. Diehl Jr., P.E.
Vice President of Marketing and Business Development
Smith Seckman Reid Inc.

There is an old adage in sales. It says, "no sales … no company." In today's increasingly competitive business environment, nothing sells itself. Therefore, a strong sales and business development program is fundamental to the life, health and wealth of your firm.

Setup

Sales/business development efforts must be part of an integrated program to be most effective. The framework of this program should be the company's marketing plan, which provides the support necessary for the marketing and sales.

Notice that marketing is mentioned first. This is intentional. The reason is that marketing is supposed to furnish the setup for sales. Marketing should provide the communications, brochures, advertising and public relations that introduce the firm to prospective clients. Marketing can also enhance the image of the firm in the client's eye.

Other chapters in this book deal with various marketing tasks in more detail. Remember, the setup that marketing provides to the sales/business development effort is invaluable.

Scorecard

Before venturing out on your business development journey, it is important for you to know the score. In other words, how much business should you attempt to obtain? This is a function of your firm's (division, team, etc.) annual sales/revenue goals. This is illustrated by the following calculation:

New Business Calculation	
1. Target gross annual sales/revenue level	$_____
2. Forecast sales from current customer base	$_____
3. Additional sales required (#1 minus #2)	$_____
4. Expected lost business from departed customers (lost to competition, out of business, etc.)	$_____
5. Total new customer sales required (#3 plus #4)	$_____

A scorecard gives you a target. One you can use to set goals, track progress and celebrate achievement. Knowing the score is a key ingredient in your business development mix.

Initiation

How does one get started? Years ago ACT, a contact management software company, distributed sales brochures with this simple message "business is a contact sport." Without question, all sales/business development efforts begin when someone contacts a prospect or client about doing some business together.

A firm's marketing plan should identify prospective targets for business development. In some cases the plan may indicate only the firm names. In other plans, individuals within those firms will be shown. In either case, it will be up to the sales force to verify who are the right people to assist your firm in winning business from each prospect.

Contacting people you do not know can be difficult for even the most outgoing. Therefore it is important whenever possible to establish a first contact through a referral. You may know someone who can bridge the gap between you and a prospect. Even if you do not know a referral candidate, someone in your firm or one of your friends may. First meetings are always easier to get and more comfortable for all parties when done through a referral.

There will be times when a referral is not available. In these cases the best method is the direct approach. Contact the prospect to set up a visit. (Be aware that your call may be intercepted by a gatekeeper.) State the purpose of your call, the nature of your services and suggest potential meeting times. Never use deception. That will ruin your chances of ever securing business from that prospect. Do not be surprised if your request for a meeting is denied. Do not give up hope. Be tactful, ask for another chance and continue to search for a possible referral.

Leads

What is a lead? Too many business developers believe that a lead is a call from a colleague about a potential project. While this is true, it misses the mark. Timing is critical (or fatal) in leads. Being first in contacting a prospect can create an advantage for your firm. An advantage your competitors will not be able to overcome. That is why I like *Webster's Dictionary's* definition of a lead as "an indication or a clue."

A lead can take any number of forms. It could be a change in codes or regulations that will produce new areas for work (ADA and IAQ are examples that come to mind). A lead could be the development of a piece of property next door to an undeveloped piece owned by one of your clients. The point is that changes in any business or business environment can generally be shown to be a lead in retrospect.

Another chapter will deal with lead development and lead tracking in more detail. Always keep your eyes and ears open. The earlier you follow up on a lead the better. Remember that leads are the DNA of a firm's business development program.

Approach

There are two basic considerations a firm must evaluate when developing its approach to sales. A firm should decide whether its program will be client-based or project-based. Likewise, your firm must decide if it will use the shotgun or the rifle approach. Your decision on each of these factors will largely determine the focus of your business development activities.

Shotgun Versus Rifle

The concept of shotgun versus rifle is fairly easy to understand. With a shotgun, you aim your sales efforts in the general area of potential work and hope to hit as many opportunities as you can. The rifle, on the other hand, takes dead aim on particular targets. Both methods can be used effectively in the right hands.

Most firms prefer the rifle approach. To them, sales is not a numbers game. Rather it is a matter of identifying, pursuing and capturing specific work that fits their marketing plan precisely — quality not quantity.

Client Versus Project

There has been an ongoing discussion for many years about the relative merits of doing business development on a client versus project basis. In the client-based mode, your firm targets and pursues certain clients assuming that you will eventually get work and keep getting work. In the project-based mode, your efforts are geared directly at obtaining certain commissions, as they become available.

Most firms prefer the client-based mode. The prospective client can be targeted based on its existing or future ability to produce work for the firm. It can also be picked based on the nature of its existing projects and how well they match up with the strengths and goals of the chasing firm. A popular trait for your accounting department is a prospect that pays on time.

Project-based business development starts with an identified opportunity. Once a project is uncovered, the firm brings its sale and business development prowess to bear in an effort to secure the commission. Even in the client-based mode, potential projects still must be identified and pursued, lest a competitor capture them. Therefore, a combination of both modes will generally prove most effective.

Being There

Woody Allen has been quoted as saying that 80 percent of success is showing up. Showing up is critical in business development. That is why business development is most effective when it is done on a face-to-face basis. Being "out there among them" is important for several reasons.

Prospects are not elephants. They may forget who you are and what your firm does. Out of sight, out of mind. Especially when your competitors are knocking on their doors or in their office. If they do not see you regularly, they will not know you anymore.

You get more information face-to-face. You see changes in their appearance, office décor or office location. You have the benefit of seeing a person's body language and facial expressions as you talk. You can better understand whether a prospect is really interested in your services or just saying so. You learn more by actions than words.

Finally, developing a personal relationship with your prospect is the key ingredient to developing lasting business. You cannot fully develop a relationship without spending time with a person. Teleconferences, e-mails and faxes are no substitute for being there. Tom Peters said that people are delighted by attention. Think of how children respond to attention. It makes them flourish. So too will your business development relationships when you spend time with your prospects.

Timing

Everyone suffers from time deprivation. There is never enough time to do all you want to do. Too often there is not enough time to do the things you need to do.

This is why timing your business development efforts is so important. A wise man once said that there are only 2,500 hours per year in which you can effectively do work. Even if you are willing to work 24 hours a day seven days a week, your prospects are not. They have other things to do than to see you or take your call. Therefore your approach must be focused. Whether you are doing business development on a full-time basis or as part of your position within a firm, you should plan and use the time you have available efficiently.

The frequency of your call pattern for a given prospect will vary based on the stage of your relationship. At first you may see or communicate with a prospect no more than once a quarter. As the prospect develops, you may move to monthly contact. Once you have identified a prospective project, you should develop a follow-up frequency appropriate for the project timing.

You must be efficient and well-organized to effectively develop a prospect. The underlying reason behind this need for efficiency is that it takes time to develop business. You plant seeds and cultivate them over long periods of time. Repetition is important. Most pros agree that it takes three or more years of consistent and concerted effort to develop an ongoing working relationship with a prospect. Sometimes it takes even longer. A word of caution: Beware of overnight success in business development. It may not last.

Persistence

Even if you are on the right track, you'll get run over if you just sit there.

— Will Rogers

One of the key differences between the winners and the losers in the business development game is persistence. Sales research statistics illustrate this point vividly:

- 43 percent of all salespeople make one call and quit.
- 25 percent make two calls and quit.
- 12 percent make three calls and quit.
- **80 percent of all sales are made after the fifth call.**

No matter how many times you hear or read these statistics they seem hard to believe. If making a sale is as easy as making five calls to a prospect, how can anyone fail? How can something so easy as a follow-up sales call to a prospect be missed? Yet every day that is exactly what happens. "How can this be?" you ask. There are a number of reasons. You may get busy on another call or assignment. You may forget to record a follow-up call on your task list. You may even put it off and then lose interest. If any of these reasons hits home, you need to ask yourself this question: Do you have the tenacity it takes to develop business for your firm?

Eighty percent of your competitors will not put enough effort into a prospect in order to make a sale. Will you? You do not have to be the brightest, most educated or most talented person to be persistent. Persistence and determination are an advantage you need to win in business development.

Advocate

The most important person to find and cultivate when developing a new client relationship is an advocate. This is someone who will sponsor and support your firm in any project decision-making process. An advocate will not always be easy to find. You must display a genuine interest in your prospects and their business to foster an advocacy. It will take time and a consistent concerted effort. Much has been written about finding the decision-maker(s). The real trick is to win their heart(s).

It will require you to develop a relationship based on personal chemistry, the perceived strengths of your firm, and the fit between your services and the client's needs. It will require you to establish a level of trust with the prospect. That trust is based on a feeling that:

- You will keep your promises.
- You will not embarrass them.
- You will be honest and fair.
- You are interested in maintaining the relationship after the sale.

Every firm that makes a short list is generally qualified to do the work. On a short list of equals, the winner will always be the one who has an advocate in the client camp.

Summary

Sales/business development is a vital part of any firm's marketing program. The effort must be vigorous, focused and ongoing to be most effective. A sound sales/business development program is the best investment you can make in your firm's future.

Kenneth G. Diehl Jr., P.E.

- Kenneth G. Diehl Jr., P.E., has more than 25 years of experience marketing professional services in the built and natural environments. He currently serves as vice president of marketing and business development for Smith Seckman Reid Inc., Nashville, Tenn.
- Diehl is a past president of the Society for Marketing Professional Services (SMPS). He is a frequent guest lecturer on a variety of marketing and sales subjects for a number of SMPS chapters.
- He is the author of several articles including "Consultants With a Winning Edge," and "Going … Going … Gone Concepts on Closing a Sale" for the SMPS *Marketer*.
- He has lectured at several national trade organization conferences, including SMPS, the Professional Construction Estimators Association, the American Consulting Engineers Council and the American Society of Healthcare Engineers.

2.2 Networking: Lead Development and Other Gains

Laurin McCracken, AIA, MCRS, FSMPS
Chief Executive Officer
Global Design Alliance

The major job of a marketer is to get work. Having an effective network enhances a marketer's ability to get work. Therefore, good networking adds to a marketer's value to their firm. A well-constructed and effectively used network will significantly improve a marketer's contribution to his or her firm's efforts to get additional projects.

What Can Be Learned from a Network?

When we think about networking, we usually think of it as a means of obtaining leads. Certainly lead generation is one of the most important uses of networking; however, there is a great deal more to be gained by having and using a network. You can use it for market research. You can find out what other firms see as market trends and where the action will be. You can get information about the competition, their strengths and their weaknesses. And, you can use a network to confirm or disqualify rumors. If Corporation X announces it is expanding, first check with the network to see if that expansion is real, if it's already been committed or if it is a potential project for your firm. An effective network can save you a lot of time and your firm a lot of money because you won't be chasing jobs that aren't real or for which you are not qualified. And if the project is real, an effective network can give you valuable information that can help you win the job.

Client Research

Perhaps the best use of a network is potential client research. Before you call on a client for the first time, call the network. Your call to this potential client is not going to be the first one this person has received from our industry. Make use of the experience of those in your network. Talk with those who have called on this client. If your network is effective, you can learn the answers to a lot of questions before you make that call: Does this person have the authority to make decisions about your services? What is the secretary's name? When is the best time of the day to call? If you work your network properly, you can change that cold call into a warm call before you pick up the phone. Your network can also help identify the client's "hot buttons." All of this can help you build instant credibility and help establish a rapport with your prospective client.

Who Is in Your Network?

There are a lot of people who are already in your network. They are people that you interface with in your normal business day. It is up to you to make them effective members of your network. The basis of your network is already there: the staff of your firm, the consultants your firm is working with on projects, your friends and associates. This can also include the people in your Rotary, church, PTA, or any group or organization in which you are active. Don't forget the most important of your already existing network: SMPS. SMPS is a ready-made national network that is always available to you.

The Rule of 250 states that if you know 250 people you can find out anything. Anyone with an active, effective network can find out anything, in any city, in three phone calls or less.

Who Should Be in Your Network?

Whom should you add to your existing base of contacts to increase the viability of your network? Most marketers and business development professionals have a number of real estate brokers, real estate lawyers and bankers in their network. Here are a few suggestions as to others whom you might add to your network.

- Suppliers of products that will be used on your projects. These should be large manufacturers that have strong marketing budgets. This will allow you to take advantage of a larger marketing budget than yours and use it effectively to gain information about the market. Think of the lighting industry, those that manufacture and supply elevators and escalators, or those in the landscape, office or furniture business, both manufacturers and dealers. You should consider only those people who also understand marketing and represent problems you know will be specified by your firm.
- Civic and government groups such as the Chamber of Commerce, the Boy Scouts, Lions. These are probably the easiest to work with because there is little or nothing expected in return for information shared except the active participation in the efforts of the organization.
- Associations and societies beyond SMPS can be very useful. Some of the more obvious are those associations made up of members of our industry such as American Institute of Architects (AIA), Associated General Contractors of America (AGC) and American Consulting Engineers Council (ACEC). The most useful organizations are those that are made up of potential clients, such as the International Association of Real Estate Executives (NACORE), International Facility Management Association (IFMA) and Urban Land Institute (ULI).
- Also add your college alumni to your network. You will be surprised how often you will find that you have access to a company or group simply by checking your alumni directory.

Some qualifiers to consider when expanding your network: Pick those people who are active in an area where you need information. If you want information about what the Corps of Engineers is doing, join Society of American Military Engineers (SAME). Pick those firms with a larger marketing effort than yours. If you are a small architectural firm, expand your network with large engineering and construction firms.

Teaming and Partnering Through Your Network

An effective network can help you identify qualified team members or partners for a project. You might find those firms right there in your network. If not, your network can tell you who has what experience and portfolio. Someone in your network has worked with almost every firm in your area. It cannot only identify firms, it can also help you sort out those firms that pull their weight and those that don't. In short, a good network can help you find the winning team for a project.

How to Network

How does one network? How does it work? For the core members of your network it starts with establishing a one-on-one relationship with that person. If requires a face-to-face meeting where you establish that you each have a mutual interest in exchanging information about the industry. This can be a breakfast, lunch or just setting aside 30 minutes over a cup of coffee. That is what networking is all about: exchanging information.

Information Exchanging

What information is valuable to others? What information should and should not be shared? Positive information about your firm is the easiest and sometimes the most valuable information you can share. That you have made a short list or better yet, that you have been awarded a new project, is fun information to share and is valuable for those further down the feeding chain that have an opportunity to provide other services or supply materials for the project.

Remember, just because you lost the job doesn't mean that you don't have valuable information. The others in your network that are still looking forward to participating on that project need to know who got it. You can make yourself equally valuable to your network by sharing with them who did get the job. It's not as much fun, but it still needs to be shared.

Information about the market is tradable information. If you went to a meeting or convention and heard a valuable speech about a market or sector of the market, think about those in your network who were not there but could profit from that information. Send them the handout or write a one-page summary and share with members of that network.

To be a valuable member of a network, you must share information that is valuable to the other person. Increase your value by thinking about how that person on the receiving end can use the information you want to share. If they are not in the health care market, information you gained at that health care conference will probably be of little use to them. Increase your value by sharing the most valuable information with only those few people in your network that help you the most or to anchor a new networking relationship. Sharing valuable information too freely decreases your value in the network.

Some information, such as information told to you in confidence, is not to be shared. Information about specific fees is usually considered not tradable. In addition, information that is internal to your firm should not be passed on. Keep your skeletons in the closet.

Keep in mind that the information you share with others has an impact on how they view you and your firm. You can use this to your advantage to enhance your position in the industry and to position your firm for future work. If your firm has a growing portfolio in a specific building type and want to grow in that market niche, let your network know of your interest. They can alert you to opportunities in the market and they will talk up your expertise to others.

The Primary Rule

The primary rule of networking is staying in touch. You don't have to take time for a personal meeting, you don't have to play a better game of telephone tag. That handout from that speech will keep you in touch with a valuable part of the network. Just don't forget to put your name on it, so they will know who sent it. Stapling a business card to what you are sending is the simplest way.

Some information is for everyone in your network, like the information you learned from an article in *Real Estate Forum* that others might have missed. Some information is for a chosen one or two — those people that you have been exchanging specific information about a specific lead because you are both in a unique position to gain information. Don't be too free with your most valuable information. If you are careful about with whom you share what, you will be a more valued member of your network.

Always keep in mind that networking is sharing information. You have to have information to share in order to receive information in return. To most it is not necessarily a *quid pro quo* arrangement. Those that sponge off of a network and don't contribute, don't stay in a network very long. Don't keep someone in your network who doesn't contribute. Your time is better spent elsewhere. This is not always easy because these may be people that you like or care for but that are not contributing to your business network. They can still be friends and you can have a different relationship with them, but not as part of your network.

The electronic age has made this, as it has so many things in our business, faster and easier. That useful bit of information you picked up at that last conference is now faster and easier to share thanks to e-mail. The Internet has become as important to your networking as printed matter used to be. Now, sending a useful URL is as helpful as copying and sending an article from a magazine.

Almost everybody has information that is valuable to you. A friendly exchange of information can most often gain that knowledge to help you and your firm. Your network can grow beyond just a vehicle to give and gain information that can help you and your firm. It can be the basis of lifelong friendships. Most of those with great networks have networks made up of people they like, and with whom they want to spend time. They take positive advantage of those good times to help their friends and in return get information that helps their firm be successful. That's networking at its best.

Laurin McCracken, AIA, MCRS, FSMPS

- Laurin McCracken, AIA, MCRS, FSMPS, is the chief executive officer of the Global Design Alliance, a strategic alliance of architects, engineers and specialty design services.
- He has more than 20 years' experience in providing services to corporate users, offering major design and management expertise in a variety of project types, including offices, hospitality, corporate headquarters, education projects and urban planning.
- He has marketed architectural and engineering services nationally and internationally.
- McCracken holds a bachelor's degree in architecture from Rice University and a master's degree in architecture and urban planning from Princeton University.
- He was the national president of SMPS in 1987-88 and is a recipient of SMPS's Marketing Achievement Award.

2.3 Professional Organizations

George Biderman, FSMPS
Director of Business Development
Fru-Con Construction Corporation

Professional organizations are groups of people in a profession or industry organized around a common interest. The Society for Marketing Professional Services (SMPS), the publisher of this book, is one example of a professional organization. Other examples in the built environment are the American Institute of Architects (AIA) and the Associated General Contractors of America (AGC).

Professional Development

The primary purpose of these organizations is to provide for the professional development of its members. Professional organizations develop educational programs, publish insightful books and studies, and, in general, constantly strive to upgrade the understanding of members in a given profession or industry, and help keep them on top of emerging technological and special developments. Conferences, both regional and national, and other types of meetings provide periodic opportunities to reaffirm shared values; establish and realign relationships; and conduct work, have fun, and thereby build relationships with other people in the same profession or industry.

Professional Certification

Approximately 18 percent of the professional organizations in the United States offer a certification program for individuals engaged in their profession or industry. Certification programs provide standards of excellence that all members of the organization can work toward. Members who gain certification benefit by increased respect and recognition in the industry or profession, increased opportunity for upward mobility, increased professional credibility and increased self-esteem.

Additional Benefits Offered by Membership

- **New business opportunities.** Membership in a professional organization breeds familiarity with the organization, familiarity builds relationships, these relationships build trust, and trusting relationships facilitate referrals, which are valuable commodities for new business opportunities. There is also the special advantage of being seen at the organization's various programs and functions, particularly at the regional and national conferences where many more members are present. Members that are in the "top of the mind" of other members have a greater chance of being contacted during the year for referrals, joint ventures and new business opportunities.

- **Communication with non-competing firms.** It is in the mutual interest of members and their firms to share information with similar non-competing firms in similar circumstances. This helps members and their firms work smarter, grow faster and avoid costly mistakes.

- **Networking and learning opportunities.** The existing membership network means it is easy for any member to get information. Conversations with other members at, or between, the various sponsored programs provide new ideas, validate existing concepts and stimulate creativity.

- **Image enhancement.** Membership in a professional organization tells everyone that the member and his or her company are actively involved in that profession or industry and making contributions to further its growth and status.

Memberships Outside Your Industry or Profession

Membership in professional organizations need not be limited to an individual's profession or industry. There are other opportunities out there to consider. Think about joining an organization or two that your company's key clients are members of. For example, let us say that hospitals are a major portion of your business. In this situation, the American Society of Hospital Engineers (A.S.H.E.) is an option. Not only would you learn more about your clients' health care business and their concerns, but you could improve your relationships by this additional time spent together.

If your clients are on any committees, it might behoove you to get on them also. This is especially important if any of your competition is trying to get closer to your clients by also joining these organizations.

Sometimes membership in your client organizations are not open to those not active in their profession or industry. If this is the case, ask about the availability of associate membership. Some professional organizations offer these restricted memberships to individuals who are remotely involved in their industry.

Selecting Professional Organizations

The first step in selecting the right professional organization(s) to join is to determine your priorities. If your primary job responsibility is marketing, they might look something like this, for example:

- Professional growth.
- Improve industry knowledge.
- Increase lead generation.
- Increase knowledge of clients' businesses.
- Improve rapport with clients.

On the other hand, if you are a senior manager in a firm and marketing is only a secondary responsibility, your priorities might look something like this:

- Enhance general management skills.
- Strengthen client relationships.
- Increase marketing skills.

After the priorities are determined, the next step is to locate the professional organization(s) that can help you the most. The best place to begin is to discuss your requirements with your business associates, peers, clients and friends. They should be able to point you in the right direction. Another place to look for options is in the business section of your city's newspaper. In most cities the Monday business section lists all the meetings and conferences scheduled for that week. Scan it for a few months and you might just uncover a relatively unknown organization that is perfect for you.

Too Many Organizations, Not Enough Budget

Sometimes you are blessed with a lot of options for joining professional organizations, but are restricted by a tight budget. The solution is to join the ones you can afford, but also keep an eye out for interesting programs sponsored by other organizations. Many of these other organizations will let you attend a few programs throughout the year as a prospective new member. You will most likely have to pay a small additional charge as a non-member, but the cost is usually small compared to the annual membership dues.

Getting the Most from Memberships

To really get the most out of any membership in a professional organization, you have to become actively involved in that organization. "You get out of it what you put into it" has been proven time and time again. Besides learning more about your profession or industry, members who take a leadership role also improve their skills in leadership, in management, and in public speaking, and they learn how to work better with clients, the media and large groups of people.

Members who are on committees, or who serve as officers of the organization, also achieve a certain added distinction and credibility, not to mention visibility. In addition, members who take a leadership role have a greater voice in how the organization will continue to contribute to their own professional development.

And, should the time ever come that you find yourself in the position of having to find a new job, prospective new employers will look very favorably on the leadership roles you had while a member of professional organizations.

George Biderman, FSMPS

- George Biderman began his sales and marketing career in 1971 with Procter and Gamble selling consumer products. A headhunter recruited him into the construction industry in 1982.
- Biderman has been a vice president of marketing for a large, family-owned general contractor, had his own sales and marketing consulting company, and is presently the director of business development for Fru-Con Construction Corp., a large national and international, construction, engineering and development firm headquartered in St. Louis, MO.
- Biderman is a Fellow Marketing Professional in the SMPS and has been a regular speaker for the SMPS and the AGC on both a local and national level since 1987.
- He has published a wide variety of articles on sales and marketing for SMPS, AGC and several other sales and marketing organizations.

2.4 Getting in the Door

Charles C. Crevo, Ph.D., FSMPS
Senior Associate
Louis Berger & Associates Inc.

Ford Harding
President
Harding & Co.

Introduction

Before addressing the process of "getting in the door," you need to identify whose door you wish to enter and for what reason. There are a variety of clients in the marketplace, and different approaches might be appropriate for different clients. A marketer could be responsible for a specific segment of the industry, such as architecture for schools, or for a larger audience sought by an architectural firm that has a general practice. Further, there are public clients and private clients. In the latter category are other architects, engineers, planners and contractors. Exhibit 1 on the next page suggests some of the more obvious client opportunities and relationships. Most of these have sub-categories, such as the federal government, which is home to a number of agencies concerned with the built environment.

Whether you wish to pursue a public- or private-sector client has a direct influence on the ease or difficulty associated with attempts to obtain meetings. Finding information about public agencies and identifying the decision-makers is relatively simple. In addition to state and federal web sites that list upcoming projects and contact references, there are published directories that list addresses and telephone numbers for state and federal agency officials. Public officials are generally accessible, although some have a policy of not granting meetings once a request for proposal (RFP) has been issued.

Private-sector clients are more difficult to identify, particularly smaller developers. Projects are not usually advertised publicly because competition is an important factor in land development projects and confidentiality is critical. Developers rely more on established relationships with architects, engineers and contractors. Time equates to money in the private sector, and decision-makers value their time accordingly. These issues pose a greater challenge to obtaining meetings with key individuals.

Because clients have different backgrounds and needs, the marketer must adjust the process employed in making the initial contact. A good example is marketing to public agencies in the state of Florida. Florida has a variety of cultures that differ in southern, central and northern areas of the state. Marketing in Miami is different from marketing in Orlando, which is different from marketing in the panhandle. To market in these three areas requires a different wardrobe, demeanor and pace. The story goes that when Robert Martinez was governor of Florida he was referred to in Miami as Roberto Martinez, in Orlando as Robert Martins and in the panhandle as Bubba Martin. The ability to adapt to the expectations of the client is a benefit. This example is not intended to suggest that we be insincere, but that we need to be aware of the environment of a prospective client's culture and adjust accordingly.

Exhibit 1 – Client Opportunities

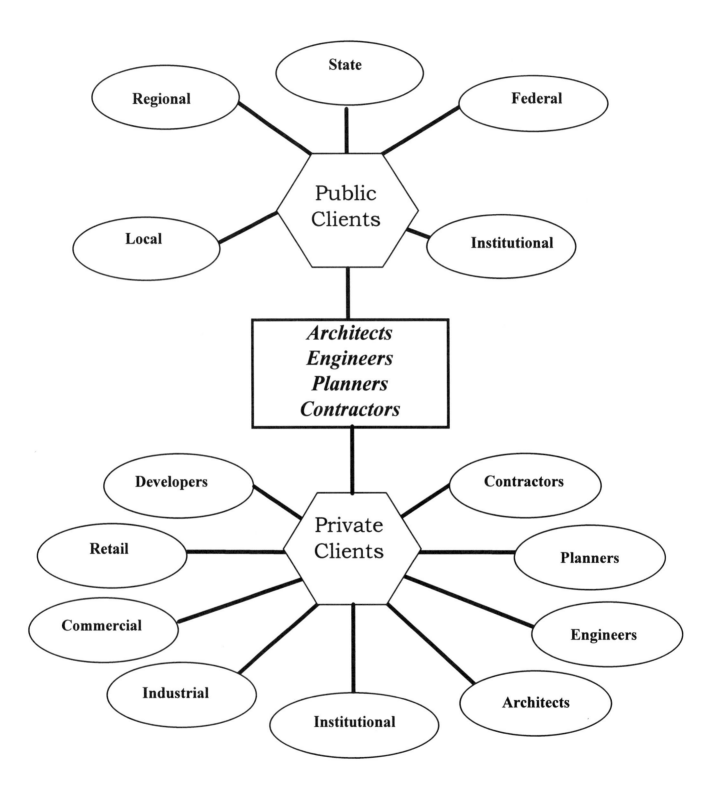

Objectives

Generally, there are two prime reasons for initiating a contact with a client. The first is you have information about a project that is going to be, or has been, advertised and you want to meet the decision-maker. The second is that you desire to conduct an exploratory meeting for the purpose of becoming known to the client and gathering information before projects become public knowledge. These are examples of reactive and proactive marketing respectively.

Subsequent to preparing a personal profile of your target, you will need to develop a plan. What do you hope to accomplish in your initial meeting? In many instances you will be forced to deal with someone, often referred to as the gatekeeper, whose responsibility is to protect and insulate the person with whom you wish to meet. There could be several reasons why you have been given a client contact assignment:

- It is your job.
- Your firm wants to penetrate a new market.
- Your firm wants to establish a new skill.
- Business is slow and your employer is putting everyone on the telephones to blitz potential clients.

The Caller

The caller is likely to have a technical background, a sales background, both or neither. Technical types are often reluctant to make initial calls to a potential client. While very skilled and competent in technical matters, they have not been exposed to the discipline of marketing professional services, either in their formal education or on the job. This person finds it very difficult to approach an unknown person and ask for work. On the other hand, the sales person has the skills to arrange a meeting but might not be able to address technical questions asked by the prospect. This person's success depends upon knowing when to hand off to a more knowledgeable colleague, which provides an opportunity to request a follow-up meeting. If you have both skills, you are well-positioned.

If you have none of the above, you should encourage your employer to provide training before sending you on a mission or assigning you a list of telephone contacts. If you are an employer, be aware that the person you are assigning to make calls should be comfortable with a knowledge of the firm's capabilities and experiences and be able to convincingly communicate that knowledge. Communication and sales skills are essential to making successful contacts.

The Purpose

You must work with two criteria when establishing a reason for making a visit: information and urgency. If you offer information of value to the prospective client and there is some urgency about the visit, you are more likely to get a meeting. If you simply want to describe your services, your chance of getting a face-to-face meeting is lower. With some thought, most professionals can come up with information that is of value to prospective clients, including:

- **Service Information.** Is there some aspect of your service that differs from your competitors? Will it solve problems that your prospect faces?

- **Project Information.** Is there a project you have recently completed that the prospective client would benefit from knowing about? One marketer worked for a year to get a meeting with the director of facilities at a pharmaceutical company and finally succeeded when the marketer learned that one of his firm's projects was built in the prospect's hometown. The prospect welcomed the opportunity to learn about it.

- **Study Results.** The results of a study can provide a sound basis for a meeting. Some firms conduct surveys to establish the potential clients' interests and needs. The survey provides an opportunity to set meetings in a fact-finding environment rather than a sales call. If the survey is conducted with a number of firms, follow-up meetings to present the cumulative results of the study can be mutually beneficial to client and marketer.

Prospects frequently receive calls from marketers and salespersons who want to introduce their companies and services, but offer no special information or claim to urgency. When making initial contacts, you should identify the value of a meeting for the prospect, thereby reducing your dependence on luck.

The Contact

You might have noticed by now that the emphasis has been on a client rather than a project. Also, the term "cold call" has been avoided. The former is a basic tenet of marketers that we look for clients and not projects. The latter is a term that instills fear in many individuals who are asked to make initial contact with an unknown person. In reality, most initial calls have some degree of familiarity and are not totally "cold." If you search a network of friends, former classmates, colleagues and other sources, you are likely to find someone who knows someone. This is not to suggest that name-dropping will guarantee success, but if legitimate, it can help establish some common ground with the gatekeeper and the prospective client. The contact does not have to be made with the top person in the organization. Depending upon the type of client, a viable approach is to establish a relationship with a lower-level individual and work your way up through the organization with internal references. This is a very effective approach, particularly in large public agencies. Remember that marketing has been, and always will be, built on individual relationships.

The recent proliferation of telemarketing is reaching into the business environment. The calls we typically receive as we sit for dinner are now being made to the office. We are experiencing competition from marketers of products as well as marketers of other professional services. You will have to find a way to overcome this situation and distinguish yourself from the product salesperson.

While the telephone is the prevalent medium associated with making an initial contact, there are other means that can be effective:

- E-mail can be successful if the prospect has an Internet connection. Relevant literature can be attached to a message. Do not flood the prospect with a lot of information that he or she will have to print. Be aware that the recipient might have different software capabilities and will not be able to convert your attachments to a readable format. With the availability of portable computers, busy prospects typically read and reply to e-mail messages outside of normal working hours, thereby enhancing your chances of getting a response. You can also send messages beyond the normal workday and expand a typical eight-hour day to 24 hours. Keep your message short and to the point.

- Facsimile transmissions can be used effectively to advance project literature and ask for a meeting to discuss its relevance to the prospect's needs. Minimize the information transmitted and focus it on what you think will prompt the prospective client to respond. Remember that the quality of faxed material is typically low, and colored graphics have no impact when received in black and white. As with all material submissions, a follow-up telephone call is essential.

- Voice mail is effective with some types of clients, particularly in the public sector. Even if you don't receive a return call, your name will be familiar on subsequent calls. You can't develop a relationship with a machine, but you can begin a one-sided relationship with the person who listens to your messages. You should be upbeat, businesslike and direct in stating the reason for your call. Ask for a return call, promising that you will keep the conversation short, a promise you must later keep. People who use voice mail, instead of a secretary, often answer their own phones when they are in the office.

- Visit the prospect's office unannounced as a last resort. Ask the gatekeeper if your prospect is available for a few minutes. Even if the probability of a meeting is slim, you will have a chance to meet the gatekeeper and establish some level of rapport that will serve you well with future attempts to arrange a meeting. You might even be able to get in the appointment book then and there. Be sure to leave business cards, one for the secretary and one for the prospect.

Whether working through secretaries or electronic channels, you will eventually be able to make contact with most of the prospects you target. If you have an urgent issue to discuss, tell the prospect just enough to pique his or her interest, then wait for a response. If the prospect cannot meet with you in the near future and puts you off, ask if you can schedule a visit in three months. If the prospect declines, acknowledge that he or she must be busy and ask if you can call back in three months. The prospect will have a hard time saying no to this request and, by granting permission, creates an obligation to take your call.

Your objective should be to keep the phone conversation to less than five minutes or you risk holding a meeting over the phone, which you must avoid. A marketer experienced this when the prospect began to question him and he responded as helpfully as he could. After the phone call, the prospect could see no reason for a face-to-face meeting. The marketer had answered all of his questions. When the prospect finally awarded the job, it went to a competitor who had a face-to-face meeting and was able to establish a more personal relationship.

Persistence differentiates the casual caller from the serious. You might experience reaching a prospect after weeks of leaving messages and will be greeted with an apology for the lack of response. An agreement to meet almost always follows and often makes the wait worthwhile.

Prior to making a contact, determine if your firm has ever done work for the client. Even though it might be your first attempt at meeting the prospect, there could be some history from years past. Neither you nor the prospect might have been in your respective positions at the time, but if the history is unfavorable, the prospect is likely to know about it. One marketer, two months after joining a firm, called on a client and was greeted with a dissertation on the dismal performance of the firm on a prior assignment. The marketer, who had a strong technical background, promised the client he would take personal responsibility for the management and performance of any new work. As a result, he was awarded a project.

When you call to ask for a meeting, your manner must communicate that it will be worthwhile. You must sound confident and well-organized. Prepare reference notes to assure coverage of the points you wish to make. Stand while you are making the call. Most people think better on their feet and have a better voice quality than when sitting.

The chance that you will be able to speak to the prospect immediately is slim. When this is the case, you should make the most of the opportunity to talk with the gatekeeper. From this person you can learn key information as described below.

Are you speaking to the prospective client's secretary? Good networkers and salespeople always learn the name of the person with whom they are speaking at the beginning of the conversation. A helpful secretary can make your job much easier. Show a personal interest by asking and remembering his or her name.

Is he or she disposed to be helpful? Some secretaries are more than willing to help than others, depending on their personality and the prospect's instructions. Those who feel it is their obligation to bar anyone trying to sell anything, with or without instructions from the prospect, present a serious obstacle. By testing a secretary's attitude with a few easy questions about the prospect's availability, you can determine whether or not your future calls should be planned to coincide with the secretary's lunch breaks.

When is the prospect expected back? This question is often answered with information on the prospect's activities: "He's in Europe this week," "She's in budget meetings all day," "We're in the midst of an acquisition and she's not around much," or "He's in the hospital" are tidbits that give you a sense of the prospect's activities and possible subjects of conversation to help you develop rapport when you do speak.

When is the best time to call? A good secretary is likely to know the time of day the prospect is most receptive to answering calls. Knowing this gets you through at a time when the prospect can focus on your concerns. If you have been playing telephone tag, setting an exact time to call is particularly important to make a successful contact.

Has the information you sent been received and what has been done with it? If you have written a letter, sent an e-mail or sent a facsimile in advance of calling, the secretary probably knows how the prospect wants you treated. If he wants to see you, the secretary will take aggressive steps to arrange a time. If the prospect has decided not to meet with you, the secretary can let you know. With this information, you can back off and plan another way of gaining access. The secretary might be willing to tell you why the prospect rejected your request.

Can the secretary schedule a meeting for you in the prospect's absence? Some secretaries have the authority to schedule meetings for their employer. If you have a sense that the prospect may have a strong reason for meeting with you, but you are having difficulty reaching each other, ask the secretary to schedule a meeting for you.

Is there information about the company or the prospect that the secretary can provide you? Most secretaries can send annual reports or brochures on their company and a biography of the prospect. The secretary might be able to help ascertain which aspects of your services might be of most interest. They are also natural sources of information on the correct spelling of a prospect's name, title and address as well as the person's direct phone line, directions to the office and similar details.

Can the secretary ask the prospect a question for you? If this isn't your first call and you are simply seeking a bit of additional information from the prospect, the secretary can probably get it for you if the prospect is unavailable.

Can you help me? When efforts to approach the prospect fail, but the secretary seems disposed to be helpful, a direct appeal for guidance can produce surprising results. The work you have devoted to develop a relationship pays off at such times.

A Final Note

Some inexperienced marketers and technical persons who cringe at the thought of making unsolicited contacts probably spend more time trying to avoid the task than attacking it. A daily investment of an hour or two is a worthwhile effort given the potential for business that might be generated. Persistence distinguishes you from the rest of the crowd. What you need is a discipline to be persistent, an untiring courteous phone voice and a measure of ingenuity.

To succeed in any marketing activity that requires relationship-building, you must have contact discipline. You have to find a way to make the telephone, e-mail, facsimile or other tool an important part of your daily activity. Many business developers spend much of the time on the telephone. Marketers who have other responsibilities often have a more difficult time scheduling contact time. Whether you set aside an hour each day, a morning each week or commit yourself to making a specific number of calls each day does not matter, as long as you make the calls.

After you succeed in arranging a meeting, be sure to send the secretary a note of thanks. Secretaries don't receive many such courtesies and it will be appreciated. The next time you call, you will be remembered.

Finally, once in the door, do not forget to listen to the prospective client and gain an understanding of his or her needs, issues and concerns. The fact that we have two ears and one mouth implies that we should listen twice as much as we talk.

Charles C. Crevo, Ph.D., FSMPS

- Charles C. Crevo is a senior associate at Louis Berger & Associates Inc.
- His educational background includes Colorado College (A.B.); University of Massachusetts (B.S.C.E.); Boston University (M.U.A.) and the University of Massachusetts (Ph.D.).
- Crevo is registered to practice engineering in eight states.
- During his 40-year career, he was a full-time marketer for nearly 20 years, and shared responsibility for marketing and project management for another 10 years. Responsible for marketing engineering and architectural services for firms in the 100 to 3,400 employee range. Focus was on opening markets for these firms in the six New England states, Delaware, Florida, Michigan, Missouri and Texas. Also procured projects with federal agencies.
- He has worked for public agencies with the states of Connecticut and Rhode Island and with the New England Regional Commission.
- Private industry work experience includes IBM and professional services consulting with Urban Transportation Systems Associates, Wilbur Smith Associates, The Maguire Group, Vanasse Hangen Brustlin Inc. and Louis Berger & Associates Inc.
- Crevo has written more than two dozen articles and papers, and made numerous presentations.
- Professional associations include the Institute of Transportation Engineers (Fellow) and Society for Marketing Professional Services (FMP).
- SMPS activities include serving as chair of the Education Committee and board member of the Boston Chapter. For National SMPS, he has served as chair of the Certification Committee and chair of the Fellows Recognition Program Task Force.
- Crevo is a member of the adjunct faculty at the University of Massachusetts.

Editor's note: This chapter is a revised and updated version of Chapter 20 "How to Get a Meeting With a Prospect," written by Charles Ford Harding and published in the first edition of the *Handbook*.

Acknowledgment

Special thanks to Ford Harding who authored the original chapter about "Getting in the Door" for the first edition of *The Handbook for Marketing Professional Services.*

2.5 Lead Tracking and Sales Reporting

Julie G. Luers, FSMPS
Director of Marketing
TSP

The process of marketing professional services demands the collection, organization and understanding of a vast body of information about prospective and current clients and their businesses. The firm with the best market intelligence is the firm best equipped to meet customer needs, and as such, has a greater chance of securing new work. Because of today's need for more and better information, a marketing tracking system has become a necessary tool to organize and retrieve data. Unfortunately, all too often a tracking system is perceived to be simply a contact-management tool. This misperception can cause the system to fall short of reaching its potential because it is not then developed to its optimum level. By providing a myriad of logically organized data, a tracking system can bring both long- and short-term benefits to the marketing effort, and be much more than a contact-management tool. It becomes a tool to leverage knowledge across your entire organization, allowing you to have more immediate information about each sales opportunity while helping manage the sales process. Conversely, because of the limitless possibilities of tracking reports, a system can also be over-designed. It then becomes a source of wasted time and money, storing useless data that may never be used. With this in mind, when setting up a tracking system the following questions should be considered:

- Why do I need a tracking system? What can it do for me?
- What information should I be able to retrieve from this system?
- How do I set it up? Must my system be computerized? Should I use off-the-shelf software or have a program designed in-house?
- How should this system be organized? What should it "look like"?

As you might expect, there are several right answers to these questions. The needs of your firm and your marketing department will drive your decisions. As with many other areas of the marketing process, the research and planning phase will be key. The planning phase should set clear objectives to ensure that the software design results in an appropriate system, one that can provide reports to meet your information needs.

Why Have a Tracking System?

The ability to store and retrieve information used for analyzing both the general marketplace and for monitoring your firm's individual marketing efforts is the primary function of a good tracking system. Additional features can then be built in to provide secondary benefits, increasing its value. For example, the system can be designed such that it forces discipline on the marketing process, helping to organize the implementation of the marketing plan. This discipline engages a specific procedure for monitoring and measuring the marketing plan, as well as providing the information from which to measure results. It also saves staff time through the efficiency of better, more accessible information.

What Can It Do for Me?

The tracking system allows you to have more immediate information about each sales opportunity while helping manage the sales process. It will help your organization gain competitive advantage through:

- Better servicing of customers and prospects.
- Providing information to improve tactical and strategic planning.
- Allowing for more efficient allocation of critical resources.
- Sharpening marketing efforts and programs.
- Improving management of the business and people.

As stated above, to be truly valuable, the tracking system needs to contain information that will address broad market issues as well as focus on the details. To ensure success, a marketing information system needs the support and approval of both management and user groups. Without management support, the system will fail due to lack of credibility; without user support, the system will fail from lack of relevant, accurate data. It must bring value to every group within the firm who will be using the information it provides. Because each group may have very different information needs, the system can become quite complicated. For example, upper management may require the system to have the ability to monitor market trends, while the business development staff needs the tickler system feature and quantitative information on customer characteristics and attitudes. The marketing support staff may focus on tracking the status of a prospect in order to project the department's work flow. To accommodate such diverse needs, the system design must allow for flexible, selective retrieval of data, regular activity reports, accessibility to firm-wide marketing information (eliminating the suppression of information by anyone within the firm), and an accurate basis for relating marketing efforts to marketing results.

Needs analysis gathered from all the user groups identified above generally will identify three main areas of marketing information to be addressed in the system's development. These areas are prospect or lead tracking and sales tracking and marketing support information, which includes project histories and company resources that are most often used in responses to request for proposals (RFPs). A single tracking system can be designed to address all areas of prospect or lead development, sales reporting and, depending on need, other marketing information as well.

Prospect/Lead Tracking

Business development requires relationship building, and relationship building requires repeat contact. When a lead is identified and qualified, a systematic process of follow-up should be carried out. Your system should track the contacts made, the results of each encounter and then provide a "tickler" for future contact. It should incorporate the usual steps of the marketing and business-development process — such as letters, telephone calls and personal visits, provide a field in which to record each activity, then have the ability to provide a report that can be plotted onto a chart or graph showing all phases from initial contact to project award and post-project client maintenance.

To easily track each lead, assign a prospect number to which both labor and expenses related to that prospect are charged. This will give you a record of how much money was spent marketing each sales opportunity. Qualified leads entered into the marketing information system can be identified by their number and stored in records, with one record for each number. Many firms set up their prospect numbers so that the first two digits indicate the year in which that record was entered with the following digits signifying the order in which the prospect was identified in that year. For example, in the year 2001, the first prospect identified would be prospect #0101. You can think of these numbered records as a kitchen recipe box with one card per recipe. Each record is then broken down into fields, as your recipes are broken down into ingredients and directions. The level of detail that you put into your fields will determine how much power you have over the information — will it be a tool or just a place for storage?

The first group of fields sets up the client record and is used for generating addresses for letters or mailing labels. These include the following fields:

1. Honorific   *Ms.*
2. First name   *Katherine*
3. Greeting name   *Kate*
4. Middle initial (optional)   *M.*
5. Last name   *Peterson*
6. Professional title   *CPSM*
7. Title   *Director of Marketing*
8. Company or affiliation   *Creative Architects*
9. Department   *Higher Education Group*
10. Street address   *1234 - 15th Avenue S.E.*
11. Suite, floor, etc.   *Suite 2100*
12. City   *Bloomington*
13. State   *MN*
14. Zip code   *55425*
15. Area code   *612*
16. Phone number   *555-1212*

Some of these fields could be combined, however, by doing so you lose your flexibility. For example, by dividing the name into the first six fields, mailings can be addressed to Mrs. Katherine M. Peterson, AIA, with the salutation "Dear Kate," and an enclosed invitation for Kate Peterson. A little more detail in the way you enter the data gives you the power of both a professional and personal touch.

Using the same level of detail, fields can be added to store the information necessary for lead tracking. These include prospect information (type of project, size, project manager, etc.), status of marketing effort (proposal, short list, award, etc.), follow-up date (reminder for the next scheduled contact), cost/budget (tracking marketing effort), the date the record was initially input, the date the record was last updated and general comments.

An important report that can be generated by your tracking system is the lead status report. This will identify the current marketing phase of each prospect. The report can be further developed to record hit rates at each of the three major junctures in the marketing process (qualification, proposal, interview). To track according to status, a menu of status codes should be created covering areas such as:

- First knowledge (of prospect or project lead)
- Letter of interest
- Qualifications requested/submitted
- Proposal requested/submitted
- Short-listed
- Interview
- Project awarded or project lost
- Ongoing client marketing

Your lead sheet or prospect report can then be formatted to sort prospects by status, marketer or by prospect number, and can be printed out to meet individual or department needs. For example, the business development staff can request their report by marketer, while marketing support can print out according to status, as in the following sample:

Prospect Status Report

Prospect Name	Prospect Number	Marketer	Project	Status	Next Action
XYZ Co.	99-001	James J. Hill	New office building	Letter of interest sent 5/12/99	RFP expected 6/15/99
Computer Giant Inc.	99-030	Thomas Peterson	New superstore	Letter of interest sent 5/01/99	Follow-up phone call by 5/07/99
Big Corp.	99-012	Rebecca Jones	Warehouse renovation	Short-listed	Interview 6/1/99
Acme Corp.	99-003	Thomas Peterson	Office warehouse	Proposal submitted 5/12/99	Awaiting decision
Phillips Co.	98-172	James J. Hill	Office renovation	Project awarded 4/29/99	Contract negotiations

Because each new prospect has been given its own number and corresponding record in your tracking system, you can easily see how many new initiatives have been identified within a given time frame and analyze if the probability of the identified opportunities will result in projects sufficient to meet your sales goals. You will also be able to identify what your hit rates are from prospect to proposal, proposal to short list, and short list to award through the status tracking feature. Additionally, because each prospect number records labor and expenses charged against the prospect number, you will be able to identify what each marketing effort costs in terms of labor and expenses.

Sales Tracking

Sales tracking reports are tools to analyze actual results against sales goals. These reports will help identify areas of strength or weakness when reported by market segment, service or individual marketer.

If attention to detail is paid when defining the lead-tracking fields, the system will also provide flexibility in tracking other sales variables. The data can be sorted to provide information such as:

- Are sales coming from new clients, repeat clients or additional services to existing clients?
- How much has been awarded ("sold") and how much is actually under contract?
- What kinds of facilities and services are clients buying?
- What is the expense to sales ratio (a form of ratio analysis in which specific cost or expense is expressed as a percentage of sales revenue)? This ratio reveals important deviations from the average.

Graphic depiction of sales data helps communicate results. Any information that can be quantified such as budget, project size, etc., can be graphed by exporting data to a spread sheet program or graphing software. The graphing features of most software packages have improved over the past few years to a level where the user simply selects the data to be graphed and presses a "graph" button. One of the most common graphs seen in sales reporting illustrates actual sales compared to yearly sales goals. A sample of this type chart appears on the next page.

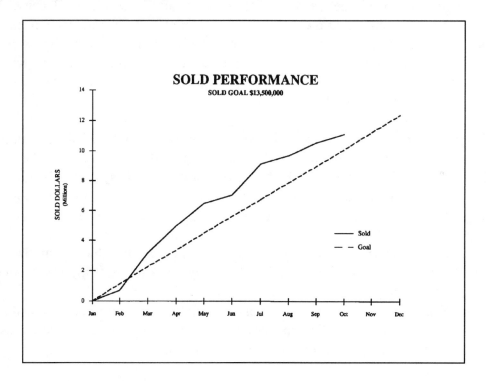

Marketing Support Information

Tracking systems will most often store information on leads and sales performance, but can also support the marketing function by storing and organizing data on firm resources and past project histories. The amount of information and detail required in RFPs is increasing as clients search for ways to differentiate between professional services firms.

Project history data fields should contain information on project costs (estimated, actual and number of change orders), schedule information, square footages, special features of the facility, project team members, including consultants or associate firms, and client references. Special firm resources and services, and staff resumes should also be included in the marketing information system. Because of the magnitude of information collected on project histories, this data base is often stand-alone and not a part of the prospect and sales-tracking data base. The decision whether to have one system for all needs or two separate systems may be driven by the capabilities of your computer systems. The option you choose is not so important, but what is important is that you do include this type of data in your total marketing information system.

How Do I Set Up a Tracking System?

To efficiently and cost effectively employ a tracking system, the firm's specific needs must be acknowledged and addressed. An internal audit to determine and understand the marketing department's needs should be the first step. Ask questions such as: How many members of the staff have some marketing responsibility? What kinds of projects are pursued? Are fees negotiated or are firm bids required? How a firm does business will determine the kind of information to be tracked. Once information needs are determined, the manager of the system can be identified. Because the data will be used primarily by the marketing department, an individual from that department will most likely be the system manager. The system manager will manage and coordinate input, including external information from project managers and accounting staff, and compile, analyze and update data and reports. During the software-development phase or when evaluating commercial software, it is essential to solicit involvement and feedback from both of these groups.

Before a marketing information system is designed or software is purchased, it is important to conduct this needs assessment. The perceived needs can then be matched to available off-the-shelf software or applied to in-house design. Most certainly, the first consideration in the system's design will be the focus of the system and its ability to retrieve the necessary information or reports. Questions must be answered such as: Will the contact list be the center of activity? Will tickler be part of the program? Can client profiles, correspondence, vital data, histories of meetings, appointments, revenues and/or expenses be tracked? Beyond reports, consideration must be given to the way in which your firm does business. Issues such as whether your company has a single office location or multiple locations will affect software decisions. Within each office will a single user be responsible for the tracking system or will there be multiple users, requiring that the system be networked? Will the software be compatible with existing computer equipment or will upgrades be necessary? Answers to each of these questions will help you begin to design the system in order to select the software that is right for your needs.

Software Selection

After the system parameters are defined, software can be selected. When evaluating software, the most important considerations are cost and function. Software developed in-house will produce a program tailored to your exact needs. Commercial software may have some shortcomings, although this is changing. Upgrades of existing product and new product have introduced more options to the market that are cost effective and flexible. Program complexity will determine cost. The more complex your needs, the more expensive the software.

When researching commercial programs, the following questions should be asked:

- Does the program do what you need it to do?
- Can it be customized?
- Can it be upgraded in the future?
- Does it link with accounting software?
- Is the size responsive to the capacity of your system?
- Can it be networked within your office, or if you have multiple locations, among all offices?
- What does it cost?
- Can the information you have on your current system be easily converted to the new system?

Many of these same questions need answers when software is designed in-house. Another important question must also be considered: Will the information systems staff be available to expeditiously set up my system?

The pros and cons of off-the-shelf versus custom software, described in the charts that follow, should be considered before making a decision as to which direction to go.

Software Pros and Cons — Off-the-Shelf Product

Pros	Cons
Off-the-shelf; ready to install	May need special hardware
Help line for operations support	May have too many or too few features
Reasonable cost	Licensing several sites may be expensive
Tested, debugged	Revisions to system difficult, if not impossible

Software Pros and Cons — Custom Designed

Pros	Cons
Compatible with other in-house systems	Hidden costs, hard to capture true cost
Can be maintained by in-house staff	Always in state of development, often over-designed
Upgrades possible	Internal staff priorities will probably not be marketing; may be difficult to keep development on schedule
Is tailored to specific needs defined by marketing	More expensive than off-the-shelf software

What Should a Tracking System Look Like?

Only you can say. Analyze what you need and why you need it. Your tracking system must be useful *to your firm, your management and your marketing staff.* I can say with certainty, however, that unless you are a very small practice with little or no resources, your system needs to be automated. There are many solutions available to meet your needs, from off-the-shelf to custom programming. The system should be simple to use, both in data collection and in keeping your information up-to-date. It must be responsive so that requests for information can be quickly processed. Reports should be easy to read and must communicate pertinent information clearly.

The ability of a well-defined marketing tracking system to provide organized, useful data to the marketing director or principal, as well as marketing support staff, will result in more effective marketing efforts and increased success for the firm. It may even spark an interest in marketing. Because uncertainty can be reduced through the ability of the marketing director or principal to assess the market, sales potential will be increased. Information will be at your fingertips. The tracking system is an essential tool, but it is important to remember it is only a tool. It will never replace staying close to the client through personal contact and human interaction. Use it accordingly.

Bibliography

Bass, Brian. "Marketing Information Systems: Micro to Mainframe." Seminar. 1993.

Berkowitz, Eric N.; Roger A. Kerin; and William Rudelius. *Marketing*. Times Mirror/Mosby College Publishing, 1986.

Cohen, William A. *The Practice of Marketing Management, Analysis, Planning & Implementation*. Macmillan Publishing Co., 1988.

Craig, Joanna. "Tracking the Business Development Function." *SMPS Marketer* (March 1990).

Julie G. Luers, FSMPS

- Certified marketing professional with more than 20 years' experience in marketing architecture, engineering and construction services.
- Bachelor's degree in marketing communications (*cum laude*) from Augsburg College in Minneapolis.
- Currently director of marketing for TSP — Architects and Engineers with offices in Minneapolis and Rochester, Minn.; responsible for strategic marketing planning, marketing reporting systems and business development.
- Formerly vice president/business development director with Ellerbe Becket, one of the largest A/E firms in the United States. While at Ellerbe Becket, was responsible for developing and managing the firm's Marketing Activity Reporting System (MARS).
- Served as president of Society for Marketing Professional Services (SMPS) — Twin Cities Chapter, national president of SMPS, and president of the SMPS Foundation.
- Teaches "Marketing for Architects," an extension class for the College of Architecture and Landscape Architecture (CALA) at the University of Minnesota.

2.6 Client Maintenance

Edward Bond Jr., FSMPS
CEO
Bond Bros. Inc.

Communication and Knowledge Sharing Build Lasting Relationships

If math can be considered the universal language around the globe, then client maintenance should be considered the universal language among marketing professionals. Where currencies influence the economies of nations, relationships with clients influence the longevity of professional services firms (PSF's). No longer does an average currency exist, nor an average client. Currencies come in different denominations and so do client relationships. Not all client relationships develop the same value — nor should they. Loyal relationships may be the only "true common currency" worthy of investment. The PSF's that are most successful know which clients fit into their firms and why.

In a client maintenance program, it is as important to understand *why* things are happening as it is to know *when* things are happening. The process of knowing why is part of the client maintenance program that PSF's need to build into their blueprints for long-term success. While all "Why?" questions are important to gathering of client information, it is the focus of this article to center on client maintenance for long-term relationships. Questions of why are not easily answered by a one-word adverb of reason and thus can lead to an improved level of understanding and dialogue with the client, thereby leading to a stronger relationship with the client.

Building a Solid Foundation

If the primary focus of marketing in your PSF is on new customers, then it needs rethinking! Inherently we know that client maintenance has no value if we have no clients. While it is hard to argue against the value of adding new customers — it is equally important to understand the danger of losing existing clients. In many PSF's, the primary focus of marketing is to develop new customers. It is not unusual for PSF's to spend more time and effort in pursuing new customers than it is to reinforce relationships with existing clients. Some PSF's do not realize that the cost of acquiring new customers could be more expensive than the cost to retain existing clients.

The thinking in some PSF's is: Why spend additional time on clients that we have successfully completed projects with? Familiar comments might include: "Our firm has always done satisfactory work for the client; they like our work and know what we can do." "If we spend non-billable time with the client we will be eating into our future income." "The client was satisfied with the project, they had no complaints, we had minimal change orders and the budget was not blown — we're happy and the client should be happy." "If the client has another project, they will call us and request our professional services." "Marketing has opened the door to the customer and now operations will take care of it from here." Do any of these sound familiar?

In order for client maintenance to have a positive impact on a PSF, marketing must not be viewed as an isolated activity. Client maintenance is a part of the marketing effort that deals with retention of clients. Many of the resources needed for new customer development also support the efforts of client maintenance. This might include individuals to support presentations, public relations, advertising, trade shows or the investment in information technology, all designed to support and reinforce your PSF's message to the client.

This is not to suggest that all clients are worth the same individual attention, or that the balance between new customers and existing clients is equally weighted. What is suggested is that you determine why your PSF is interested in pursuing a customer, and evaluate if that customer has the qualities to become a loyal client of your PSF. Thinking about client maintenance and the retention of clients should start at the beginning of your business development program.

Client maintenance has more to do with accelerating, enhancing and improving your ongoing client relationship so that your PSF will benefit with more work opportunities from these clients. Ideally, these relationships should provide additional opportunities that would not have occurred without the relationship.

At Bond Bros., we provide building, utility and civil construction services. When seeking relationships with clients, we always seek large capital end users, such as energy firms that require buildings, pipelines and power plants. Our blueprint has developed around clients that can use all of our services. While one of our services may have initially attracted the client, it becomes a concerted effort within our firm to learn more about that client at all levels. With this knowledge, we are better able to develop relationships in other areas and procure work on a negotiated basis. These relationships also lead to other relationships where health and education clients have similar infrastructure demands and our clients are willing to recommend us for the work.

The Changing Marketplace

As the onslaught of mergers and acquisitions has taken hold of the banking and energy markets, many clients are looking for PSF's that offer a larger diversity of professional services. "Much of this trending is centered on economies of scale," according to James Alley, president of Aberthaw Construction, one of the oldest construction firms in the country. "The need to meet more of our clients' diverse needs has motivated us to seek more alliances with firms of similar cultures. The building of facilities is important, but equally important to some is the ability to work in teams and form expanded relationships with PSF's that will meet my client's needs. Having solid knowledge of the real issues and concerns is why client maintenance is beneficial and integral to our marketing efforts." The PSF that can ascertain and validate important information about its client has a competitive advantage over other PSF's in meeting the real needs of its client.

The same body of knowledge that is required to do the job for new clients is not necessarily the same body of knowledge required for client maintenance. Just as each project is different, each client is different. The skills to build a dormitory building are similar to the skills to build an apartment building, but they are not the same. Clients want you to talk their talk — not generalities. Profoundly enough, the ability to gain an improved body of knowledge for *why* is more acutely realized by working closely with the process: the project, the client and the industry.

Getting close to the client involves everyone in the PSF. More common among the PSF is the ability to get close to the client who is using your service. Meeting face-to-face is far better than sending e-mails or exchanging telephone calls. Developing a one-to-one relationship with the client can greatly accelerate the learning curve. Studies have indicated that face-to-face knowledge sharing can be twice as effective as written communication.

Client maintenance is about serving more than it is about selling and should meld more toward knowledge sharing. While the professional skills to sell and to serve are similar, they are not always the same. In client maintenance, it is more important to listen and understand the client than it is to sell the client on an immediate solution. Communication is an important link to the success of any client maintenance program. The success of knowledge sharing will be linked to the ability to communicate in a timely and effective manner with your team. Keeping team members posted about what is happening, when it is happening, how it is happening, where it is happening and why it is happening is the key. These are all compelling components for the client maintenance program and each has a level of importance and timeliness within the PSF.

Is the Client Really on Board?

Is the client a strong advocate of your PSF? Have you given them a good reason to be? Are there valid reasons to suggest that the client is real*y* happy? If a client is not truly elated with your PSF then there should be concerns that the level of service or way in which they are being served needs refinement. Knowing whether a client is on a short trip or long trip with your PSF can guide your firm more accurately into the future.

Donnelly, Berry and Thompson in their book *Marketing Financial Services* suggest some differences between how we view customers and clients:

> Customers may be nameless to the institution; clients cannot be nameless. Customers are served as part of the mass or as part of larger segments; clients are served on an individual basis. Customers are statistics; their needs are reflected on computer printout summaries. Clients are entities in and of themselves; specifics about them — background data, services used, special requirements — are captured in a database. Customers are served by anyone who happens to be available; clients are served — at least for nonroutine needs — by the professional … assigned to them.

Clients will not always be able to explain why one PSF is more favored than another — sometimes it is nothing more than the way in which they are being served. The PSF that is capable of measuring its level of service in terms of meeting or exceeding expectations will retain a higher level of loyal clients. Knowing what the expectations of the client were in the beginning, how they might have changed during the project and why they have changed can lead to an improved understanding within your PSF of changes that the client is facing.

Information Transformation

Assisting clients in using technology for their projects has been a driver of success for many PSF's. "There has been an increased level of PSF's bringing information technology to the client" according to Tom Viehl, CPA and president of CIS, a Boston-based information and technology firm. "Many of my PSF clients are taking the lead in orchestrating the project information and communications systems, making them a valuable part of the client program. Through the aid of networking systems and software programs, project web sites are providing data, voice and video information."

The tools of information technology have been equally important to many PSF's and should be viewed as a strategic instrument for client maintenance. Some of the benefits listed above for clients have also translated into benefits for many PSF's that use this information technology wisely. By improving the cost of doing business, PSF's have been able to improve their bottom lines while providing a more competitive and complete service to their client. Many PSF's are making productive use of technology by increasing their level of connection with their clients. Information technology has assisted PSF's with an improved understanding and ability to customize issues central to what their clients need, how they need it and why they need it a certain way.

The Importance of Knowledge Sharing Among Professionals

Understanding *why* is more than a repository of book knowledge. It is the learning that comes from working with the client. Part of it is learning how to work with the different cognitive preferences of individuals. Realizing that each individual has his or her own way of learning is important to the effective design of systems for knowledge sharing. Being aware of the visual, auditory and kinesthetic areas of learning will guide you in developing a system for building rapport with your client.

Much of the knowledge sharing for client maintenance should take place with the client and hopefully while on the project. Project executives and project managers can play a pivotal role in the ability to gather knowledge from the client and share that with the rest of the team. Knowledge without sharing will never fully enhance the organization to its greatest potential. Having systems in place to cross-fertilize the PSF with knowledge is how the PSF will benefit.

It is also important to realize that relationships on a project will take time. As many project relationships develop over time, the strength of its foundation will be developing. The integrity and compassion that develops from a strong foundation will simplify the sharing of knowledge. People who work well together have a proclivity to trust each other. Taking extra interest in a client and their industry is part of the equation for loyal clients. This interest cannot be superficial and should never be forced.

Managing the Professional Service Firm by David Maister presents a view of attitudes that some professionals need to overcome to be effective:

> "Because of the proclivity of professionals to become more fascinated with the intellectual challenge of their craft than with being responsive to clients, all too often clients are mocked

for their lack of professional knowledge, despised because of their demands, and resented because they control the purse strings and hence the autonomy of the professional."

The blueprint that is designed for client maintenance should include more than just the marketing department. Each department or component of the PSF can play a role in client maintenance. While a great project delivery program is but one goal, total enthrallment of the client may be an overall objective. Having a client that is pleased with the project work but uncomfortable with the accounting department's attention to invoicing, or lack of responsiveness to questions, will certainly not leave them enthralled with your total service. To enthrall clients takes the total PSF effort.

The role of creating an atmosphere to assist in facilitating these occurrences is just as important. Designing a blueprint for your PSF that will assist everyone in understanding what types of clients are most beneficial and why will greatly enhance your marketing efforts and result in a more highly committed and measurable business development plan.

The Details!

The "devil is in the details" is one of many trite axioms that can be heard in business. In client maintenance, the attention to the total process is the details. People are serving people, and actions cannot be forced. Relationships do not develop because of time; they develop because of trust. People have emotions, and sometimes these emotions can influence decisions. The need for understanding, compassion and sincerity are even greater in a highly trusted relationship. The people skills in client maintenance almost become as important as the professional skills that brought the client to your PSF.

Far too often, it is easier to forego the efforts of client maintenance and direct those efforts toward new customers. While in reality both old and new clients are needed, don't give in. Exchanging one new customer for one existing customer is not a good investment. Adding a new customer and retaining a good client is better! The odds are better for getting work from existing clients than they are for getting work with a potential customer. Remember Pareto's Rule (20/80): 80 percent of your profits come from 20 percent of your clients.

In theory, most businesses have a common denominator: Keep good customers. Bringing in new customers to make into loyal clients is a goal of any good business. It will take a combination of influencing service drivers to impact the level of service. These drivers can be readily seen in the Internet environment: certain influencing factors of convenience, accessibility, attractions and support are important drivers for service firms. These are all words found in the Internet arena, and as such, there is much to be gained by watching other industries.

Treating customers with special consideration is important. Since we are service providers, it is in our best interest to serve the customer, show the desire, understand their need and recommend solutions. When convenience, dependability, personal attention and follow-through are not in alignment with the product being delivered, most customers never complain and also never return. Customers know that low price is not always a direct correlation to low cost, especially when service is involved with the purchase.

One need not be a student of graphology to see the writing on the wall. Could a PSF learn more about its own business by observing the changes in a client's business? Is there more to learn about our own business through the eyes of the customer? Is there more value to the PSF than just monetary by working with a client? Can the knowledge and experience gained with one client serve another client? Does the knowledge gained provide greater opportunity for the PSF? These are only a few of the investment questions that should be addressed in a PSF's blueprint when seeking the "right clients" for the firm's future.

Clients know that the economic cycle has changed from one of demand to that of supply. We see the effects of alliances, joint ventures, partnerships and teaming efforts in our own backyard. With the steady stream of mergers, acquisitions, deregulation and general changes in business practices, clients have come to expect more. A common denominator that appears off the balance sheet is the strength of the relationship with a client. This in itself can have a major role in the decision-making of why good things happen.

The level of a relationship with a client can be extremely valuable. Doing good work with a particular client may be what got you in the door, but is not necessarily the strongest part of the equation to keep you there. Hanging around and waiting for a client to hand you its next project is not likely to happen. Earning the respect and endorsement of the client is an ongoing process.

Moving Forward

Listening to a client can be either passive or active. Listening to the client and knowing what to really listen for is the part of the client maintenance program that needs attention. Noted author Tom Peters in a *Fast Track* magazine article suggests that project management is emotion management, and listening has a tremendous amount of emotional involvement.

Asking clients (internal and external) what they like, why they like it and all the other important questions is one way of cementing a stronger bond with them. The saying, "People don't care how much you know until they know how much you care" is vital to creating a loyal client base.

How can we show that we're listening to the client? Take a sincere interest in not only our portion of the project, but in the whole process. Keep communications open and uncluttered to help facilitate discussion. Make sure clients understand what they are buying and how it can be delivered best. The ability to think like a client by assisting them in saving time, saving money, preventing redundancy or any part of the consultative process will send positive signals.

Spending time knowing the client's interests, business, industry, special needs, challenges and working to become a trusted adviser are all worthy investments. These investments will show a level of service and commitment that cannot be easily duplicated. Clients like to be treated as individuals, to be treated special. They like familiarity, the good feeling of being with peers and the camaraderie that comes with being a part of a winning team.

In an article for *Fast Company* magazine, Tom Peters speaks about selling your WOW Project. He notes that all work of economic value can be defined as project work. He reminds us that projects, especially those that can change the shape of the future, have a tremendous amount of emotion to them. And certainly the crux of any strong program that deals with client relationships comes down to one thing: project management. As Peters puts it, "If you read the literature on project management carefully, there is one word that I guarantee that you won't find: 'selling'." He continues: "The assumption seems to be that, like a better mousetrap, a worthy project will sell itself. Although the project-management experts may not appreciate the need to sell, there is a group of businesspeople who do understand the critical role of selling projects. They are the people who inhabit the 'real' professional-services firms: Every management consultant, every ad-agency wizard, every stock-market jock is a salesperson. They're selling their strong point of view, their recognized expertise, and their scintillating services to customers [clients] on the outside, and they're selling their reliability, dependability, and talent to colleagues on the inside. It's just another part of our old friend the Brand Called You. Your project and your brand go hand in hand: Both depend on your ability to sell yourself and to sell your project. If you want your WOW Project to happen, you have to learn how to sell it — smart, hard, and from beginning to end."[1]

The challenges ahead for PSF's will have only the propensity to pick up speed. The markets change quickly, the rules change, and people change. Even though we may not be as fast to market as some Internet firms, the expectations are as great. While firms of the past built businesses, firms of the future will build projects. The difference is similar to that of a customer and a client — WOW!

Endnotes

[1] Tom Peters, "The WOW Project" *Fast Company* (May 1999): 122.

Bibliography

Client Maintenance

Bell, Chip, and Ron Zemke. *Managing Knock Your Socks Off Service*. New York: AMACOM, 1992.

Berry, Leonard. *Discovering the Soul of Service*. New York: The Free Press, 1999.

Berry, Leonard, and A. Parasuraman. *Marketing Services*. New York: The Free Press, 1991.

Cathcart, Jim. *Relationship Selling*. New York: The Berkley Publishing Group, 1990.

Christopher, Martin, Adrian Payne, and David Ballantyne. *Relationship Marketing*. Oxford: Butterworth-Heinemann Ltd., 1991.

Dimitrius, Jo-Ellan, and Mark Mazzarella. *Reading People*. New York: Random House, 1998.

Gitomer, Jeffrey. *Customer Satisfaction is Worthless, Customer Loyalty is Priceless*. Austin, TX: Bard Press, 1998.

Heil, Gary, Tom Parker, and Deborah Stephens. *One Size Fits One*. New York: Van Nostrand Reinhold, 1997.

Kotler, Philip. *Marketing Professional Services*. Englewood Cliffs, NJ: Prentice-Hall, 1984.

Maister, David. *Managing the Professional Service Firm*. New York: The Free Press, 1993.

— . *True Professionalism*. New York: The Free Press, 1997.

McKenna, Regis. *Real Time*. Boston: Harvard Business School Press, 1997.

Pine II, Joseph. *Mass Customization*. Boston: Harvard Business School Press, 1993.

Seybold, Patricia, and Ronni Marshak. *Customers.Com*. New York: Times Books, 1998.

Vilas, Donna, and Sandy. *Power Networking*. Austin, TX: MoutainHarbour Publications, 1991.

Wall, Bob, Mark Sobol, and Robert Solum. *The Mission Driven Organization*. Rocklin, CA: Prima Publishing, 1992.

Wellmin, John. *Successful Customer Care*. Hauppauge, NY: Barron's Educational Series, 1997.

Audiocassettes

Davenport, Thomas, and Laurance Prusak. *Working Knowledge*. Harvard Business School Press.

Christensen, Clayton. *The Innovator's Dilemma*. Harvard Business School Press.

Leonard, Dorothy, and James Brian Quinn. *Leveraging Knowledge Assets*. Harvard Business School Press.

Hagell III, John, and Arthur Armstrong. *net.gain*. Harvard Business School Press.

Edward A. Bond Jr., FSMPS

- CEO, Bond Bros. Inc., fourth-generation (1907) building and utility construction management firm.
- Director, NEUCO Inc., research and development firm.
- Director, Innerseal Inc., technology firm.
- Trustee, Spring Realty Trust, real estate development firm.
- Trustee, Quantitative Group of Funds, publicly traded mutual funds.
- Corporator, Wentworth Institute of Technology.
- SMPS past national president.
- SMPS Boston Chapter past president.
- Harvard Business School, OPM.
- New Hampshire College, M.B.A.
- Cambridge College, M.Ed.
- New England College, B.A.
- Licensed instrument pilot.

Part 3:
Winning Work

3.1 The "Go" or "No Go" Decision: Choices and Consequences

C. Ronald Capps
Managing Director and Partner
The Beck Group

You have done your research, written your plan, defined your budget and have the technology tools in place to move forward. You are out there selling and actively engaged in the business-development process. The fun part is about to begin: winning work.

The work you and your associates have been doing will result in invitations to submit qualifications, proposals and bids for work. As soon as that process happens, the key principals, officers and business development manager must sit down and make the first of several key decisions: to go or not to go. This activity is a critical part of achieving the firm's business and marketing plan. More time and money are about to be committed and it is vital to be sure that resources are available and that this opportunity is evaluated against others that the firm is pursuing. Regardless of title, the head of business development must take the leaders of the firm through a strategic exercise that helps all involved understand the commitment that is about to be made by submitting to the request. Before that meeting is called, there is work to be done. Let's look first at why it is necessary.

Once the request for quotation/request for proposal (RFQ/RFP) process is initiated, expectations are set. These are both internal and external. It is the responsibility of the business development leader to guide these expectations and set them in accordance with the business plan and the direction in which the firm's officers have said they want to go. The following items need to be considered:

- Culture match between your firm and the prospect.
- Selection process (proposal, fee competition, design competition, hard bid, etc.).
- The estimated cost to pursue the work.
- Size of project and resources required (money, time, people, etc.).
- Financial ability of the prospect to pay for the services.
- Type of project and alignment to firm's capabilities.
- Risk the firm will bear if the project is won.
- Potential fee income.
- Surety and insurance requirements beyond the norm.
- Location and the firm's ability to service the work.
- Consultants already involved.
- Fit with the firm's marketing plan.
- Competitive position of your firm.
- Impact of the project on the firm, preventing it from pursuing other work.
- Political ramifications.
- Past relationship with this contact or with the prospect.

There are a variety of ways to organize the collected data. Two of the easiest methods include either a questionnaire or a matrix. Much of the above can be turned into questions that can be asked for any customer or project. The same can be said for a matrix. The repetition of a standard format works because it helps organize the thoughts of the participants and gets them accustomed to thinking about prospects in an organized and business-like manner. The business points of the opportunity become the discussion points, not aesthetic issues, volume or other less important points. The author has had experiences with both the verbal and a standard format approach to evaluations. The culture of your firm and your own style of management should be considered as you proceed. You may find that a combination of both questions and a matrix works best in your culture, but a format that is repeated will yield benefits over time. It is an excellent discipline and a way to involve others in the marketing and selling process.

If the marketing plan is aimed at developing specific industries and types of business, it may be helpful to utilize a "go, no go" process on prospects before the projects cloud the issue. A customer matrix or assessment might include an evaluation of the following:

1. Does the nature of the prospect's business result in a culture that is adversarial, making them hard to deal with and resistant to a cooperative environment? Is there a cultural match with your firm?
2. Is the business growing or declining? What will be the impact over time to your firm?
3. Has the prospect shown a history of choosing new service providers every time they need new facilities?
4. Typically, what size projects does this company require? How frequently?
5. Have they shown any indication that they are willing to try new methods, designs, services or innovative techniques?
6. What is the financial condition of the firm?
7. How does their approach to business compare with the firm's approach?

Some or all of these questions may be important to you and your firm. There may be others that should be considered. A good check is to revisit the marketing plan's objectives and see what had been agreed on when it was written. One firm that was researched for this chapter is so concerned about the right mix of customers that it has a unique customer matrix evaluation for each industry in which it pursues business. The firm's research showed that there are significant differences in customers within its primary markets. The company wants to choose the ones that best fit its culture and approach to business. The advantage of the "customer evaluation" is that it puts you in a decision mode and will save you time in the long run. This will result in a better "hit rate" of projects won if you measure yourself in this manner.

Assuming that you have proceeded beyond the evaluation of the customer, let's take a look at a matrix approach to the "go, no go" decision for a project. The example on the next page shows what might be created and made available to any member of the firm who is engaged in the business-development process. It is an excellent means of communicating items that are important in seeking customers to members of the firm. You might create a customized chart and, as an experiment, run some of your existing work through the evaluation process. Would you have gone after all of it? Would you have priced it differently if you had known the answers to the questions? This exercise will help you refine the points of your evaluation.

Sample Project Preference Matrix

Contract Issues					
1. Size *5 points*	$25M - $50M (5 Points)	Above $50M (4 Points)	$10M - $25M (3 Points)	$5M - $10M (2 Points)	Below $5M (1 Point)
2. Type/Risk *10 Points*	Standard Firm Contract (10 Points)	Revised Firm Contract (8 Points)	Good Terms on Owner's Contract (6 Points)	Government Contract (4 Points)	Unreasonable Terms (2 Points)
3. Fee *15 Points*	5% and Up (15 Points)	3.25% - 4.99% (12 Points)	2.4% - 3.24% (9 Points)	2% - 2.49% (6 Points)	Below 1.99% (3 Points)
Project Issues					
4. Type *5 Points*	Health Care (5 Points)	Retail/Airport (4 Points)	Industrial (3 Points)	Office (2 Points)	Multifamily (1 Point)
5. Location *10 Points*	Local City (10 Points)	Local State (8 Points)	Surrounding States (6 Points)	Regional Area (4 Points)	Non-Regional (2 Points)
6. Team/ Consultants *5 Points*	Know Team Members Good Relationship (5 Points)	Know Team Members Fair Relationship (4 Points)	Local Team Members (3 Points)	Do Not Know Team (2 Points)	Bad Relationship (1 Point)
Client					
7. Desirability (Target Client) *10 Points*	Past Client Good Relationship (10 Points)	New Client w/ Good Contact (8 Points)	Past Client Fair Relationship (6 Points)	New Client (4 Points)	Past Client – Bad Experience (0 Points)
Personnel					
8. Experience/ Availability *10 Points*	Right People Available (10 Points)	People Available (8 Points)	People Available by Shifting (6 Points)	May Have to Double Up (4 Points)	Not Available Must Hire (2 Points)
Subjective					
9. Other *5 Points*	Have an Advantage Over Competition (5 Points)	High Success w/ This Type of Project (4 Points)	Know Client Well (3 Points)	High Visibility (2 Points)	Good Feeling About Project (1 Point)

Maximum of 70 Points

Note: Be sure to make the categories, evaluation points and the numerical rating fit your approach to business and the culture of the firm.

If the members of your firm are analytical, you may want to use numerical ratings, as shown above, in order to arrive at a total score for comparison with other opportunities. A ranking can be created and an agreement can be reached that serves as a cutoff below which a project will not even be considered. The chart might look like this:

60 – 70	Great Prospect
50 – 59	Good Prospect
40 – 49	Average Prospect
Below 40	No Way

While this may seem too left-brained for most of the creative marketers, it really does help the analytical members of the firm. The scale can easily be changed for market conditions and capacity growth of the firm. At the author's firm the matrix is a part of the marketing plan and they are both updated together. In addition to formalizing the "go, no go" decision process, a key result of this is to get buy-in with all concerned. If the key members of the firm have participated in this process, it should be much easier for the marketing team to get the assistance needed in developing the response to the RFQ/RFP. Another advantage is the assistance it provides in the choices and consequences when there are more opportunities than capabilities of either the firm or of the marketing team's ability to produce the responses. Everything cannot be a number one priority and this will go a long way in helping to establish the priorities. Time and other resources are limited for all of us.

If you and your firm leaders are less analytical and prefer more of a case study approach, the same kind of thought process might take place. Consider the following:

- Firm position.
- Market intensity.
- Competition.
- Services desired.
- Financial commitment and opportunity.
- Relationship with the decision-makers.

Consideration of the elements listed above could cause an analysis based on questions such as:

- What is our firm's total capacity and does this opportunity fit our strategic plan?
- Are the right professional resources available to staff the project?
- Can the project be completed in the time allowed by the prospect?
- Is the market such that the services will be bought as a pure commodity or will the customer pay for value-added services?
- Do we need the work?
- Are there opportunities where we are better positioned than this one?
- Who are the likely competitors for this project?
- How fierce will the competition be?
- Do we know the decision-makers?
- Is it our kind of project?
- If specialized knowledge is required, do we have it?
- Will the services require teaming with others to propose a complete package?
- Can we identify and quantify the financial risk and potential reward?
- Does the reward justify the investment in the pursuit of the opportunity?
- Who will make the decision and is it a level playing field for us?
- Is this a past customer who expects us to respond?
- Is the decision-maker a past customer who is new with this prospect?

If a case study approach seems to suit your firm's culture the best, you might do an executive summary after the research is completed. This could then be circulated before the "go, no go" meeting is held preparing everyone for the upcoming discussion and decision process.

After the team has met, analyzed the many facets, and discussed the risk and reward potential, a decision must be made to either decline the opportunity or to pursue it. While nearly all of the items your team will have considered require some subjectivity, you will have agreement among the firm's leaders where you invest your best efforts. The result should be a unified approach to doing everything within your firm's control to win the opportunity.

Assuming that the decision is to "go," you really have some work to do. Be sure to appoint a leader of the proposal team before leaving the strategy session. It is a good idea to convene a meeting with the proposal team leader and all of the marketing support people for the next steps. You need to determine a schedule of events to meet the due date, complete a check list to organize the collection of data for the response and prepare a proposal strategy. The prospect should be contacted to let them know that you will be responding. This is a great time to introduce your team leader, if they do not already know each other. Beginning the switch from marketing to operations now will make it seem very natural when you go to the interview or sit down to negotiate your contract because your proposal was so responsive.

But what if you make the decision to not pursue an invitation? As the marketing leader, you will still have some work to do. You need to thoughtfully decide who will respond because this is still a selling opportunity. For most prospects, they will be back in the marketplace at some point and you may want your firm to be considered again. Be straightforward in your response and try to do it in person. You might hand deliver a short letter confirming why you will not be submitting a proposal or bid. If you present your reasons, and they are based on sound business decisions for your firm, the prospect should respect that. It is a good idea to follow up and get the results of the competition so that you will have this information for your future use.

If the "go, no go" decision is formalized and organized, the leaders of the firm will see the marketing effort differently. It will be perceived as a much more business-like approach to an area of the professional services business that they have never been totally comfortable with. You will have raised the odds by being thoroughly prepared to lead the strategic discussion of the many variables that should be considered before investing the firm's resources. The business-development process and you will be seen in an organized and professional light.

C. Ronald Capps

- Ronald Capps is a managing director and partner in The Beck Group, a real estate and construction firm based in Dallas with 10 offices. Capps is responsible for the development of new business for the firm on a national basis. Using his 38 years of experience in the industry, he has been able to refocus his firm from one whose primary customers were speculative developers to one whose primary focus is the corporate users of space. Beck has grown to an organization of 460 people that provides a variety of services to its customers.

Among Capp's accomplishments are:
- Sales and marketing experience of 17 years with a major vertical transportation company, including positions as national sales manager and regional manager with P & L responsibility.
- A number of building and real estate programs for Fortune 500 companies, including MetLife, Fidelity Investments, Xerox and American Hospital Corp. (now Baxter Health Care).
- Provided market evaluations of potential commercial real estate investments for a major regional bank's trust department.
- Developed and managed a partnership between a Fortune 100 firm and the United States' largest developer. The team developed an industrial park in suburban Chicago.
- Served as a national accounts manager at Trammell Crow Co.

- Capps is a long-time member of SMPS and has served on the board and as the president of the Dallas Chapter. He is currently treasurer of the SMPS Foundation board.
- He is a past president of the Commercial Council of NACORE, the International Association of Corporate Real Estate Executives, in which he is still active. Currently active in International Development Research Council (IDRC), International Council of Shopping Centers (ICSC), a member of the Texas Marketing Team for the State of Texas and a mentor for the Southern Methodist University MBA Program.
- Capps has a bachelor's degree in business from Michigan State University.
- He may be contacted at **roncapps@beckgroup.com**.

Acknowledgment

Special thanks to Kathy M. Kondor who authored the original chapter on "The RFP Decision Making Process" for the first edition of *The Handbook for Marketing Professional Services.*

3.2 Joint Ventures, Alliances and Teaming Strategies

Ron W. Garikes, FSMPS
Senior Vice President
Karlsberger

In the pursuit of a new market, client, project or when expanding opportunities with existing clients, assembling the right team is often the difference between success and failure. Successful team-building strategies are both an art and science. The art of team building includes intangible factors such as team chemistry and the development of a team culture that is compatible with the prospective client. Components of the scientific approach include research methods, data base development and quantitative-based analysis. The focus of this chapter will be on both the science and art of successful team-building strategies.

Topics addressed in this chapter include characteristics of a successful team, intelligence gathering, team structures, evaluation criteria of potential team members, minority and small business participation, exclusivity, and benefits of successful team building.

Characteristics of a Successful Team

The success of a team is contingent upon the group's ability to communicate effectively, develop high levels of trust and shared values. The ultimate success of a teaming strategy is the team's ability to secure and profitably produce work. A major factor in a team's success is in its ability to communicate effectively to the client the benefits and added value the team will bring to a project. Most clients are seeking consultants that can provide a single source of contact and accountability. Clients need to understand the distinguishing characteristics of a team and why a particular team structure will benefit their project. Like any human endeavor, effective team-building strategies rely on solid relationships. A successful relationship requires a high level of commitment, trust and effective communications. Figure 1 below lists 10 characteristics of a highly effective team.

Figure 1

Characteristics of a Highly Effective Team	
1	Clear purpose
2	Informality
3	Participation
4	Listening
5	Civilized disagreement
6	Consensus decisions
7	Open communication
8	Clear roles and assignments
9	Shared leadership
10	Style diversity

It is critical to maintain a good working relationship with team members during the execution of a project. An unsuccessful relationship may result in the client serving as the referee for issues in dispute between team members. Warning signs of a team headed for trouble include a lack of responsiveness, a lot of talk with little action and a low level of trust between team members. Ten common warning signs are listed in Figure 2.

Figure 2

	Ten Warning Signs
1	Formal meetings—stuffy, tense
2	A lot of participation with little accomplished
3	A lot of talk; no real communication
4	Assignments discussed in private after the meeting
5	No trust or mutual respect
6	Confusion about jobs and responsibilities
7	Not enough diversity of ideas
8	Corporate culture clashes
9	Inconsistent core values
10	Decisions made by formal leader with limited participation

Intelligence Gathering

The access to and availability of information about potential teaming partners have never been greater. Several options that should be considered when gathering intelligence about potential team members are described below.

The Internet

With the current revolution in information technology, particularly the Internet, information can be gathered about a company's project experience, services, staffing, resources and office locations in a matter of minutes. Visiting a firm's web site can also provide clues about its past teaming relationships, design ability, creativity and corporate culture. The absence of a corporate web site can also be revealing. This would certainly bring into question the firm's commitment to invest in new technology and its ability to communicate effectively. Although the Internet is a powerful tool, it is not the only effective resource for gathering intelligence about potential partners.

Clients

Client user groups have probably always been, and will remain, the best resource for gathering information about partnering opportunities. For example, to find out about the best firms doing children's hospitals, call several CEOs and facility managers at children's hospitals, preferably ones who have recently completed projects. If you are looking for someone who does a lot of pulp and paper plants, contact several plant managers who, again, have recently gone through this process. For any project type or service, 99 percent of the time, someone, somewhere, has recently completed a similar project.

Associations and Trade Publications

Other effective resources for gathering information are professional and client-related association web sites and membership directories. SMPS is an excellent resource for researching potential partnering firms. Its web site provides information about services and project-type expertise of all member firms. The *Construction Market Data ProFile* is also a treasure house of information, with member firms' areas of specialty, focus and staff resources included.

Many industry trade magazines publish annual surveys ranking firms by market sector, service orientation, sales volume and staff size. Several magazines that publish these surveys are *Engineering News Record—Building Design and Construction* and *Modern Health Care.*

Vendors and Consultants

Vendors and equipment manufacturers can also provide reliable information regarding potential partnering opportunities. Many of these companies work internationally and have worked with A/E/C-related firms on a global basis.

Information should be gathered, evaluated and disseminated for continuous monitoring and update. There are many software applications that provide data base capabilities for information retrieval. FileMaker Pro, RFP and custom-designed systems are all effective tools for managing the data base. Hard-copy files should also be kept on potential partnering firms, including a general brochure, 254/255 data and related materials. These files should be updated annually at a minimum.

Team Structures

"One size fits all" does not apply for a successful team-building strategy. Almost every market, project and client requires a different strategy and team structure. Typically, teams are structured as a joint venture—association, alliance, design/build, or as a prime/sub-consultant relationship.

Joint Ventures

A joint venture is a separate legal corporate entity that usually provides services for a specific project or client. Because of legal and liability considerations, legal counsel and professional liability carrier should always be consulted prior to entering into a joint venture agreement. The formation of a joint venture to pursue and execute a project is most commonly used on large, complex and technically demanding projects. Many clients, including some federal agencies, state governments and many private sector businesses, prefer working with consultants that have a joint venture team structure. From the client's perspective, the advantages of working with a joint venture include a clearly defined single source of contact and legal responsibility for the project.

Most professional associations provide their members with a standard joint venture agreement form. When discussing this agreement with your joint venture partners, you should address these questions:

* Who will be the primary contact?
* What specific personnel will be assigned, including their duties and responsibilities?
* Where will the work be performed?
* Who will supervise the work?
* Who will be responsible for financial and administrative functions?
* How will the fees be allocated?
* How will profits and losses be shared?
* What information technology and CADD format will be utilized?
* Who will be responsible for developing a project web site?
* How will marketing expenses be allocated?
* What provisions must be made for insurance?
* What method of dispute resolution will be acceptable to each firm?

These and other issues should be thoroughly discussed when entering into a joint venture agreement and when developing other team structures.

Associations

Forming an association does not require the creation of a separate corporate entity. An association is typically less formal than a joint venture, although many of the same issues addressed in the joint venture section of this chapter should be reviewed when entering into an association agreement.

The prime consultant in the association must be determined, as this firm will usually enter into a direct contractual relationship with the client. Firm responsibilities, staff assignments and allocation of fees must also be determined. Associations allow for greater flexibility when structuring the team. Design and construction-related firms usually form associations to augment their experience, resources and capabilities. Associations are also effective team structures for pursuing work in remote geographic markets where a local presence will enhance the chances of winning the project.

Alliances

Probably the fastest growing approach to teaming in the A/E/C industry is the formation of alliances or what is often referred to as strategic alliances. The primary difference between alliances, joint ventures and associations is the long-term relationship and commitment by alliances to pursuing and executing projects in predetermined markets. Successful alliances have been formed to serve very specific market sectors, including education, criminal justice, hospitality, infrastructure development, biotechnology and health care.

Many successful alliances consist of only two firms that complement each other by providing one another with broader geographic opportunities, diversified services and more extensive portfolios in a specific market. Other alliances consist of multiple firms with a broad range of disciplines, services and geographic locations.

Design-Build

An effective and commonly utilized project delivery method that many private sector and institutional clients are using in the execution of a project is design-build. Design-build provides a single source of contact and contractual responsibility between a project team and owner. A successful design-build approach requires a high level of trust, commitment and effective communication between team members. Any company can take the lead in a design-build team structure. Client expectations and project requirements will usually dictate the optimal structure for a design-build team.

A design-build project-delivery approach is similar to a turnkey-delivery approach where the project team provides a single source of contact and contract responsibility for a variety of services. Services included in a turnkey approach can include financing, development, management contracts, maintenance and other support services.

Prime/Sub-consultant Relationships

Most firms still pursue and execute work utilizing the traditional prime and sub-consultant team structure. Many clients still prefer this project-delivery approach as well. When utilizing this team structure, select the most qualified and capable sub-consultants that have relevant project experience and qualified staff for a specific client or project. More specialized project types or services require a higher level of expertise from sub-consultants.

Evaluation Criteria of Potential Team Members

There is no standard set of evaluation criteria for evaluating potential team members for the wide variety of new client and project opportunities. For example, identifying potential candidates for local affiliations would be necessary only when exporting services or project-type expertise to remote project locations. Other project opportunities may require importing a signature design firm, specialty service consultant or the vast resources of a large national firm.

There are several general criteria that should be considered when assembling a project team that are usually necessitated by client expectations. Important factors to consider are the core values of each organization and an evaluation if the partnership will truly be a mutually beneficial and reciprocal relationship. For example, if one firm is primarily motivated by profit potential, a firm that places a higher value on quality design may not be a good match for a partnering relationship. A reciprocal relationship is also an important criterion to consider, especially in the development of long-term opportunities with potential associate firms and consultants. Following in Figure 3 is a list of general evaluation criteria that should be considered when evaluating potential team members.

Figure 3

	Evaluation Criteria for Potential Team Members
1	Firm compatibility
2	Complementary services and experience
3	Market position and reputation
4	Common core values
5	Reciprocal relationship
6	Flexibility
7	Successful prior teaming experiences
8	Views of past and current clients
9	Financial stability
10	Size, resources and technical capability

Minority, Small and Disadvantaged Business Participation

Minority, small and disadvantaged business enterprise (MBE, SBE and DBE) utilization goals have been established to assist disadvantaged businesses in obtaining a fair share of design and construction dollars. Utilization goals vary depending on the jurisdiction of the contract. Many federal and local government agencies have established goals expressed as a percentage of the contract dollars awarded. Many private organizations have established goals as well. Be sure to verify the specific requirements of a perspective client.

As mentioned above, client jurisdictions have varying utilization goals for MBE, DBE and SBE participation. Federal, state and local government agencies not only have different utilization goals but also a variety of designations for MBE, DBE and SBE classifications. The Small Business Administration, the Department of Commerce, the Department of Justice, the Corps of Engineers and other federal government agencies have guidelines, regulations and certification criteria for MBE, DBE and SBE utilization. In most states, the department of transportation is an ideal resource for information about utilization goals and the various designations in its jurisdiction. State departments of transportation usually have a directory of certified firms that work in their jurisdictions. Although designations greatly vary by jurisdiction, following in Figure 4 is a list of commonly used designations:

Figure 4

DBE	Disadvantaged Business Enterprise
SBE	Small Business Enterprise
MBE	Minority Business Enterprise
WBE	Woman-owned Business Enterprise
WDBE	Woman-owned Disadvantaged Business Enterprise
MWDBE	Minority Woman-owned Disadvantaged Business Enterprise
AABE	African American Business Enterprise
ABE	Asian Business Enterprise
HBE	Hispanic Business Enterprise
NABE	Native American Business Enterprise
SDB	Small Disadvantaged Business Concern
HBCUs	Historically Black Colleges and Universities
MIs	Minority Institutions
HUBZ	HUB Zone Small Business Concerns
VSB	Very Small Business
SBA 8(a)	Certified Small Business

A number of client agencies also encourage and support a mentoring approach for MBE/DBE/WBE/SBE firms. This is an excellent opportunity for prime consultants to work with new and growing disadvantaged businesses while, at the same time, enabling their firms to achieve client utilization goals. One other factor to consider when assembling project teams is the inclusion of suppliers/vendors as part of the utilization goal. Many jurisdictions will allow inclusion of small and disadvantaged businesses such as reproduction companies and paper suppliers.

Exclusivity

Exclusivity can be one of the most contentious issues in the team-development process. Prime consultants, understandably, seek an exclusive arrangement with associate firms and consultants, especially when the consultant's expertise or client relationship will provide a competitive advantage. Consultants and associate firms that receive a large percentage of the fee are also viewed as prime candidates for an exclusive by the lead firm. Team members that normally work in a sub-consulting capacity or provide specialty services have legitimate and valid reasons for not granting exclusives. The potential of jeopardizing an existing relationship with another firm the consultant is working with currently or has had a long-term and profitable working relationship with is usually at the top of the list.

There are creative options that should be considered by both parties when evaluating the pros and cons of exclusives. Options to consider include: (1) Limited exclusives: Sub-consultants or specialty firms agree not to actively solicit other firms for inclusion on their team and also agree not to participate on a team they are not currently working with or have a prior relationship with; and (2) Prime consultants requesting exclusives should be prepared to offer incentives such as higher compensation, more involvement with the project and guarantees of prominent consultant identification in all project-related public relations and publication materials.

Benefits of Successful Team Building

A successful team is a group of firms with a high degree of interdependence geared toward the achievement of the common goal of securing new and profitable work in a new market, with a new or existing client or for a specific project. Additional benefits realized from successful team building include the following:

Photo courtesy of Karlsberger

- **The effective use of limited resources.** Combining the resources of a multi-firm project team is an ideal method for effectively utilizing limited, and in many instances, over-committed resources. Larger staffs to draw from, combined with greater technological capabilities, will greatly enhance a team's chances of securing projects.

- **Better problem-solving ability.** The old adage "two heads are better than one" certainly applies to successful team-building strategies. Diverse opinions and different perspectives are crucial elements for solving complex problems.

- **Greater productivity.** Greater productivity results in higher success rates in pursuing work and larger profit margins in the execution of the work.

- **Enhances creativity and innovation.** The synergy generated in a successful team environment is a breeding ground for creative and innovative ideas and solutions.

A Final Thought

"All your strength is in your union. All your danger is in discord..."

— Henry Wadsworth Longfellow

The ultimate success or failure to infiltrate new markets, secure new clients, expand opportunities with existing clients, increase market share and win new projects is profoundly influenced by a firm's ability to implement effective team-building strategies. Utilizing both scientific and artistic team-building strategies will greatly enhance a firm's ability to achieve ultimate success.

Ron W. Garikes, FSMPS

- Ron Garikes is senior vice president at Karlsberger.
- Twenty years of marketing and business development experience in the A/E/C industry.
- Lead international marketing efforts for the Karlsberger Laboratory and Technology Group.
- Responsible for the formation of more than 1,500 A/E/C project teams.
- Professional memberships: SMPS, ASHE, SCUP and AURRP.
- SMPS activities: past national president; southeast regional director; distinguished life member; fellow; SMPS Alabama Chapter: past president, charter member and Distinguished Service Award.
- Workshops and presentations:
  ⇒ **SMPS** – More than 40 programs at regional conferences and local chapters, including "Team Building/Partnering," "Market Trends," "Niche Marketing" and "The Marketing Plan."
  ⇒ **AIA** – "Profit by Specialization."
  ⇒ **NAWIC** – "Maximizing Your Marketing Effort."
  ⇒ **CSI** – "Construction Industry in 20 Years."
  ⇒ **Door and Hardware Institute** – "The Marketing Plan."
- Publications:
  Author of numerous A/E/C marketing-related articles for local, state, regional and national publications. Topics include "Niche Marketing," "Profit by Specialization" and "The Marketing Plan."

Acknowledgment

Special thanks to Robert S. Barnett, AIA, who authored the original chapter on joint ventures for the first edition of *The Handbook for Marketing Professional Services*.

3.3 Marketing the Design-Build Team

Betty Hearn, FSMPS
Business Development Manager
Carlson

Marketing the design-build team can be challenging and fun. There are many forms of design-build and each has many elements. The fun part is educating the client on the methodology while determining which method you think is right for the client's project. This has to be done in conjunction with selling the team or firm you represent. So the fun part is selling several services at the same time and changing the structure of the team as you progress. Before we can discuss how we market the team, a discussion and understanding of the ever-changing structure of design-build should be addressed.

History

Design-build remains controversial although it has been around for decades. There are stories of the early pyramids of Egypt and medieval churches of Europe being created through the design-build method. A GSA report documented the fact that "design-build is applicable to all types of projects, regardless of size or complexity, as long as the project's requirements are relatively known and stable." The use of design-build in both the public and private sectors has increased over 200% since 1986 to over $50 billion per year. The first year into the millennium, approximately 50% of all construction will be some form of design-build.

Design-Build Project Delivery commonly means that the single point of responsibility for both design and construction of a project is one entity in the prime contract with the Client (Owner). The Design-Builder Contract can have various provisions for performance, price and schedule, and some may have operations and/or maintenance responsibilities subsequent to commissioning of the project. The Design-Build Institute now has a design-build package available to include a contractual form much like the Architectural Institute of America standard form that has been used for years.

Projects that are large, complex, fast track, or just complicated in some way are ideal for design-build. Using the design-build method, problems that come with this type of project are worked out up front due to the emphasis placed on early and detailed planning. It is important for the marketer to be able to identify projects best suited for design-build. My first experience with this method of delivery was in 1953 when I watched (and sometimes was allowed to participate in) the raising of the family barn. My father was definitely the program manager. He did a lot of early programming: planning the stall for each animal, the storage for crops and an open flow for convenience in integrating the two. After carefully laying out the plan and estimating the cost of materials he discussed his plan with several family members, neighbors and friends who were going to participate in the construction. He considered their suggestions and made appropriate changes. Our barn was built in two days, within budget and with no change orders. Because I had helped with handing supplies and running errands, and did some intense negotiations up front, Dad split the savings with me at the end of the project. He had just enough lumber left to build a new doghouse for the animal closest to my heart.

Design-Build

The design-build industry has gained considerable popularity in the last few years, as more people become familiar with the concept. Design-build can be adapted to any project. It has a profitable place in the built environment. The industrial market carries the strongest support for design-build because of the nature of the building type. Most industrial projects have only the need to house what takes place inside. The exterior looks rarely matter. The owner or programmer can determine size, shape, internal basic needs and budget, giving the design-builder all the information he needs for his delivery method. Most design-build projects are not design driven but are more engineering and construction oriented. This methodology of building can **save a conservative owner about 30% in the overall cost of construction**. It does however put more responsibility on the owner for early planning input and involvement throughout the project, to strengthen the design.

When approaching a potential client about a project, mention that your firm has design-build capability. The potential client's reaction to this statement will direct your next move. If there is a strong negative reaction, drop the subject for the time and move on. You may want to research later the client's experience with design-build and try to establish what happened to cause the negative opinion. You can then address the situation or leave it alone. If you can successfully address the situation then give it a try but realize you are there to give the client what they want in services. If the potential client indicates a lack of knowledge about design-build, then it might be appropriate to offer a presentation on the subject. On the other hand, if you get a positive reaction, then more discussion can take place on the possibility of structuring the team and moving forward in the design-build process.

It is often suggested to the client who wants a traditional proposal but has an open attitude about design-build that the proposal be structured in the traditional method of delivery with an additional section addressing the design-build methodology. It should include a schedule that shows the client the savings in time, which is a strong selling point. This can also be done in a presentation, depending on which situation you are in with the client. Adding the design-build section to the proposal has two benefits: 1) It educates the client on time (money) savings and 2) it gives the client a choice in method of delivery. Figure 1 is a tool often used in demonstrating this idea:

Figure 1

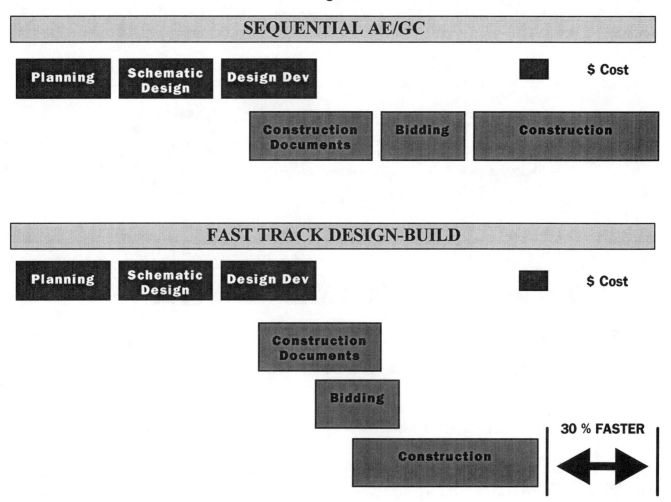

While my barn story is pretty basic in nature, it covers many of the aspects of design-build. Five points set design-build apart from other methods of delivery:

1. Single-source delivery
2. Fast track
3. Cost savings
4. Fewer change orders
5. Competitive purchasing of long lead items

These points should be discussed at length with the client/owner so they clearly understand the benefits of this delivery method. I often use storyboards for this and leave the boards up in the room for the client to refer to during the discussion.

There are three basic types of delivery methods. While our main focus is on the design-build, it is important to understand the design-bid-build and Construction Manager (CM) at Risk structure (See Figure 2):

Figure 2

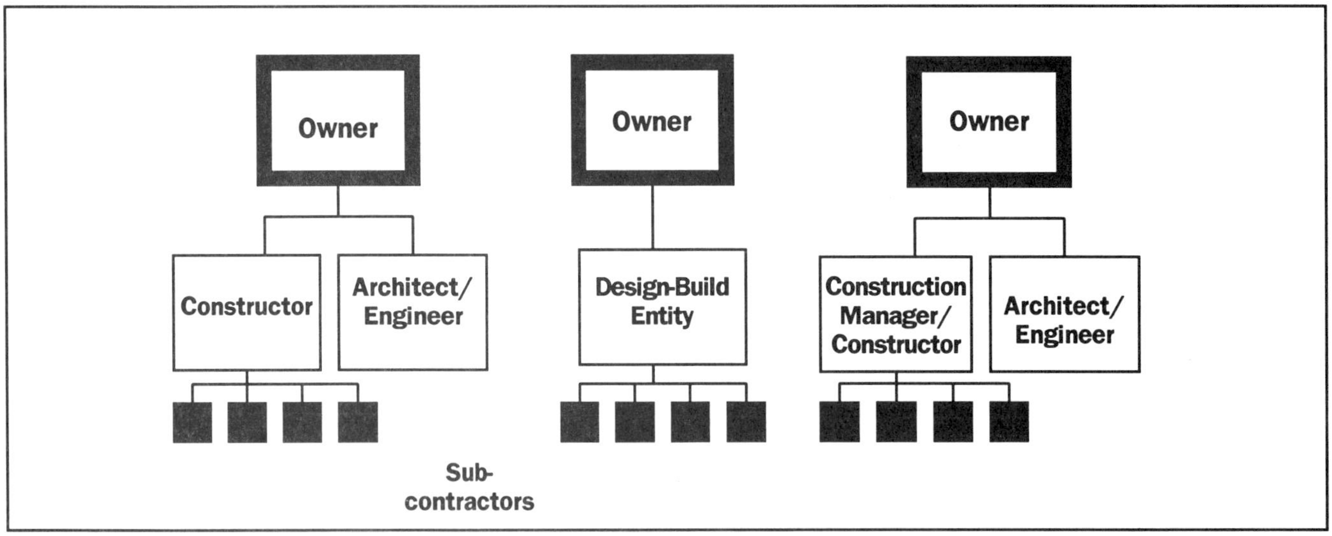

Design-Bid-Build   Design-Build   CM At Risk

Who Are Clients for Design-Build?

Basically, all owners are potential design-build clients. The private sector prevalently uses the design-build method of delivery. Owners who are design-conscious about their facility should be careful in selecting a firm for the design-build method. The multi-discipline design-build firm usually has a strong design (architectural) element that controls the project. This is difficult to find when the design-build team is organized through a general contractor. A large number of owners send Requests for Proposal for design-build projects to contractors. The contractor then assembles the architect and engineer to complete the team but it is typically managed through the general contractor. This method puts more emphasis on construction than design but is good if the major concern is cost. Full-service design-build firms have a better chance of having a more balanced emphasis on the project. If the client has concern about the design, they can always ask for the project manager to be selected from the architectural discipline. Since I personally am more design oriented, it is my opinion that a full-service firm is the ideal option for a true design-build project.

We would be remiss in leaving the developer out of this list (see Figure 3). So many major clients are into the developer lease-back arrangement which goes along with our current trend for outsourcing. This is a situation where design-build fits well, again depending on the type of facility. Certain facilities in the public sector are now being offered to design-build teams and sometimes through a developer in a lease back arrangement. Even large privately held corporate groups are choosing the developer lease back arrangement in order to build corporate campuses. The lease back arrangement frees up corporate money for more profitable investments and strengthens the bottom line figures on their financial reports.

Figure 3
TYPES OF PROJECTS BEST SUITED FOR DESIGN-BUILD

Industrial	Corporate Campus	Commercial Office
Large Complex Projects	Retail	Health Care
Mixed Use	Airports	Rapid Rail/Transportation
Fast Track Projects	Cargo Facilities	Multi-story Dwellings
Data, Call & Operation Centers	Reservation Centers	Information Technology
POP Sites	Broadcasting	Interior Renovations

Single Source

When a full-service firm is hired for a design-build project the program manager is the single point of contact. Having a **single source** of delivery can benefit the owner through accountability. All activities are handled through that single source. The program manager is familiar with other team members, having experience with them on similar projects. The most successful team will be a team that has worked together for years on projects. The team that is put together for one assignment will often have internal struggles because they are learning to work together for the first time. The day-to-day experience of working together has created a very efficient and cost-effective delivery process. Throughout the project, each discipline continuously challenges the other so that quality of the project and obligation to the client are never compromised. The design-build delivery makes the firm responsible for the project (at risk) and eliminates the possibility of finger pointing among firms if something goes wrong. This type of blame is prevalent with the more traditional approach where the client selects firms from each discipline. Most clients have experienced this type of behavior and will respond in a positive way to this selling point.

Guaranteed Maximum Price

Some owners prefer a single-source program management approach that makes it possible for a **guaranteed maximum price (GMP)** during the early design phases. The design-build firm **assumes the risk** so the client can proceed with funding approval and fiscal budgeting during the early stages of the project, rather than months later as is traditionally the case. If the firm is not supporting the client with all aspects of the project, it is not possible to provide a GMP. This form of design-build cuts back or eliminates change orders. Some firms build in a contingency to cover any unexpected expenses. Contingencies are often built into each phase of the project and can be moved around as needed during the process. It is always wise to define the scope exactly and tie the GMP to that defined scope. If the client/owner then changes the scope, the GMP can be adjusted accordingly.

Some studies indicate schedule savings can be between 10% to 30%, depending on the type and size of project. When the GMP is established in the early design stage, the owner and the design-builder sometime agree to become partners. The owner then becomes involved in expediting the permitting and regulatory review process. With this arrangement, they can at times split whatever difference there is in the savings at the end of the project.

In other scenarios, the client keeps the savings. In traditional methods, the general contractor keeps the savings. Savings can be achieved by overlapping the schedule to fast track the project, early purchase of supplies and equipment, and value engineering developed throughout the project. When the owner agrees to share his savings it is often on a 60/40 split with the design-builder. This can be negotiated at the time of contracting. The negative part of this arrangement can be that the project team can squeeze the project so tightly that the final product is of lower quality than the owner originally planned.

Pros & Cons

There are many terms used to describe forms of design-build projects: project management, CM at risk, design and construction, full service, turnkey, PM/CM, design and implementation and many others. Each delivery method offers different ways to create a team. Different geographic areas use different terminology to describe design-build. As stated earlier, it can be a great way of building if the situation is right. It provides considerable cost savings to the client but the client can lose control of the project very quickly. In presenting this method of delivery, make sure you include steps throughout the process where the client is included or involved in the project, such as weekly meetings, reports and computer programs where the client can review the daily posting of activities. You need to emphasize to the owner that they can have immediate contact with the program manager via telephone, cell phone or beeper.

Some of the most negative comments you will hear about design-build is "the fox in the hen house" syndrome or "who's watching out for the owner." The traditional method of delivery has the architect acting as the owner's agent to ensure compliance with the contract documents. The general contractor's role is accountability for the construction and construction cost of the project. With the design-build method, the design-builder is in charge of himself. This is a perceived problem to some owners but the cost savings and other benefits of design-build help to balance this negative perception. Two points help to elevate this negative syndrome: 1) Design-build is basically an extension of the client's internal team; and 2) the practice of an open-book approach leaves no secrets. Trust and integrity are a big part of this relationship. Any examples of these statements could be presented as a positive scenario before the client introduces the subject as negative.

Program Management

One major benefit of program management is the organizational infrastructure put in place to support the client's project manager or management team. The program manager is responsible for orchestrating all aspects of the project and for presenting the client with the information he needs to make decisions. **Open-book** competitive bidding, pre-qualification of trade contractors, guiding the design team, writing subcontracts and purchase orders and a host of other actions are all part of his responsibility. This single-source approach greatly enhances the client's program manager's ability to perform his job.

The strongest tool in selling a design-build project is your program manager. This is the daily contact person for the client over the life of the project. In describing this position, note I have included some personal traits that are unusual to find in a resume. You may want to use a standard resume then list the personal traits separately on a storyboard to talk about at the presentation. The only reason to list them in the resume (they could be on a separate sheet of paper attached to the traditional resume) or proposal is that they sometimes help the firm get on the shortlist. The program manager profile should fit a similar outline, emphasizing the following characteristics (you may come up with your own list):

Credentials/Resume: Education
Experience
Personality
Flexibility
Percentage of time allocated for this project
Management skills
Cost savings on similar projects
Ethics
Communication skills
Creativity
Quality control

The experience listed above should always relate to projects that are similar in nature to your client's project. You should find a place or situation to show the personality of this program manager (e.g., Halloween costume contest winner, office leader of entertainment, biggest joker in the office). This is difficult to create and difficult to get support from your firm, and especially from the program manager. Remember that this person will work with the owner daily and coordinate with the project architect, engineer and construction manager. The relationship is sometimes referred to as "a marriage." The flexibility of this person will be very important to the success of the project.

Including a paragraph in this person's resume that includes personality, flexibility, ethics and creativity can be most impressive. Show the client cost savings on previous projects this program manager managed. It shows credibility as well as good management. I often take the major monthly report of another similar project to show the open-book approach and what the client can expect from our team. Even if the client does not examine these reports, it expresses and promotes the feelings you want to create with the client: trustworthy, open, and communicative. Any other documents related to communication skills and creativity are helpful. Quality control methods or programs have become important to the client and are often tied to the type of owner financing available.

The program manager should be the lead in the presentation to the client. This enhances the chance for bonding with the client. The marketer should practice with this person privately. Eye contact with the client is an important point to emphasize. Use charts, storyboards, PowerPoint, overheads, models or whatever the person feels most comfortable using. It is more important for the program manager to be comfortable than what method is used. If the program manager prefers to sit during the presentation, structure the program around this preference. The program manager's position of leadership for the entire project (architecture, engineering and construction) can make or break the sale, especially in design-build. Remember this is the fox! Developing that trust level is important. Your job as the marketer is to pump this person up and make them feel the importance of their role in making this project successful for the client.

Fast Track

It often seems that all projects are fast track. Design-build firms make more money using this method of delivery and the owner saves more money. The key is early and near-complete planning for the project from all disciplines involved. This is why I feel it is better to have a full-service firm (A/E/C) doing the entire project. It saves time by having everyone in-house working together for the same goal. After a certain point the team leader can release the other members to resume work on other projects. These team members are still available for questions and working out situations on the project if needed but are not tied to the project unnecessarily.

Another way to fast track a project is to purchase the long lead items early. Even though they are purchased early these items are competitively bid, usually getting three bids per item. Steel is a major item with a long lead-time. It should be ordered early in the project — as soon as the scope is completely identified. Specialty equipment, power systems, heating and cooling systems and any technical equipment necessary to complete the project should be purchased through vendors with which the firm has established relationships. Ongoing relationships with vendors can help achieve better prices and facilitate corrections in equipment or products ordered if changes occur during the later process of the delivery.

Where to Find the Clients?

Design-build clients are in all the same places your regular clients are located. The largest following of design-build is in the private sector and the industrial markets. They are usually a more sophisticated client with knowledge of the building process or general construction. I have found that most clients either like or hate design-build. There are few clients that are borderline. I usually will attempt to change a negative attitude but find that, once this idea is implanted, it is difficult to change. The best tool is a trip to a similar project and a discussion with the owner of that project. As mentioned earlier, if a client has had a bad experience with design-build, I usually drop the design-build subject and sell the team with traditional delivery methods or just use different terminology.

The industries listed earlier are where I find most clients. There are lead sources that identify design-build projects and these are mixed into your regular lead sources: newspaper clippings, corporate financial statements, real estate groups, developers, state economic developers, lending institutions and your ever-loyal networking buddies. Most leads on design-build are found through large companies that use the design-build method. Once you have identified the company, try to penetrate their facility or construction departments. The One List is a great tool in finding the contacts for such a firm. The Internet has many resources for getting information such as financial, long-term plans and geographic areas of growth for companies and contacts. You can often find background information about the methods of delivery the company has used and with which firms they have worked.

There are certain words in a request for proposal, scope of services or article written on upcoming projects that lead me to believe they might be open to the design-build method. You have something to work with in selling design-build services if time is a factor, if they are having trouble matching scope with their budget, if there are many complex parts to the project or if there are many owners involved. Most of these concerns can be solved through the design-build methodology.

Involvement Through the Project

Marketers and business development managers should always stay involved throughout the project. This all goes back to relationships, trust, commitment and all the warm fuzzies we created along the way in selling the client. Let your client know that you are the point person in your firm. If the client isn't happy, someone had better know about it and be in a position to correct the situation. I feel so strongly about this involvement that I suggest the business development manager be placed on the organization chart as the client relation contact. This opens other doors about the empowerment of the business developer and how their title has significant influence with the client. Business developers should carry a title of importance — vice president, principal, director and/or manager — as long as it says to the client, "I can influence or make decisions within my firm." This is the point where certification could play an important role. If the business development person is not technical or a principal in the firm, how does the client know they have the ability to perform in this role? They can gain creditability through their association with the client by obtaining certification credentials. These credentials prove ability by a certified testing procedure. This helps to give you an upper hand in involvement throughout the project.

As mentioned earlier, most of the clients in design-build are from the private sector and the industrial market. If you are awarded a project and your involvement ends there, how will you get their next project in our competitive marketplace today? If you have the correct relationship with the program manager and they can pick up on the importance of information about a new project and if they relay it to you, then you might have a chance. I have never been fortunate enough to be in this situation. I suggest you stay involved. There are certain places during the project that are key spots to connect with the client. These should be discussed with the program manager so you will be included. I prefer to do this by attending a meeting where all the key players are present. If there are any adverse emotions present, I can pick up on them. Sometimes my technical people are not aware of any discomfort with the client because they are too close to the project and are not looking at the emotions from the client side. Catching a situation like this early during the project can turn it into a positive and successful project and increase repeat business. It is far more profitable to get repeat business than to develop a new client. The ratio is 5 to 1: It takes five times as much time and money to find a new client as it does to retain the existing one.

Involvement is not an easy thing to balance. It is fine with the client but internally it can be tough. You sold this project using all the adjectives you could think of about the program manager. Now you're going back to that person and telling them they have a problem with the client. It can be difficult, and finesse is the only way to handle it. You have to be good friends with that program manager and be very tactful but honest about the business situation. Developing reporting forms with the program manager early in the project can help in this situation. Also helping the program manager understand your role in the project is important. Work together and only go around the program manager when problems can not be resolved to the benefit of the client and your firm. You have a responsibility to the client and to your firm, so stay involved to drive the relationship with the client. It is also important to let the program manager manage the project; this is the role they have in the project. Your role is to stay involved in the customer satisfaction and public relations processes with the client. Sometimes it is easy to get overly involved and confuse these leadership roles.

When my firm is awarded a project, I meet with the client privately and let them know that I am the point person if they have any problems they can't resolve with the technical team. I let them know that I will not be as active with them during the project, as that is the role of the program manager, but I will check in with them from time to time. I also let them know that if they need me, they can call. This gives the client a comfort level with you and your firm about their project without taking away from the technical side. I try to spend time with the client that is not always focused on their project. If things are going well, why rock the boat? Just being there is enough to say, "I care and I'm here if you need me."

Another relationship building technique is to call the client every few weeks to see how things are progressing. This lets you stay in touch without being annoying. Send them newspaper clippings about similar projects or articles of interest to them. Most clients really appreciate this. When the project is finished get a debriefing to help with the next one. This is where you find out if your firm performed well enough on this project to be considered for the next one.

Fun

We stated at the beginning that selling a team and a method of delivery could be challenging and fun. Marketers love a challenge — and they are fun-loving people. Selling design-build services is indeed a challenge. It keeps many balls in the air simultaneously and it can take a different form at any given moment. You have to have a lot of concentration, a lot of involvement and a direct focus to sell the team and the delivery method. It takes a specialized professional firm to follow your sale and deliver what you promised. Marketing the design-build team takes knowledge and a comfort level for the different scenarios. For true success add to your knowledge creativity, flexibility and — most of all — a great sense of humor.

Betty S. Hearn, FSMPS

Betty Hearn has worked with professional services firms for over 20 years. She serves as business development manager for Carlson, a national, full-service design and implementation firm listed 16th in ENR's top 100 Design-Build Firms. She has served as principal, partner, director and manager of architectural and engineering service firms in Atlanta, GA, during her career. A former President of the Georgia Chapter of SMPS and a Past-President of SMPS National, she holds a Life Member Designation. Under her leadership as National President of SMPS, the Board of Directors inaugurated the Foundation and the certification program. She has authored many articles for the SMPS *Marketer*, conducted workshops and is often an invited speaker at national, regional and local SMPS meetings.

3.4   Proposals/Qualifications

Sheryl B. Maibach, FSMPS
Vice President
Barton Malow Co.

Introduction

As marketers, we are in the business of securing profitable work for our firm.   Proposals and qualifications help prospective clients determine what firm(s) they wish to hire.

It is rare that a proposal alone can secure a coveted project award.   Pre-selling the job with face-to-face meetings and relationship building — prior to qualifications or proposal submittal — is often the most important element in securing work. Still, in our industry, qualifications and proposals are a reality; we must create them efficiently and effectively.   To do that, we need to pose and respond to these questions:

- How can you weed out owner request for qualifications (RFQ) and request for proposals (RFP) that your firm has no business responding to?
- What tools or information do you need to produce high-quality documents?
- What can you do to make your submission special?

Answers to these important questions, and others, are covered in this chapter.

Organizing for Success

At least 90 percent of your proposals should make an owner's short list — it takes the same amount of time to prepare a winning proposal as it does to create one that falls short of the mark.   And improving your short list percentage conserves the time and patience of your busy marketing staff, and retains experienced team members who may otherwise tire of the pressures and leave your firm.

Low-winning percentages are often symptomatic of underlying procedural problems; getting organized reduces stress and proposal rework and results in a better product.   The following steps are suggested to improve the document planning and preparation process.   All will help you get "busy work" out of the way, and focus your efforts on addressing client needs:

- Create databases of frequently used information.
- Institute a formal "go, no-go" decision process.
- Follow a proposal work plan process.
- Strengthen your proposal leadership.

Proposal-Related Databases

If you are reinventing the wheel for each proposal, stop immediately and create a set of important tools: linked databases. After all, a large percentage of the information in proposals and qualifications (experience, resumes, past litigation, firm financial status, personnel count, awards and firm history, for example) is needed over and over again. Having information available on a marketing database at a moment's notice allows you to respond quickly and devote more time to project-specific RFP questions.

A staff person must be assigned to update information regularly. This task should have priority status on someone's job description and should not be left up to a marketing coordinator to do in "downtimes." Marketing databases will help reduce staff stress and overtime, speed up the learning curve of marketing personnel and enhance the quality of your proposal documents.

While databases can make your marketing department more efficient, be careful not to fall into the trap of your proposals reading like canned text. Custom writing is required to tailor answers to your client's needs.

The databases you need depend on your firm services. The following list will give you some ideas regarding possibilities for firms in the built industry.

Sample Marketing Databases

- Experience lists
- Reference letters
- Project photography
- Resumes
- Peer professionals
- Customer satisfaction statistics
- Client quotes
- Proposal text
- Statistics
- Graphics

Experience Lists

The experience list stores project information about current and completed projects, including project scope, owner, architect, contact people and services provided. It can be sorted by any of the field elements. FileMaker Pro software is commonly used for this type of database.

Reference Letters

Located within the experience list, the reference letter field indicates whether or not a given project has received a letter of reference from the project owner. It includes the date of the letter and refers the user to a file location where the hard copies of reference letters are stored. Some firms scan client reference letters and have them available electronically.

Project Photography

This database catalogues architectural photography stored electronically on compact discs. Sorting is possible by owner name, building type and specific building locations (kitchen, lobby, classroom, operating room, etc.).

Resumes

To maintain consistency of project cost and description information, it is helpful to link the resume database to the experience list database. Include the automatic calculation of an employee's total years' experience within the built industry, easily interchangeable project role descriptions and custom project sorting within each resume.

Peer Professionals Database

The names, mailing addresses and phone numbers of peer professional organizations your firm has done business with are maintained in this database. Like the personnel resume database, it is linked to the experience list to maintain consistency of project information. Firm names, addresses and phone numbers of peer professionals frequently change. Linking the databases means that when a change is made, all the information is updated at the same time.

Customer Satisfaction Statistics

This database contains customer satisfaction scores, a useful marketing tool. Each month, the database is updated with new scores for projects still in progress. Statistical proof of performance provides prospective clients with a third-party endorsement of your great service.

Client Quotes Database

A client-quote database for use in the margins of a proposal also gets endorsements across. Sort categories can be made by client name, market, building type or any grouping you choose. This is especially useful when the proposal you are preparing has strict page limitations and you cannot include an entire letter.

Proposal Text Database

Nothing is more frustrating than coming across RFP questions you know you have answered before but simply cannot find. A proposal text database is organized alphabetically by *subject* (cost control, project approach, scheduling, etc.) and not the name of the client.

At the conclusion of each proposal, cut and paste great answers into the proposal text database. Keep only the best answers. As you update proposal responses, delete the old and replace them.

Store all proposal text in the same format so information can easily be cut and pasted into a document without having to waste time reformatting.

A proposal text database is a powerful learning tool for junior marketing coordinators. It allows them to provide answers for proposals they could not have written themselves. It also allows them to learn by reading the text more experienced personnel have written. This database allows the firm to capture the writing talents of many in a central location to benefit the entire firm. And if one of your talented writers elects to leave the firm, some of his or her best writing stays.

Statistics

This database contains Excel files detailing numerical and statistical information for the following areas: human resources/employee headcount, firm financial and historical accounting numbers and industry ranking statistics. This information is updated on either a monthly or quarterly basis.

Graphics

Ready-to-use graphics and PowerPoint slides are stored by subject matter for use in marketing material. Useful marketing databases have accurate information that is easily accessible.

Weighing Opportunity: The "Go, No Go" Decision

Producing qualifications and proposals can be an expensive endeavor. Firms in the built environment are faced with limited resources and a desire to get the most return for their business development investment. Increasing the firm's win rate is high on the list of marketers' goals.

There are two ways to increase your firm's win rate: (1) Win more jobs or (2) Submit fewer proposals. Few marketing coordinators need the practice of creating documents for projects your firm doesn't have a prayer of winning.

One of the most difficult business decisions is saying "no" to a new project opportunity. Yet an evaluation of most unsuccessful submittals typically indicates that some emotional factor took precedence over sound business logic when the decision was made to pursue the project. One of the main reasons the "go, no go" decision is difficult is timing. Ideally, the decision should be made prior to pursuit of the opportunity. Unfortunately, at this early stage in the process, many of the determining considerations are still unknown.

Successful firms have developed a process to evaluate each RFP. Upon receipt of an RFP, think about the following strategic issues and weigh the project opportunity:

- Does the project meet specific marketing plan goals for profitability?
- Does the project mirror the firm's market-niche expertise?
- Are necessary personnel resources available to produce quality work?
- Does the project offer opportunity for repeat business?

To overcome the subjectivity of this process, use a "go, no go" decision form. Exhibit 1 on the next page contains a sample; you should create a form that reflects the priorities and strategic goals of your firm.

Exhibit 1. Go/No-Go Decision Form

**PROJECT
NAME:**_____   **DATE:**_____

**PROJECT
DESCRIPTION:**_____

ANTICIPATED CONTRACT VALUE:_____

COMPLETED BY:_____

Scale: 1 is poor, 4 is excellent

ISSUES	1	2	3	4	REMARKS
STRATEGIC ISSUES					
Does the project fall into our existing project niches?					
Are there expanded service opportunities?					
Does the project aid geographic expansion?					
Does the project help balance our market mix portfolio?					
Does the project have outstanding public relations value?					
CLIENT ISSUES					
Have we devoted time to pre-selling?					
Do we have experience with this client?					
Is the client financial position adequate?					
Does the project have a 60% chance (or better) of being funded?					
RISK ISSUES					
Is the contract form known to us at this time?					
Is the contract language reasonable?					
Has a risk analysis been conducted?					
Will we be able to limit our exposure to consequential damages?					
COMPETITIVE ISSUES					
Do we have similar project experience?					
Is a project manager available?					
If known "low-ball" competitors will be in the market, do we have a clear non-price advantage?					
Do we have experience with the Architect?					
TIMING ISSUES					
Are resources available to market, estimate, design and manage project?					
PRICING ISSUES					
Is the "real" and anticipated fee fair?					
Is price the primary selection criteria?					
Will we be able to be competitive in the local marketplace?					
Is there opportunity for additional fee on self-performed work?					

DESIGN/BUILD WORK					
Have the teaming subcontractors been identified?					
Do the Arch., Eng., subs and vendors with design responsibility have adequate E & O insurance?					
Will the selling fees be adequate to offset the added costs and risks of DB development?					
Is the cost of preparation in our business plan?					
Does the buyer understand design/build?					
CUSTOMER-DRIVEN DEVELOPER WORK					
Is the facility user a company we want to work for?					
Reputation of developer and its key personnel assigned to project.					
Financial condition of facility user.					
Financial condition of developer.					
Opportunity for enhanced fee for added risk.					
Developers capacity to pay for contract increases (e.g.: scope, force majeure, damages)					
Project scope is within funding amount					
Column totals					
TOTAL SCORE					

* Highest possible score for projects other than design/build or developer work is 88.
* Scores 50 and above indicate "Go" possibility.
* Scores below 50 indicate "No-go" status.
* Highest possible score for design/build projects is 108.
* Highest possible score for developer work is 120.

A firm principal or officer should review the RFP for non-standard insurance, bond requirements, indemnification, environmental concerns, hazardous materials, etc. If these conditions or requirements are present, legal counsel (for consequential or liquidated damages, damage clauses, environmental issues, indemnification issues, etc.) or the officer in charge of insurance and bonding should review the requirements. These conditions may influence a "go, no go" decision, and the costs or approach associated with these issues must be addressed in the development of the proposal.

The "go, no go" decision form should be filled out jointly with the salesperson and firm principal or operations officer who would have to deliver the work. Care should be taken to make a business decision and leave emotions out of the equation. If a "no go" decision is reached, contact the originator of the RFP and send a letter of regrets.

If a "go" decision is reached, begin the proposal-planning process. Forward a copy of the RFP and the completed "go, no go" decision form to the marketing department manager, who will assign a marketing coordinator to help develop the submission.

If critical project factors affecting the "go, no go" decision matrix should change at any point in the submittal process (such as a sample contract made public), re-evaluate the decision.

Joint Venture Teaming

It is common for firms in the industry to team up in pursuit of a project. The following teaming agreement (Exhibit 2) provides you with sample text to consider to ensure all parties understand their responsibilities during the pre-award marketing effort. Your legal counsel should draft language that protects your interests for any joint venture.

Exhibit 2. Teaming Agreement to Provide a Proposal

This Agreement is entered into by and between FIRM NAME and _____, both hereinafter designated at times jointly as "Participants" or individually as "Participant," to prepare a proposal ("Proposal") for _____ ("Project").

RECITALS

A. Both Participants have positive industry reputations. Recognizing the complimentary capabilities of each Participant, this Agreement is entered into to establish the Participants' mutual rights and obligations during the period of preparing, submitting and negotiating the Proposal, so as to result in a team for providing the client with the optimum combination of capabilities to achieve its Project objectives.

B. Upon the award of the Project to the Participants, they intend to negotiate in good faith a Joint Venture Agreement ("Joint Venture") to be executed by them for the purpose of entering into a contract with the client to perform the services set out in the Proposal, which will reflect the requirements of the Project.

TERMS AND CONDITIONS

1. Participants shall mutually compile and agree to a Proposal for the Project for submittal to the client and shall jointly agree in writing on all subsequent amendments and changes to the Proposal.

2. In the preparation of the Proposal each Participant shall utilize its personnel necessary to develop in a timely manner pertinent data including without limitation technical approach and analysis, resumes, research, company background and experience, necessary cost breakdown data, required certifications and other special requirements of client's request for proposal. Participants shall jointly prepare and mutually agree upon written materials for the Proposal and for use in the oral presentation of the Proposal.

3. Each Participant shall participate in the planning for the Proposal. In this connection, the Participants will more fully define the scope of services to be included in the Proposal and the portion which will be the responsibility of each Participant. The Participants shall sit together in working sessions during the period of this Agreement. At each session, each Participant shall fully inform the other of the progress of its work on the Proposal.

4. The Participants shall exert all reasonable and proper efforts to develop and submit a competitive proposal to the client including the above scope of services.

5. The Participants shall deal exclusively with each other with the object of obtaining the award of the contract for the Project. Neither of the Participants without the written consent of the other, either

directly or through any subsidiary or affiliated company, will enter into or negotiate any contracts for any construction management, or program management services, or any construction or consulting services in connection with the Project, except pursuant to the Proposal which is the subject of this Agreement.

6.   Each Participant represents to the other that it will employ no personnel which, because of a conflict of interest, may make it undesirable, illegal or impossible to proceed with the Proposal for obtaining the contract for the Project or to perform such contract if awarded pursuant to the Proposal of the Participants.

7.   Each Participant shall bear its own costs incurred in preparation of the Proposal, except that Proposal printing costs and similar jointly used items of cost shall be shared on a pro rata basis.

8.   Each Participant shall supply the other throughout the period of preparation and presenting of the Proposal with information and copies of materials and documentation prepared by it ("materials") relating to the Proposal and Project. All such information is considered confidential by the Participant providing same. The Participants agree that _____ shall manage the proposal/presentation process.

Neither Participant shall, without the prior written consent of the Participant, use the other's information or materials for any purposes other than the preparation, submission and presentation of a Proposal under this Agreement. The Participant receiving confidential information shall protect such information utilizing the same controls such Participant employs to avoid disclosure of its own confidential information. Disclosure of confidential materials and information may be made to the client.

Upon the termination of this Agreement in accordance with its terms, each Participant will, within a reasonable period of time thereafter, return all materials and information received from the other Participant under the terms of this Agreement.

This Agreement does not offer or grant to the receiving Participant any rights in, or license to use, any drawings, data, plans, ideas or methods disclosed pursuant to this Agreement except in connection with the Proposal and its presentation to the client.

9.   This Agreement shall terminate when any of the following events occur, without further obligation or liability between the Participants:

A. By mutual agreement of the Participants,

B. Upon rejection of the Proposal or the public disclosure that the requirements for the Project have been canceled or that the contract for the Project has been awarded to another party, or

C. Upon negotiation, execution and delivery of a Joint Venture Agreement between the Participants for the Project, to the extent provided therein.

10. Each Participant represents that it has full authority to enter into this Agreement, to make the Proposal to obtain a contract and to enter into a joint venture to perform the contract.

11. Nothing in this Agreement shall grant to any Participant the right to make commitments of any kind for the other Participant without prior written consent of the other Participant.

12. No news releases, including photographs and films, public announcement or confirmation shall be made by a Participant concerning the subject matter of this Agreement without the consent of the other Participant and client first obtained.

13. Neither Participant shall have any liability to the other arising out of this Agreement in the event the client does not award a contract to the Participants except with respect to the obligation of each Participant to pay a pro rata portion of the costs as provided in section 7.

14. All notices, requests, demands and other communications required or permitted hereunder shall be deemed to have been duly given if delivered or mailed by certified or registered first class mail with postage prepaid, or sent by facsimile or other electronic transmission (confirmed by such first class mail provided that the failure to so confirm shall not affect the validity of such communications) addressed as follows:

TO:	YOUR FIRM NAME	TO:	[Insert Company Name]
	Attention:		[Attention:]
	ADDRESS		[Address:]
	CITY, STATE, ZIP CODE		[Address:]
	FAX NUMBER		[Telefax:]

15. The Participants intend to add other members to the Proposal team as consultants. Those consultants will be mutually agreed upon by the Participants. It is anticipated that they will participate in the Proposal process at no expense to the Participants.

16. Upon the award of the Project to the Participants, they shall promptly negotiate in good faith, execute and deliver to each other a Joint Venture Agreement which shall provide that the Joint Venture is formed to enter into a contract with the client to perform management services for the Project in accordance with the Proposal. The compensation to be received by each of the Participants for performing the work of the Joint Venture shall be equally shared and shall be a fixed 50 percent of the profit or loss from the performance of the contract. The Joint Venture will treat all actual costs and expenses (including direct personnel expenses and consultants) as a cost of the work. The amount of compensation received over the total costs of the work will be considered profit, which will be equally shared by the Participants. Should the amount of compensation received be less than the total cost of the work, the loss will be shared equally by the parties, and each party will indemnify the other for losses in excess of their 50 percent share.

17. This Agreement may be executed in one or more counterparts, all of which together shall constitute one and the same instrument. This Agreement shall become effective when a counterpart has been signed by each party.

18. Neither this Agreement nor any of the rights, interests and obligations hereunder shall be assigned or delegated without the prior written consent of the other party.

19. This Agreement shall be governed by and construed in accordance with the laws of the State of
_____.

IN WITNESS WHEREOF, the parties hereto have caused this Agreement to be executed by their respective officers duly authorized as of the _____ day of _____, 20____.

FIRM NAME	FIRM NAME
a _____ corporation	a _____ corporation
By: _____	By: _____
Title: _____	Title: _____

Proposal Planning Process

An organized proposal development process begins immediately upon a "go" decision. A work plan is the foundation of early, careful proposal development; it will help to produce an effective document with little rework. It will help ensure that all people involved in creating the proposal understand their task assignments and deadlines. Customize a work plan form to reflect your services and how your firm assigns proposals and qualifications.

A work plan is most effective when individual assignments are discussed by the proposal development team and there is shared ownership to meet deadlines. The work plan is completed at the proposal planning meeting.

Proposal Planning Meeting

The marketing director is responsible for determining who should be involved with proposal development and setting up a proposal planning meeting. It is generally productive to invite these participants:

- Operations officer or principal.
- Account director or salesperson.
- Project architect or manager.
- Lead estimator, if required.
- Joint venture (JV) team members, if applicable.
- Proposal coordinator.

It is helpful to distribute a copy of the RFP and proposal-meeting planning agenda to involved staff prior to the proposal planning meeting.

Agenda items should include the following:

- Discuss owner requirements.
- Discuss and list your firm's competitive advantages.
- Discuss competitors and their strengths and weaknesses.
- Determine if any business utilization (MBE/DBE/WBE, etc.) or EEO/affirmative action is required by the owner or a government agency, or if the use of an MBE/DBE or WBE firm(s) would give the firm a competitive advantage.
- Identify project team members.
- Determine whether or not it is necessary to create a project budget, cost model, schedule or project management plan.
- Identify a proposal theme.
- Review RFP questions and determine who will answer each specific question. Complete the Proposal Work Plan form (See Exhibit 3, page 193).
- Establish deadlines for all proposal development activities allowing for sufficient review and editing time.
- Determine if there are unique project insurance or bonding needs that require a certificate from an insurance carrier or a letter from your bonding company.
- Identify scope and approach for required design or estimating efforts.
- Review Proposal Page Layout (Exhibit 5, page 200) and Resume Format (Exhibit 6, page 202), especially if joint venture partners are involved.
- Firms that track marketing expenditures by project should take out a marketing job number and communicate the account number to participants in order to track proposal expenses.

Exhibit 3. Sample Proposal Work Plan

PROJECT NAME: _____ DATE: _____

COMPLETED BY: _____

RFP Distribution List:

1. _____
2. _____
3. _____
4. _____

Points to Emphasize:

1. _____
2. _____
3. _____
4. _____

Person	Task	Due Date	Completed
	Design schedule		
	Management plan		
	Construction schedule		
	DPE plan		
	Staffing plan		
	Safety plan		
	Cost model/estimate		

Joint Venture Information:

Is this project a joint venture?   Yes ☐   No ☐

List names of JV partner(s), percentage of contract, phone number and contact person.

JV Name	Contact Person	Phone #	Phone #

Proposal Copies

Total number of copies: _____

_____ In-house   _____ Main Office

_____ Client

Proposal Delivery

☐ Federal Express

☐ Hand Delivered by: _____

☐ Other _____

Copies of the completed proposal work plan should be distributed to all people who attend the proposal-planning meeting and others who are assigned tasks. The proposal coordinator should update the work plan every few days and send it via e-mail to proposal participants, so all can monitor progress.

The marketing director must demonstrate leadership to ensure that team members understand how their efforts contribute to a quality document. The RFP may require project-specific information from respondents — for example, a cost model, schedule or project approach — or an evaluation of technical project elements requiring the participation of operations and technical personnel. Good leadership means that everyone called upon for participation will contribute the necessary information in a timely manner. A proposal coordinator should never have to beg for information.

Proposals should be approached just like a project. Firms would not think of embarking on a project without a schedule or matrix of responsibilities. And yet they routinely approach proposals, a critical component of winning work, without enthusiasm or a defined process. *The proposal process is important to the lifeblood of your organization.* Insist on a proposal-planning meeting and a written proposal work plan; the marketing director should hold people accountable for assignments.

Identifying the Project Team

The success of your firm in delivering services and meeting customer expectations is largely based upon the composition of your team and the ability of project team members. Depending on the nature of the RFP, the contracting structure and services required, selection of the project team may involve members from your staff and also joint venture personnel.

Review project requirements and develop an understanding of the talent and qualifications that are needed. Criteria should include the following:

- **Market type experience:** health, automotive, education, stadium, etc.
- **Project complexity:** highly sophisticated versus simple.
- **Contract type:** at-risk versus non-risk.
- **Services offered:** architectural design, building design, construction management or consulting.
- **Project location.**
- **Political connections.**
- **Experience with associated team members:** architect/engineer, prime contractor, etc.

Review personnel availability with human resources to get a complete picture of whom in the firm is available for a new assignment. Human resources can review the training/skills matrices for candidates to determine strengths and weaknesses for the project assignment and identify training needs. Final selection of project team members should take into consideration personality fit with the owner and other team members, as well as any special requests made by the owner. Develop a preliminary organization chart for the project that features reporting relationships, key project positions and the names of individuals assigned to each position on the team.

Creating a Memorable Proposal

Competitive Advantage

The objective of a proposal or qualification submission is to convince owners that your firm is the best choice to meet their needs.

Before you begin assembling information for your submission, write down your firm's *unique* competitive advantages. A competitive advantage is something your firm can offer over another firm. Once you have established your competitive advantages, use every opportunity to reinforce these points in your submission.

Owner-Centered Content

It is important to do your homework and find out what the owner needs and wants. If your proposal or qualification submission is focused on issues that are meaningful to the owner, and clearly presents the benefits the client will gain by hiring your firm, you are on your way to securing a contract.

Test material you include in your submission against these critical questions:

- Is the material relevant to the project?
- Does this material reinforce our competitive advantages?
- Is this material written in terms the owner can understand?
- Are the benefits to the owner clear?

Proposal Theme

Great books and plays have strong themes. So do proposals. What was *Hamlet* about? It was about the consequences of indecision. Take a look at your last proposal. Is the theme evident? Is it clear what the proposal is about? A theme will provide unity and coherence to your proposal. Without one, your proposal will appear disjointed and lose impact.

An effective theme has the following characteristics:

- Brings clear value to the owner.
- Is provable by data or testimonials.
- Is believable to the owner.

GREAT themes include something your firm *alone* can offer above competing firms and the client must believe only you can do it.

Proposal Schedule

It is important that proposals be completed efficiently and that client requirements are fulfilled. The following instructions are intended to provide a framework for timely and thorough proposal completion:

- Arrange for long lead items and/or specialized materials (e.g., bonding or banking letters, logos, custom binders or tabs).
- If it's a joint venture project, send partner(s) a list of questions they need to answer and request logos/graphs/photos that are needed. Forward the Proposal Page Layout (Exhibit 5) and Resume Format (Exhibit 6) to JV partner(s).
- Proposal coordinator should review the proposal database and select the answer that best answers each RFP question, and tailor that answer for the project type.
- Through interviews, Internet, firm resource library, etc., research and write new text for RFP questions that have not been answered in the past.
- Gather answers being prepared by other people. Edit these answers and insert into the proposal document.
- Make sure that the text is complete, proofed, spell-checked and fully responsive to the RFP questions.
- Tailor resumes to the project, cross-reference project costs to experience list figures. Verify the resume title matches the organization chart position. Read through the document to make sure that the text tells a consistent "story" that addresses the owner's specific project requirements.
- Submit the document draft to the designated team representative(s) for review. Incorporate changes and review the revised document; re-submit for review, if required, and make any new changes.
- Arrange for help, if necessary, in printing, copying, collating and shipping the approved document.
- Obtain final approval from the operations officer and obtain signature for the cover letter.
- Follow up with the person who hand-delivered the package or shipping company to confirm that the package was received by the owner.
- Copy the new proposal answers and place in the proposal database .
- Log the master proposal copy in the proposal log and file the document in the proposal files.

A Proposal Check List (Exhibit 4) can help make sure production tasks do not fall through the cracks.

Exhibit 4. Proposal Check List

PROJECT
NAME _____

DATE: _____

COMPLETED BY: _____

☐ Read RFP (Request for Proposal)
☐ Identify project team
☐ Set up proposal-planning meeting
☐ Hold proposal-planning meeting and complete proposal work plan
☐ Send the work plan to everyone who must submit information. Include:
  • information needed
  • deadline
☐ Draft a proposal table of contents
☐ Create proposal cover and tabs
☐ Type in RFP questions
☐ Check proposal text database for appropriate answers
☐ Gather information from sources and assemble answers in document
☐ Distribute draft proposal to editor for review
☐ Make corrections/changes
☐ Distribute draft proposal to operations officer for review
☐ Final changes
☐ Copy and bind
☐ Get required signatures
☐ Deliver/send
☐ Verify that proposal was received

Production Tips

☐ Make color copies early
☐ Copy sections as they are ready
☐ Have mailing label, box, label, etc., ready

Proposal Close Out

☐ File proposal electronically and enter in proposal log
☐ Enter new proposal text information into database
☐ Distribute in-house proposal copies to team personnel
☐ Send proposal copies to JV team members

Proposal Elements

Proposal Cover

The proposal cover should be about the owner, not about your firm. The cover must draw the owner's attention to your submittal. If six proposals are sitting on a table, you want the owner to pick up your submission first. Make the cover emotional to spark the owner's interest and launch your proposal on a positive note.

Cover Letter

Limit the cover letter to one page. Focus on your *unique* competitive advantages. Use the cover letter to highlight the key points in your proposal. Use personal pronouns to help owners feel that they are getting personal attention. Remember, you are writing to people just like you. The human connection is as important as the qualifications you bring to the table.

Executive Summary

An executive summary highlights the main points of your submission in a few pages. Write the executive summary first, and make sure your submission contents accurately reflect the summary. A good executive summary will provide the owner with sound business reasons to select your firm.

Submission Format

Follow the format outlined in the RFP or the RFQ. Many clients use an evaluation form that mirrors the RFP or RFQ outline. A sure way to annoy the evaluator is to answer questions out of order.

Answer all questions. Skipping questions sends up a red flag to the evaluator that your firm does not have expertise or experience in a specific area or you do not know the answer.

Use tabs to separate the different proposal sections as indicated by the RFP. Section tabs "establish a rhythm" to the proposal, and make it easier for the reader to find areas of interest.

Page Layout and Text

If you are still using the old standard one-inch side margins for submissions, stop immediately. The most readable proposals or qualifications have text running four inches or *less* across the page with graphics in side margins or within the text (Exhibit 5, page 200). The magic of word processing allows for creativity. Use pictures and charts in lieu of words to enhance reader retention.

Include the proposal questions, in bold or italic, before each answer to keep the reader focused on your proposal. When RFP questions are not included, the reader must refer to the RFP, which is distracting and difficult to follow.

Clear, concise writing is essential. Make sure your submission is proofread more than once. If you preach total quality management in your submission and fail to catch errors in spelling and grammar, your credibility goes down the drain.

Address all the RFP requirements, regardless of how insignificant they seem to you. Give owners what they ask for, not what you think they should want. Spell out the benefits of your approach and services so the client cannot help but see them. Substantiate all your claims with facts.

Give proposal raters the ammunition they can use to defend their decision to hire your firm to their management.

Exhibit 5. Proposal Page Layout

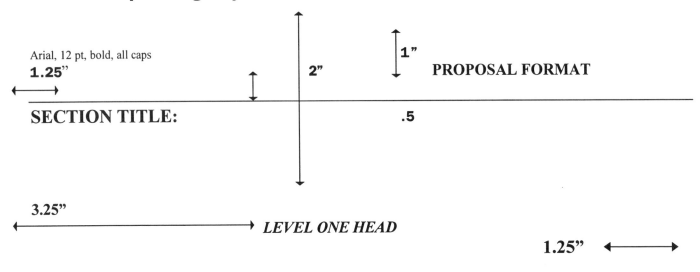

Arial, 12 pt, bold, all caps
1.25"

2" 1" **PROPOSAL FORMAT**

SECTION TITLE: .5

3.25"

LEVEL ONE HEAD

1.25"

Level 2 head

Normal text, normal text norm

Styles:
Level 1 Head - Times New Roman 12 pt, bold, italic, all caps
Level 2 Head - Times New Roman 11 pt, 13.2 lead bold, italic
Normal - Times New Roman 11 pt, 13.2 lead, justify

←→ .25"
- Normal text, normal text normal text normal text normal
- Normal text, normal text normal text normal text normal
- Normal text, normal text normal text normal text normal
- Normal text, normal text normal text normal text normal

Normal text, normal text normal text normal text normal text normal text normal text normal text normal text normal text normal text normal text normal text normal text normal text normal text normal text normal text

Normal text normal text normal text normal text normal text normal text normal text normal text normal text normal text normal text normal text

Normal text normal text normal text normal text normal text normal text normal text normal text normal

*NOTE: Please do not use spaces in place of tabs. Also do not use caps lock key for all caps, use style sheet

.5"

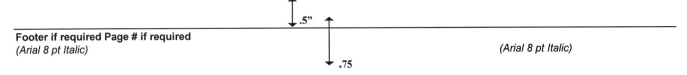

.75

Pictures and Graphics

Research conducted at the University of Minnesota has proven that pictures and graphics help increase reader retention by 300 percent. Effective use of photography can be a very powerful tool. Software today makes it easy to incorporate graphics, client quotes, architectural photography and owner graphics into marketing material. Take advantage of this software and incorporate visuals where appropriate to enhance your message to the owner. Rest assured your competitors are using visuals even if you aren't.

Proposal pictures say a thousand words if they are of good quality and *relevant*. Do not put industrial or commercial photos in a proposal for an education owner. Use discipline and stay focused on relevant graphics and architectural photography.

Visuals allow you to "show" instead of "tell." Avoid sweeping generalities like: "Our team brings extensive experience to the project." Instead, *show* your experience by including photos of similar projects and bullet the benefits you brought to the client.

Resumes

If possible, keep resumes to *one* page and highlight the following information:

- Project role description.
- *Relevant* experience.
- Special registrations/certifications.
- Educational background.

If you include a consultant resume, put the resume in your format and indicate that the individual is a consultant. Be aware that many firms use the same consultant. If one firm tries to claim a consultant as an employee, and the next firm indicates that the person is a consultant, guess which firm gains credibility for being honest? Refer to Exhibit 6 on the next page for a sample resume format.

Relevant project experience is the key. Do *not* list extraneous experience if at all possible. If you are pursuing a hospital project, leave off the project manager's experience on a famous Disney resort. No doubt the project is the pride and joy of the proposed project manager; however, it will come across as "Mickey Mouse" to the selection committee.

Exhibit 6. Resume Format

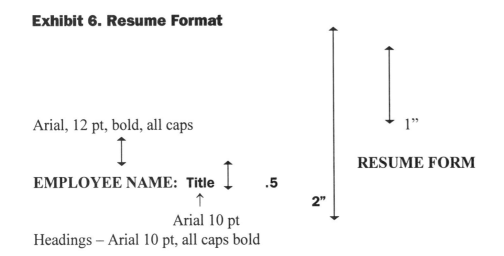

Arial, 12 pt, bold, all caps

EMPLOYEE NAME: Title ↕ **.5**

↑
Arial 10 pt

Headings – Arial 10 pt, all caps bold

PROJECT ROLE: List project role here

Brief description of individual's role or job responsibilities→→**Justify**

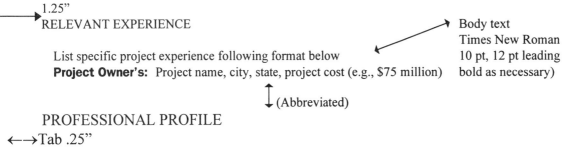

1.25"
RELEVANT EXPERIENCE

List specific project experience following format below
Project Owner's: Project name, city, state, project cost (e.g., $75 million)

Body text
Times New Roman
10 pt, 12 pt leading
bold as necessary)

↕ (Abbreviated)

PROFESSIONAL PROFILE
←→Tab .25"

Brief paragraph, including:

Years in construction industry, years with company
Other relevant experience
Specific areas of expertise (field management, mechanical, controls, safety, accounting, estimating, etc.)
Specific building-type expertise (Sports facilities, hospital, schools, etc.) 1.25"←→

EDUCATION, LICENSES and APPLICATIONS

Degree(s)
Registration(s)
Professional/Organization Affiliations
Awards
Works published
Professional presentations

.5"

1'

Experience List

If the owner requests that you list manufacturing experience, that is exactly what you should provide. Discipline is important. If the RFP clearly asks for firms to list five relevant projects, list only five. And then go the extra mile. Smart firms will list five projects and then highlight a similarity between the owner's project and each project listed.

Tough Questions

Answer questions directly, without hype. The shorter the answer, the better. Selection committee members love one-word answers. *Will your project manager attend weekly team meetings?* Yes.

The best way *not* to have your answer read is to put it in four or more paragraphs. Use bullets in lieu of paragraphs when possible. Do *not* refer the reader to another section (see section three) in your proposal to find an answer. Proposal rating forms typically follow the outline in the RFP. Make it easy for the rater to find the answer to each question.

What is your policy regarding errors or omission in plans and specifications? How many hours per week will you commit to site visitations during construction? You must provide straightforward answers to tough questions. Many highly qualified firms stumble by trying to beat around the bush. For example, "biweekly site visits are contemplated." This is not a quantifiable answer. Be honest and *specific*. If the owner is confused by your answer, ratings tend to go down.

What is your proposed fee, stated as a percentage of construction costs, for each of the projects (A, B and C) you are interested in? Most firms will answer this question by providing a fee for *all* the work. Smart firms will provide compensation options (fees for A + B, A + C, B + C, and so on). When owners ask for individual fees on multiple projects, they are often considering breaking down the total program into more than one contract. You can increase your odds of at least getting a part of the work if you are flexible.

Selection committee members are tolerant when firms provide more information than requested on project-specific questions. For example: What is your understanding of our needs? What is your approach for involving owner staff personnel in the design process for the new training facility? On non-project-specific questions, such as firm credentials, service and experience, provide only the information requested. And keep it short.

Conditions on fees or other items listed in the proposals are perceived negatively. For example, some firms list the cost of reports and documents required for owner design approvals and governmental agency approvals as an additional expense. Interestingly, these firms tend to have the lowest fees, but are often removed from the short list because owners think they are going to get nickel-and-dimed to death.

Editing

It is common for a number of employees to contribute to the proposal effort. That means many different writing styles, and possibly, a wide range of writing talent. An editor is needed to craft the document into a single voice and to ensure that the proposal theme is honored in each section of the proposal, regardless of who wrote it.

Proposal accuracy has a direct reflection on the credibility of your firm. Having a technical writer on staff can be a wise investment. Owners with multimillion-dollar projects don't want to see proposals littered with errors. Use your word processor spell-check and grammar functions. Make sure your proposal is edited before it goes into printing production.

Winning Elements

The highest-rated proposals can be half the size of losing proposals. Quality, not quantity, is the key to success. The worst offender is canned text. Very few people (if any) actually read the canned material, especially the *pages* of text that explain your services. Simply list your services with bullets, and provide a short paragraph for each that explains the benefit to the owner.

The common denominators among winning proposals are listed below — and should *all* be presented in a memorable, readable fashion:

- Honest, straightforward answers.
- Snappy graphics.
- Clear understanding of the owner's needs.
- Experienced project team.
- Owner benefits clear.
- Solid qualifications.

Winning submissions are fun to read, with wonderful graphics, short answers and no inflated credentials. And most importantly, the benefits the owner will gain by hiring your firm are crystal clear.

Continuous Learning

Firms faithfully debrief after a presentation and routinely miss an opportunity to learn from the proposal process. Win or lose, conduct an interview with a member of the selection committee to determine the merits and shortcomings of your proposal. If you don't ask, you miss a golden opportunity to enhance future proposals.

Sample proposal debriefing questions:

- Did the executive summary highlight key points?
- What was the proposal theme?
- Did we communicate an understanding of your needs?

- What were our competitive advantages?
- What benefits would you gain by hiring our firm?
- Was material easy to find?
- What did you like best about the winning proposal?
- What could we do differently next time to earn a higher rating?

Share the results of the proposal debriefing with your team members so everyone can be smarter the next time around.

Celebrate Your Success

Creating proposals day after day can be tedious work, especially under demanding deadlines. Make a special effort to celebrate your wins and reinforce the good work of your proposal team. An appreciated and motivated team produces better work. And since this is all about winning work, anything you can do to enhance proposal quality is worthwhile.

Bibliography

Barton Malow Company. *Proposal Development.* Southfield, MI: Quality Operating System Documents, 1999.

Campbell, John M. "Make It Clear," *Technology Century* (Jan. 1999): 36-39.

Cohen, Janet. Personal interview. 26 August 1999.

Kotler, Philip, and Paul N. Bloom. *Marketing Professional Services.* Englewood Cliffs, N.J.: Prentice-Hall, 1998.

Henshall, Ruth, and Meredith Bena. *Proposals.* Alexandria, VA: Society for Marketing Professional Services, Core Series, 1991.

Safford, Dan. *Proposal Writing Tips & Techniques.* Vashon, WA: PS Associates, Inc. Summer, 1997.

Sheryl B. Maibach, FSMPS

- Sheryl Maibach, FSMPS, is a fellow in the Society for Marketing Professional Services (SMPS) and vice president of marketing for Barton Malow Co. Barton Malow is a national design and construction services firm with six offices. She is a graduate of the University of Michigan and has more than 20 years of marketing experience in the built environment.

- Maibach is past president of the SMPS Michigan Chapter and served for three years on the national board of directors. She has served as SMPS National Foundation president and championed the original *SMPS Marketing Handbook* and this revised edition published in 1999.

- Maibach has written and published 23 marketing articles and is a frequent guest speaker on marketing-related topics.

Education

- Fellow, Society for Marketing Professional Services.
- University of Michigan, School of Business Administration, Management Program Graduate.
- University of Michigan, bachelor's degree; triple major in business, communications and history.

3.5 Winning Presentations

Janet S. Sanders, Ph.D., CPSM
Clayton Consulting Group

"It's yours to lose." That's the message when you discover your firm made the short list for a project. All your earlier client cultivation, marketing, and sales efforts got you on that list, acknowledging that your firm can do *what* the client desires. The final phase of the client's decision process determines *whom* they want to do it, and that takes face-to-face communication in a presentation. Only one team will win — the team that does the best job of selling its message and itself. Everyone else loses.

This chapter highlights the three basic elements of winning presentations — strategy, structure, and style.

Strategy

Sell, Don't Tell

The purpose of the presentation is to sell the decision-makers on why they should select your firm, not to tell them about your firm or that your firm can do the project. Telling got you to the presentation; selling is what will win it.

Telling how your firm approaches programming, design, project management, or construction usually doesn't sell. While some firms have innovative labels for a task, function, or project phase, face it: everyone in the industry does about the same thing. You're not giving the client a reason to select you if you're saying the same thing as everyone else.

Even those firms with a truly unique wrinkle on some aspect of work should think twice about spending much time telling the client how they do what they do so uniquely. Generally, the client cares more about the outcome of our process than its inner workings.

What does sell is talking about what your firm will do to program, design, manage, or construct the client's specific project, and stressing how what you'll do will be to the client's advantage. Describe your approach in project-specific terms, stressing how the process and results will benefit the client. Emphasize what you're going to do for *them,* rather than what you do in general.

Creating that project-specific content requires good in-depth information about the project, accurate understanding of the client's needs and desires, and savvy advance work in developing the specific project approach. Marketing wizards generally can't transform stale boilerplate into targeted fresh text, nor can they make up a highly project-specific yet innovative technical approach. The *sine que non* for winning presentations is solid, substantive content reflecting the firm's genuine discriminators focused upon the client's true needs. Without that content, a presentation will be some semblance of dogs and ponies cavorting with smoke and mirrors.

Sell What Will Win the Job

Some firms have a standard approach to presentations: An executive opens and says the team is happy to present its credentials. The firm's history is recounted and a string of comparable projects is listed. The team is introduced; the project approach is described in detail and various people who'll handle aspects of it explain their processes and describe their experience. The executive asks for the work and closes. Sound familiar? If we've heard it before, certainly the client has. When you not only say what the competition says but also say it in the same format, you're definitely not on the winning track.

The strategy for every presentation will be different and must be tailored to the idiosyncrasies of your team, your competition, the client, the job and the selection panel — not quick and easy but necessary to win. Advance intelligence gathering, what the military calls "G2," is the most important step in creating a winning presentation.

Clients select firms based on their specific needs, goals, preferences, and constraints. If you don't know those things, you don't know what you must present to convince the client to select your firm. Telling about you doesn't sell them on selecting you; selling your firm's solutions to meet the client's own needs, goals, preferences, and constraints does.

Based on your firm's G2, identify at least two (in case the client rejects one) and no more than five (because most minds can't cope with more than five ideas simultaneously) *strategic selling points.* Think of these points as the client's reasons to select your firm and *only* your firm. If the competition would list the same points, you know that either your G2 isn't deep enough or you haven't sufficiently differentiated your firm. Or maybe your firm *isn't* the best one for the job!

Those selling points will be the major topic areas of your presentation and almost everything else said during the presentation should support them. If your firm's history isn't a strategic selling point there's no reason to use precious minutes retelling the stirring saga of its founding and growth. Unless you really expect the client to be sold by an in-depth explanation of the seventeen elements of effective project management, don't let the project manager give that explanation.

The presentation shouldn't repeat the proposal. Most proposals are ordered and organized to "answer the mail" of an RFP, and to make it easy for a reader to compare the response with the RFP requirement and compare one firm's response with others'. Most proposals go into detail that would bore decision-makers if it were recited. Most proposals include graphics that are too complex to be usable or even visible if converted to presentation visuals. An oral presentation is a person-to-person communication setting. To be effective, information, organizational structure and graphics must be appropriate to that communication setting, which usually means that they must be different from those used in the written text medium.

Essentially, the only thing that counts is this: How will your team *better* satisfy the client's needs and provide *more* and better specific benefits to the client than will the competition? Remember — talk more about them (the client) and their needs than you and your history and features.

Schedule for Presentation Development

When do you begin work on the presentation's strategy? As early as possible is the easy answer. Faced with the pragmatics and logistics of most pursuits, start working on the presentation strategy the day after the proposal is submitted. *Don't* wait until short-list notification if you believe your firm probably will be short-listed. Build the presentation schedule working backward from the anticipated delivery date.

The presentation schedule will be driven by the time required to develop the strategy and the content and visuals that will support it. In my experience, the absolute bare minimum for a decent effort is one full day strategizing, another developing the bullet point outline and storyboarding the visuals, a third day to get management approval of all that, and at least two additional days collecting and developing the content, images, and graphics that will support the content. Add a couple of more days minimum for circulating drafts and receiving suggestions and revisions. So count on at least a week — with most winning efforts requiring more than those two days for collecting and developing the content and visuals.

Allow at least two days (three if you possibly can) immediately before the delivery date for rehearsal. The assumption is that the presentation team will arrive for the first day of rehearsal ready to walk and talk through the presentation. Even if everyone arrives with that level of preparation, the team will need at least two days to tweak and solidify (*not* debate and create) the strategic content, fine tune and become comfortable with (*not* debate and create) the visuals, develop coordination and chemistry with (*not* meet for the first time) one another, and work on potential Q&A topics and responses as well as the presentation itself.

Structure

After you've determined your unique strategy — what must be sold to win this specific job — plug it into a basic structure that's used for almost every presentation.

Connect with the Client

In the first 30 seconds of each presenter's talk, he or she must establish rapport with the listeners and win their attention. This *doesn't* happen with opening lines like "Good morning, we're pleased to be here …" and "Thank you. My name is Jon Doe and today I'm pleased to be able to introduce a great team …" First words must refer to what the client cares about, which *isn't* the time of day ("Good afternoon!"), your feelings ("I'm delighted to be here today to present to you …") or other ritual words ("Hello, my name is Jo Blow and I'm here today to …").   To catch and focus their attention and to create a positive pre-disposition toward all they are about to hear, you must — in real-life language rather than stilted "presentation-speak" — show the client you understand and value the same things they do.

I call this technique the "hook." To illustrate, let me go back a few years to an architect starting his presentation to the selection panel for a university's football stadium renovation. That selection panel was composed of the school's football coach, its athletic director and the head of the alumni athletic committee – none of whom knew a rodent's posterior about design!

The usual way to begin would be to say: *"Good afternoon, gentlemen. I'm Joe Blow, principal with Blow, Hard & Associates, and I'm delighted to be with you this afternoon to present the qualifications of our team for the redesign of East Makota State College football stadium."* Ho hum.

Instead, following the concept of the "hook," Joe begins by addressing what's most important to his listeners: *"Football (pause) is a game of individual effort and coordinated teamwork. This presentation will show how Blow, Hard & Associates will provide top-notch individual effort in design — to give you the high-impact stadium you want – and great teamwork, in coordinating with you, the College and your contractor."*

When the *real* "Joe Blow" delivered that hook in an actual presentation, the coach's head snapped up and all eyes, attention and positive attitudes were riveted on him!

Educate by Defining and Clarifying

Before you get into the content that will *really* sell your team, you usually must cover content that provides the selection panel with a basic orientation. Such content often includes a positive overview of the "corporate" team (firms, their key qualifications and why they have united to serve the client on this project), the "people" team (the individuals being proposed to do the work, and why out of all the available resources they are the *best* to meet the client's needs), and the project team leader (and the specific expertise he/she brings to serve the client and project).

Keep in mind that *all* your competitors will be extolling their team's experience and their people's virtues, and showing the project organization chart (which will have the client at the top, the project manager/designer right underneath as "single point of contact" and the various disciplines arrayed below). The challenge here, immediately after the hook, is to present the basic information from a client-benefit "here's what it means to you" perspective rather than from a firm-oriented "here's who we are" outlook. This is where creativity — focused on known client hot buttons — really pays off by keeping positive attention focused on your presentation.

Prepare the client for the sell by sharing information that will expand his or her perspective. To see your strategic points (which will be raised soon in the presentation) in the same way you do, the client must understand those points as you do. For example, naming the members of a joint venture doesn't prepare the client to see that venture as *the* solution to their problem. Before the venture is stressed as a selling point, the client might need to learn what a joint venture is, why it is the best approach for this project, why these particular firms came together, and why they are the best combination to meet the client's needs.

Remember, *before* you raise your strategic selling points you must *educate* your audience to understand them and *motivate* them to desire them. *That's* what you're really doing when you present what often is considered "boilerplate" information at the start of most presentations.

Demonstrate How You'll Provide More and Better Specific Benefits

"Our people" is *not* a strategic selling point, and reciting background and experience isn't proof. What firm would say and show *anything* other than they had super people with expertise and experience sufficient to meet project requirements! Selling your strengths isn't enough. Strengths must be matched to the client's needs and be demonstrably superior to what the competition will offer. Rule of thumb: 60% of your content should be about the client, 40% about you. And that 40% must be linked in some clear way to the 60% client content. Talk about the client's needs and project, and the ideas and techniques you will employ to solve the client's problems.

Here's where straight, direct talk by a project team that *connects* with the selection panel is vital. DON'T let your presentation team write out their content and memorize it. Most will fall back to passive voice, impersonal and multiple-clause written language that will make them sound stilted and artificial. Tape the team as they actually talk to one another about how they'll meet the project challenges. Then present them with an outline of key words that will lead them through a replication of that discussion. They'll sound more genuine, honest and committed.

Develop Visuals That Support the Sell

NEVER let the team plan their visuals *before* they have their strategic content organized. They can't know what to *show* until they know what they'll *say*. Working on visuals before taut, targeted content is finalized is a sure-fire way to have the presentation degenerate into meandering minutiae while overrunning your budget with complex visuals that won't advance your winning strategy.

When it comes to visuals, match the medium to the strategy. Computer-based presentations provide great visual volume and versatility at low cost. But if one of your major selling points is the *personal relationship* of your project team with the client, realize that you want the selection panel to focus most of their attention and eye contact on that team rather than on some whiz-bang animation on a 52" screen. Similarly, if you're selling the bleeding-edge technological advantage of your team, you're selling against yourself as the presenters manhandle large boards on easels.

Forget about what your team is "used to" and "comfortable with." The only criteria that matter in making decisions for the presentation are "What will the client want?" and "What will advance our strategy best?"

Finish with an Energy Surge

"We *want* this project. Thank you. Do you have any questions?" is the standard, trite, and weak close. The winning presentation close is a brief, memorable review of the strategic selling points and an energetic finish that carries emotional impact. Lincoln didn't say, "So America's going to be around for awhile. Thank you." He said, "And the government of the people, by the people, and for the people shall not perish from the earth."

Likewise, architect Joe Blow finished his presentation to the College selection panel by saying, *"And so Blow, Hard & Associates will deliver the best individual design for a high-impact stadium renovation, and will work as part of a coordinated team with you, the College and the contractor, to ensure that the renovated facility reflects both your proud heritage and your winning future!"*

Going back to the device used as the "hook" is often an artful and effective way to end the presentation.

Style

Keep It Conversational

A presentation is spoken and shouldn't sound like writing. In reading, you skip back to words earlier in the paragraph or sentence to clarify. In listening, you must make sense of what you hear within about 15 seconds or it drops from short-term memory, so sentences should be short and clear. When people talk they use more colloquial language, more colorful images, more active verbs and express more personality than when they write. So, if the team writes out a "script" of what they want to say, they'll be locked into words and phrases that will sound stilted, artificial and insincere. The best way to get conversational, rapport-building style is to not write out the presentation. Develop presentation content as a detailed bullet-point outline and have speakers practice — *from the very first rehearsal* — based upon that outline.

Here's where you'll encounter strong opposition, but persevere. *Do not* allow rehearsal from notes, even on the first run-through. The *only* thing people learn from practicing with notes is when to look down, or back at the visual, to prompt themselves. You build memory the same way you build muscles: work it to the point of failure. Rehearsing speakers have to go until they honestly can't recall what comes next. Then you help them build a mental link from the last idea they remembered to the next one.

Sure, speakers will never say exactly the same thing twice. That's ok, so long as they communicate the *idea* that was on the bullet point outline. They don't have to have every word 100% perfect. Even with grammatical errors and idiosyncratic expressions, they'll sell better than if they sound — and act — as if they're reading or reciting something canned.

Keep Them Moving

People uncomfortable with presenting tend to freeze into rigid statues or fidget. What feels and looks better is movement, especially of hands and arms. *Never* let presenters hold anything — pen, pointer, note card — in both hands. They'll get a death grip on it or fiddle with it. With at least one empty hand at about waist level at all times, that hand usually moves naturally. Don't require presenters to plant themselves in one location. They look and feel more relaxed if they stroll through their presentation. Continuous pacing like a caged lion isn't acceptable, but taking three or four steps as they move from one content point to another is great. Body movement creates vocal movement, putting energy into the voice and breaking monotony.

The firm that wins the selection is the one that the client thinks stands out from the competition. The winning presentation that helps create that perception must be different from and better than the others in its three key elements: strategy, style, and structure.

Janet S. Sanders, Ph.D., CPSM

- Ph.D. in Speech Communication and Human Relations.
- College professor for 15 years, teaching at the universities of Maryland, Kansas and Missouri-St. Louis.
- From 1985 to 1993, as president of the Clayton Consulting Group, served as a communication and marketing consultant to scores of A/E firms across the country.
- Her "hit rate" was over 70% on competitive marketing presentations on projects totaling over $23 billion.
- In March 1993, she became vice president of business planning and marketing for Sverdrup Civil Inc. (As one of the Jacobs companies, Sverdrup Civil is part of the nation's third-largest engineering firm.) She conducted the company's sales training and directed the marketing strategy, marketing information, and marketing support units.
- In January 2000 she returned to the Clayton Consulting Group and conducts sales, marketing and communication training and consultation.
- Contact her at **DocSanders@aol.com**.

3.6   SF 254/255 Preparation

Rose M. Dela Vega
Vice President
RTKL Associates Inc.

The federal government is required by law to base the procurement of A/E services on qualifications, rather than fees. Public Law 92-582, originally enacted in 1972 and amended 40 USC 541-544, effective July 25, 1991, is commonly referred to as the Brooks Act after its sponsor, Texas Representative Jack Brooks. This Act mandates qualifications-based selection for A/E and related services.[1] Regulatory implementing guidance for federal agencies is found in the Federal Acquisition Regulation (FAR), a procurement regulation used by both civilian and defense organizations. Part 36.6 of the FAR provides the implementing regulations.[2]

Federal jobs are advertised to the general public in the *Commerce Business Daily* (CBD), published weekdays by the U.S. Department of Commerce. The CBD lists U.S. government procurement invitations, contract awards, subcontracting leads, sales of surplus property and foreign business opportunities in all areas, not just A/E and construction services. With certain exceptions, federal procurement offices are required to announce in the CBD proposed procurement actions over $25,000 and contract awards over $25,000 that are likely to result in the award of any subcontracts. Each edition of the CBD contains 500 to 1,000 entries, and each notice appears only once. Subscriptions are available from the superintendent of documents of the Government Printing Office, on the Internet at cbdnet.gpo.gov and other commercial sources.

Within this framework of fairness — qualifications-based selection and a procurement system open to all — A/E selection is made on the basis of two documents: Standard Forms 254 and 255. The purpose of both documents, particularly the SF 255, is to make firm selection easier via evaluation of responses to the selection criteria listed in the CBD within a standard format.[3] This makes comparing credentials among firms straightforward, fair and undistracted by extravagant presentations materials. An agency's slate (short list) and selection boards, composed of government-registered architects and engineers and contract specialists, review the SF 254s and 255s and interview the short-listed firms. To ensure impartiality, some agencies prohibit a member of one board from serving on another board for the same project. Specific procedures for the control of slate and selection boards will vary from agency to agency and can be influenced by the involvement of the headquarters elements of those agencies, depending on the respective approval authorities delegated.[4]

SF 254

The SF 254 offers slate and selection boards a profile of your firm by office location, staff, disciplines, project types and billings. It is not project-specific and should be submitted to agencies for which you are interested in performing A/E services. It is best to include an SF 254 whenever you submit an SF 255, even if one is on file with the agency.

Architect-Engineer Contract Administration Support System (ACASS) serves as the repository for A/E qualifications data. It was established to reduce the burden and expense to the A/E community in the reproduction and distribution of multiple SF 254s. A copy of your SF 254 must be submitted to the Department of the Army, Corps of Engineers, Portland District, Attention: ACASS, P.O. Box 2946, Portland, OR 97208-2946, (503) 808-4591, for inclusion in this system. Each Corps office has ready access to information on all firms in the system, including performance evaluations, contracts and modifications awarded to the firm by the Department of Defense. The Corps will not release any information about your firm to other A/E firms, but you may request a computer print-out of the information on your firm.

Federal Acquisition Regulation, Subpart 36.603, mandates that A/E firms update their SF 254s annually. The form can be prepared on government-created forms, developed with commercially prepared software, or created in-house with page layout software. The latest SF 254 version, revised November 1992, must be used. The SF 254 requests the following information:

- Firm name/business address.
- Year established.
- Date prepared.
- Type of ownership (small, small disadvantaged business, woman-owned business, large business).
- Name of parent company, if any.
- Former parent company and year established.
- Firm contact names.
- Office addresses and size.
- Personnel by discipline.
- Summary professional fees received for the past five years.
- Profile of firm's project experience for past five years (by profile code).
- Project examples for past five years (by profile code).

If the diversity of project types warrants, separate SF 254s can be created by project type (for example, planning-oriented, retail-oriented, health care-oriented).

SF 255

Unlike the SF 254, the SF 255 is project-specific. Slate and selection boards trying to identify the A/E firm that best meets a list of specific criteria scrutinize the form. Qualifications, past performance on government projects, the consultant team and individuals involved are significant factors. Like the SF 254, the SF 255 can be prepared using government-created forms with commercially prepared software or created in-house with page layout software. Again, remember to use the latest version dated November 1992.

Before responding to the SF 255, firms should make certain they are qualified to perform the work. Read the CBD announcement thoroughly to determine what services the government is seeking. Qualified firms should then follow several steps. First, ask yourself if your firm has performed 10 relevant projects in the last five years and if team members responsible for those projects are still with the firm. Corporate experience means nothing — the federal government wants to see the individuals who worked on the relevant projects.

Depending on the project, it is not unusual for an agency to receive 45 to 75 submittals or more. To reduce the number, board members look for reasons to eliminate firms (including the obvious one of missing a due date). Make sure you follow instructions.

Instructions for completing the SF 255 are as follows:

- Section 1. Project name/location for which the SF 255 is being submitted.
- Section 2.
    2a. Date of CBD in which the project announcement appeared.
    2b. Solicitation/contract number provided in CBD.
- Section 3. Firm (or joint venture) name and address. When requested by the agency, show your firm's contractor establishment code (CEC), commercial and government entity (CAGE number), and architect/engineer contractor administration support system (ACASS number).
    3a. Name, title and telephone number of the principal to contact.
    3b. Address of office that will perform work if the office submitting the SF 255 will not.
- Section 4. Personnel by discipline in the office who will perform the services. This should be the same as that listed in 3 or 3b. The capacity of the office that will perform the work must be easily ascertained. Use the blank spaces to fill in non-standard discipline categories (graphic designers, computer programmers, model makers and so on). List each person only once, by primary discipline. Show consultants in parentheses. The SF 255 (November 1992) requires this.
- Section 5. Answer this section only if the SF 255 is submitted by a joint venture of two or more entities. If a joint venture submittal is being prepared, list the participating firms and outline the specific areas of responsibility each entity of the joint venture will have (for example, administration, technical and financial).
    5a. Indicate whether the proposed joint venture has worked together before.
- Section 6. List key outside consultants with address, role/roles they will perform and whether your firms have worked together before. A project's teaming arrangements are critical. Teams should be composed of the best and most qualified subconsultants for the specific project. It helps if the team has worked together before, ideally on the relevant projects listed.
- Section 7. Provide resumes only for those individuals who will have major project responsibilities. Tailor resumes so that the experience and qualifications are relevant to the proposed project and make sure all questions "a" through "g" are answered. Include personnel who have worked on the projects listed in Section 8 and their role in the project. Highlight the relevant projects on which the individual has worked and provide a brief description of the project.
- Section 8. List no more than 10 projects that best illustrate current qualifications relevant to this project. Projects in this section should be similar in scope and magnitude to the proposed project and may reflect a combination of projects completed by the prime and major subconsultants within the 10-project limit. Make sure questions "a" through "e" are answered. If illustrations and lengthy descriptions are used, list only one or two projects per page. Make sure relevancy of the projects is listed.

- Section 9. List all work by your firm, or joint venture, currently being performed directly for federal/Department of Defense agencies. Provide all of the information required in questions "a" through "e."
- Section 10. Provide a narrative description of why your firm, or joint venture, is most qualified to perform the services required. The organization of this information should follow the selection criteria listed in the CBD and should be as precise as possible. If a numbered note is referenced in the CBD announcement (for example, "see note 24"), it must be read as part of the text. Numbered notes are footnotes and are used to reduce the amount of text and repetition in the announcements. A full text of the numbered notes is included only in the Monday edition of the CBD.

  A brief description of the key individuals and consultant firms is helpful. Include a description of your CADD capabilities. Provide an outline of the techniques you employ to assure a quality design product, including a discussion of your procedures to maintain the project schedule and budget. Outline your procedures for effective contract document checks and reviews for the discovery of design errors and omissions.
- Section 11. A principal of the firm who is authorized to commit the resources of the firm and the team should sign the completed forms.

Other Suggestions

- Know the agency with which you are dealing. Although all agencies must follow the FAR, their requirements for submission of SF 255s and SF 254s may differ.
- Include a clear, easy-to-follow organization chart before Section 7 so the reviewers can determine the roles of the individuals proposed for the project.
- On large projects with multiple requirements, incorporating an experience matrix, schedules and other illustrations in Section 10 will help reviewers visualize your firm's method and approach to accomplishing the project.
- Make sure your subconsultants provide you with SF 255 information of comparable quality and relevance.
- Submit supplemental data only if the agency has indicated that this is acceptable. Keep in mind that only the SF 255 is used during the evaluation process. Cover letters may also be disregarded.
- Use dividers to separate SF 255 and SF 254 and bind them together. Custom covers with the project name, your firm's logo and the agency's logo will help distinguish your submission from others.
- Finally, remember that your SF 255 is the only chance your firm has to make the short list. Its appearance should convey that it was organized, managed and executed with the same care that your firm will organize, manage and execute the proposed project.
- If you are not short-listed, request a debriefing. Most agencies will ask you to put your request in writing and will schedule a debriefing after the contract with the selected firm is negotiated.
- Finally, before preparing SF254s and SF255s, read and follow instructions attached to these forms.

Endnotes

[1] See FAR 36.601 for typical "architect-engineer services." Examples include: studies, investigations, surveying, tests, evaluations, consultations, comprehensive planning, program management, conceptual designs, value engineering, construction phase services, soils engineering, drawing reviews, preparation of operating and maintenance manuals, and other related services that logically or justifiably require performance by registered architects or engineers or their employees.

[2] See also FAR 36.602-5, which allows short selection process for contracts not exceeding the Simplified Acquisition Threshold now $100,000 (FAR 2.101).

[3] See FAR PART 36.602-1 for selection criteria. The regulations permit agencies to add other appropriate evaluation criteria. It is critical that the proposer responds to each and every evaluation criteria listed in the CBD announcement.

[4] See FAR PART 36.602.3 Evaluation Board Functions.

Bibliography

Commerce Business Daily. Washington, D.C.: U.S. Government Printing Office, Superintendent of Documents. (For subscription information, call (202) 512-1800.)

Defense Acquisition Regulation. Washington, D.C.: U.S. Government Printing Office, Superintendent of Documents. (To order, call (202) 512-1800.)

Federal Acquisition Regulation. Washington, D.C.: U.S. Government Printing Office, Superintendent of Documents. (To order, call (202) 512-1800.)

Public Law 92-582. Washington, D.C.: U.S. Government Printing Office, Superintendent of Documents. (To order, call (202) 512-1803.)

Rose M. Dela Vega

- Rose Dela Vega is a vice president and partner with RTKL Associates Inc. and director of federal contracts and marketing.
- Before joining RTKL in 1991, Dela Vega held management positions at CRSS Inc. and KCI Technologies Inc.
- Prior to her positions in private practice, Dela Vega served as manager of the Architect and Engineer Contracts Branch of NAVFAC's Chesapeake Division for 18 years.
- While with the Navy, Dela Vega evaluated thousands of SF 255 submittals, was a voting member of the A/E selection board, and negotiated and administered A/E contracts as a warranted contracting officer.

3.7 Debriefing: Building Positive Relationships from Client Feedback

Nadine R. Yates, FSMPS
Principal
N.R. Yates and Associates

As marketing professionals, we may profess to understand our clients' needs and perhaps those of prospects. However, if we fail to ask these people directly, we miss opportunities to establish clearer communication, learn client standards of quality, improve service, and develop a favorable image for ourselves. When we seize these opportunities and act on the information we gain, we nurture positive long-term relationships with clients and capture both repeat business and strong referrals to make our work enjoyable as well as profitable.

We invest in these relationships by conducting debriefing interviews, also called client reviews. In these private meetings, we learn the clients' impressions of our proposals (and performance in the case of long-standing clients) as well as their perceptions of our image and reputation. When they are well planned and executed, these interviews demonstrate our sincere interest in clients and prospects and assure credible technical work by removing assumptions.

Firms commonly develop proposals based on an appraisal of the fit between their skills and the needs of the client or prospective client. Debriefing interviews are a smart way to increase the proposal hit rate. Debriefings are appropriate at any of three stages in the proposal consideration process: before any decision has been reached, after a favorable decision, and after an unfavorable decision. Debriefings may also be held during projects, immediately after projects, and between projects. The purpose is always the same: to elicit constructive feedback and reinforce positive regard.

Information to be Gained

A debriefing interview establishes a time to talk privately with a client or prospective client. The critical task of the interviewer is to pose open-ended questions in a manner that encourages complete answers from the client, especially regarding expectations about process and outcome. All marketing professionals advocate quality products and excellent service but to achieve client satisfaction, we must allow clients to confirm their definition of quality. We may then fulfill their needs better than the competition and secure ongoing business.

This discussion also gives clients an opportunity to make special requests about the project at hand. Such new or updated information about a project or an untapped market may provide an important competitive edge.

The client's message may contain more than just the technical or unique aspects of the project. It may spell out the types of working relationships desired among team members and other consultants on the project. Plans for ongoing communication or reporting throughout the project should be noted and followed.

As ongoing, honest communication is developing, a debriefing may be the occasion for a firm to learn of a specific dissatisfaction that has not been previously expressed by a client. Once aware of the problem, the firm is usually able to fully resolve the difficulty and restore its client's trust. When such communication continues, loyalty develops and becomes the basis for repeat business and a solid reputation.

Advance Marketing

Before a sharpshooter takes aim, he or she sizes up the target and proceeds only after taking into consideration a multitude of factors that will affect the likelihood of success. Similarly, we have an opportunity to increase our success rate when we first assess our target clients, then create a strategy to satisfy their needs. Jones and Sasser (1995) write, "A completely satisfied customer typically believes that the company excels in understanding and addressing his or her personal preferences, values, needs, or problems. To figure out how to satisfy customers in this fashion, a company has to excel at listening to customers and interpreting what they are saying." Thus the debriefing is an important tool for gathering advance marketing information before deciding to prepare a proposal.

A debriefing may be held with potential clients *prior* to their putting a project out to bid or publishing a request for proposal (RFP) or seeking sole source work. This meeting is an informal introduction of our services and interest. We discuss the clients' needs and interests while listening for their expectations and values; we may casually present our qualifications, especially pointing out where our skills and experience meet their criteria. We may then learn how to position our services in future proposals and increase the effectiveness of its presentation.

A Proposal Under Consideration

We may ask to speak with a prospective client after submitting a proposal, before a decision is made. This contact, whether as a meeting or a telephone discussion, is to emphasize our interest, to find out whether anything further is desired from us, and to clarify when to expect the next step in the decision-making process.

An Accepted Proposal

The opportunity to debrief after winning a new project is often lost in the excitement of the victory. However, it is an important chance to ask why your proposal was selected. Hearing what the client valued about the proposal and its presentation, as well as the client's perception of a firm's professional reputation, allows for more meaningful differentiation from the competition.

Debriefing also clarifies the client's expectations from the start of the project and reveals if anything has changed from the initial parameters. Gathering such information for the strategic planning of the project gets the working relationship off on the right foot and avoids potential misunderstandings. This concerted display of interest demonstrates a willingness to work cooperatively and opens channels for further communication. It is also an opportunity for the client to clarify the level and amount of communication desired, which is important in developing compatibility and trust.

Because acting upon what is learned is imperative to a successful debriefing, the debriefing of an accepted proposal should probably be conducted by the project manager or principal-in-charge, someone with the authority to implement the client's instructions. This person must also make certain that the information gained from the debriefing is passed along to *everyone* who works on the project. When all team members know what the client expects, the project will progress more smoothly and the client will receive the work proposed by the firm selected.

A Rejected Proposal

A debriefing interview after a proposal has been turned down is not a time to defensively argue the decision. Rather, the meeting is an opportunity for soliciting and accepting beneficial feedback from the client. Being given undivided attention impresses upon clients a firm's sincere desire to learn from an honest assessment of its performance.

To be constructive, the debriefing session must be conducted as objectively as possible. It is perfectly appropriate to express disappointment at not getting the project and appreciation for the meeting as a chance to increase understanding of the client's needs. Resist the temptation to make another presentation, to clarify or add points that may have been unclear or omitted; focus on the future rather than the past. To lower any defensiveness on either side, maintain a positive attitude. For example, consider asking, "What made the winners win?" rather than, "Why did we lose?"

The client may offer compliments on aspects of your firm's proposal or presentation; accept them graciously without downplaying the efforts made, then note them to share later with other members of the firm as a morale-booster following this loss.

Work to establish and maintain rapport. Rapport is built on the ability to convey empathy and understanding without judgment. Throughout the interview, tacitly show that the knowledge, experiences, attitudes, and feelings being shared are important, yet no judgment is being passed on the content of what is expressed. Control personal reactions (frowning, head shaking) to ease the client's delivery of sensitive information.

Phrase carefully prepared questions in a manner that encourages a client to answer candidly. Demonstrate active listening (eye contact, head nodding) and summarize major points. Work hard to gain as much information from the potential client as possible.

Close with an optimistic discussion of future work. However, refrain from launching into a sales pitch. Some clients perceive future-oriented talk as too aggressive, so keep the conversation focused on improving future performance and becoming better prepared to meet anticipated needs.

Before leaving, establish how to best stay in contact (how frequently and in what manner: telephone call, appointment, conversation at a professional meeting). Depart with confidence to leave behind a positive impression.

An Ongoing Project

Regular communication throughout a project is perhaps the most important key to a successful outcome. Research conducted by the author indicates that all too often clients fail to hire firms a second time not for technical reasons but for subjective ones. Debriefings provide a qualitative measure of a firm's performance to complement the quantitative measures of the project's progress. When conducted regularly, debriefings become increasingly beneficial, just as exercising a muscle regularly makes it stronger and more capable with less effort.

Debriefings of ongoing projects should address four key areas: technical competence, communication, the working relationship, and future opportunities. Apart from noting progress, a firm should ask about technical competence to discern whether it is undervaluing its services or overestimating its skills. The frequency and means of communication should be reviewed for effectiveness. Are people receiving the information they need in a timely manner? The working relationship should be assessed for efficiency; duplication of effort is one symptom of a poor working relationship. An ideal situation is one of synergy, where the two firms working together produce results greater than the sum of the results achieved by the firms working individually. Future opportunities may evolve out of present projects or anticipated growth in other areas and may be easily discussed if communication has been open thus far.

Keep in mind that different people working on the project will have different perspectives on a firm's working relationship with the client. For example, an outside consultant conducting debriefings will elicit different information than a team member. A project manager will interpret information differently than a marketing professional. This is desirable because the variety serves to widen the view. Remember, we interview people to find out from them those things we cannot directly observe. Debriefing as a process begins with the assumption that the perspective of others is meaningful when allowed to be communicated clearly. Consider carefully whom to involve in the debriefing meetings, then contact them regularly. Major clients should be interviewed at least once a year to discuss the "big picture" aspects of the working relationship as an adjunct to weekly job meetings which tend to focus on day-to-day activities and technical considerations.

The Right Questions

A successful debriefing session results from determining in advance what information to elicit. The quality of the information obtained during an interview is largely dependent on the interviewer's preparation. Firms may prepare by asking:

- What is the specific purpose of this debriefing session?
- Which members of the client organization should be interviewed?
- What specifically do we want to learn?

From the answers to these questions, prepare debriefing and probing follow-up questions for the client, then call to schedule the meeting.

Coming to the meeting with a prepared list of questions and a notepad for writing down answers shows the clients that their responses are being taken seriously. Faced with thoughtful preparation, clients usually give questions thoughtful consideration before answering.

During the interview, maintain flexibility to be able to pursue information in whatever direction appears to be appropriate, depending on what emerges from a given response. Allow the questions to flow from the immediate context and build a conversation rather than automatically reading them in order. Use the list of prepared questions to keep the interaction focused but encourage opinions and emotions to surface.

Also use the prepared questions as a guide for listening to what is not being said. These areas should be brought up, albeit with great tact.

Phrase questions in a manner that encourages a client to talk freely. Such questions often start with *how, what*, and *where*. Be careful with questions starting with *why*; they may inadvertently sound threatening. Avoid questions which may be answered with a curt *yes* or *no* or with a terse factual answer. Review the questions to assure that the wording does not suggest an expected answer. For example, when asked "How satisfied were you with our communication?" the client might feel limited to a modifier as an answer: "pretty satisfied," "kind of satisfied," "mostly satisfied," and so on. A better question would be, "What is your opinion of our communication?"

Make certain to ask only one question at a time and wait for a complete response before asking the next one. Multiple questions may seem to be related and even efficient but they are likely to confuse the client about what is really being asked, and confusion generates tension that interferes with frank communication. Similarly, it is the responsibility of the interviewer to make it clear to the client what is being asked. Asking questions that are understandable is an important part of establishing rapport.

Use preliminary statements to let the client know what is going to be asked before it is asked, especially when making a transition from one topic to another. For example, "Now I'd like to ask you about our proposal organization." This serves two functions. First, it alerts the client to the nature of the question that is coming, it directs their awareness, and it focuses their attention. Second, a cue about the upcoming topic gives the client a few seconds to organize some thoughts before a question is actually asked. This technique often reduces the time spent in awkward silence as a result of an abrupt transition.

The value of the answer is often determined by the value of the question. Asking simple or meaningless questions will only elicit simple or meaningless answers. Dare to ask important questions to evoke thoughtful answers. Below are some appropriate questions for each of the debriefing opportunities.

Advance Marketing
- What is most important in this client's selection of a firm?
- What kind of information and materials may we provide to help the client in the selection process?
- How may we best stay in contact with this potential client?

A Proposal Under Consideration
- What additional materials or information may we provide to help the client in the selection process?
- When may we expect the next step in the decision-making process?
- Is there someone else or a group of people we should talk to?

An Accepted Proposal
- What were the factors influencing the client's selection?
- What do we have that other firms don't? Is there anything they have that we don't?
- What are the client's expectations for this project? Has anything changed from the RFP?

A Rejected Proposal
- What were the factors influencing the client's selection?
- What factors led the client to believe that the firm selected will be successful?
- How effective were our proposal and presentation?

- What else could we do, or what could we do differently, to be considered another time?

An Ongoing Project
- How effective are our frequency and means of communication?
- How is our on-site staff relating to the client's staff?
- What would the client like us to pay more attention to?
- What areas of disappointment may we rectify?

The Debriefing Process

Debriefing may be conducted on projects or proposals of any size. Debriefing is contingent only on the importance of a project or proposal to the client and our commitment to act upon what is learned.

Clients are most receptive to debriefing interviews at their offices at their convenience. The interviews are most effective when conducted in person, but they may take place over the phone. Whether conducted by a trained team member or an outside consultant, it is the interviewer's responsibility to build an atmosphere of trust and open dialogue. Set the tone by demonstrating friendliness and a willingness to listen with an accepting attitude. The critical task is to pose open-ended questions in a manner that encourages complete answers. Taking notes during the discussion shows the client that such feedback is deemed worthy of further consideration.

To reinforce the position of listener, end the debriefing session by asking, "Is there anything else you'd like to tell me?" When the client has finished, offer assurance that any shortcomings mentioned will be dealt with. This is not the time to insert a sales pitch. Remember that this is a time of learning; clients will be more open and offer more information when they're confident that there's no sales pressure. Be sure to thank the client for taking the time to provide honest, informative answers.

Make sure to follow with a letter reiterating the value of the meeting. Such thoughtfulness will reinforce sincerity and leave a favorable impression.

Analysis

To maximize the benefits from the debriefing session, the information should be processed through the following steps.

1. Immediately after the meeting, find a time and place free of distractions in which to review the debriefing notes and make additions and corrections. This time of reflection and elaboration is critical to guarantee that the information generated will be accurate and useful.
2. Send a letter of appreciation to the client. Cite one or two key discussion points as being especially beneficial.
3. Transcribe the debriefing notes so they remain useful–spell out shorthand abbreviations, write complete sentences, arrange information under headings. Clearly indicate ideas and interpretations that arise following the interview.
4. Write a summary of the meeting with recommended steps for improving proposals and presentations.

5. List any remaining questions and issues to be probed with key people. If areas of vagueness are found, check back with the client for clarification. A brief phone call indicates the seriousness with which the information is being treated.
6. Pass along relevant information to those who will benefit from it. Talk personally with the project leader, management, and marketing personnel. Be certain that compliments are passed along to those who deserve them. Similarly, make certain that areas in need of improvement are brought to the attention of the appropriate people, including management.
7. Solicit ideas from these people on future debriefings–what information would be useful to them?
8. Write a report stating the value of the debriefing and submit it to management, marketing, and perhaps the company newsletter.
9. Review the debriefing session with someone objective to determine what could be done differently next time. Did we find out what we really wanted to find out in the interview? If not, what was the problem? Poorly worded questions? Wrong topics? Poor rapport?
10. Determine an appropriate strategy for remaining in contact with the client for future opportunities.

Summary

My research findings from conducting debriefings for 16 firms over 10 years indicate that a firm gains the following six benefits:

- A clearer understanding of market needs. Clients invariably describe precisely what services and products they're looking for and the kind of working relationship they desire.
- Increased esteem from clients. Clients recognize that a firm is demonstrating genuine concern for them by planning and financing debriefing interviews and reward the effort with higher regard.
- Insights applicable to strategic planning. Many firms report that client feedback brings focus to their strategic planning by providing additional perspective or by reinforcing corporate goals.
- Revelation and resolution of client dissatisfaction. Clients are often hesitant to initiate a complaint; in a debriefing situation, they may raise issues in a constructive and cooperative forum with the reasonable expectation of attentive resolution.
- Ongoing, honest communication with clients. Such feedback may prompt an advantageous change in procedures and alert a firm to the clients' lines of thinking.
- Opportunities for additional work and revenue. Most firms that conduct debriefing interviews are able to document additional revenue gained as a direct result of the debriefing, either in ongoing client work or new work from client referrals.

A variation of the debriefing interview is especially effective in determining the availability of work in a market new to the client's current niche. When clients are interviewed by an outside consultant, they are typically willing to answer questions about what they look for in selecting a firm and how a new firm could effectively solicit their business.

The majority of debriefing interviews are enlightening and many even dramatically so. However, in rare instances, an interview may not go well. The possibility exists of meeting an uncooperative client, a person who seems overly sensitive (perhaps from poor treatment by another firm at a previous debriefing), or someone who seems to talk too long on one point. However, it remains the challenge and the responsibility of the interviewer to find a way to unlock the internal perspectives of each client. The interviewer must establish an interview climate that facilitates open responses and find which interviewing style and which question format will work with a particular respondent personality.

We need to guard against dismissing portions of the interview that we don't believe to be relevant or important. The client may have a valid point that we're missing or be simply giving us insights into how that client thinks or operates. All feedback must be given due consideration.

The purpose of conducting debriefing interviews is to understand how clients and prospective clients view projects and the firms they hire, to learn their values and judgments, and to capture the complexities of their individual perceptions and experiences. By conducting debriefing interviews, firms develop greater client focus, improve their proposal effectiveness, enhance client satisfaction, and earn a more favorable image in the process. Listening intently to more fully understand the client's needs and wants is one of the most important activities marketing professionals perform to succeed in today's competitive business climate.

Biography

Nadine R. Yates, FSMPS
- Principal of N.R. Yates and Associates, Maynard MA
- Fellow in the Society of Marketing Professional Services [SMPS]
- Experienced strategic marketing and management consultant
- Conductor of hundreds of debriefing interviews on behalf of clients
- Coach to clients' staffs for conducting debriefings themselves
- Researcher of debriefing interviews since 1987
- Published author on the value and benefits of debriefing interviews

Selected Readings

Coben, Richard S., "How to Maximize Client Retention and Provide a Client Advocacy Role for Marketing Staff," *SMPS Marketer*, August-September, 1994

Jones, Thomas O. and Sasser, W. Earl, Jr., "Why Satisfied Customers Defect," *Harvard Business Review*, November-December, 1995

Reichheld, Frederick F., *The Loyalty Effect*, Harvard Business School Press, 1996

Reichheld, Frederick F., "Learning From Customer Defections," *Harvard Business Review*, March-April, 1996

Yates, Nadine R., "Six Benefits of Debriefing Interviews," *Marketing Tactics,* PSMJ, December 1998

Yates, Nadine R., "Client Reviews: The Value of Asking," *A/E Marketing Journal,* PSMJ, July 1997

Yates, Nadine R., "Debriefing: Improve Project Success While Taking Care of Your Clients," *Project Management*, PSMJ, July 1997

3.8 Marketing During Project Execution

Philip F. Valence, FSMPS
President
Blackridge Ltd.

Establishment of a strong relationship with clients and colleagues has long been the foundation of professional services marketing. Because codes of ethics of many professional organizations strictly disavowed or censured "self-promotion," professional services firms relied primarily on doing a good job, forging strong relationships (the "old boy" network), and referrals to build reputation, recognition and business.

Then came the revolution: the acceptance, in the mid-1960s, of self-promotion (marketing) by most professional organizations. Since that time, firms have embraced marketing and business development and incrementally expanded its purview. While continuing to focus on doing good work, they have developed solid expertise in the range of marketing/business development/sales techniques and systems: intelligence gathering rivaling some governmental agencies; sophisticated public relations/communications techniques involving all forms of print, graphic, video and electronic media; quality promotional materials that are differentiated as to purpose (marketing vs. sales); and a wealth of tailored sales and marketing management tools and database systems.

Thanks to our own marketing prowess and enthusiasm, we have created an environment in which the playing field has been leveled, competition is more intense and client expectations have continuously been raised. In an effort to maximize the return on marketing resources, we have differentiated, we have segmented, we have formed strategic alliances, and we have continued to fine-tune our techniques and systems to convince our clients they should retain our services.

And then it dawned on us that, in our efforts to market ourselves, we had lost sight of the most important — and constant — factor in the equation of success: the client. And thus began a renewed focus on "client satisfaction" and on building strong relationships.

There is little argument that client satisfaction is a key factor in successful marketing, client development and client retention efforts of professional services firms. The mantra has become: "Do a good job, clients will be happy and return to us with future work; they will be 'loyal'."

Yet, we need to be careful. Frederick Reichheld, in *The Loyalty Effect*, writes:

> "Customer retention ... has three dimensions — customer loyalty, employee loyalty, and investor loyalty ... Loyalty has implications that extend to every corner of every business system that seeks the benefit of steady customers. Retention is not simply one more operating statistic; it is the central gauge that integrates all the dimensions of a business and measures how well the firm is creating value for its customers."[1]

Research into customer satisfaction and loyalty (retention) indicates that client satisfaction does not guarantee loyalty; that loyalty is driven by four factors:[2]

- **Needs/values fit:** the extent to which the client's needs/values are satisfied in our dealings with them (responsiveness, access, services, performance, results).
- **Involvement:** the extent to which the client is/was involved by/with us before, during and after our dealings with them (input, communication, decision-making).
- **Disposition to alternatives:** the extent of the attraction the client feels toward competitors.
- **Depth of ambivalence:** the extent to which the attraction to alternatives creates indecision about which to choose.

Of these four, we have the ability to control two: the needs/values fit and our involvement with clients.

Our clients want to be engaged by and with us. When asked in surveys to describe what makes a service firm stand out in their mind, the responses by many (but not all) client representatives repeat common themes:[3]

- "I want firms that respect my experience and knowledge (related to my responsibilities), and that respond with solutions which meet my objectives (not theirs)."

- "I want firms that do not walk away after the project is done (after they have my business)."

- "I want firms that make themselves accessible to me to answer questions and give me help when I need it, even if I have no project (work) for them."

- "I want consultants to spend their time figuring out how they can help me do my job better; how to keep me informed about things of value to me without wasting my time."

Professional expertise and doing a good job — in and of themselves — do not impress clients; that's why they hire us. The basic expectation is that we will provide the services we promised, we will do a good job, and the results will be what they wanted. For this we get a "D" (or maybe a "C"). We become heroes ("B+"/ "A"), and clients become satisfied, by the *way* we provide service, how we connect with and engage them over and above the service itself. The single most effective link to future work is the person-to-person connection we make with clients — before, during and following a project. (For a brief discussion about the process of building relationships, see page 240.)

This chapter on marketing during project execution is divided into three sections:

- Section I discusses the marketer's continuing role following acquisition of a project.
- Section II discusses four key marketing responsibilities of the project team during project performance.
- Section III discusses briefly how a firm can utilize the quality objectives of ISO 9000 to promote customer satisfaction and enhance its marketing effort during project execution.

I. The Marketer's Role

Melanie Cornell, in the previous version of this chapter, wrote:

> "Most senior marketers excel in developing relationships with potential clients; relationships that should place the marketer on the team chart. ... Clients who place (a high level) of confidence in the marketer expect that individual to be their representative throughout the project."

The marketer's work does not end with the award of a project. In fact, some client-focused firms are expecting senior marketers to become more involved in active management of key clients — as account manager/project executive. This expanded role for the marketer may be project-focused (one time) or for the long-term. Most typically, it is employed for clients with whom the firm expects to have an extended working relationship, and is intended to strengthen and support the project team's relationship with the client and provide continuity for the firm over the longer term.

Whether or not the account manager/project executive role is an official responsibility for the marketer within a firm, there are four distinct roles he or she can and should assume during project execution. These roles are:

- Interpreter
- Advocate/Mediator
- Coach
- Contributor
- Noodge

Interpreter

As a result of the strong relationships developed with clients prior to the award of a project (see sidebar), most marketers develop a solid understanding of the client's personality, goals and objectives. In addition, during the pre-award period, the marketer is also instrumental in creating the environment that establishes (for good or evil) the client's expectations.

Therefore, the first important role of the marketer is that of interpreter; he or she should play an important part in the following three areas:

1. Translating the client's goals, objectives and expectations into the final contractual agreement between the parties.

2. Interpreting the client's goals, objectives and expectations for the project team, and ensuring the team understands and incorporates them into the project.

3. Selecting the project team — including sub-consultants as appropriate — and matching to the extent possible what he or she knows of the client's personality with the appropriate personalities of the firm.

Advocate/Mediator

As the individual who best understands the client's personality, goals, objectives and expectations, the marketer is the objective link between the client and the project team. He or she is *de facto* the client's alter ego within the project team; the next-to-last point of last resort (we cannot absolve the principals from being the point of last resort). In this capacity, he or she should be continuously aware of project status vis-à-vis the client's goals, objectives and expectations.

Can this be accomplished? Yes, and here are three suggestions that will minimize disruption of schedules and routines.

1. Periodically attend regular in-house project team meetings (depending on project size and schedule, at least monthly). Consult with the project team leader to have client service issues included on the meeting agenda (as the *first* item!). Be prepared with questions about issues or concerns that might interfere with the team's ability to meet the client's goals, objectives and expectations; and press discussion as to how the team intends to resolve those issues or concerns.

2. Depending on project size and schedule, insist on attending at least one (perhaps more) project team meeting with the client. Observe and assess the dynamics between the client and the team (communication, personalities, etc.). Verify that the client's goals, objectives and expectations are being met. As follow-up to this meeting, provide useful feedback to team members that helps enhance their skills and keeps the project focused on the client.

3. Independently maintain personal contact with the client as the firm's ombudsman. The opportunity afforded by these one-on-one meetings can be invaluable to the firm and its relationship with the client. Listen objectively to the client's experiences with the firm and the project team; avoid becoming defensive or pointing fingers. The goal is to learn of issues (e.g., project performance, billing, responding to questions) that may not have been communicated to or heard by the firm or the project team.

As advocate for the client, voice these concerns immediately to the appropriate individual(s) within the firm or team. If a client is experiencing problems or has concerns with any aspect of the project and cannot find solutions, it is up to the marketer to become the mediator and to help find satisfactory resolution that is in the best interests of all parties.

Coach

Another outcome of the marketer's advocate/mediator role: he or she can serve as a coach for other staff. In this capacity, marketers can provide "real-time" support to staff by adopting the "lessons learned" approach in his or her involvement with clients and the project teams during a project. To be effective in this role as coach, the marketer must have outstanding interpersonal skills and sensitivity to how individuals react and respond to suggestions and critique.

Through the lessons learned process, the marketer can use actual project situations as coaching opportunities to develop and enhance the skills of both principals and staff in a variety of critical areas including: interpersonal and client relations, responding to and resolving conflict, running effective meetings and presenting difficult information. Depending on the specific situation and personalities involved, this coaching role is carried out either through one-on-one interaction or small group activity, or through a more structured internal or external professional development program.

Contributor

The particular skills and background a marketer possesses (be they marketing, finance, public relations, communications, advertising or technical) can be transformed into a valuable service to assist clients in a variety of ways during a project. The opportunities are limited only by time, resources and creativity; and by our understanding (or lack thereof) of the client's business and needs.

The job of the marketer is to develop that understanding, and to identify opportunities that will maximize his or her potential for contribution to a successful client project and client relationship and that make sense for the firm.

Examples of how some marketers have used their skills to support a client during a project (may even be billable time) include:

- Helping prepare necessary documents for, and participating in, public hearings to assist clients obtain essential permits and funding approvals, e.g., public facility funding (bond issue campaigns), siting/zoning issues, environmental permits.

- Preparing materials to help the client market new or newly renovated facilities, e.g., high-end office space, retirement/congregate care facilities for seniors, patient care/treatment centers for health care providers, college recruitment brochures featuring specialized learning spaces.

- Preparing materials for and/or arranging and participating in special events, e.g., community outreach programs; ground breaking, topping-off and ribbon-cutting ceremonies; helping a client celebrate milestones (not necessarily on a project); special fund-raising events for projects or client-supported charitable organizations.

- Using a specialized non-technical background to the client's benefit, e.g., a financial background to perform pro forma cash-flow analyses of project scenarios for a development project, or to help a client arrange financing for a new project; a nursing background to help evaluate project options for a new CCU/ICU patient care facility; an educational background to assist a client in the training of staff.

To quote Microsoft: "Where do you want to go today?" What do you want to do with your talent?

Noodge

This is perhaps the marketer's most unique role (it applies before and after as well as during a project) because the marketer is the only individual within a firm who, almost with impunity, can stick his or her nose into every aspect of the business.

As noodge, the marketer asks questions — about everything. Why something has or has not happened. How and when commitments are going to be met, and if necessary why they have not. What will be required to enable an individual or a project team to fulfill a task or assignment. It is, of course, essential that the noodge be beyond reproach, that he or she has carried out the responsibilities of his or her position to satisfy the objectives and expectations of the firm's principals.

As noodge during a project, the marketer's role always is to remind project team members of their critical role in marketing as they work through the project with the client. The marketer must continually ask the project team members to provide information. What have they learned about the client, the organization, the business, future plans? Is there potential work coming up for another group/discipline/office? Has the team informed the client of our other capabilities? What are next steps to ensure the firm is considered/selected for the next project?

These questions may be perceived as threatening to some. Therefore, as with the coaching role, the marketer's role as noodge demands well-developed interpersonal skills so as not to alienate others within the firm and diminish the marketer's effectiveness as noodge and other roles.

II. The Project Team's Role

Perhaps the greatest marketing opportunity for a firm, and the one used least effectively, occurs during project execution. This is the time when we (the firm) have the most continuous contact with, and greatest potential influence over, the client. And yet, we frequently do not maximize our advantage.

Every marketer has heard a project manager or team member say: "We're working on a project with them; they know who we are and what we can do. I don't need to market them." AARRGH!! Or, "I'm too busy doing the work to do marketing." Yikes!! The project team, and especially the team leader, has the primary responsibility for the client relationship during the performance of a project, supported as necessary by the marketer and the principals.

Before going any further, let's define what is meant by "project team." Clearly, it includes *all* the technical members of the team (PM, PA/E, field staff, designers, drafters and technical administrative staff). Additionally, we include receptionists, accounting/financial staff and others who might have even occasional contact with a client during the performance of a project. There are more "project team members" than meet the eye.

So, how does the project team contribute to the marketing effort during a project? Besides doing a good job (meeting client goals, objectives and expectations on time and within budget), there are four key roles:

- Providing hassle-free service.
- Stealth marketing.
- Cross-selling.
- Keeping marketing informed.

Providing Hassle-Free Service

Every point of contact between our firm and the client is a potential marketing opportunity (or disaster). Clients are extremely sensitive to how our services are delivered, and the project team is on the front line.

The marketer's classic nightmare: Our firm delivers a technically excellent project (on time, on budget) of which we are justifiably proud; everything seems fine. Yet, the client turns around and gives the next project to another firm. When asked why, the client responds: "I wasn't happy with your service." HUH? How and why did this happen? When pressed for an answer, the client explains that whenever she made inquiries about aspects of the project, she felt it was a hassle.

What might be viewed as "a hassle" by a client? Some typical examples:

The Situation	The Hassle Producer	The Hassle-Free Response
The client asks project manager for clarification of information on an invoice.	"I don't know; call the accounting department, they should know the answer."	"I don't know, but I will find out the answer and call you with information tomorrow."
Our client calls irate about her treatment by our JV partner's "male chauvinist" project manager.	Arguing that she misunderstood. Trying to defend the PM as "a good PM; he was only joking."	"I'll speak to our JV partner and let you know tomorrow what we propose to get the issue resolved."
Hours before a client meeting, we discover an error in documentation.	We conduct the meeting as usual, hope the client won't notice the error, planning to address the issues afterward.	Communicate at once with the team to determine ramifications. Bring issues to the client's attention to let them know we are on top of the situation.
A problem develops between team members on the project.	"It is/was the (engineer's, builder's, architect's) responsibility." Pointing fingers, assigning blame between team members.	Acknowledge the problem; work together to find a solution that is in the best interest of the project.
To serve our client, with whom we have an excellent relationship, we associate with an out-of-town firm with specific skills.	The client calls to say that our associated partner is pitching their services behind our back.	Thank our client; call a summit with our partner.
The client calls the office.	"ABC, Inc.; please hold." The client gets put on hold, and is promptly forgotten.	Give the option of being put on hold, leaving a message or going to voice mail.
The client requests a change that will extend the schedule and/or increase costs in the project.	Nothing is said about the schedule change or cost increase until the work has been completed; then an invoice/change is submitted.	Inform the client about changes or delays, and the impact on cost/schedule, as soon as they are known; no last-minute surprises.
The client calls unexpectedly to discuss the project status.	The PM is not available and no one knows where he or she is, or who can talk to the client.	Leave a complete message on how/when we can be reached, and update the message often.

The possibilities to hassle are endless; the project team must be alert to them and avoid them at all costs. What can you do? Develop your own list of "hassles" (your clients can help) and remedies; distribute the list to *all* employees to raise their level of awareness about hassle-free service.

Stealth Marketing

Stealth marketing supplements the overt, direct marketing and client maintenance activities of the firm. Encourage the project team to practice "stealth marketing" as an off-agenda part of every project encounter with the client. Four proven simple techniques that project leaders and team members can utilize are: research, 10-minute marketing, marketing by walking around (espionage) and pollination.

Research: Risky as some might feel this is (it might open Pandora's box), research is simply asking the questions: "How are we doing? Are we meeting your expectations? What might we do to enhance our service?" Regular project "checkups" can provide valuable information, identify potential problems early, and go a long way toward solidifying client relationships and fostering client satisfaction (cf. Section III ISO 9000).

Ten-minute marketing: The project team leader can allocate (in his or her schedule) a period of five to 10 minutes at the end of each project meeting to have a one-on-one conversation with the client about issues not related to the project; i.e., internal or external events affecting the client's business, changes in the client organization, how our firm (or we) can help him or her do his or her job better. Client project meetings provide a natural forum for learning more about the client's organization, how it is changing and why, and how we can serve the client better.

Marketing by walking around (or espionage): Visits to the client's office for project meetings provide an excellent opportunity to market. By using their keen powers of observation while walking around, project team members can turn up valuable clues or hard information about future client plans early in their development. Tactfully asked questions can provide additional information. A critical element of this technique is knowing when and how to inquire about what has been observed, so that the client is not offended.

Pollination: To raise the client's level of knowledge about the depth of our organization, when project team meetings take place in our office, the project team leader should take the opportunity to introduce the client to other members of the staff, to the principals and to the marketing department. Similarly, when visiting the client's office for a project meeting, the team leader can ask to meet others in the client's organization. As appropriate, he or she can suggest that the client's project manager invite another individual (a peer, his or her supervisor) to attend a project meeting.

By incorporating stealth marketing into the regimen of project meetings with the client, project team leaders and members will be rewarded with opportunities to extol all the virtues and capabilities of the firm (cross-sell) to the client.

Cross-selling

Even though promotional materials list and describe all our capabilities, often a client's knowledge of our firm and its capabilities is based on and limited to current or previous project work, which may not represent the firm's full range of expertise.

Again, a marketer's classic nightmare: A multidiscipline engineering firm (transportation, environmental, water/resources and site/civil) is retained to prepare an environmental impact assessment related to the design of a new highway, including bridges. Later, the same client hires another firm for the highway and bridge design work. Why? Because the client did not know the first consultant had highway and bridge design capabilities.

A firm's exposure to, contact with and potential influence over the client during a project provides an excellent opportunity to reinforce the firm's full range of experience and capabilities. It is the responsibility of every member of the firm to have a basic understanding of the firm's complete range of services and capabilities, and to be able to explain them, at least broadly, to clients and colleagues when successful stealth marketing presents an opportunity.

Keeping Marketing Informed

Successful stealth marketing and cross-selling by the project team will expand their information about the client, about potential project opportunities with the client and about problems or issues that might affect the long-term relationship with the client. To be of maximum value to the firm, this information must be reported to marketing for tracking and future action.

Sounds like such a simple thing, a motherhood-and-apple-pie kind of statement. Yet, while a project is in progress, there is often a disconnect between marketing and client teams that interferes with the effective flow of information. Again, it is the responsibility of the project team to inform marketing of any and all information they learn about a client — good and bad.

For his or her part, the marketer must keep the reporting process as simple as possible by providing clear mechanisms for the teams to use. Develop a reporting form that can be completed quickly, yet will allow team members to provide essential information about clients and opportunities (see Figure 1 on the next page).

Figure 1

CONTACT REPORT FORM
(Provide as much information as possible.)
(Bolded items are essential.)

NAME: FIRST _____ M.I. ____ LAST _____

SALUTATION: (Mr., Mrs., Ms., Miss, Dr.)_____   **NICKNAME:**_____

TITLE: _____   **SECRETARY:** _____

    DIRECT TEL: _____   **DIRECT TEL:** _____

COMPANY: _____

ADDRESS: _____

_____

CITY: _____   **STATE:** ____ **ZIP:** _____

    MAIN TEL: _____   **FAX:** _____

CONTACT BY: _____   **DATE:** _____

FOLLOW-UP DATE: _____ **BY:** _____

FOLLOW-UP ACTION: _____

CONTACT COMMENTS/INFORMATION

III. ISO 9000 — Impact on Marketing

As was stated at the outset of this chapter, there is little argument that client satisfaction is a key factor in successful marketing, client development and client retention efforts of professional services firms. It requires that we forge a strong connection with the client; that we understand the client's personality, goals, objectives, and expectations and incorporate them into our firm's plan for serving that client; and that we constantly identify opportunities to improve the quality of service our clients experience.

This is the premise of ISO 9000: formalizing procedures for improving service quality.

Chapter 1.9 discusses the ramifications of ISO 9000 on professional services firms. The primary focus of ISO 9000 is process improvement within a firm; raising the quality of service and product delivered to clients by developing and implementing systems and processes that ensure that quality is an integral part of a firm's business practices. How does this relate to marketing? Improving quality of service and product can enhance client satisfaction and lead to increased client retention and referrals — a bonus for any marketing effort.

With respect to project delivery, implementation of ISO 9000 within a firm may include active processes that involve both the firm and the client in codifying project parameters and client expectations in a range of performance areas, defining measurables against which to gauge performance and objectively evaluating the firm's performance against the measurables. As a result of the evaluation process, the firm is able to identify areas of performance that fall below desired standards and to initiate corrective actions to improve internal processes.

To be effective, the project delivery procedures adopted should require that a project leader and/or team meet face-to-face with the client several times during a project:

- First, to define the client's (and the firm's) expectations for the project and to establish how the firm will be measured against those expectations.
- To review performance on a regular schedule (monthly, quarterly) and discuss issues or concerns against expectations. Corrective action can be taken rapidly on performance problems, and they can be slated for review at subsequent meetings.
- To conduct a post-project evaluation.

According to Amanda Palookas of Barton Malow:

"The process results in early identification and remediation of performance problems. Corrective actions taken as a result of individual project performance issues are reviewed at the corporate level and incorporated into broader process improvement initiatives. From a marketing perspective, because the client is an integral part of the process, it opens the lines of communication and provides another opportunity to enhance the relationship."

Summary

Marketing is a continuous, ongoing process involving everyone in the firm. While the need for a strong marketing effort to acquire work is generally acknowledged as important, too often the need to maintain that strong marketing effort is forgotten once a project has been acquired. This chapter has focused on the importance of marketing during project delivery to establish strong client relationships, and the critical role of both the marketing staff and the project team in that effort.

Let's summarize the key points outlined.

1. The marketer should have an active role in management of key client accounts.

2. The marketer should assume responsibility for five roles within the firm:

   - **Interpreter and translator** of client goals, objectives and expectations.
   - **Advocate/mediator**, the client's alter ego within the firm and a project team.
   - **Coach** to help enhance the skills of principals and staff.
   - **Contributor** to client projects in his or her specific area of expertise.
   - **Noodge**, asking questions that others do not or cannot ask to ensure that the firm is doing everything possible to provide quality service to clients.

3. From a client service perspective, the project team includes finance/accounting and administrative/support staff as well as technical staff.

4. The project team is responsible for critical client service tasks beyond doing a good job; these tasks are:

   - **Providing hassle-free service** — what's in the client's best interest, responsive, client-focused, non-confrontational.
   - **Cross-selling** — understanding all of the firm's capabilities and how they can be applied to a client's needs, and regularly keeping clients informed of those capabilities.
   - **Stealth marketing** — constantly expanding the firm's information base about clients with whom they are working.
   - **Keeping marketing informed** — communicating new information learned about clients and opportunities.

The marketing responsibilities outlined in Sections I and II for the marketer and the project team should assist the process of improving client satisfaction, loyalty and retention.

Building Relationships — Connecting with Others

Building enduring relationships with others is a complex process involving a range of philosophical, ethical, practical and emotional issues. The process typically takes place over a period of time, during which both parties are constantly evaluating — objectively and subjectively — how well they connect in terms of these critical issues as well as their general interests.

Blackridge, Ltd. developed the **Curve of Relationships**© (Figure 2) as a model from which to describe and discuss the relationship-building process. The curve can best be understood by thinking about your closest personal (non-professional) relationship (spouse, partner, fiancée, mentor, school chum or whomever) and how that close relationship developed over time.

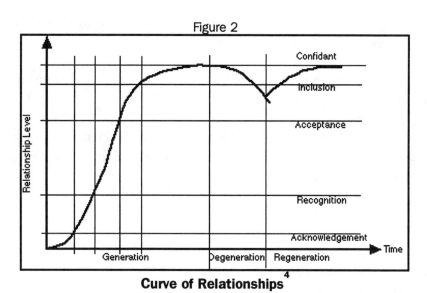

Curve of Relationships[4]

As the curve illustrates, you will recognize at least four, and perhaps five, specific levels of connection that were achieved as the relationship matured and three separate phases of evolution. Those five levels are:

Acknowledgment: the first meeting/introduction following which basic information is exchanged.

Recognition: subsequent encounters, casual or arranged ("dates"), at which there is mutual recall of previous conversations; there is mutual understanding of respective interests, skills and capabilities.

Acceptance: recognition of similar interests, values, ethics, philosophies; an initial level of trust exists; we are invited into the "outer circle" of acquaintances and colleagues.

Inclusion: recognition that interests, values, ethics, philosophies are the same; the level of "trust" has increased; we become part of the "inner circle" of friends and colleagues; we are privy to information others are not.

Confidant: high level of trust; perceived as true advisor; highly personal; sought out for advice/counsel; willingness/ability to be a resource; confront issues directly, unafraid to speak up.

In an ideal world, all relationships would develop smoothly and continuously from the initial meeting (the Acknowledgment level) through Inclusion to Confidant. Unfortunately, the world is not always ideal; not all relationships develop smoothly or continuously. There are times when the parties disagree or they are out of contact and the relationship begins to degenerate, requiring a period of recovery. So we find that the relationship curve can, and usually does, involve three phases of evolution, which are defined as:

Generation: moving up the curve from Acknowledgment to, ultimately, Confidant.

Degeneration: that point at which a relationship begins to falter and break down; can occur at any time and for any reason if we are not alert.

Regeneration: the intense effort required to reverse degeneration of the relationship and move back up the curve.

Development of a professional or business relationship proceeds in the same fashion as a personal relationship. By understanding the five levels and three phases of the Curve of Relationships, we can identify where we are in our business relationships.

Endnotes

[1] Frederick F. Reichheld, *The Loyalty Effect* 3.

[2] Trevor Richards and Jan Hofmeyer, *The Conversion Model.*

[3] Blackridge, Ltd., owner surveys, 1995-1997, owner identity privileged.

[4] Copyright, 1994-1999, Blackridge, Ltd. All rights reserved.

Bibliography

Bennis, Warren G. *Managing People is Like Herding Cats.* Provo, UT: Executive Excellence Publishing, 1997.

—. *On Becoming a Leader.* Reading, MA: Addison-Wesley Publishing Co., 1989.

Bolman, Lee G., and Terrence E. Deal. *Reframing Organizations.* San Francisco: Jossey-Bass Publishers, 1997.

de Geus, Arie. *The Living Company.* Boston: Harvard Business School Press, 1997.

McKenna, Regis. *Relationship Marketing.* Reading, MA: Addison-Wesley Publishing Co., 1991.

Reichheld, Frederick F. *The Loyalty Effect.* Boston: Harvard Business School Press, 1996.

Richards, Trevor, and Jan Hofmeyer. *The Conversion Model,* "Marketing Professional Services '95," London: Financial Times Conferences, April 1995.

Schneider, Benjamin, and David E. Bowen. *The Service Organization: Human Resource Management is Crucial.* American Management Association, "Organizational Dynamics," Spring 1993.

Treacy, Michael, and Fred Wiersema. *The Discipline of Market Leaders.* Reading, MA: Addison-Wesley, 1995.

Philip F. Valence, FSMPS

- Philip F. Valence, FSMPS, is president of Blackridge Ltd., management and marketing consultants located in Wellesley Hills, Mass. He has more than 30 years' experience in marketing, management and operations of technical consulting and construction firms.
- Former vice president of marketing of Earth Technology Corp., the George B.H. Macomber Co., construction manager/builder, and Vanderweil Engineers; responsible for marketing and business development activities.
- Responsibilities included directing the client maintenance and development activities of professional technical teams, and for training technical staff in client maintenance activities during the performance of a project.
- Well-versed in the creation of internal organizations and information systems to support the marketing and business development activities of professional services firms.
- At Blackridge, assists architects, engineers and construction firms with issues ranging from ownership and management transition planning to leadership development, marketing and business development planning and training.
- Former SMPS National secretary, treasurer and regional director; a founder, past president and treasurer of the Boston Chapter.
- Recipient of SMPS Boston's award for Outstanding Contribution to Marketing.
- Frequent speaker at programs of the Society for Marketing Professional Services, the American Institute of Architects, the American Consulting Engineers Council, the Associated General Contractors of America and the American Marketing Association.
- Master's degree in business administration; bachelor's degree in electrical engineering.

Acknowledgment

Special thanks to Melanie M. Cornell who authored the original chapter on marketing throughout project execution for the first edition of *The Handbook for Marketing Professional Services*.

Part 4:
Public
Relations

4.1   Communications Planning

Rolf Fuessler, APR
President
Fuessler Group Inc.

Professional services marketing is about relationship building, and strong relationships are built, in part, on good communications. Communications is the ignition switch of professional services marketing. It starts conversations, which lead to relationships that may result in work. Many professional services firms have developed sophisticated, synergistic tactics to help them communicate with their varied audiences. Other firms rely on one or two simple tools to keep their name in front of clients and prospects. In either case, successful programs are those that contain the right message for the audience.

How does a professional services firm separate itself from the clutter and the competition? Simply, with a clear and compelling message, delivered creatively, to the right decision-maker. And communications planning is a critical element to help you accomplish this.

Communications planning is a five-step process that involves message development and positioning, audience identification, tactical analysis, delivery mechanism selection and post-program analysis.

Message Development and Positioning

The development of a clear and compelling message is the crucial first step in communications planning. Successful message development relies on differentiation: breaking away from the crowded field of similar firms to clearly position your firm as different.

Developing a message that results in a response is about more than background and experience. It can be about projecting a unique corporate personality, differences in approach and attitude toward projects, strengths in a niche market or positioning yourself as the low-cost service provider. It can also be about projecting a razor-sharp understanding of special needs and concerns of clients within a specific market sector. Whatever your positioning strategy and message, they must emerge out of a focused sense of where the firm is headed and what clients are seeking.

Thus, message development and positioning involve a two-part process of rigorous self-analysis and market research. Message development evolves out of internal factors — strengths and weaknesses, background and experience, principal goals, business plans and organizational goals. Positioning derives its roots from the marketplace: expectations, foibles, competitive analysis and image. Firms that undergo rigorous self-analysis and accumulate a large amount of market intelligence will develop the right message and positioning strategy. This can be accomplished through market and image research. The results from a properly formulated and implemented research program can give a firm a wealth of information to create a competitive edge.

Without both extensive self-analysis and market-based attitudinal research many communications programs will fail. For example, an expensive, high-quality, six-color, award-winning brochure developed to communicate to potential clients in a market that has become highly cost-conscious will fail. It is sending the wrong message. However, a series of articles or workshops on ways to cut costs in the design, engineering and construction process will get serious interest. In the first example, use of the brochure, with a cost in the high five figures, was quickly abandoned once the firm's principals began receiving negative feedback about the "expense." In the second example, the workshops helped another firm start conversations with potential clients that ultimately led to work.

A finely honed positioning and targeted message strategy must also be consistent across all communications platforms that a firm uses. The messages contained in your newsletter must be consistent with those in your corporate brochure; your web site must be in synch with your media-relations strategy. A communications audit, which reviews all material used in marketing, public relations and communications efforts, will uncover glaring inconsistencies in message and content.

Audience Identification

Developing a set of market-focused messages is meaningless if a firm hasn't gone through an exercise to identify potential client targets. Without a qualified, finely honed target list, you could be sending the right message to the wrong folks.

Research about and experience with a market can help a firm accumulate data about decision factors, selection processes and likely level of interest in your services within various parts of an organization. Knowing with whom you want to communicate is a major factor in developing your messages. Is your audience the 26 closest colleges/universities to your office or is it all colleges east of the Mississippi? Is your ideal target college facility managers or college boards of trustee members? To what messages does each level of client respond?

Lists of potential clients can range from highly targeted and accurate to those containing inaccurate information and poor quality leads. List companies tout their product as containing the latest information with minimal mistakes. However, bought lists rarely live up to the hype in the quality of information and abound in inaccuracies, duplication and off-target listings. A better source of potential client lists are the ones that can be obtained from professional organizations or trade and client-read publications. While these lists tend to be more targeted, they will contain many more listings than are practical or useful.

The ideal target list is one that a firm has carefully assembled over time through networking; one-on-one situations at trade shows, conferences and presentations; or developed by calling a targeted list of companies or institutions for the names of persons occupying positions identified as key in the decision-making process.

Having a well-qualified list of 25 or 1,000 potential clients versus a list of 10,000 prospects of unknown quality and validity will bring you to the next step in communications planning: tactical analysis.

Tactical Analysis

Professional services firms have a host of communications tools and tactics at their disposal. Some have long been used in the A/E/C industry, for example, newsletters, brochures and project sheets. Some are relied upon less frequently, such as advertising, trade shows and annual reports. Others, like web sites and CD-ROMs have entered our tactical grab bag only in recent years.

Communications tools range from the simple and inexpensive, such as a press release to several trade magazines or a quick note to clients about a new project, to the complex and expensive, such as direct mail programs and advertising campaigns. Other chapters in this section of the handbook are devoted to detailed discussions of these tools and tactics.

Part of communications planning is coming up with the mix of tactics or tools that best communicate your message to the right audience. Initially, the decision you need to make is whether to approach your client universe directly or indirectly. Direct approaches to prospects are ideal. Networking, presentations to potential clients, professional organizational involvement, conducting workshops, showcasing at trade shows, or any other tactic that places you within eyeball and handshaking distance of clients should be a first priority. Indirect approaches, like using media relations, direct mail campaigns without response mechanisms or web sites, can create name recognition and visibility for a firm but does less to establish relationships.

Recently, I had a conversation with a marketing director with a local engineering firm. He was thinking of developing a postcard mailer to announce a new service that his firm was offering. In the discussion, it came out that his "potential" client universe in fact was less than 25 existing clients. Rather than use an indirect approach, I urged him to start making appointments to meet with each client personally to discuss the new service. If his potential client universe were 1,000 — made up of clients and potential clients — the tactics used would have been different. Most likely, the communications program would have been a mix of direct approaches to existing clients and a mailer or announcement to potential clients, with follow-up to selected potential clients.

Using direct approaches to clients supports relationship marketing. Potential clients have an opportunity to form preliminary opinions about a firm and probe about services and experience. Your firm principal or marketer can gauge whether this potential client is appropriate to pursue further and can gain valuable insight and intelligence about plans and philosophy.

In market surveys, clients tend to value direct marketing tactics and information gleaned from peers higher than indirect communications tools. Consistently scoring poorly are advertising, firm brochures and newsletters.

Picking the appropriate communications tool or tactics to use in bringing your message to a subset of your potential client universe involves answering a series of questions. For the sake of discussion, let's use the K-12 market as an example. An architectural firm located in Ohio wants to grow this part of its practice, both in-state and within neighboring states, and has conducted extensive market research.

How much is budgeted for the communications program? If a modest amount, a single tactic may be the only option. First choice would be a direct communications tactic, such as attendance or presentation at the annual meetings of several state educational professional groups or targeting a select list of potential school district officials with in-person meetings. Advertising is rarely the single option used because of cost. With a more ample budget, these tactics can be supplemented with articles in school trade publications, workshops and even select advertising in regional professional magazines or newsletters. Advertising may not be appropriate even when a firm has an ample budget because there may not be a regional publication that cost effectively reaches the targeted Midwest school audience.

How big is your potential client universe? Is it every school district in a four-state region above a certain size? A program of sending information packets to several districts a week, with scheduled follow-up telephone discussions, may be an option. Have you targeted the 10 largest districts in Ohio? Do you already know their concerns and needs? Can existing clients provide you with entree to this small universe of potential clients? You have a situation here where a finely targeted, in-person presentation to each district may be appropriate. Do you want every school district in the four-state region to associate your firm with the K-12 market? Your research has uncovered low name recognition in several states. Because the challenge here is raising name recognition, using multiple communications platforms usually works best. Media relations, direct mail campaigns, trade show participation, professional meetings and workshops, newsletters, your web site and advertising.

Do you have a good mailing list? Why develop an expensive brochure or direct mail campaign to send out to an unqualified purchased list? Spend the money on hiring an outside consultant to cold call and identify clients and potential leads. Then, develop a program to reach those pre-qualified prospects.

What is the best tactic for my message? If you are trying to establish recognition for a niche expertise and have a growing track record of success, developing an article for a key client-read publication may be a good tactical candidate. Touting your expertise in a brochure or your newsletter may be less believable.

How much time do you have to grow this market? If you have a five-year plan, a steadily increasing mix of communications tools will help cover all bases. Eventually, potential clients will read about you in the trade press, see you at conferences and trade shows, attend one of your focused workshops, skim your advertising, meet your key folks, file away your brochure and quietly view your web site. If you have less than a year to see growth in the schools market, you will need to jump-start the communications process. Tactically, you need to find the quickest way to identify leads and then ways to communicate to those leads. Usually, the direct approach and heavy networking works best.

There is no one communications tactic that works in all situations. A careful analysis of budget, timing, audience and message will lead you to the right mix for your firm

Delivery Mechanism Selection

Selecting how you deliver your message has become an important consideration. The methods used to deliver a firm's message have increased dramatically through the advent of technology. The traditional methods of hand delivering a brochure during a meeting or mailing a newsletter continue. These methods are now joined by faxed direct mail campaigns, bulletin board mailboxes, e-mail cold calling, CD-ROM brochures and interactive videos.

The delivery mechanism you use is key and often will determine if something is read. Put yourself in your clients' shoes. What computer systems do your clients use? Send them information on a compatible disk. What magazines do your key prospects read? Write bylined articles or run advertising to attract their attention. What impact will regulatory changes have on industry? Fax targeted clients and prospects in that industry a fact-filled analysis outlining implications and alternatives.

Even if you use traditional snail-mail forms of delivery, how you package your message becomes important. Everyone is inundated with mail every day. Sending your brochure or press kit in an unusual way or using special packaging increases the chances that it will be opened, read and kept.

In addition to having become an increasingly important tactic and form of communication, web sites should be viewed as an alternative delivery mechanism. Why? Your web site is basically a floating information kiosk, easily accessed by anyone who wants information about your firm. The design, information content, personality is accessed (delivered) many times daily by a diversity of folks, including competitors, those seeking employment, researchers and possible clients. When your web site comes up on some far away screen, you must make sure that you are presenting the best possible view of the firm.

Post-Program Analysis

So how do you know that your communications program has been a success or failure? There are two ways. The first is through post-program follow-up research. You compare growth in recognition and identity or change in attitudes toward your firm with the initial research conducted prior to beginning the program. The initial market research that you completed should contain some questions that benchmark attitudes and recognition factors.

For example, the firm in Ohio learned through its initial round of benchmarking research that it had a 65 percent name recognition in Ohio and less than 25 percent name recognition in neighboring states. Asking a similar universe of school officials similar questions after its communications program is completed, the firm finds out that name recognition has risen to over 80 percent in its home state and to more than 50 percent in neighboring states. These numbers underline a successful campaign. However, if the recognition numbers rose less than 10 percent in the neighboring states, the program should be analyzed for the reasons. In both cases, the follow-up survey should probe respondents about their reactions to the various tactics used.

A second way of gauging success or failure is related to bottom-line impact and anecdotal information. Was there a cause and effect? Did the $50,000 campaign targeting school board members and superintendents result in establishing conversations and relationships with some of the districts, leading to an increase in requests for proposal (RFPs) and projects? Did the firm capture two $10 million school projects or only one $200,000 study? Analysis and in-depth discussions with selected school officials can help uncover some of the triggers for a program's success or failure.

Several years ago, an A/E firm had developed a brochure targeting the K-12 schools market. The brochure was mailed to a combination of past, existing and potential clients. In two cases, the brochure sparked a telephone call from potential clients for further information, which led to multi-million dollar contracts. The cause and effect here were clear.

Often, communications programs results are less clear, particularly if no benchmarks were established. In these cases, anecdotal information can help establish some measure. Asking every new prospect who calls how they heard about your firm, the responses you receive from direct mail solicitations or through your web site, and comments you receive from colleagues and peers, all begin to answer the question of success or failure.

Communicate Your Difference

Planning is a critical first step to take in creating an effective and successful communications program. In today's world of 10-second sound bites, 15 minutes of fame, 150 channels of cable programming and the Internet, the information clutter is overwhelming. Communications planning helps a professional services firm find a personality, message and positioning strategy that breaks through the clutter and connects with its audience.

Successful communications tools or tactics are those that clearly communicate a difference, an edge, a reason for someone to pick up the phone or respond. Find your difference and use the helpful hints throughout this section of the handbook to start you on your way toward using the right communication tools and tactics for your firm.

Bibliography

Beckwith, Harry. *Selling the Invisible: A Field Guide to Modern Marketing.* New York: Warner Books, 1997.

Cutlip, Scott M., and Allen H. Center. *Effective Public Relations.* Englewood Cliffs, N.J.: Prentice Hall, 1985.

Dilenschneider, Robert L. *Power and Influence: The Art of Persuasion.* New York: Prentice Hall Press, 1990.

Kliment, Stephen A., FAIA, *Writing for Design Professionals. A Guide to Writing Successful Proposals, Letters, Brochures, Portfolios, Reports, Presentations, and Job Applications.* W.W. Norton & Co., 1998.

Ross, Robert D. *The Management of Public Relations.* New York: John Wiley & Sons, 1977.

Schwerin, Horace S., and Henry H. Newell. *Persuasion in Marketing.* New York: John Wiley & Sons, 1981.

Sonnenberg, Frank K. *Marketing to Win ... Strategies for Building Competitive Advantage in Service Industries.* Harper Business, 1990.

Stephenson, Howard, editor in chief. *Handbook of Public Relations.* New York: McGraw-Hill, 1971.

Wilcox, Denis L., and Lawrence W. Nolte. *Public Relations Writing & Media Techniques.* Addison-Wesley Educational Publishers Inc., 1997.

Rolf Fuessler, APR

- Rolf Fuessler, APR, is president of the Fuessler Group Inc., a marketing communications firm based in Boston. The Fuessler Group is publisher of the *Publicity Directory for the A/E/C Industry.*
- Over the last 15 years he has helped almost 200 professional services firms nationwide attract attention, change perceptions, build image and broadcast accomplishments.
- In former professional lives, he was an editor with *Engineering News Record* and vice president of corporate communications for Camp Dresser & McKee.
- He is an accredited member of the Public Relations Society of America and a 20-year member of SMPS.
- He can be reached at **fuessler@fuessler.com**.

4.2 Hiring Consultants and Managing Consultant Relationships

Craig Park, FSMPS
Vice President, Integrated Solutions
Intellisys Group Inc.

Dana L. Birkes, CPSM

Professional services firms face a myriad of challenges where outside consultants can help. As the representative of your firm's marketing department, you will often need to hire outside expertise to support the marketing effort. These consultants can include firms and individuals with expertise in public relations, photography, graphic arts, web design and corporate identity. These roles are typically outside the purview, expertise or capacity of your internal marketing staff. Consultants, as experts, can provide new information, interpret existing information or support organizational objectives in ways that are unavailable to internal resources. Whether picking a consulting firm for a project in support of some aspect of the marketing effort, it is important to understand the aspects of selection and management that will ensure success for your endeavor.

Selecting the right consultant for your firm's project teams can sometimes mean the difference between getting a job or not. Similarly, selecting and properly managing the marketing support consulting effort can also determine the success (or failure) of any project you may undertake. The same detailed analysis that the marketer uses to evaluate a potential project opportunity should be used to set the criteria, scope and deliverables for outside consultants.

Defining the Project Requirements

Regardless of the consulting discipline or support required, a well-managed selection process will set the stage for a successful project. In preparing a request for proposal (RFP), avoid generalities and presumptions that will hinder the ability of the consultant to perform the work. If the scope of work seems vague, you should clarify the expectations for performance and the metrics used to evaluate the result. If your internal organization structure is bureaucratic (i.e., the work is being managed by the marketing department for some other department's use), specify the requirement to communicate extensively with the end-users to ensure that the project meets their desired result.

If the project budget is set, determine if the funding is based on a current and relevant estimate or modeled after a similar project. If the schedule is established, it is important to verify that the completion date is realistic. Do you have design standards from prior work that the consultant will be expected to apply to this project? Are there any implied liabilities for the performance of the work that are outside of the norm? Are there contractual methods established to deal with changes to the scope or schedule? If the contract is awarded based on technical qualifications only, take a proactive approach in establishing the value of the consulting fees.

Unfortunately, client (your) expectations are rarely in harmony with the consultant's reality. What you expect for the delivery of quality service is often at odds with the vendor's methods or practice. Thus, it becomes extraordinarily important that the initial communication between you and the consultant establish and define deliverables and the metrics that will be used for measuring the success of the completed project. Contracts based on a clear understanding of expectation are complete and inclusive of protections from the vagaries of less-than-clear desire on the part of the client.

Finding the Right Consultant

In the hiring process for a consultant, the first step is determining the kind of consultant that you need. Make sure the project fits the company's strategic agenda and will not compete for time, funds or staff with other projects. Otherwise both the consultants and your staff assigned to the project will become frustrated, and costly consultant hours will be wasted.

From the generalist to the specialist, consultants come in many flavors. Through research and investigation, you can develop a network of experienced consultants. By using your network you can build long-term working relationships and have the resources needed to locate a specialty consultant to fulfill a unique project requirement. Some common sense considerations in developing a list of consulting resources include:

- **Expertise:** Look for consultants who have specific experience in the type of project you are undertaking. Usually there are many firms capable of producing the project. Selecting the firm that has specific experience assists in marketing the team and minimizes the learning curve during production. Ask your peers in other firms for referrals (and ask whom they wouldn't work with and why.) Look at the consultants included in the teams of published projects that are similar to the work your firm does.

- **References:** Ask for them and check them. Ask for current references that are relevant to the project you are undertaking. If possible, ask the potential client whom they would recommend using. Ask others in your firm for their opinions of the consultant.

- **Key project personnel:** Ask for the names of the individuals who worked on the projects that are relevant to your project. Some consultants promote work produced by people who are no longer on staff. Others will solicit your work with experienced staff and assign someone else to the project once it is underway. Get written confirmation that those individuals will commit a specified amount of time to your project. Request their current and projected work loads. Minimize the potential of being handed off by asking these questions and getting commitments prior to project start-up.

- **Financial stability:** Check the consultant's financial status and stability, years in business and so on. More than once a consultant firm has gone out of business or gone bankrupt at a critical juncture in project development.

- **Exclusivity:** When selecting consultants for your firm's projects, determine whether they will provide personnel on an exclusive basis. Will they be challenged because they are working on multiple projects (that may compete for time with yours)? If you work with a particular consultant on a regular basis, the strength of an ongoing relationship will often be a motivation for exclusivity. This will strengthen your teamwork and assist in the project's efforts.

Find firms and people to work with whom you like and respect and who like and respect you. Consultants are professionals and react and perform best when they are treated with mutual respect. When you are in a pressure situation, it helps to know that everyone is doing their best and working toward the common goal. Socializing professionally with your regular consultants is a simple investment in time that can greatly enhance the collaborative effort. Good consultants interact with many clients and can be a wealth of competitive information and market research.

Keep current experience, qualifications and resumes of your regular consultants on file for quick access. Keep this information up to date; personnel changes can radically change a consultant's ability to provide the quality service you may have grown to expect. If you have standard proposal formats and contract terms and conditions, provide them to the consultant. That way, when you are pressed for time, you are not as dependent on them to provide you with standard information.

Preparing a Solicitation for Consulting

When a project needs are well-defined, prepare a request for qualifications (RFQ) or RFP. You may want to include a formal presentation/interview process when a group of people will be involved in working with the consultant. It not only provides an equal opportunity for the consultants/vendors to present their qualifications, it has the additional benefit of generating project support from everyone involved in the selection process. The process of selecting a consultant is easier if the terms of reference for the project (which are formalized in the contract) contain the following elements.

- **Context and background:** Create a clear description of the background to the project, its relevant characteristics and the details of the specific issues under examination.

- **Project purpose:** Write a description of the objectives for the assignment and state the expected project results and their intended end use.

- **Resource requirements:** Define the internal resources available to the consultant and the relationship of these resources to the consultant's role and position.

- **Process:** Describe your desired process. It should describe the basic phase requirements (e.g., needs analysis, concept development, approach and fulfillment). If you want the consultant to suggest appropriate processes, this should be so stated.

- **Detail:** State the level of detail and documentation that is expected. How many interim reports, presentations or design alternatives, etc., are required? How many copies of both the analysis and the final report are required? What are the type and number of coordination meetings? Is there flexibility in the terms of reference and other matters?

- **Responsibilities:** Provide an overview of the day-to-day project administration, hierarchies and protocols; what constitutes, in your terms, the final acceptance of the project's results; the use of steering, advisory or other review committees; the methods for gathering of basic data; and the responsibility for project direction.

- **References and standards:** State what other information will be available to the consultant (e.g., previous reports, survey data). Provide, or note availability, of existing standards that the consultants work must meet or reflect. Document whether working space, clerical, research assistants or other resources are available.

- **Time line and budget:** Prepare a schedule indicating the required start, mid-term milestones and completion dates. Provide an estimated range for professional fees that fit within your budget. However, do not make price the sole basis for consultant selection. Cost overruns due to lack of experience can cost more during the course of a project than hiring a specialist at a slightly higher rate.

- **Evaluation criteria:** Provide a clear specification of proposal evaluation criteria (e.g., experience, costs, time to be spent on-site, innovative methodology), and the weight placed on each, so the selection can be informed, fair and efficient.

Selecting the Consultant

After the qualifications submissions have been received, it's time to select the consultant that will be hired for the project. There are several methods for making this decision. Single-source selection is justified when there is one consultant who clearly stands out with the special skills required for the project. This also applies when time constraints make it impractical to have an extensive search process. Often there is one consultant who is familiar with the specifics of the project to create the potential for substantial cost savings, or, by the unique location of the project, save travel costs and be more cost effective.

More often, negotiated-contract is the preferred method for consultant selection. By widening the group receiving solicitations, you can negotiate with a pre-selected group of consultants who may all be suitable for the project. These firms should be interviewed, their references checked, and their proposals evaluated against the selection criteria and available budget. This type of negotiated procurement is suitable for larger budget projects and for projects on which it is important to tap a large pool of consultants for a more creative approach.

When only a limited and select number of firms compete for the job, they are more likely to spend the time and effort on a more creative approach. The careful preparation of objectives prior to the proposal call will make evaluation easier, fairer and will enable selection of the best proposal. Evaluation should consider:

- Professional and technical competence in meeting proposal objectives.
- Understanding of the project and the logic of the project methodology.
- Technical approach to the project program.
- Cost and ability to work within the project schedule.
- Experience of the staff, and the application of staff resources to the task.
- Experience working with your firm.
- Management and organization.
- Consultants resources offered.
- Use of innovative and imaginative approaches.

The primary emphasis should always be on professional and technical merit. Provided all proposals are in a reasonable range, cost should play a relatively small role. Professional and technical competence has far-reaching and major financial implications well beyond the consultant assignment itself. The evaluation process should never be a contest of experience or cost alone.

Everything else being equal, you are often best served by hiring the consultant you have worked with before. An existing relationship means they have some familiarity with your method of operations and you with theirs. Having this understanding in place will facilitate both project development and communication.

Contracting for Consulting Services

Establishing a contract for any consulting services can use much of the information prepared during the solicitation and selection processes as the basis for the more formal contract for services. However, as a legal document, binding on both the firm and the consultant, contractual language should always be in the form of direct statements of work to be performed. A well-written contract is the key to managing the consultant relationship. Because of the variations in legal requirements on a state-by-state and local level, as always, it is safe, if not pleasant, to check with an attorney before finalizing any contractual language. The elements of a consulting contract follow many of the steps of the selection process. At a minimum, the contract should include a definition of the following:

- **Parties:** the individuals or firm that represents the "client," and which firm and individuals represent the "consultant."
- **Scope:** what is the nature of the project.
- **Deliverables:** what will be the consultant's output or contribution.
- **Metrics:** the method by which the completeness of the work will be judged.
- **Schedule:** when does the project start and when does it end.
- **Billing:** the method and timing of payment.

Special circumstances often dictate special terms and conditions. Issues like "prepayment" or "retainage" should be reviewed and established. If the project will take one month or less to complete, it is not unheard of for a consultant to request 100 percent of the fee up-front. If the project will last longer, the request should be for a proportionally lesser amount.

Because consultants may forego potentially significant revenues from other projects because they have contracted for yours, be prepared to pay a project cancellation fee if your project is delayed or cancelled. This is especially true on large projects where you will demand a great percentage of the consultant's resources. This cancellation fee should decrease the longer the project has run, as the consultant earns a greater portion of the expected revenues.

Change order contingencies should be reviewed and agreed upon. The purpose of this is to allow for payment for any unanticipated changes that occur during the course of the project. It is safer to budget extra funds in the initial financing to cover contingencies that may not be anticipated at the beginning of the project (e.g., unknown site conditions, schedule extensions, product changes), than to haggle over them when the schedule is more pressing. The funds to cover these contingencies may not be as easily secured later in the project.

Invoicing formats and procedures should be spelled out. Provide the consultant with a sample of how you require invoices to be formatted.

Define the number of alternatives you expect the consultant to provide. Although you are hiring the "expert," it is reasonable to expect more than a single choice or recommendation for your review. The limitations should also reflect the schedule for the project, allowing you to make an informed decision within a time frame that allows for cost-effective implementation.

Recognize that when projects extend over long periods there should be budget to account for the escalation of the consultant's costs and rates. Most consulting firms put a clause in their contracts stating that after some date, "all fees will be subject to renegotiations." It may be safer to specify a specific percentage increase that begins at a given point in the project schedule. Open-ended renegotiations could result in significantly increased costs for the work being performed.

Limit the liability. Your contract should include a statement that acknowledges the liabilities incurred by the consultant throughout the course of the project. Limit liabilities to a maximum of the net contract amount received, not including reimbursable expenses and subcontractors, for all services rendered on the project. This is simply a more reasonable limit of liability than that of the total fee or the costs of the work the consultant is designing or specifying.

Contract validity can be established by including names of those authorized to approve the contract. Similarly, there should be a date that sets a limited time for acceptance. Do not make open-ended commitments that you may not want to live up to in the future. This clause helps define the time of the project completion.

Ownership and copyright of documents (particularly photographs) is often an area of contention. Establish in your contract that all documents produced under the terms of the agreement are your property. Be aware, however, that documents used for other than their original purpose may result in liability to the original design firm.

Establish which reimbursable expenses you will pay in addition to the consultant's fees. Typically, these include expenses associated with travel, subsistence, telephone and facsimile charges, blueprint, messenger, delivery and postage associated with the project. Consider making reimbursable expenses a small percentage (e.g., 3 to 5 percent) of the consultant's monthly billings. This simplifies your accounting and may actually save money. It also eliminates the need to keep track of mountains of detailed backup.

Contract terms should be used only after consultation with a competent attorney knowledgeable in contract law in your area of practice and locale. This does not diminish the importance of solid contracts that reflect your requirements. They are, in the end, key to the successful business relationship with outside consultants, as well as with your practice and long-term viability.

At the End of the Day

Before project start-up, define a system to communicate while the project is in progress. It is critical that both you and the consultant communicate consistently during the project's development. It is usually recommended that project communication happen a minimum of five times (at 20 percent completion milestones) to ensure the project stays on track. Follow up each meeting with a memo documenting your understanding of the actions required, deadlines, presumed costs and major decisions so there can be no room for confusion or error.

When hiring consultants, remember that you are the client. If you will apply the same considerations and procedures in hiring a consultant that you would like your clients to in selecting your firm, you can improve the consulting experience. Look at this process as an educational opportunity to learn how your firm can better position it to be selected.

Though there may be no escaping the need for consultants — if anything, you'll be using them more — there is no reason for despair if you follow one basic rule: Stay involved. Like your personal physician, your consultants can only know how to help if you communicate and share responsibility with them. If you do, you should have fewer horror stories and many conclusions that are more successful.

Craig Park, FSMPS

- Craig Park is a fellow of the Society for Marketing Professional Services (SMPS) and marketing professional with nearly 30 years' experience in professional services, consulting engineering and systems integration firms.
- His experience includes business development, marketing management and the development of promotional marketing materials.
- Park is vice president of integrated solutions at Intellisys Group, engineered design-builders of multimedia communication systems, based in Mountain View, Calif. (**www.intellisysgroup.com**), and is responsible for their corporate design and national business development activities.
- Park received his bachelor's degree in architecture from California State Polytechnic University, San Luis Obispo.
- He currently serves as Fellows Delegate to the national board of directors of the SMPS and is past president of the San Francisco/Bay Area Chapter. Park has presented programs on technology and marketing to SMPS, the American Institute of Architects (AIA), the International Institute of Interior Designers (IIDA), the Institute of Business Designers (IBD) and the International Facilities Management Association (IFMA).
- Park has published more than 50 articles on technology and marketing, and writes a regular column titled "On Virtuality," in *Systems Contractor News* magazine, which focuses on improving business processes for the multimedia systems integration industry.
- Park can be reached by phone at (415) 472-0930, by fax at (415) 472-0934, by e-mail at **craig@craigpark.com**, **www.craigpark.com**.

Acknowledgment

I want to acknowledge the fine original chapter on this subject prepared by Dana L. Birkes, CPSM, for the first edition of this book. It helped form the outline for my writing, and I have tried to include much of her original information.

4.3 Image and Corporate Identity: Strategically Positioning Who You Are

Dianne Ludman Frank, FSMPS
Principal
Dianne Ludman Frank Public Relations

Every action, every form of communication reveals a great deal about a firm and the way it does business — its vision and values, its culture and character, its expertise and strengths. The receptionist at the front desk and the tone of e-mail messages have as much to do with conveying who a firm is and what it stands for as the actual process of securing and serving clients.

Image and corporate identity are powerful and all-encompassing marketing tools that can strategically position a firm in the marketplace. They are long-term investments upon which a firm can forge better business relationships, build positive perceptions, inspire loyalty and differentiate itself within its markets. Image and corporate identity are two of the most valuable assets a firm can have, and, as such, need to be managed as any real asset should. Through strategically planned programs, a firm can use its image and identity to create value in the marketplace and a better understanding of the firm on the part of its clients, staff, allies and publics.

Understanding, Creating and Building Image

In "The Brand Called You," published in *Fast Company*, August/September 1997, Tom Peters states: "Today brands are everything, and all kinds of products and services — from accounting firms to sneaker makers to restaurants — are figuring out how to transcend the narrow boundaries of their categories and become a brand. ... The brand is a promise of value you'll receive."[1]

Whether viewed within marketing concepts such as branding or differentiating or creating experiences, it is the "promise of value" to which Peters refers that is essential to professional services and thus communicated through a firm's image. Image has traditionally been defined as the collective perceptions, impressions and experiences that audiences have about who the firm is, what it stands for and how it conducts its business. Infiltrating every aspect of a firm's business, image can be a powerful influence and determinant in the selection and decision-making process. A firm, therefore, needs to not only create and control a good image, but manage it as an important element in market-positioning strategy. While image can be built and developed, its success ultimately depends upon how fully it represents reality and experience. If the "value promised" is undelivered, no amount of enhanced packaging will be able to support a positive image.

There are a number of factors that contribute to image — firsthand experience, opinions and word of mouth, publicity, media coverage, electronic media, advertising, promotional literature, financial stability, standing in the community, reputation in the industry and the attitudes of a firm's own staff, both past and present. These subjective feelings can be consistent or inconsistent with reality, and favorable, unfavorable or neutral, in varying degrees.

Each encounter with clients and potential customers presents an opportunity to radiate and reinforce image. These encounters may be direct and personal, or through indirect means such as print and electronic media. How are visitors greeted? Is the office ambiance and dress code formal or informal? To what extent are staff members empowered to make decisions? How are problems resolved? What is the level of involvement of the principals? How is the web site navigated? How "user-friendly" are telephone systems, invoices, proposal responses? What is the protocol for meetings? How open is the firm to innovation? How does the firm respond to change? What is the character of collateral materials? How visible is the firm in the press? How active are staff members in professional and industry organizations? Regardless of style or substance, obvious or subtle actions, each experience can be used to communicate qualities about the firm that are fundamental to understanding who it is.

In an interview for *Fast Company*, "What Great Brands Do," August/September 1997, Scott Bedbury, the marketer responsible for the well-known campaigns for both Nike Inc. footwear and apparel and Starbucks Coffee Co., outlines eight principles for brand-building. Among these are: "a great brand is in it for the long haul," "a great brand knows itself," "a great brand has design consistency," and "a great brand is relevant" — key success factors for building corporate image.[2]

In "knowing oneself," it is important to remember that what a firm's own principal and staff perceive to be the firm's image may or may not be the same as a client's perceptions and preferences. One of the best ways to determine and assess image is to undertake serious research, which will answer questions such as:

- How well is the firm known?
- How well are the firm's services and capabilities known?
- What are the firm's strengths and weaknesses?
- What value does the firm bring?
- Who is the firm's competition?
- What is the firm's competitive edge?
- What market position does the firm hold?
- How does the firm's performance rate on: delivery of service, project management, design, technology, innovation, pricing?
- How effective are the firm's communications materials and promotional programs?

Based on the results of the study, an assessment can be made to carve or defend a leadership position, work to penetrate market share or define a market niche.

The most thorough image study is one that surveys a sample of past, current and prospective clients in a firm's respective markets. It should also assess feedback from senior management and staff, significant associates, colleagues, consultants and vendors to gain internal as well as external evaluations. The study should clearly define at the outset the goals and information to be gathered. Whether an independent, outside research company is used to conduct an image study, or the firm embarks on a structured debriefing study, the usefulness of such research depends upon securing information that will help the firm position itself effectively in its markets.

It is also important to note that a firm's image is not one specifically defined perception, but composed of a number of relevant perceptions and notions that build up to a larger whole. Underneath the "umbrella" image, for example, is the firm's significance locally, regionally, nationally, internationally. As the firm's image is applied to individual market sectors or to individual areas of expertise, nuances and patterns of relevancy emerge. A firm's image in the public sector may differ from that in the private sector. The same characteristic of the firm that is perceived as a plus in one market may be a negative in another. An understanding of those notions and relevant differences allows a firm to strengthen them or counteract them in promotion and communications materials targeted at each specific audience — clients, industry and community leaders, allies and colleagues, shareholders, employees, potential recruits.

Communication in each market sector in which the firm is active must, nevertheless, be consistent with the firm's overall image. For example, a firm fluent in the knowledge-based specialties will be able to cross-market easily in such sectors as health care, research and development, and higher education. But it would be inappropriate for that same firm to send the message that it is lowest-price if indeed it has built its practice on value-added service. There is a danger in trying to be "all things to all people," giving "mixed messages," or stretching an image too thin. Marketer Al Ries, in his writings with Jack Trout and Laura Ries, warns against line extension (applying the name or image of an established product to new products), and gives numerous examples in product marketing and advertising. In *The 22 Immutable Laws of Branding*, the Rieses state, "A brand becomes stronger when you narrow its focus."[3] This advice applies to the service industry as well.

Building a positive image requires long-range planning before a crisis occurs. After a firm gains an understanding of its image, it should concentrate on strengths, evaluate its niche areas, formulate public relations and promotional strategies, create effective themes and messages, and focus every communication on supporting and reinforcing the image in a consistent way.

Consistency characterizes the image of Cambridge Seven Associates Inc., an international firm based in Cambridge, Mass. Having based its success and reputation on creativity, collaboration and diversity of practice, the AIA award-winning firm continually positions itself with an identifiable image that reflects its fresh-thinking, collaborative approach to design. All forms of communications, from personal presentations to colorful, engaging three-dimensional mailings to an interactive web site, are developed to convey the themes of participation, vitality and invention that infuse the firm's practice and projects.

Achieving the Full Potential of Corporate Identity

While image is based on perceptions and feelings, some controllable and many uncontrollable, corporate identity, on the other hand, is a graphic expression based on the substantive resources and actual realities of a firm — its services, markets, offices, staff, vision, mission and approach. A firm's name, trademark and logo all carry associations with these real attributes. Thus, a corporate identity can and should be carefully planned, designed and implemented by the firm to achieve its full potential and desired effect.

Often, a significant event or major change precipitates a new corporate identity, such as a firm transition, changes in organizational goals, culture or structure, new name, new address, new market focus or business lines, or geographic expansion. An existing identity may no longer reflect the current image of a firm, thus requiring an upgrade. Before embarking on a new identity or enhancing an existing one, it is important that a firm have a clear understanding of its image and the goals for the identity program: What are the firm's strengths and weaknesses? What makes the firm unique? What does the firm want to achieve? How does the firm want to position itself in its markets? The answers can help provide the criteria for developing a corporate identity program.

A client perception survey conducted by a consultant for the architectural and planning firm Wimberly Allison Tong & Goo (WAT&G) of Honolulu, Hawaii, indicated, among a number of significant findings, a disparity between the firm's presentation materials and the high quality of the firm's work. The survey was extended by a critique of the existing identity program by an independent graphic design firm and in-house questionnaire to principals. The results included management's decision to change the firm's name by eliminating one name of a non-participating partner and redesigning the corporate identity and logo to place the firm in its historic, cultural and marketing context. (See Exhibit 1.)

Exhibit 1

Wimberly Allison Tong & Goo
Architects and Planners

Courtesy of WAT&G; Graphic design by The GNU Group

Likewise, WAT&G's planning subsidiary, Helber Hastert & Kimura, used a client perception survey and image/identity analysis on the occasion of its 10th anniversary to develop a more sophisticated and appropriate look for the firm. A fresh, new logo was created by drawing from the ancient Hawaiian system of land tenure, depicting wedges stretching from the mountains to the sea, as a symbol for the integration of environmental, economic and social factors within contemporary land planning.

Every element in a corporate identity program should be used to maximum advantage. Name, symbol, color, graphics, typeface, composition and even the texture of paper stock can express character, corporate values and market strengths. The final graphic representation should express and reinforce the firm's goals, vision, markets, characteristics or traits.

Graphic designers Laughlin/Winkler of Boston recommend developing an identity program that serves as a structure for all of the printed and electronically transferred information generated by a firm. It establishes a hierarchy of information, flexibility, consistency and readability. With the structural identity in place, the cornerstone visual, or logo, can then be developed. This image or aesthetic identity of the company expresses its personality through the careful use of color, form and texture. A sophisticated identity program for R F Walsh of Boston unifies three separate companies representing construction management, property management and development management. A solid triangle, symbolizing the unity of the three areas, refers to the built environment, while alternating line weights create movement as the active element to providing professional services. Their integration in the identity expresses harmony between management and the environment, as well as suggesting the letter *W*. (See Exhibit 2.)

Exhibit 2

For senior partners founding the new marketing and management consulting firm Blackridge of Wellesley Hills, Mass., the corporate identity needed to express experience, sophistication and stability. A logo, symbolizing the unity of marketing and management and embossed with a ridge, was created to aid in name recognition and convey a world-class emphasis that would appeal to the top-level executives the firm would contact. Black typeface of varying boldness and textured paper selected for standard stock created a sense of richness while remaining economical. (See Exhibit 3.)

Exhibit 3

Management and Marketing Consultants

In creating a corporate identity, consider the range, ease and suitability of the design and its applications in the full range of electronic as well as printed media. The identity program should be used deliberately and consistently in the full range of communications media — job signs and hard hats as well as business cards, stationery, brochures and web sites. A complete graphics standard program applies the corporate identity to every aspect of a firm's communications, including technical documents and drawings in all formats, ensuring a unified and cohesive image for the firm. Logo and identity elements must be designed to be structurally sound during the transfer of information into new formats and meet the requirements for communication on the Internet, such as the size of the file, time needed to load, resolution and the ability to incorporate links to other sites. Flexibility and applications become particularly important for marketing in an electronic age in which corporate identity must present a firm on the web, bind branch offices of an organization together or adapt to constantly developing strategic alliances. Conducting business globally is placing new demands on the application of corporate identity. Graphic design must become increasingly versatile as the need for carrying additional amounts of information — such as e-mail addresses, mobile numbers and multilingual text on business cards and stationery — increases, and other unpredictable requirements emerge.

Janet M. Baetz, CPSM, president of Moran Design Associates, cautions firms to use corporate identity programs and funds wisely. She emphasizes good design, consistency and affordability when developing and implementing identity programs. Building corporate image through careful and effective visibility campaigns achieves greater returns than a costly identity program leaving no remaining funds for its implementation. An example of successful corporate image building through direct visibility is that of Giffels Hoyem Basso, LLC, architects, engineers and planners of Troy, Mich. A bright and vibrant identity upgrade expresses the young and fresh, problem-solving approach of the firm to its educational and health care markets. These qualities are communicated through colorful and visually appealing marketing materials, including business stationery, proposal systems, market segment handouts and a phased direct mail program.

Identity should be a memorable, clear and readily identifiable visual image that contributes to name recognition, enhanced visibility, differentiation and positioning. As the visual representative of a firm in all of its business, corporate identity goes hand in hand with corporate image as powerful position strategies in the marketplace.

Endnotes

[1] Tom Peters, "The Brand Called You," *Fast Company* (Aug./Sept. 1997): 84.
[2] Alan Weber, "What Great Brands Do," Interview with Scott Bedbury, *Fast Company* (Aug./Sept. 1997): 98, 100.
[3] Al Ries and Laura Ries, *The 22 Immutable Laws of Branding*. (New York: HarperBusiness, A Division of HarperCollins Publishers, 1998) 17.

Bibliography

Anagnostis, Randy. "The Value of Image Studies." SMPS *Marketer* (Nov. 1990): 5-6.

Frank, Dianne Ludman, and Jane Cohn. "Who Are You?" *Contract Design* (March 1995): 66-67.

Hannah, June. "A/E Image Power: Sales Tool or Nightmare." *Marketing Insight* (Fall 1986), 1-2.

Marken, G.A. "Corporate Image — We All Have One, But Few Work to Protect and Project It," *Public Relations Quarterly* (Spring 1990): 21-23.

Newmann, Lynn. "Image Assessment." SMPS *Marketer* (Feb. 1989): 4-5.

Peters, Tom. "The Brand Called You." *Fast Company* (Aug./Sept. 1997): 83-94.

Raymond, Cary G. "Chance or Strategy: Your Firm's Image." SMPS *Marketer* (Feb. 1992): 1-3.

Ries, Al, and Laura Ries. *The 22 Immutable Laws of Branding*. New York: HarperBusiness, A Division of HarperCollins Publishers, 1998.

Ries, Al, and Jack Trout. *Positioning: The Battle for Your Mind*. New York: McGraw-Hill, Inc., (Warner Books Edition), 1981.

Smith, Patrick J. "How to Present Your Firm to the World." *The Journal of Business Strategy* (Jan./Feb. 1990): 32-36.

Strong, David. "Corporate Identity: Communicating the Essence." SMPS *Marketer* (Aug. 1990): 6-7.

Weber, Alan. "What Great Brands Do." Interview with Scott Bedbury. *Fast Company* (Aug./Sept. 1997): 96-100.

Dianne Ludman Frank, FSMPS

Dianne Ludman Frank, FSMPS, is the principal of Dianne Ludman Frank, Public Relations of Birmingham, Mich., established to focus on national promotional and communications programs for the professional services industries.

Dianne Frank has lectured for:
- Society for Marketing Professional Services (SMPS).
- American Marketing Association (AMA).
- Michigan Society of Architects.
- Chicago Women in Architecture.
- Boston Architectural Center.

Her professional involvement includes:
- Past president of the Boston Chapter of SMPS.
- Founding member of the Upstate New York Chapter of SMPS.
- Chair of the National SMPS Awards and Editorial Committees.
- Chair of the Michigan Chapter SMPS "Thumbs Up" Awards Program.
- Member, Awards Committee of the Detroit Chapter AIA.

She has received numerous awards for marketing communications programs including:
- Hatch Award sponsored by the Advertising Club of Boston.
- *Outstanding Professional Achievement Award* from the Boston Chapter SMPS, 1990.
- *Best of Show*, 1991, National Awards Program, SMPS.
- Numerous other national and chapter awards from SMPS.
- Awards from IABC and the Business and Industry Communicators Council.

Dianne Frank has been widely published in national real estate and marketing journals, including:
- *Promotion Through Publications*, author, Core Series, SMPS, 1991.
- Co-author of articles on public relations for *Architectural Record, Progressive Architecture* and *Contract* magazines.
- A certified Fellow Marketing Professional of SMPS, Frank received her master's degree in fine arts from Syracuse University, and her bachelor's degree, Phi Beta Kappa, from Hofstra University.

Acknowledgment

The author wishes to acknowledge her collaborative work with colleague and co-author Jane Cohn, FSMPS, in developing positioning concepts referred to in this chapter.

4.4 Guidelines for Working with the Media

Lois E. Boemer, FSMPS
Principal
BA Communications

In the June 1998 issue of *Architecture Magazine,* the "Practice" section included a very comprehensive article by Contributing Editor Elizabeth Padjen entitled "Getting Noticed" with the sidebar: "Journalists Are People Too," her "helpful hints" included:

- Return media calls promptly.
- Don't be surprised if you are contacted but not included in a story.
- Since you are in a service profession, win a friend or at least a higher position on the journalist's call list.
- Bland is boring.
- Don't ask to review a story before it is published.
- Don't send unsolicited slides or photos.
- Label photos.
- Be succinct.
- There are no guarantees in journalism.

Introduction

It is no secret Ronald Reagan was the great communicator of the 1980s. The former president and his administration made quite certain everyone who communicated with the outside world had the same message. From the time the evening news beamed into our living rooms, until the next morning's newspapers arrived at our doorstep, the President's message was always concise, clear and to the point.

Why is it professional services firms have trouble conveying this kind of message about their firm and services? Experience teaches us it is because the staff is usually giving out one message, the principals another, and the publicity sent to the outside world yet a third. It is not possible to train technical and other marketing staff to interact with the media without first defining the message *in-house.* It is also not possible to interact with the media unless there is a clear understanding of the firm's potential markets and clients. Only then can targeted media be defined and staff assigned to cultivate individual editors and reporters. This chapter, therefore, will cover the following areas:

- Defining the message.
- Establishing the public relations media plan.
- Targeting the media.
- Contacting the media.
- Duties and responsibilities.

Defining the Message

Goals, Objectives and Desired Image

The staff responsible for the public relations effort, including working with the media, should be well versed in the firm's goals, objectives and desired image. This includes being privy to the marketing plan and knowing which markets the firm plans to target over a given period of time. All too often, the staff is expected to "get something published" without much background on the who, what, where and why of doing so. To be effective in the media, the firm must first identify these key areas:

- Markets and audiences.
- Messages for individual markets.
- Targeted media for these markets.
- A realistic timetable.
- Person(s) responsible for working with the media.

Key Messages

The goals and objectives form an umbrella over *all* of the firm's messages including:

- Verbal.
- Written.
- Collateral.
- In-house newsletters.
- Outside publications.
- Events and celebrations.

It is especially important in today's technically advanced world for collateral materials and web sites to be updated and appealing. You cannot *say* you are capable of being out front and look like you're running behind the pack. Web sites are being used by potential clients to check out the firm's background; they are also being used by the press for backup information. Before training staff to work with the media, all collateral, visual and background material should be thoroughly reviewed, including the quality of photographs and the web site.

What is being said about the firm in and outside of the office is equally important. Marketing, after all, is everyone's business, and so is public relations. I once phoned an architect's office and asked for the principal. The receptionist said: "He's not here (sigh); I have no idea where he is (sigh), and I don't know when he will be back!" Would you hire a firm if its principal were among the missing? Or, would you keep that person on your rolodex, or in your computer, for future reference if you were a member of the press? Negative and conflicting messages are often conveyed by principals and staff at company open houses, cocktail parties and other events. When everyone understands the firm's goals, objectives and desired image, all of the messages, in whatever medium, will glean positive, rather than negative, results.

Establishing the Public Relations Media Plan

Once the goals, objectives and desired image are defined, a media plan can be put in place. Based on the marketing plan, the markets should be identified and matched with the messages and the audiences. Although there are many facets to public relations, including events, direct mail, newsletters, community involvement and other activities, for purposes of this chapter, only the publicity portion of the public relations plan is presented. Ideally, if you were sending out a direct mail piece on your latest health care project, you would also simultaneously publish information in a health care magazine, and perhaps advertise as well.

Market Media Research

Market media research is crucial and the key to a successful publicity program. Someone should be assigned to do this research prior to formulating a media plan. One way to obtain information is to telephone the editorial assistant or advertising person at each periodical and ask for a media kit. Although designed for advertising, the kit will tell you the demographics, readership and other pertinent information. A sample of the periodical will also be sent to you.

In the public relations media plan, the media is matched with the markets and the audiences. Each magazine and/or trade publication usually has an editorial calendar, as do the special focus sections of daily and weekly newspapers. Editorial calendars are helpful in planning for publicity in targeted markets and included in the media kit. The editorial calendar is also usually available from the editorial assistant who can be reached by telephone.

Topics and Submissions

If the potential information is project oriented there are key milestones along the way. It should be noted, however, most daily newspapers, the trade press and the design press are not interested in awards, dedications or ground breakings. Specific magazines and newspapers oriented to the real estate community, design professionals and the built environment will usually accept the milestones, if presented in a timely and concise manner. The format for these news announcements should be simple and the information limited to one page. Backgrounders can be included containing additional information but only if it is relevant to the one-pager. The press does not have time to read through your entire brochure and/or background material. You need to be prepared, however, should they ask you for more material.

Since the media plan will include a timetable, here are several milestones occurring in most professional design, engineering and construction firms:

- Awarding of the project.
- Ground breaking.
- Dedication.
- Special awards for the project.
- Staff announcements and promotions.

- Community affairs announcements.
- Public speaking events.
- Academic announcements.
- Staff announcements and promotions.

News items and announcements are just one part of publicity; more extensive publicity includes:

- Special features regarding projects, process and other timely matters in the general, business, design, professional, trade and specific market media.
- Authored articles by members of the staff in targeted publications.
- Principals and key staff serving as a resource for the press.

These features, and sometimes "ghost authored" informative articles, require a commitment of both time and personnel. Recently, an editor of a focus section in a weekly real estate newspaper phoned looking for an informative article because someone had let her down. That is not good news for the person who made a commitment and didn't keep it. If you want to build relationships you absolutely must keep your word.

The first step in all of this, however, is writing a public relations media plan. This can be as simple or as complicated as you want to make it.

Criteria for Media Plan

The following criteria will assist the staff in formulating this media plan:

- Set priorities.
- Categorize by markets.
- Divide the media into local, regional and national press.
- Assign someone to research the media.
- Determine each periodical's focus, their editors and reporters.
- Check the media web sites.

Media Plan Format

Message	Audience	Periodical	Special Focus	Calendar Dates Due – Publish	Person Responsible
The firm uses new technology *before* the design process begins.	Colleges & Universities Presidents Chief Financial Officers Directors of Facilities	XYZ College Planning Jane Doe, Editor Editorial: Yes Advertising: No	Technology	5/99 - 9/99	LEB

Preparing this public relations media plan, and scheduling it at least six months in advance, will greatly increase the chances of being published and of having all the proper materials by the due date. In addition, an individual data base sheet for each periodical should be maintained. Again, this must be updated each time someone talks to the press or receives new information. Advertising should also be factored in to the publicity, as well as web site costs. All of this adds up to the question: How much is allowed in your marketing and public relations budget for publicity? *Remember: The more cohesive your public relations, the better understanding your clients will have of your message.*

Targeting the Media

Thousands of news releases marked "For Immediate Release" are discarded daily; hence, the phrase "canned press releases." As a former newspaper columnist, and as a correspondent for the *Boston Globe*, I am convinced you need a direct link to an individual when working with the media. In my many years in the communication business, no news release, to the best of my knowledge, has ever left my office without the name of an individual and the name of the periodical.

If you target the media, and specific editors and publications, and cultivate relationships, you will have a better chance to interest them in a process or information article. An event or project is not as important as the story behind them, and the people who are interested in writing the story are the ones you need to know.

Market media research is invaluable for targeting the media. Editors, contributing editors, writers, reporters all change periodically, and if you are attempting to really target the media, this information needs to be continually updated. Several good manuals are available in our industry that will help you begin this process, especially if you are training staff not familiar with the media.

Helpful Hints

In a pamphlet entitled *Helpful Hints for Public Relations Strategies*, prepared for a joint Associated General Contractors of Massachusetts and SMPS/Boston luncheon, the following information from the Public Relations Committee of Associated General Contractors of America was offered.

Each medium (publication) selected should pass five separate tests:

- Will it reach the target audience?
- Will it accept the message you wish to convey?
- Can you create and afford the type of vehicle it will require?
- Can it get the message out fast enough to be effective?
- Will there be any negative consequences of the use of the media (will the media reach undesired audiences that might misinterpret your messages)?

Contacting the Media

During my eight-year tenure with newspapers, I found most people pleasant and outgoing when they telephoned. The press releases I received were another story. Because I used only one or two lines in a section of my "Scene & Heard" column, why in the world would anyone send me three or four pages? (This includes schools of communication in the area.) Provide the press with the who, what, where, when and why in the first line or two. You'll have a much better chance of getting your news published and not having it "canned."

Rules for Making Contacts

Your own personal set of rules in dealing with the press is a good idea. Here are 10 items on my list:

1. Get to know potential editors and reporters by attending functions where you can speak to them informally. If they have never met you, don't pitch a story. If they know you, they will probably ask you, "What's been happening?"

2. Present a potential feature story to the press in one or two lines; if it doesn't grab them right away, it's probably not right for them.

3. If you are phoning, and they answer, always ask, "Are you in the middle of something?" They probably are, but if you are polite and ask this question, it will serve you in good stead.

4. Use voice mail to your advantage. Think before you begin to speak and speak slowly and clearly. Practice out loud if you need to. Voice mail is being used by many busy editors and reporters as a tool for screening calls. It is necessary to be upbeat and state the reason for your call in a succinct manner. If you do this, and have a great article idea or news story, an editor might even pick up the phone.

5. Some e-mails, in national magazines for example, are easily attainable. Always introduce yourself if the editor or reporter has not met you. And be polite, not flip! E-mail is a great way to get your name in front of the press by sending out "information" rather than "press releases."

6. If the person you've contacted is not interested, don't be afraid to ask: Is there someone else I should contact? If they say, "no," take no for an answer and do more homework.

7. Never ever badger.

8. Don't follow up on short news items. What's to follow up? It's either usable or it isn't.

9. On story ideas and project features, do follow up within several weeks, but then only as a courtesy. Ask if they need any additional information or anything else that might be helpful to them. Sometimes, editorial decisions take months. Other times, it happens quickly.

10. When something is published, send a short thank you even if it is "only" a news item. Once a group of editors, participating in a panel I was moderating, asked each other on the dais (in front of everyone) if *they* received notes from me. The audience laughed, and I was embarrassed, but thank you notes continue to be one of my trademarks.

Targeting Specific Press

All print publications have special areas of expertise, as does the broadcast media. In daily and weekly newspapers this is referred to as "Special Sections" or "Focus Sections." In trade and/or business publications it can be separate departments or special sections. On television or radio this can be the "special reporter" or a news magazine. For this reason, identifying the areas of expertise for each medium of interest must be part of the market media research.

Most of these different sections have their own editors, and many use "correspondents" or freelancers. It is important to read several editions of a publication prior to approaching someone, and to watch, or listen to, any broadcast media several times before approaching them. Again, a separate sheet in the database for each periodical and for different reporters and editors is a very valuable tool.

Duties and Responsibilities

Which brings us to: How in the world is all of this going to get done? First, you can assign someone inside the firm to be responsible for public relations and publicity. The problem is: How much time will you allow your staff away from its *real* work, like getting out proposals for example? The publicity is often the last thing to go out the door, and then only when the principal sees a competitor with a feature or news article. If you can find the resources (even on a part-time basis) to have someone take on *only* this responsibility, you will be on the road to reaching out to the media. Or, you can look outside the firm for assistance. Many firms who have successful publicity programs use a combination of both outside and inside public relations people.

The duties and responsibilities to accomplish what we have been talking about in this chapter are many. For clarity, they are divided here into research, news announcements, features and informative articles.

Research

The duties assigned to the media researcher must include an awareness of the marketing plan and the firm's goals, objectives and desired image. Otherwise, the research will be in vain. Responsibilities include:

- Identify with the principal's key markets, messages and audiences.
- Create a media data base.
- Prepare individual media sheets within the database for separate markets including addresses, telephone and fax numbers, e-mails, web sites and areas of expertise.
- Collect media kits and editorial calendars from the selected media.
- Review web sites.
- Prepare a public relations media plan based on this research.
- Update the media database on an ongoing basis.

News Releases

- Secure appropriate background information from staff and/or client.
- Prepare targeted media lists based on database.
- Interview key staff.
- Write draft for principal and client's approval.
- Secure any photos or graphics.
- Contact the press (if appropriate).
- Write and place news releases in keeping with the short, concise format previously discussed and distribute to individual editors and reporters.

Features and Information Articles

- Review editorial calendars for special sections and focus.
- Match the opportunities with the availability of projects and/or information.
- Secure client approval prior to contacting the press.
- Interview key staff for timely topics and interesting aspects of projects.
- Phone or e-mail targeted press with an idea or story line.
- Write outlines.
- Write "ghost authored" articles for key staff.
- Secure photographs and graphic materials.
- Place materials with the media.
- Follow up.

There are many other responsibilities for the person assigned to the media. This could include the following:

- Attend functions where the media will be in attendance.
- Provide media with information *not* related to the firm.
- Write bylined articles for certain periodicals if requested by media.
- Propose principals and key staff to media for resource information.

Since no one person can probably handle all of these items in-house, it is best to set priorities as referred to earlier. Looking inside of your firm for key personnel who are good at working with the media, as well as community and social affairs related to business development, is one way to "double-up" responsibilities. The person adept at this will, in fact, probably introduce clients, principals and the media to one another. It should also be evident that the person selected is a good writer. This means a "people person" writer, not necessarily a technical writer.

George M. Cohan is quoted as saying, "I don't care what they call me as long as they mention my name."

This formula might work for a songwriter, but it can prove fatal to a professional services firm. Although we want our name mentioned, we also want the media to spell it correctly, to be accurate in stating what it is we *really* do, and to help us get new clients through name recognition and, ultimately, our expertise.

A successful communications program, including publicity and public relations as an integral part of the marketing plan, will reap many rewards both inside and outside of the firm. Publicity based on the same goals and objectives as the marketing plan will also enhance your image. You will know your program is successful because you will have reprints to distribute to your clients. You and your staff will also have a sense of accomplishment for a job well done.

Bibliography

Boemer, Lois E. "Road to Successful Sales — A Three-Step Process." *Journal of Management in Engineering,* Volume 5, No. 4 (Oct. 1989). ASCE, ISSN 0742-597X/89/0004-0351. (Or contact the author for a copyright reprint.)

Padjen, Elizabeth. "Getting Noticed." *Architecture Magazine* (June 1998): 154-156.

Lois E. Boemer, FSMPS

- Lois E. Boemer is a principal at BA Communications in Boston, a public relations firm specializing in the built environment since 1984.
- Representative clients include architects, construction firms, engineers, interior designers and numerous non-profit institutions such as the Boston Architectural Center, the Massachusetts Institute of Technology (MIT) and the Boston Society of Architects.
- Currently a *Boston Globe* correspondent in special sections.
- Previously a newspaper columnist.
- SMPS Fellow.
- Founding member of SMPS/Boston.
- Named an Honorary Life Member by SMPS/Boston in 1996.
- Former northeast regional director of SMPS, and former editor of the SMPS national newsletter.
- Winner of various marketing and communications awards.

4.5 Brochures

Rena Frankle, CPSM
Principal
Reichman Frankle Inc.

A corporate brochure is an important marketing tool — and a major marketing investment. Despite the proliferation of corporate web sites, CDs and videos, a print brochure most often remains the centerpiece of a firm's marketing materials. Nothing yet has been invented that will replace the immediate impact and portability of a well-written, well-designed brochure. It can present the salient facts about your firm at a glance, elicit a favorable response based on color, design, text and photographs — as well as quality of paper and printing — and exhibit a tactile presence that has yet to be matched by electronic media.

The basic advantages of a brochure are still valid — a brochure provides an introduction to new clients; is a reminder of your total capabilities and a cross-selling tool for existing clients; and can be a source of inspiration and renewed pride for employees. At its best, a brochure explains who you are, what services you provide and how you can benefit your clients. It presents a quality image and delivers a clear consistent message.

Yet today, when brochures coexist and vie for marketing dollars with web sites and other electronic media, it is more important than ever that a print brochure have a clearly defined purpose in a firm's marketing program. And a brochure must respond to the realities of the 21st century. The video age has tuned us into writing less and presenting information in the print equivalent of "sound bites." And the way that web sites are structured has caused us to consider ways to personalize a brochure so that recipients get the information they are most interested in. Corporate brochures in the 21st century will probably be shorter, and they will be accompanied by related brochures and information pieces that can be targeted to particular audiences. In other words, the trend to personalization and modularization will accelerate.

The following discussion, focusing on corporate brochures but applicable to special market brochures as well, covers the essentials of developing an effective brochure and includes a "basic 10" list of questions to help a professional services firm define its message and audience.

Establish a Purpose and Need

Before you embark on producing a brochure, use the "basic 10" questions in the box to help you create a preliminary statement outlining why you need a brochure, how you will use it, who you are targeting, what is your message and how the brochure will fit into your firm's marketing plan. This information will be refined later in the brochure development process, but it is important to at least get started. This preliminary information may help you decide if a brochure is the best way to deliver your message, or if you can more effectively use some other medium.

It is important to understand what a brochure cannot do — it cannot follow up on leads, establish a relationship, close a sale. It cannot do your marketing for you, but it can be an extremely useful tool that should be integrated into a total marketing plan.

Gather Information

Have a clear idea about who your firm is and where it is headed before you begin a brochure. Think about why you need a brochure and how you will use it. If your firm is in the process of reorganization or is having internal conflicts, this is not the time to begin a brochure. The brochure process is not a corporate therapy session, although it can help to sharpen goals. And it is not a substitute for a marketing plan. Your firm should have a marketing plan — if only a two- or three-page list of goals and target markets — before you undertake a brochure.

To gain an understanding of how you would like to represent your firm, collect examples of writing styles and design that you like — in brochures, annual reports, advertising and other print materials, not only from other professional services firms, but also from other professions and businesses.

Although a brochure can be produced in-house if you have the resources, be realistic in assessing your capabilities. Most firms will choose to work with a brochure consultant. The first step is to identify a number of consultants who can write, design and produce the brochure. Get recommendations from other professional services firms that have produced successful brochures. And meet with the brochure consultants, look at samples of their work, discuss format options, get "ballpark" costs for various types and sizes of brochures, and see if the chemistry is right — you'll be working with these people for several months.

These discussions with consultants will help you make a preliminary decision on size and format — enough to prepare a request for proposal (RFP), get proposals from two or three consultants (including an estimate of printing costs), and select a consultant. (You may later refine the size and format, but at least you'll have some basis at this point on which to compare consultants.) The earlier you get a consultant involved, the more he or she will be able to help you.

Set the Ground Rules

As in any design or construction project, it is important to appoint a project manager and establish lines of communication and responsibility. Make sure you know which key decision-makers in your organization need to have input, and who will sign off on the text and design — and make sure they have input early in the process and approve initial drafts and design concepts. This procedure will help to avoid major changes in the final stages of brochure production.

- Appoint one in-house person to lead the brochure development effort. That person may be supported by a committee, but should have the authority to decide among conflicting comments and be responsible for final approvals to the text and design.
- Develop a list of in-house reviewers who will comment on and approve the first and second drafts

of the text. Include top management and experts from various disciplines, and let them know that they will be responsible for signing off on factual information and for returning comments on time.

- Decide who will review the design concepts. This should be a smaller group than the text reviewers. You want input and support, but you don't want design by committee.

Sharpen Your Focus — The Basic 10 Questions

Early in the brochure development process, it is critically important to ask — and answer — some questions that will bring into focus the purpose, message, audience and desired results. Get input from the brochure committee and top management. If necessary, do some market research to get accurate answers. Don't skip this step. The more specific the answers to the questions, the more on-target the brochure will be, and the answers will help to shape and position the brochure to further your firm's marketing strategy.

Answer the following "basic 10" questions to establish a purpose and need when you first begin to think about developing a new brochure, and then again — with your consultant — before beginning the writing, design and selection of a format. Depending on your firm's circumstances, you may want to add a few more questions to elicit additional information.

The questions can be answered by each participant in writing, but they work best if they are reviewed by the participants in advance, and then discussed by all involved in the give-and-take of a round-table discussion.

1. What is your objective in producing this brochure?

2. Who are your clients? Describe your current client base and list future target clients/market sectors. Focus on the next three years.

3. What are your client concerns and problems, and how do you respond to those concerns?

4. What are your firm's strengths? Weaknesses or perceived weaknesses?

5. Who are your competitors and how do you differentiate yourself?

6. What are the most important projects/services/geographic areas to be included in the brochure?

7. How do you get projects? Is the process likely to change?

8. What is the overall impression you want to make with the brochure?

9. How will you be distributing the brochure so that it supports your marketing program?

10. How many copies will you need, and what is your budget?

Define Your Message and Target Audience

Once you have answered the basic 10 questions, you'll have a lot of information, and you'll have to make some decisions — sifting and paring down the information until you can write, in a concise statement, the message that you want to convey with the brochure. Another concise statement should define your target audience. Don't include too much in a brochure. It will lose its focus, and therefore its effectiveness. Once you've defined the message and the audience, you'll be able to define the medium — the brochure and its format.

Choose a Format

There are no hard-and-fast rules on format, and the variety is almost infinite. Format is closely linked to budget, but there are other considerations. Think about the amount of information you must include, the types and numbers of photographs, how often the information will need to be changed or updated, and the overall impression you want to make.

- A small or start-up firm can be well-served by a four- or six-panel brochure that folds to fit into a #10 business envelope. But paper and design must be top quality, or clients will treat it as a throw-away piece.
- A young firm with a rapidly growing portfolio of projects may find that a flexible format of a pocket folder plus insert pages makes the most sense.
- A large company with many disciplines may find that a single brochure won't meet their needs; it will need a corporate brochure that covers general capabilities, specialty brochures on various disciplines and perhaps a folder to hold these materials.
- Most firms opt for a finished size of 8½ inches by 11 inches (fits neatly with letters and standard qualifications materials) to 9 inches by 12 inches — of four, six or eight panels, or eight, 12 or 16 pages plus a cover.
- Many architecture and interior firms prefer a customized brochure approach — preprinted cover, back cover, and individual pages that can be assembled in various configurations and wire-bound into an attractive presentation book to meet the needs of individual clients. This type of brochure requires an investment in the binding equipment, but — if well-designed — makes an impressive presentation.

A pocket folder or a pocket on the inside back cover of a brochure is useful for including project descriptions, resumes or information that is likely to change or need updating — but pockets should be used only for a limited number of pages designed specifically as part of the brochure package, and not as a catchall for miscellaneous information.

Some of the most successful brochures break the rules, but you should have a good reason for doing so. Think very carefully before you produce a brochure that will not fit into a legal size file folder. And be aware that oversize or square formats will need custom-mailing envelopes.

Establish a Budget

Be realistic. If you do not have an adequate budget to produce a quality brochure with good photographs, good writing and design, and quality paper stock and printing, stop here and re-evaluate your program. It is better to have a smaller brochure or even just a well-designed folder holding a few pages of information than to send out a poorly produced brochure.

Elements that affect the printing budget include size of the page and number of pages; number of photographs; use of color; varnishes, embossing, foil stamping, die-cutting, foldouts or other special techniques; paper stock; and quantity.

A brochure generally has a shelf life of about three years, so be sure to order a quantity large enough to serve your needs. Increasing the quantity of the initial printing, for example from 3,000 to 4,000 copies, adds only a small incremental cost — basically the cost of the additional paper and binding. Reprinting 1,000 copies at a later date is much more costly.

Set Up a Schedule

A realistic schedule for brochure production is six months, from consultant selection to delivery of final brochure. This allows adequate time for approvals and printing, but moves the process along at a steady pace.

Where most brochures bog down is in the internal approval process, and this is where the in-house person in charge of the brochure must exercise his or her authority to provide guidelines for the review committee and get comments in on time.

A typical production schedule follows. In actuality, some "months" may be five to six weeks long, with the tasks in one month overlapping the next. Allow about two weeks for in-house review of the first draft of text, and up to one week each for the second draft, design concepts, comprehensives and blues.

- Month one: gather information; develop list of questions; interview principals and key people; make final decision on format; collect and review existing photographs, drawings or graphics; prepare first draft of text.
- Month two: present design concepts; prepare preliminary list of photographs; prepare second draft of text.
- Month three: refine design concepts; prepare final list of photos; schedule and take new photos; make final adjustments to text.
- Month four: develop full "comprehensive" (mock-up of the brochure with type, graphics and photos in place); make any minor changes; get sign-off on design and text.
- Month five: prepare disk for printer; solicit and evaluate printers' bids.
- Month six: print brochure.

If reviews are turned around quickly, this process can be shortened considerably — but never produce a corporate brochure under pressure. The investment of time and money and the process of brochure development are too important to rush. If you need to convey information about your firm within a tight deadline, find another approach.

Writing and Content

The common wisdom is that a client will spend only a minute or two on your brochure — glance at the photographs, read the heads and subheads, scan the client or project list and maybe read the first paragraph or two. This may be true in many cases, so make the best use of these elements to give a quick and accurate picture of your firm at a glance.

But also write and design for clients who will read all of your brochure, especially if they see some information of benefit to them. So hook them with a discussion of their concerns. Instead of starting a brochure with "Smith, Jones, and White is a consulting engineering company with expertise in a wide range of disciplines...," try talking directly to clients about their problems and how your services can help solve those problems. Then back it up with examples.

The trick is to say just enough to convey the essential information a prospective client needs, while giving a flavor of what sets your firm apart. Most clients will want to have a description and brief history of your firm; an understanding of how you work with clients (approach or philosophy); a list or description of services; information on types of projects, representative projects and/or representative clients; and a list of offices. Detailed project or process information is best left to a specialty brochure or to project description pages that can accompany the brochure or be sent as a follow-up.

Writing should be economical and direct. Write not only about what you do but also about your clients' concerns and needs, and how your services meet those needs. Avoid clichés and empty superlatives. If you think you are the best at something, provide some examples to illustrate why. Avoid information that will make the brochure out of date quickly. And consider client testimonials — if you can get them, they add an element of credibility that's hard to beat.

Important messages should be brief and stand out clearly. Headlines, subheads, call-outs and bullets are useful to break up dense blocks of text and present key points so that they can be understood at a glance.

Above all, be honest. Don't try — even by implication — to take credit for more of a project than you have actually done.

Design

The design should evolve from and reinforce the message; it should be reader-friendly — attractive, uncluttered, inviting. A good design will make your firm look like it confidently belongs in the 21st century.

If you have a strong corporate graphic identity program, the brochure should follow the guidelines of that program. If, on the other hand, your corporate graphic identity is weak, the design of the brochure could be the impetus for upgrading your graphic identity — from a subtle change in logo size and color to a complete new logo and graphic identity program. Elements of the brochure design then can be incorporated in other print materials, such as proposal covers and project description pages.

The type should be large enough, with enough leading (space between the lines) to be easily read. Many brochures treat a block of type as a design element only, with no thought given to the fact that it should be readable and inviting.

Avoid the temptation to fill every available inch of paper. White space is absolutely necessary around text and photos to create a frame for the important images and allow your message to be absorbed.

Other elements contribute to the overall look of the brochure. Color adds visual interest and helps to define the mood of a brochure. Embossing, metallic ink, varnishes and other techniques add richness. And the selection, weight and quality of paper stock are very important. Your consultant should present samples of recommended stock in a brochure format so you can visualize how it will look and feel.

Photography

It is better to have no photographs in a brochure than to have poor quality photographs — in fact, many elegant brochures have only text and graphic elements. If you use photos, and most brochures do, be ruthless in photo selection; a brochure is only as good as its worst photo. Your photos should represent the diversity of project types, sizes and geographic locations that you want to market. ·

The best approach, if you have the budget, is to take new photographs expressly for the brochure. Photography should take place after the design is developed, so you know exactly what projects to use, the point of view, whether or not to include people and even the approximate proportions of the photo.

If you cannot afford to take all new photos, contact your clients. Most will have professional photographs of projects you have worked on and will allow you to use them.

Stock photography is also an option for photos that convey a mood, setting or theme. Stock photo houses offer one-time use of a photo; the cost generally depends on the size and position of the photo and the number of copies of the brochure.

Keep safety in mind during photo shoots and photo selection. When photographing on construction sites, make sure that all personnel and project activities depicted are following accepted construction safety procedures. In addition, have a construction safety professional review all selected photos for any construction safety violations.

Editing and Proofreading

Every element of your brochure should reflect quality and attention to detail — and that means paying attention to basics such as editing and proofreading. Be sure to allow enough time in the brochure production schedule for these critical tasks.

Once you have a draft of the text, read it three or four times, preferably over several days.

- First look at the tone and content. Are you comfortable with the way your firm is portrayed? Are all the important projects included? Is there a balance of disciplines, project types and geographic location? Are there too many words (most likely) or not enough?
- Second, check for consistency of voice, for parallel construction of subheads, for inelegant or pompous phrases or clichés. Do you have some nagging doubt about a phrase or sentence? Now is the time to resolve those doubts. Don't let it slide until later in the process. A handy rule: When in doubt, take it out.
- Third, test the brochure copy by reading it aloud. If you stumble over clumps of multisyllabic words, chances are your readers will too — and you'll lose them.

One additional note about editing: Make sure that when modifications or changes are made, they are consistent in tone and format with the rest of the brochure.

As for proofreading, the rule is to check, check and check again. You can never read a brochure too many times before it goes to press. Some experts advocate reading the text backwards — it forces you to look carefully at every word. Pay particular attention to numerals, addresses, phone numbers, photo credits, project names and locations — and, if you have a client list, make sure you have the correct names and spellings, down to the commas.

After the final color comp is prepared, it should be read carefully by at least three people — and each person should read it twice, once for sense and once for typos and format. Check for correct hyphenation at ends of lines, consistency of heads and design elements (rules, etc.) from page to page, page numbers (if used) on every page and in the correct position, etc.

Be especially vigilant when last-minute corrections are made. Very often that's when new errors get introduced. Proofread not only the corrected line of text but also the whole paragraph, and scan the rest of the page for good measure. And when all corrections are made, and the disk is prepared for the printer, get a print-out of the disk and read it carefully to catch any errors *before* the disk goes to the printer.

Approvals and Sign-offs

Reviewers should take their responsibilities seriously. They should check facts, numbers, project names and client names, and provide their comments in a timely manner. A designated reviewer should also determine if client approval is needed to include client names, projects and photographs in the brochure, and obtain timely sign-offs.

Don't let nagging details go unresolved — changes made at the last minute will incur additional costs. The most costly place to make changes is when you review the printer's blues — and it happens much too often. The printer has to make new plates, driving up costs and delaying the schedule. This is the surprise line on the printing invoice called "Author's Alterations."

Printing

Printing is a critical element of the brochure production process. No matter how good the writing, design and photography, it is the printing that translates these to paper. Modern, computer-controlled presses allow a greater degree of control than formerly, but printing is still an art and not an exact science.

Your brochure consultant should supervise every step of the printing process, from recommending printers and evaluating bids, to reviewing and adjusting color separations, reviewing blues and being "on-press" when the brochure is actually printed. Here is where subtle adjustments in ink color and coverage make the difference from simply OK to fantastic. Here is where you need a sharp eye to make sure the color registration is correct and to catch the stray spots of ink that invariably appear in the middle of an expanse of white.

New ink formulations, using less volatile solvents, take longer to dry, so don't ask the printer to rush this part of the process, and allow enough time for binding and delivery.

Using Your New Brochure

Remember question No. 9 of our 10 basic questions? Early in the brochure process you should have developed a plan for using your new brochure as an integral part of your marketing program. Now you can put that plan into action.

One of the first items in your plan should be a mailing. Send your new brochure with a personalized cover note to all existing clients and prospective clients on your corporate or special market mailing list. (You should begin to upgrade your mailing list as soon as you begin the brochure, so that the mailing list will be ready when the brochure is.) The plan should also include the development and distribution of in-house guidelines for using the brochure at trade shows, seminars and meetings. For example, at a trade show, do you want to hand out the brochure to all who pass by, or send it as a follow-up to contacts made? There should be some centralized monitoring, but everyone in contact with clients — project managers as well as marketers — should be encouraged to use the brochure and instructed in the most effective ways to use it.

Bibliography

Beckwith, Harry. *Selling the Invisible: A Field Guide to Modern Marketing*. Warner Books, 1997.

Frankle, Rena. *Creating an Effective Brochure for the 21st Century*. SMPS Marketing Information Report, 1997.

Frost, Susan, et al. *Blueprint for Marketing: Comprehensive Marketing Guide for Design Professionals*. SEF Publications, 1995.

Newsom, Doug, and Bob Carrell. *Public Relations Writing: Form and Style*. Wadsworth Publishing Co., 1997.

Ries, Al, and Jack Trout. *Positioning: The Battle for Your Mind*. Warner Books, 1993.

Yudkin, Marcia. *Persuading on Paper: The Complete Guide to Writing Copy that Pulls in Business*. Plume Paperback, 1996.

Rena Frankle, CPSM

Rena Frankle, CPSM, a marketing communications consultant with more than 20 years' experience, is a recognized expert in marketing strategy, brochure development and communication of technical information. A principal of Reichman Frankle Inc. (RFI) of Englewood Cliffs, N.J., a marketing communications firm that specializes in promotional materials for professional services firms, she has a wide range of experience that includes:

- Consulting on a full range of marketing communications materials and programs.
- Production of more than 100 brochures, many of them award winners.
- Leadership roles in SMPS and other professional organizations — past chair of the SMPS Publications Committee.
- Serving on the board of advisors of *Construction Company Strategist* newsletter and frequent contributor to *Design-Build Strategies* newsletter.
- Presentations on professional services marketing to audiences that include SMPS, American Institute of Architects, American Consulting Engineers Council and the National Innovation Workshop.
- A member of SMPS New York Chapter and the Society for Technical Communication, she can be reached through RFI's web site at **www.reichmanfrankle.com**.

4.6   What Is Advertising and How Can It Be Used to Benefit the Professional Services Firm?

J. Rossi
Vice President
HLM Design

"Advertising is the art of enclosing a sales proposition in an attention-getting, involving vehicle and positioning the product (or service) uniquely in the consumer's mind."

— **Kenneth Roman and Jane Maas**
The New How to Advertise[1]

In other words, advertising is a marketing tool that uses purchased space to deliver a message to a targeted audience to help sell a firm's service.

There's a short history of advertising by professional services firms. Only since 1978 have professionals — architects, engineers, accountants, lawyers — been permitted by law to advertise. Many firms do use advertising as one component of the overall marketing mix.

Tactics used by professional services firms (for the built environment) include advertisements on television, either in a straight "plug" format or as sponsors on public television, radio spots, print ads, and more recently, banner ads on the web. Some large firms have used print advertising to effectively reach their targeted clients. Firms, especially those with sophisticated engineering specialties or those in the construction business, advertise in trade magazines read by their clients.

What Can Advertising Do for a Professional Services Firm?

E. Jerome McCarthy, in *Basic Marketing — A Managerial Approach,* states that "every advertisement and every advertising campaign should be seeking clearly defined objectives." McCarthy says that basic advertising objectives should:

- Aid in the introduction of new services to specific targets.
- Assist in the expansion or maintenance of an identified market.
- Enhance the firm's personal selling efforts.
- Keep the firm's name before targets.
- Provide information regarding the availability of new services and possible application of other services.
- Aid in the establishment of a firm's image.

- Induce the target market to take swift action (for example, get in touch with your firm).
- Help clients to confirm their decision to hire your firm.[2]

There are also a number of things advertising can't do:

- Sell a service to someone not in the market for you.
- Sell a service to someone who can't afford it.
- Make a satisfied customer.
- Save a bad service.

Categories of Advertising

Different forms of advertising can be utilized to enable a firm to fulfill its objectives. The different categories of advertising include:

- Institutional, or image, advertising.
- Service advertising.
- Direct mail.
- Tombstone ads.
- Yellow page advertising.
- Broadcast advertising.
- Banner ads.

Institutional, or image, advertising is designed solely to enhance the name recognition or reputations of a firm without focusing on a specific service. For example, Morris Aubry Architects, in the 1980s, pioneered advertising for an architectural firm with a campaign that ran in *The Wall Street Journal*. Recently a civil engineering firm used a series of ads that played on the name of the firm. The ads featured an interesting visual, for instance, a cow with zebra stripes and a headline that read "Unique approaches to environmental problems." The firm was not really selling a particular benefit, but attempting to generate name recognition in its target market.

Institutional advertising is useful but should not be used to generate immediate new business. It does, however, have its place as part of a larger campaign.

Service advertising is display or promotional advertising in which a service or capability is described in a selling context. These are highly focused ads that describe a particular service to a clearly defined audience. For example, a consultant who specializes in selling a marketing management database program to architectural firms would use this kind of advertising.

Direct mail allows you to target your marketing efforts to selected prospective clients. It is particularly effective for professional services firms because it delivers a specific message to a clearly defined audience. It can address specific problems and can be used as a door opener to sell to a prospective client personally. Like other forms of service advertising, it cannot produce clients by return mail.

Tombstone ads are simple, straightforward announcements. They are used to announce a significant event like a merger, major personnel change, acquisition or new office. It is one additional technique to provide visibility for a firm or to convey an impression to prospective clients.

Yellow page advertising is another form of marketing used by professional services firms but is not necessarily an effective way to differentiate one firm from another.

Broadcast advertising — radio and television — is used by attorneys and accountants to sell their services but has not been used by architects, engineers and contractors. An architectural and engineering firm used radio advertising in western Pennsylvania to generate name recognition and enhance its position as a leader in that region. The format used was "information marketing," a 60-second spot offering specific information on a wide variety of subjects of architectural interest with a tagline that identified the firm. Broadcast and print are being used to promote every member firm of the American Institute of Architects through its national ad campaign "Building on Your Vision." Two different 30-second television ads run several times a week on programs like NBC Nightly News and Larry King Live. Print ads appear in business magazines like *Inc.* and radio spots are run on National Public Radio. Each ad directs viewers to a web site specifically designed to help consumers find and understand how to work with architects.

Banner ads on the web are a relatively new form of advertising being used by professional services firms to attract attention. The banner ad is the web's answer to display advertising in print or outdoor advertising on a billboard. It is a simple and bold ad with the ability to attract the viewer's attention for long enough to make a simple point. One architecture and engineering firm placed a banner ad on the web site of its local chamber of commerce. Visitors to the chamber site immediately saw the name and message of the A/E firm and were able to link directly to its site.

Start with the Basics

Before embarking on an advertising campaign, a professional services firm should examine all avenues for promotion to determine whether advertising is the best way to get its message delivered to its target markets. Advertising is only one element of the marketing program and should be consistent with the objectives of the overall marketing program — brand positioning, image and strategy. A systematic approach to planning and strategy should be employed. Advertising should be well-conceived, planned and executed.

As with any marketing program, promotional campaign or public relations program, you have to begin with the basics. Objectives must be clearly defined; ads must be well-planned and designed, and the media chosen wisely. Consider these key questions:

- What do you want to accomplish? (objective)
- Whom do you wish to reach? (market)
- What do you wish to convey? (message)
- Which is the best format for conveying the message? (medium)
- What can you afford to spend? (budget)
- How will you know it worked? (evaluation)

Once it is determined that the use of advertising will allow the professional services firm to fulfill its objective, a plan is developed. The plan can be simple, but should consist of the following elements:

- Objective
- Audience
- Message
- Medium (from categories listed above)
- Budget
- Who is to manage
- Expectations and time frame (frequency and coverage)
- Evaluation

To Go It Alone, or to Hire an Agency?

Advertising is a finely tuned art. Professional services firm advertising is a very specialized discipline. Although the advertising program has to be managed by someone within the firm — principal or marketing professional — it's a mistake, and possibly a very costly one, to embark on an advertising program without the aid of experienced counsel. How does one go about selecting an appropriate agency?

The answer parallels how clients approach the selection of a professional services firm:

1. Define your needs.
2. Make an agency short list.
3. Select a few finalists.
4. Check references.
5. Manage the presentation.

At the end of the selection process, there should be a comfort level with the selected agency. They should know the professional services firm's business. Great advertising can be created through a great partnership with an agency with great results!

A Case Study

An Architectural Firm Embarks on an Advertising Program

A lengthy reorganization had caused confusion and misconceptions in the justice/corrections community about the future direction of a large national firm specializing in justice architecture. A year had elapsed without a coherent strategy to address this vital market segment.

Three primary objectives were set by the justice marketing team to be accomplished in a calendar year:

1. Reinforce continuing commitment to justice/corrections facilities community.
2. Craft service message to differentiate the firm and present it to the market in an impactful way.
3. Position the firm's experience to attract business from developing niche markets.

The Strategy

Media Plan. The team planned a comprehensive campaign using the four most well-read publications, representing the best mix of justice/corrections decision-makers: *American Jails Magazine, Corrections Forum, Corrections Today* and *Court Manager.* After studying competitors' often-inconsistent spending and frequency patterns, a more balanced media plan was designed to maximize exposure. The schedules provided full representation around key editorial issues and industry events. Throughout the year, full pages ran in annuals and programs, while single half-pages and half-page, three-ad clusters ran in bi-monthly magazines, alternating among the four to give constant coverage. (See ads on pages 296-299.)

Creative Plan. Further analysis of competing advertising revealed that most firms listed services or referenced projects. Many lacked a clear identity or personality. The team determined that the firm could create differentiation by consistent, bold graphics, and achieve the other objectives with simple text and a clear message. The ads would **pledge commitment, sell experience** and **demonstrate creativity.** Care was taken to keep ads appropriate to the medium — primarily a black and white format, appropriate to the audience — straightforward and hard-hitting and appropriate to the client — dignified, but not without a sense of humor. In the world of deadly serious corrections, the firm chose to be lighter in tone, but not in intent.

Results

Reader response vehicles and an 800 number generated numerous leads. Editorial coverage was invigorated and the firm's architectural projects were selected for covers twice in six months. Market reception and recognition was noticeably enhanced. Rumors were diminished. Specialty markets were addressed. The firm differentiated itself in the justice market — it got noticed.

Body of Evidence

HLM has a convincing record of building a better courthouse facility. Judge for yourself.

Call 1-800-333-3310. Experience counts.

JUSTICE
ARCHITECTURE ENGINEERING PLANNING

Charlotte	Chicago	Denver	Houston	Iowa City	New Orleans	New York	Orlando	Philadelphia	Sacramento	Washington
N CAROLINA	ILLINOIS	COLORADO	TEXAS	IOWA	LOUISIANA	NEW YORK	FLORIDA	PENNSYLVANIA	CALIFORNIA	D C

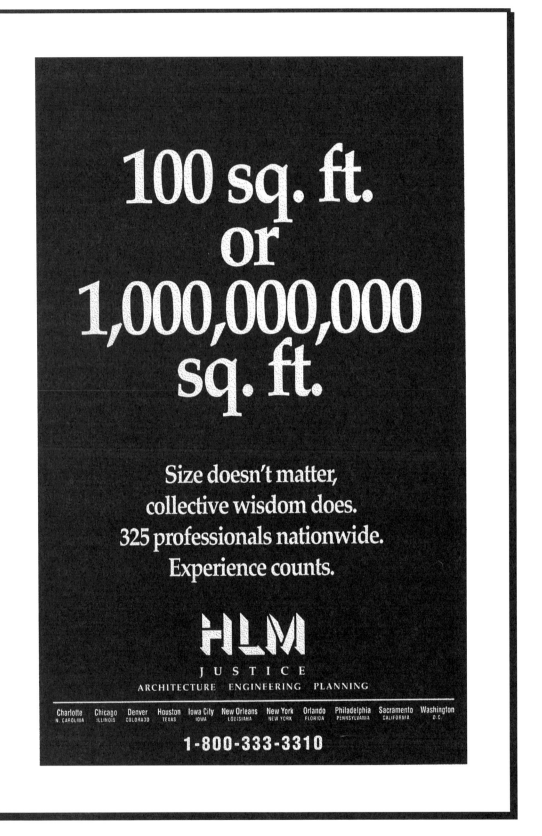

How Do You Get Your Advertising Noticed and Acted Upon?

An increasing amount of information (messages) assaults the public daily. Taking that into consideration, what does your advertising have to do to be noticed and acted upon? Frank Grazian, in an article written for *Communications Briefings* entitled "Getting More Mileage from Your Advertising," states that ads and commercials should be:

- *Attention getting.* Advertising should be distinctive. A fresh approach will make it stand out among the thousands of messages competing for attention. But attention-getting techniques that have little relationship to the message or that overpower the message should be avoided. Make the message distinctive.

- *Aimed at the right audience.* Time and money should be spent researching your audience. Your ads should be designed for those who might be interested in your service. Advertising that appeals to everyone — and misses your prime target — should be avoided.

- *Related to an objective.* Obvious, yes. However, many advertisers set objectives that are so vague they're useless.

- *Appropriate to the marketing mix.* Advertising is only one element in the total marketing plan. Advertising messages should fit in with and enhance the marketing strategy, including the public relations efforts.

- *Placed in the right media.* Most media offer demographic breakdowns of their audiences. These breakdowns should be obtained and used to help in determining if your audience will be reached with that particular medium.

- *Rewarding.* People purchase a service because they perceive they will benefit from it. Advertising that simply entertains or attempts to be clever and gimmicky often fails. If your service will provide a benefit, state it. If it won't, then it won't sell anyway.

- *Planned around a major concept.* Some advertisers call this "the great idea" concept. David Ogilvy, one of the great advertisers of our time, says, "unless your campaign is built around a great idea, it will flop."[3]

- *Designed with a single focus.* Once a great idea is established, an entire ad campaign should be built around it. Don't allow less important ideas to share the spotlight with it. As many selling points as needed should be included, but each one should contribute to the great idea.

- *Credible.* Today's consumers have to believe what is said or they won't budge. Even if the right concept and strong selling points have been selected, the ads will fail if they are not believable. Claims have to be supported with evidence that people can accept.

- *Constructed with a call to action.* Exactly what you want the consumer to do, or think, should be spelled out. Nothing should be taken for granted.

Keys to Success

In *The New How to Advertise,* Roman and Maas state that advertising must be delivered with sufficient frequency to be effective. People have short memories. They forget 60 percent of what they learn within half a day. The more repetition there is, the better the retention. Advertisers who seek to reach a broad audience at the expense of sufficient frequency among key prospects risk wasting much of the investment.[4]

A case can also be made for impact — concentrating everything on a dramatic program that rises above the clutter and commands attention, rather than spreading it over a long period of time. It's a seductive concept that relies on the hope that people will remember.

Studies by the Advertising Research Foundation and the Association of Business Publishers by Alfred Politz Media Studies and by W. R. Simmons & Associates Research conclude: "It's clear that creating a strong message is only a start. The more you repeat it, the stronger it gets."[5]

Why So Much Advertising Fails

If we learn from our mistakes, then there are lessons to be garnered from Jay Conrad Levinson's book *Guerrilla Advertising.* A sampling of reasons why advertising doesn't work, according to Levinson, include:

- *Premature abandonment.* Most advertising is discarded too soon. Patience should be part of the strategy.
- *Silly positioning.* Services should be positioned in such a way as to tempt buyers.
- *Failure to focus.* Advertisers fail to make the essential link between the glories of their offering and how it relates to their prospects.
- *Beginning without a written plan of attack.* A written plan lets you see where you've been, where you are and where you're going. You should always know how much you're spending on advertising and if the profits generated are commensurate with your efforts.
- *Picking the wrong media for the right audience.* Market research enables you to ascertain to which media your audience pays attention.
- *Being unclear to prospects.* Lack of clarity will probably cause prospects to think you'll be the same if they buy. So they pass.
- *Not understanding customers.* People tend to buy what they want instead of what they need. Your business will fare better if you're attuned to filling the wants of your customers instead of their needs.
- *Exaggeration that undermines truth.* Don't overstate a case past the point of believability.
- *Not keeping up with change.* The changes that cause much advertising to fall on its face occur on the competitive scene, in the marketing field, in the national or local economy, in the media or in current events. If you're not moving ahead, you're falling behind.
- *Unrealistic expectations.* Impatient advertisers expect profits to come in faster and larger than reality dictates.

- *Saving money in the wrong places.* Use a professional to write your ad copy, plan your media, do your research or design your ads.
- *Thinking it can be done without hard work.* The homework that goes into knowing how to say the right things to the right people in the right place at the right time is formidable.
- *Committees and layers of management.* Committees tend to dilute great ad ideas.
- *Not supporting advertising with other marketing.* Millions of dollars are wasted daily because naive advertisers expect ads to do the whole job.
- *Starting out in the wrong direction.* A great deal of advertising fails because crucial market and motivational research did not precede it.
- *Boring advertising.* Boring advertising comes at you in waves of invisibility, looking, sounding, feeling and acting like everything else in the sea of advertising.

Have a Target, Hit the Bull's Eye

Advertising can be a potent element in a professional services firm's marketing program. However, professional services firms that advertise must know what they want to gain from their advertising, how to achieve their objectives and where to direct their message. When a program is focused, the gain can be tremendous.

Endnotes

[1] Kenneth Roman and Jane Maas, *The New How to Advertise,* (New York: St. Martin's Press, 1992) 2.

[2] E. Jerome McCarthy, *Basic Marketing — A Managerial Approach,* (Burr Ridge, IL: Richard D. Irwin). This excerpt appeared in Richard A. Connor Jr. and Jeffrey P. Davidson's book, *Marketing Your Consulting and Professional Services,* (New York: John Wiley & Sons, 1985, 1990) 144.

[3] David Ogilvy, *Confessions of an Advertising Man,* (New York: First Atheneum, 1983) 95.

[4] Roman and Maas, 84.

[5] Roman and Maas, 86.

Bibliography

Connor, Richard A., Jr., and Jeffrey P. Davidson. *Marketing Your Consulting and Professional Services.* New York: John Wiley & Sons, 1985, 1990.

Levinson, Jay Conrad. *Guerilla Advertising.* New York: Houghton Mifflin Co., 1994.

Ogilvy, David. *Confessions of an Advertising Man.* New York: First Atheneum, 1983.

Roman, Kenneth, and Jane Maas. *The New How to Advertise.* New York: St. Martin's Press, 1992.

Seiden, Hank. *Advertising Pure and Simple.* New York: AMACOM, 1978.

J. Rossi

- J. Rossi is vice president of marketing/communications at HLM Design.
- She has a broad range of experience in marketing professional services. She began her career in this field in 1979 as a marketing coordinator of an architectural firm, went on to become that firm's marketing director, and subsequently joined another firm where she served as director of business development for six years.
- She was director of communications at Burt Hill Kosar Rittlemann Associates for three years prior to starting her own consulting practice and joining HLM Design.
- The advertising program she developed for HLM Design, the subject of this chapter's case study, was recognized with Best of Show and a First Place in the advertising category of the SMPS Marketing Communications Awards Program.

4.7 Publicity in Good Times and Bad

Joan Capelin, FSMPS, Hon. AIA, Fellow PRSA
President
Capelin Communications

What's the one question on the mind of the consumer of news — any news, including yours?

So what?

Answer that to your readers' or viewers' satisfaction, and you will be successful with your publicity. Problem is, much of the time, firms in the design and building industry have little to offer in the way of hard news and a limited number of people inside or outside the community that would find their news interesting and helpful. Nonetheless, since this book is all about how your firm handles competition, leadership and excellence, publicity needs to be center-stage in your marketing plans.

Publicity — **dealing with the media**, and therefore persuading a third party to tell your story — is far more than putting down who, what, where, when and why, which are the celebrated five W's, plus "how." Rather, publicity is a crucial part of establishing your reputation, which is your business's most precious asset.

The purpose of this chapter about publicity in good times and bad — an activity that is not for the faint at heart or indecisive — is to present ways to answer that provocative "So what?" question. It is also about *how to* communicate who you are (in this case, to the media), *how often* that needs to happen, *who* needs to know about you and how, and *how much* you need to invest for the results you want.

Warning Label

With all the scrutiny of the media and its behavior in Clintonian times, I don't need to use this space to describe today's rough-and-tumble world of media relations. William Raspberry, the *Washington Post*'s Pulitzer Prize-winning, good-times columnist, told an audience at Brown University at a recent graduation that an editor nowadays would consider a good story to be conflict or scandal. "What's gone wrong?" sells far more papers than "What works?" Only on the sports pages is it clear that the reporters root for the home team; any other section, one would wonder if they wouldn't be happier if their community and the whole nation imploded.

Reporters can be accurate and perceptive, or sloppy, lazy and even hostile; then again, so can the communications staff members or outside publicists who represent our professions. If your mission and message are clear, if you make every reasonable effort to control what is issued in writing or conveyed in an interview, if you trust no one on the news-gathering side, if you accept the premise that their job is *not* to do your publicity for you, if you have a responsible answer for every question that might be asked … then you have a fighting chance of getting your story told. But told accurately, appropriately or "exactly as we wanted" is another matter.

Definitions

Publicity — or media relations, as it is also called — is only part of the public relations arsenal. Public relations is the full gamut of activities that creates a climate of acceptance for your organization. Public relations yields visibility, credibility and access to people in a position to advance your business. And public relations, properly practiced, is a function of a firm's management, not a handmaiden to its marketing department.

Soap Box

Given this perspective, publicity that is not integrated into the rest of a firm's policy-making, positioning and marketing is wasteful and potentially dangerous. Everything must be congruent, must work together, to establish a firm's distinction and distinctiveness.

Too often, publicity — even when it is integrated into all the firm's communications — deals solely with what has already happened, period. Telling only part of the story in essence slows down the firm, instead of propelling it forward. For professionals, the real excitement lies in what it knows that no one else does, what is first happening, what motivates the practice to go into uncharted territory. By my definition, really effective publicity discloses achievements only in the context of what lies ahead for the firm, its clients and the world in which both navigate.

Who *Are* You?

Each press release must clearly enunciate why your firm should be considered an expert about the subject discussed. State this up front — "for 30 years, the ranking authority in school building design," "the region's largest civil engineer practice, according to [whatever indicator]," "one of the handful of firms internationally to design big bridges" — so the editor immediately knows to trust your information and therefore will read past the opening paragraph.

By the same token, if your release deals with something designed or built for another organization, a similar brief description is needed for them. In fact, this entity may be far more interesting to the editors than your firm, particularly if they are publicly traded or a major institution in the area.

Releases are written in a reverse pyramid format; that is, the most important information must be in the top three paragraphs, sometimes less. To save space, editors cut information from the bottom towards the top of the release. Include in the second or third paragraph something truly significant about the company, so if everything else is cut, this will remain.

(Said another way: You are not building to a climax or storytelling in your press release. Pack your payload up front.)

In any event, the last paragraph of your release should be a tightly written description about the company that can even be in italics to signal it is a boilerplate statement. This information will move from release to release, so make it powerful but general.

What Goes Into a Press Kit

A press release or query letter about a professional services firm is often insufficient by itself to impress an editor or reporter. To persuade the media about your story's newsworthiness or usefulness, you might also send a selection of the following items. (*Note*: No ranking is implied by their order.)

Even if you don't send the backup, "chance favors the prepared mind"; that is, when an editor asks for more information, she wants it *now*. That request is not the moment to first start pulling your kit together. Unless — even if — you are a seasoned pro who can generate these materials in your sleep, it's best not to launch a publicity campaign until you have everything you need in hand.

- News or feature press release.
- Query letter to gauge editorial interest.
- Pertinent recent company press releases.
- Detailed fact sheet about the project.
- Design statement.
- Project chronology.
- "Did you know?" factoids.
- Renderings and/or photos with captions.
- Local or regional map showing the site.
- Site plan, selected floor plans, sections, elevations.
- Company backgrounder(s), but not your brochure.
- Company fact sheet.
- White paper and/or case studies.
- A related interview or Q-and-A you might have done.
- In the case of a controversy, any internal memos or letters that can be made public.
- Client backgrounder, if germane.
- Biographies for the company principal(s) involved.
- Biographies for the client leader(s) involved.
- Articles featuring your company.
- Relevant articles that have featured your business/industry or your client, even if they don't mention you.
- Relevant research on the topic at hand.
- A list of additional experts willing to be interviewed on the subject at hand, with their phone numbers.
- A formal invitation to a forthcoming event where the media are included.
- A copy of the home page of your web site, marked to indicate where additional information might be found.
- For a public company: financials, including the 10K, annual report and research reports.
- Your business card (provide someone else's and you lose control).

A sample press release appears on the next page.

A B C ARCHITECTS & ENGINEERS, INTERNATIONAL

Contact: The name and phone number
of one or two people who
are available <u>and</u> informed

PUNCHY DECLARATIVE STATEMENT ABOUT SOMETHING YOUR READER IS CERTAIN TO WANT TO READ GOES HERE IN A TWO- OR THREE-LINE, ALL-CAPS FORMAT

A Secondary Headline Might Be Useful; It Reinforces Your Focus and Provides Added News; This Can Be a More Informal Format

(Some space left here aids editors, who need room for their own headlines and re-writes.)

Place, date of the release (not the event) — In the first paragraph, introduce yourself briefly and tell what your story is all about: Who, What, Where, When and Why. If there is room, also tell How.

The second paragraph elaborates on the first. Make all your points by its end and be sure to include **your firm's name**, since this may be all the room the publication gives you. News releases are developed in a reverse pyramid; that is, the most important information is at the top, in descending order.

"You are not telling a story that builds to a conclusion," editors explain. The third paragraph is a good time to put a pithy quotation. Place it in the mouth of your most influential source — not necessarily yours, quite possibly your client's.

SUBHEADS ARE HELPFUL
Subheads guide editors, who are often on deadline, so they know what's coming and where they can cut. If the release is brief, you won't need them.

[More]

```
Brief Identifying Head Here
[Page number] of [total number of pages]


If the release runs to more than one page, then note [More] at the bottom of
each page.  Do not break a paragraph in the middle when going from one page to
the next.  Ideally, no release is more than two, perhaps three pages long.

If your news is of sure-fire interest and if you have the time and money to do
so, consider including additional pieces: a fact sheet (background data in
bullet form), captioned visuals and other pertinent materials.  If this
package starts to become unwieldy, you probably need to send your information
in a press kit.
```

FORMAT IS IMPORTANT

```
It is courteous to follow conventional rules about news release presentation:
white paper, generous margins, 8½-inch by 11-inch sheets, and 1½- or two-line
spacing.  Before it was considered wasteful, releases were printed on one side
of a sheet; now, they can go front-and-back.  Photos can be smaller than 8
inches by 10 inches, even 5 inches by 7 inches, but they must be reproducible;
always caption them, since they might become separated from your other
information.

Keep paragraphs short.  Print your news in a large, readable typeface.
Consider printing your release in bold face for additional legibility, if your
printing equipment reproduces faintly.

Although it provides credibility, you do not really need special "news"
letterhead.  Plain bond will do, so long as there is an address and official
source.  If you are relying on a public relations firm, decide whether to use
its news release letterhead or your own.  Generally, an agency can write more
colorfully and boastfully about your achievements than you can.
```

The last paragraph is a good place to tell about your firm, using your standard boilerplate. If you place it in italics, the editors immediately recognize it as background.

```
At the end of your release, put either - 30 - or three hatch marks in a row.
# # #
```

Frequency

What's news? Answer: What the editor says is newsworthy. To paraphrase an old anecdote: There are balls and strikes, and an umpire may call them as he sees them — but they are nothing until he calls them.

News has to be deeply interesting to the readers or viewers. It has to be timely. Much of what we consider exciting news — a new commission, a ground breaking — is meaningless to the rest of the world. We must collectively help the nation's media to understand the contribution of our industry to the national or the local economy before this starts to change. But we are then obliged to provide important stories — important, that is, in the context of the reader, not the provider.

Small firms don't often make news; then again, big firms don't necessarily make riveting news just because of their size. Our most successful, most attention-grabbing, and, for us, award-winning campaign ever was a tiny story with a tiny public relations budget about a tiny (890-square foot) ice cream parlor.

But the angle was big for that precise moment (architect does *pro bono* work to help the sponsoring shelter for homeless men), the owner was politically as well as socially active in the community (Harlem) and appreciative of his architect, and 12,000 people turned out for a joyful dedication at the same time Los Angeles was in flames. No wonder the media turned out in droves. Serendipity or good publicity? Both. After all, someone had to take the story forward, before it could go on national television and into *People* magazine; in this case, it was the architect, a firm of three, on a good day.

By the same token, we were once asked by one of the industry giants to develop a campaign that would distribute 365 releases a year. That would have been a lucrative assignment, but I said no. Why? It would have been impossible to achieve logistically — imagine the data-gathering and sign-offs, for starters — and I was willing to bet they didn't have that many truly newsworthy items.

But even more crucially, that unrelenting dissemination of stories would overwhelm, and bore, the press with their releases, and thus devalue their credibility. Too much visibility is as much a problem as too little.

Who Gets the Story?

There are several layers of media, each with its own needs:

Local/regional media, which only cares about what effect your news has upon the area. Are you growing? What new structure or infrastructure is going into the ground, and why the investment? What part of the community's history is being destroyed or preserved? What will improve the quality of life, or line someone's pockets? Or, can you offer a local perspective on a story of national import?

You need to know this layer of media well — professionally, that is. They can help your business or kill you in a nanosecond. A civil engineering firm of considerable reputation and some size ignored this truism a few years back. Based in a small town, this office was selected for its impeccable credentials to design the county's new dump site. It had almost successfully completed the project when the county's politics shifted, the dump became a volatile campaign issue, a lawsuit started ... and the rest is a very unpleasant tale.

It's included here because the press tore them to shreds — even though they never corrected or even contacted them, at least to offer to explain the complex *engineering* issues and advances involved. This practice, despite its long history in the region, had never made its presence, reputation or impact known to the local press.

So, there was no comprehension, no appreciation or good will, no archive of past stories to which to refer. And thus there was no one in that hometown media to say, "But they seem very responsible; let's give them the benefit of a doubt and ask them for their take on the story." They are no longer in business.

The trade and professional media of the design and building industry, which is totally absorbed by what you do, for whom and to what standards. We are fortunate to have national weekly coverage in at least one industry publication, *Engineering News-Record* (*ENR*), and bi-weekly coverage in a few business-oriented newsletters, *DesignIntelligence* and *The Zweig Letter*, among others.

Most of the remaining design and construction publications are monthly. Their goal is to show how the best of your colleagues succeed (or not), by a variety of definitions of success. In good times, there is tough competition to get into their well (feature story section), but opportunities abound to appear in other sections that discuss different facets of design practice.

Interestingly, these days when it is so difficult to attract good personnel, people are very keen on being published in the industry press, on the theory that name recognition helps enormously. When times are leaner and photography, for instance, is difficult to budget, people don't pursue these magazines as aggressively.

Proving your expertise to them is challenging, since firms that make it through the editorial gamut are at the top of their game. Still, the magazines compete intensely against each other, and firms that haven't yet been published are particularly tantalizing. Study them carefully. Track each editor across a few months of articles. Consider your own work, stash of visuals and information or insights that you uniquely can provide. Draft a query, pare it down to the essential message — and pick up the phone. Don't bluff, though; that costs dearly, perhaps forever.

Your clients' trade and professional media, which follows the industries or communities where your clients operate. Articles in these publications are golden. What *this* industry does has enormous impact on its *clients'* industries. Health care, education, research and development, roads and bridges, entertainment, convention centers, retail — all are constantly building or upgrading. Those that aren't, should be — for reasons that a well-worded, strategically placed opinion-editorial piece could make clear and persuasive.

One caveat, though: The client media is really not interested in your side of the story. Rather, they want to know about and assess your tale's impact on their readership. How did you do something faster, better, cheaper? How did you enable someone to make or save money? Avoid or get them out of trouble? Improve or create a reputation? Enable people to heal faster, learn easier, play harder? No matter what your story, it must ultimately answer that first question I raised: *So what? Why should I spend my limited time reading this?*

If you appear in these publications, don't neglect to clip the pages and distribute them on a turnaround to the related local media. The very fact you've had national trade press visibility could open doors. Certainly, national attention for a local installation is a cause of pride for the owner, whether public or private — and those publications will want to carry the story. Telling your story over the fence extends your publicity budget — and your credibility — immeasurably.

National media, but how many firms in our industry get to play in this arena? Not many. The *Wall Street Journal*'s "Property Report" is receptive to a really good angle. The major national business press, however, traditionally doesn't track privately owned companies because of their limited appeal and closely guarded financial information. That leaves the small-business, entrepreneurially focused publications, which are no less difficult to crack for their own set of reasons.

As for the popular shelter magazines, on the opposite end of the publishing spectrum, houses published in *Architectural Digest* axiomatically attract more work for their architects and designers. But *Digest* plays by its own rules — including complete control over the photography until the property is published. The other shelter magazines follow this leader, with their own set of restrictions. It surprises me that design firms with this focus don't try more aggressively and realistically to be placed in their regional style publications or pages, rather than lock up their work and their expensive photography.

Press Lists

Directories — print or CD-ROM — abound that will give you information about media outlets: *Bacon's, Burrelle's, Editor & Publisher*, among others. Some cities and regions have their own directories. You should be able to find these in the public library. If you are serious about publicity, you will want to purchase the one that you find most comfortable to use. One of the design professions' newsletter publishers sporadically produces a reputable directory that can get you started, though by definition it isn't complete and dates quickly.

Public or university library databases are another good place to start a press list. While you are there, if you have time and curiosity, check client associations for their publications, starting with a directory like *Gale's* or *NTPA*. AIA members also have an excellent resource in their well-stocked library at headquarters.

The Internet can be endlessly scanned for information, including the sites of those of your competitors that include articles on their firms among the offerings. Dow Jones has a formidable interactive web-based service, also useful for marketing research. Cruising its offerings gets expensive, but you can see which publications and writers track certain types of stories.

In New York, and I imagine in other major cities, a number of news dealers have comprehensive offerings on their racks. I like to browse to see what new national and special-interest publications are out that could be useful to our clients.

Once you have identified monthly publications that could be helpful to the firm — you'll know instinctively which they are because they will be familiar and agreeable to you:

- Subscribe or regularly track them somehow.
- Track their competing publications as well.
- Obtain the editorial calendar (which is actually an advertising vehicle), usually cast in August and issued in late fall and balance your work against the publication's interests.
- Call editors that you respect and ask for what they specifically are looking.
- Start your strategy accordingly.

Creating a Press Release

The press list for professional services firms is not a scattershot compilation. Leave that to the major organizations that must reach millions of constituents. In fact, the number of publications that carry our news is relatively limited; this enables us to concentrate on being carefully targeted.

It remains important to have the correct name of the journalist targeted. That precision is becoming less and less easy to achieve, however, because today's print and electronic media are prone to constant personnel changes. Further, journalists with overflowing real or virtual in-boxes are apt to discard mailings to a predecessor.

Because media relations is a considerable part of my firm's work, we have across the years developed press lists from hundreds of sources — direct experience with the press being prime. Still, before we start to develop any new list, we go through the following exercise to be sure we are approaching the right media outlets and recipients. This process should apply to anyone who needs to develop a press list, especially those who don't do this for their living.

- Are we clear about what the release is supposed to achieve?
- What categories of audiences do we need to inform?
- How quickly does this release have to get out?
- Have we done any list like this before, and how long ago was that? How long will it take to refresh that list?
- How much time and budget do we have to develop or reconstruct the press list?
- If not, where is it possible to reduce our efforts?
- How readily can we get any missing information?
- Where are the people targeted to receive this news located?
- How broadly is this release to travel?
- Are there any media people with whom our client [read: your firm] has had contact — or we, on behalf of the client — that should be given priority?
- Are there any journalists that should be excluded?
- Is there a particular industry focus?
- Will visuals be needed to make our point? Are they readily available?
- Is there a chance that radio, television or the Internet may be involved? Do we have the budget to develop their special materials?
- Are the particular publications the right size and profile of readership?
- What kind and level of editor or reporter should receive the release?
- Have we dealt with any of them before? Here, or at another media outlet? What are their preferences?
- Do we have recent copies of the publication on hand?
- Do their mastheads (or web sites) reveal any changes in publication ownership, assignments, new names, new bureaus that could give us new insights into their thinking about news?
- Are we going to contact all the media at once, or will this be a tiered effort?
- Are there any influential industry, association or community leaders who should receive this release as well?

- Does a line-for-line reading of the first draft of the release yield any opportunities that we might not have considered?
- Is everyone on this list essential?
- Does anyone else need to review the list? At what point? With how much influence?

Investing in Publicity Wisely

Publicity costs what it costs, with few shortcuts. It involves:

- Time to gather and verify facts, interview the people involved and relevant experts, and then transcribe those conversations.
- Generating artwork, notably photography and drawings.
- Time to write and edit.
- Costs of circulating text for comments and approvals.
- Production and dissemination of the final materials.
- Entertaining editors (not as much as it used to).
- Travel to whatever site.
- Online and other telephone charges.
- Fees to an outside public relations professional (optional).
- Ultimately, the rights to reproduce an article or pictures.
- Generating and distributing the reprints.

Early in my consulting work, we achieved miracles for a structural and civil engineering firm, getting its breakthrough project published broadly everywhere — locally, regionally, trades and professional publications, client-read publications, even nationally. But we discovered that when it finished with the costs of developing the campaign, it had no money left for reprints! That's how I learned that:

> **The real goal of publicity is to get something that can be distributed to clients and prospective clients, bound into proposals and placed in the waiting area — not "just" to get published.**

Achtung!

Here are a few warnings that aren't always immediately apparent:

- Get your client's permission *before* you start a publicity campaign using his or her project. The client relationship is more important than the ink.
- There is no longer anything "off the record."
- Coordination of publicity with the outside companies that support your outreach is crucial. This has become an approach in itself, called integrated communications; whole university departments are now devoted to it. Those who need to be coordinated: public relations, graphics, advertising, web site developers, investor relations.
- If a key employee leaves the firm disaffected, you can anticipate a kiss-and-tell negative story about the firm in the press soon after, perhaps even unverified. The "deep throat" mode remains

endlessly appealing to some journalists. Since you probably can't stop this from happening, you might as well be prepared.

- Your firm's leader may be the wrong person to speak for the company. Assess his or her ability to communicate before inviting a reporter for an interview. Get that partner media or, at least, public speaking training. Or, find another spokesperson in the partner ranks.
- Before you set one of your firm's clients in front of the media, be sure that he or she won't place his or her own abilities and contribution before that of his or her design consultants. It doesn't take some people too much prompting to say: "They did what I told them to draw" or, more ambiguously, "I'll never do that again!"

Bad News

As the saying goes, "Scandal has a thousand stringers, but good news doesn't know the editor's phone number."

This is the construction industry; things will go thump. Then why are so few firms prepared to cope with bad news of any stripe? Human nature, perhaps. But crises are highly disruptive. If you are the person responsible for a firm's publicity, let alone its public relations, you had better be prepared — just as you had better have a nature that stays calm under intense pressure. Here are some key elements to help you be prepared for the crisis.

- Do you have the firm's leadership's home phone number?
- Does the leadership know where and how to find you off-hours?
- Have you designated and trained the spokesperson? The backup person?
- Do you have a way to get a story out quickly?
- If a crisis occurs, who from the administrative staff would be available to work with you to produce and get out stories?
- Do you have a public relations firm lined up, in case you need that firepower? How do you reach your account executive off-hours?
- Is there embedded in the collective memory of everyone in the firm a statement about the level of service and quality for which you stand — the mission statement will do if it has been worded effectively — so they can measure any crisis-related action against your stated ethic?
- Do you have any documentation that indicates how many projects like this failed one you've done successfully? What has been your firm's track record for safety over the years?
- Is your master press list up to date for this locale and for the one where the crisis has occurred? Is your relationship with at least one person in each pertinent publication strong enough to gain you the critical benefit of doubt?
- Are you clear that the problem may *not* be the fault of the firm ... but that your client will be under such stress, you might be blamed just from faulty speculation? ... that leaving it to the client to tell the story is tantamount to handing over the management of your reputation?
- Are you clear who are all the constituencies of the firm (Marketing 101) so you can assess the impact of this bad news on each and then determine how to mitigate it?
- Are your firm's key people aware that they should turn to you immediately in case of a crisis — not just to their lawyer?

- Is there someone you can count on to get you organized in case of a crisis — setting up the logs, files, supply of background and new materials? Does that person know what these should be, with a sample readily available?
- Have you done any reading on crisis communications? It abounds. If not, contact the Public Relations Society of America's library at (212) 995-2230 today.

If nothing else, knowing how to handle bad news will sharpen your wits and materials when you distribute the abundant good news your firm generates.

For More Information

For more information about public relations, check with your local public or university library. Another source for information is the national headquarters of the Public Relations Society of America in New York at (212) 995-2230.

Joan L. Capelin, FSMPS, Hon. AIA, Fellow PRSA

- Third recipient of the SMPS Marketing Achievement Award as "our consummate communicator."
- Named to SMPS Fellowship in the first class.
- Pioneer in marketing professional services, including developing many of the tools and techniques routinely used today.
- In-house director of communications in the 1970s.
- Founder of the first public relations agency to concentrate on professional services firms, with clients exclusively from the design and building industry.
- Honorary member of the American Institute of Architects (1997), its highest recognition of a person who is not an architect, for "her optimism, actions, and efforts to persuade clients and inform society of architects' effectiveness [that] have enhanced our ... reputation and brought us untold opportunities."
- Columnist, author of hundreds of articles, and perennial speaker on public relations and marketing professional services.
- Highly visible member of the Public Relations Society of America, 1999 chairman of the PRSA College of Fellows, and member of the Professional Services Section, which she helped to found.
- "Accredited in Public Relations," recognition accorded by PRSA after an examination and a peer review.
- Recipient of multiple honors and awards from SMPS, PRSA and AIA, as well as perennial juror and jury chairman.
- Past member of the board of directors and counsel, Professional Services Management Association.
- Past president, Women Executives in Public Relations.
- Editor, *40 Effective Newsletters for A/E Firms* (a Professional Management Associates book).
- Author, *Marketing Professional Services in the Decade of Integrity,* a PRSA Professional Services Section monograph.
- Education: bachelor's degree, Wellesley College, master's degree, Middlebury Graduate School of French in Paris. Fulbright Scholar (France).

4.8   The Visual Voice of Photography

Wendy Sherrill
Marketing Coordinator
Wade-Trim

Photography brings your work to life. It is a window to your professional expertise that makes technical issues easier to understand and design concepts more emotionally appealing. It is a visual voice, communicating your firm's story across all cultures and languages. As a marketer, you are responsible for creating the best images to support your marketing efforts. This chapter will help you undertake a professional photography program to successfully create and guide your firm's visual voice.

Who Needs Professional Photography?

Depending on your firm's willingness to budget photography, you are most likely going to be limited to a few projects a year that warrant the expense of hiring a professional. This means determining which projects will best showcase your firm's design skills and expertise and which projects best represent the markets you will be pursuing. In short, which images will give you the most mileage. This can be a difficult challenge when you are faced with several projects nearing completion simultaneously or others in your firm who think their project "deserves" to be professionally photographed. Use your best judgment. You know what works in your communication pieces. You know which images you are always scrambling to find.

Start by determining what you need the images for. Are you creating a new brochure? Are you submitting a specific project for an award? Do you need examples of specific skills for proposals? Are you pitching a cover article to a national magazine? Look for images that can be used to fulfill a variety of your marketing needs.

Determine project completion dates to plan your photography. It is a good idea to have a couple of alternate projects in mind in case something doesn't go as smoothly as planned. Create a list of projects to be photographed, including location and the appropriate time frame and use it to begin your discussions with photographers. Be prepared. The more you understand about your own needs, the better you will be able to communicate them to your photographer.

Finding a Photographer

There are many good photographers. Ask other marketers or professional associations in your industry who they have used. This will probably give you the best perspective because they will be able to give you insight into what the photographer was like to work with. Ask your clients. They may have worked with photographers on other occasions or projects. Magazines always feature professional photography. Look through current and old issues to find some photography that you like and track the photographer down from the photo credit. Look for image styles or projects that are similar to what you have in mind.

Are you looking for a photographer that merely records your project in a well-focused photo or are you looking for someone who may offer a more creative approach? Do you want someone who is easy to work with and open to your suggestions or do you prefer someone with their own strong ideas about how and when to photograph a project?

Interview your photographer. Discuss what your expectations are and what kind of work he or she has done. Take the time to find someone who specializes in architectural and engineering subjects. Look through his or her professional portfolio for images that you like. Explain to the photographer what in particular you like about an image or how the approach could be changed to meet your needs. Make sure you are comfortable with his or her ability to handle the scope of your shoot. If you are shooting only interiors, be sure the photographer demonstrates the ability to handle lighting to create a natural appearance. Make sure you are talking with the person who is going to take the photos. If your photographer is sending someone else to take the pictures, you may want to think twice about using him or her, or have another meeting with the actual person who will be doing the shoot.

Understand the photographer's costs and make sure that it is within your budget. Typical expenses include time, travel, photographic medium (negatives or slides), proof sheets and prints. Is the photographer willing to sell you the negatives or will you have to order all prints from him or her? Securing ownership of the negatives gives you unlimited rights to use the images. Is the photographer willing to use multiple cameras during a single shoot to produce slides and negatives simultaneously? Will you be able to cut costs by scanning the photos yourself and outputting them as slides?

Guiding Your Photographer

Guide your photographer with specific information about the images you desire. There is no way for the photographer to know you are dying for a close-up of a crane unless you tell him or her. Do you want ground shots or aerials from a plane or helicopter? Explain who your audience is and what the images will be used for. Reveal how many different images you are expecting. If your subject is a one-time event such as a construction milestone, ground breaking or dedication ceremony, make sure your photographer is aware that these images will never be able to be captured again so he or she can prioritize your shoot accordingly.

Think about the major end uses for your images. Clarify specific issues such as time, budget, location and what format the images need to be in (slides, prints, transparencies). If you are going to enlarge the images for display purposes, larger format negatives will give you the best results. The photographer should also shoot the images close to final size so cropping will not compromise the quality of your print when enlarged.

Listen to your photographer's ideas. They often have good suggestions for camera angles, props to enhance the image, composition and lighting. A single soccer ball placed in the foreground of a soccer field can give the image much greater impact. For interior spaces, you may want to bring additional furniture or flowers to the site. It is important to give your photographer some room for creativity. Make sure he or she gets the exact images you want and, budget provided, encourage the photographer to play a bit on his or her own. Your photographer's eye may catch a unique and refreshing image that you would have never thought to capture. You may find that these images are your favorites because of their ability to reveal something unique or creative about your project. The expense of a few more exposures once the photographer is on-site and set up is minor compared with the overall cost.

If possible, accompany your photographer on the shoot so you can provide input on the fly. Often photographers will come up with new ideas on-site and may want your input as to whether you agree. If you are unable to attend the shoot, it may be helpful to take some 35mm shots of the site before you meet with the photographer. This will allow you to point out specific areas you want to feature and help the photographer get the lay of the land.

If you will not be present, make sure your photographer has a confirmed contact person on-site, if needed. Your field people and those who are directly involved with the project are the best contacts. Most likely, these are the people who can best direct the photographer's efforts and coordinate any project scheduling issues. If your project is under construction, you may want a safety person on-site to make sure no violations are photographed. Although the violation may be minor, the photograph will speak poorly of your firm and most likely be unusable. It is best if the photographer speaks directly with the on-site contact to verify meeting time and location. If your photography shoot impacts the project schedule, explain the importance of your photographer's mission to your personnel so they are not frustrated and angry when they have to work around the photographer for a day.

Plan Ahead

Good photography depends on many factors: photographer's talent and equipment, cost, your ability to communicate what you want, project location, site constraints, weather, seasons, etc. Planning ahead can help you make the most of each of these components to achieve your best images.

Site location may determine which projects get professionally photographed. The photographer's travel time may be cost-prohibitive for distant sites. You may be able to reduce costs by having several nearby projects photographed in the same day. It may also be more cost effective to work with several photographers that are located near different projects. Site constraints may hinder a photographer's ability to capture good images. If your site is too difficult to access or just not worth the extra cost, consider others.

Take advantage of the seasons, when possible. Whether you desire the lush green of summer grass, a forested background of fall colors, or a clean, snowy foreground, you can take advantage of seasonal dynamics with proper planning. Seasonal changes also include project use times. If you are photographing a golf course or other recreational facility, you may want to wait until people are actually using it to give your photos a human appeal. Or you may have an interior space that needs to be scheduled at a specific time when no one will be around to interfere with the shot. If you are going to spend the money for professional photography, make sure your efforts are well-timed to give you the results you desire. Keep in mind that good timing also means photographing a project early enough in its completion that it still appears clean and new. Waiting a year to photograph something just to catch a season can compromise your images in other ways.

Don't rely on others to tell you it is ready. If possible, visit the site yourself to make sure the grass is in good shape, the landscaping is complete and all construction materials have been properly removed. For interior spaces you may want to remove trash cans or other incidental objects that can detract from your image. What looks "finished" to others, may not mean camera-ready to you. It is not solely the photographer's responsibility to make your project look good.

Mother Nature does not care about your photography budget. If the site is to be shot outdoors, your photographer should be prepared for inclement weather. Good photographers book up quickly so make sure you select an alternative date when you are scheduling to get a second chance if the weather is miserable. Sometimes a not-so-sunny day can actually produce better images because your photographer doesn't have to contend with sunspots. Consider the time of day. East- or west-facing structures should be shot early or late in the day for best detail. Building shadows can be very large and distracting at certain times of the day. Taking shots at dusk can be very dramatic. Keep in mind, however, that striking sunset colors captured at dusk may not reproduce well if you use the image in a single color due to the lack of contrast.

Obtain client approval to photograph any project. An uninformed or unwilling client can put a stop to photography in a hurry. They should be informed about when the photographer will be on-site. There may be sensitive photographic issues to consider for some clients such as schools or churches.

Consider undertaking a joint photo shoot. Often other members of a project team, such as contractors, suppliers and owners, are willing to share in the cost of project photography. Additional costs may be incurred when shooting for multiple parties because more aspects of the project must be covered, but the end result should be lower costs for everyone. Make sure your photographer is well-informed about what images specific parties want. You may not be willing to pay for a close-up of a specific pump that a supplier has requested. Negotiate costs and usage rights with additional parties before the shoot.

The Power of Images

Although marketers typically strive for a perfect photo that reveals an entire finished project in one dramatic image, sometimes photos taken during a project can be equally engaging. Construction images are excellent to use in proposals to demonstrate a particular service. They project a hands-on image of your firm's capabilities that is sometimes difficult to portray once the project is complete. Some projects, such as underground sewers, are only truly visible during construction. They can also work well in award submittals and other marketing materials that need to show a variety of images for one project. Before and after comparison photos can effectively show architectural and engineering accomplishments.

Consider creating images that represent your firm's capabilities in a new way. Perhaps the most important thing to feature about a recently completed project isn't the project itself, but the end use. For instance, if your firm completed a major water improvement project you could photograph installing the water mains during construction, the project area after completion, or the nearby water treatment plant that the mains lead to. This approach would obviously demonstrate that your firm knows how to design and construct water mains. Another approach would be to photograph some children playing with a garden hose or running through a sprinkler. With the proper explanation, this image could be much more eye-catching and demonstrate that your firm understands the overall importance of clean water to the end-user. Brainstorm possible ideas and present them to your photographer. He or she may be able to create some of these images at a more leisurely pace at a lower overall cost to you.

A wide variety of stock photography companies sell images. Depending on the company, you can purchase a single image or an entire collection of images for unlimited use at a fairly reasonable price. If you are in a hurry for a specific image or don't have the budget to undertake a professional photography program, you may want to browse image libraries through the Internet. Try www.corbisimages.com, www.eyewire.com and www.dgusa.com.

Modeling 101

Featuring people in photographs is an effective way to portray professional services. However, working with people usually makes the photographer's job more difficult. These may be people that are actually working on the job site during the photo shoot or they may be your own staff members whom you have coordinated with in advance to pose in the photos. Regardless of who they are, make sure you communicate what you are trying to accomplish. Discuss with your photographer what clothing colors and styles will work best for the images you want and advise your models accordingly. Keep in mind the end use of your images. For instance, if you will be reproducing your images in one color only, you may want clothing combinations with high contrast. If you will be using your images in four color, you will be able to discern between color shades, even if they are all dark.

Choose your models wisely. Don't waste your time and budget with models who are going to fight the photographer. If you are using employees, be aware of their lasting effect on the image if they leave your firm. You may need a photo release if you are using a highly recognizable person. Initially, your models may lose their ability to look and act naturally when they are in front of the camera. Be prepared to allow for a little giggle time. Make sure they understand the amount of time involved. Often people are unaware of the set-up time that photographers need to make lighting adjustments, lens changes, test photographs, etc. Don't ask someone to just drop in who is going to be looking at his or her watch because what he or she perceived would take five minutes ends up being half an hour. Treat your models and your photographer fairly to get the best results.

Getting the Most Mileage Out of Your Photography

Strong photography greatly enhances your firm's image. Get the most mileage out of your photographic efforts by planning the use of your photos. Look at the results of your photography shoot together when creating a new brochure. Consider whether you want to use all the images simultaneously or save some for future pieces. Effective use of your photographs is critical to maintaining your firm's visual voice.

In today's digital age, a photograph can be manipulated through software programs such as Adobe PhotoShop to achieve varied results. Consider using these techniques to lengthen the usable life of your images. For instance, you could apply different filters to the same image to achieve drastically different looks. The more you use one particular image, the less overall impact it will have. If you are forced to shoot a subject before it is ready, digital manipulation can help. Unwanted scaffolding or a construction barrel can be removed. Green grass can be added to a sparse area or a gray sky can be made blue to improve your image. Be aware that digital manipulation has raised serious legal and ethical questions. Architectural and engineering firms are advised to use good judgment when manipulating photos. Changing the color of the sky or making other alterations to simply improve the image are acceptable. Altering the facade of a building or adding details that vary from the actual structure are not. Take care not to make changes that lower the integrity of your image.

Pitch your photography to magazines that your clients read. Magazines are interested in good photography. An appealing photograph can help you get your foot in the door to author an article. Contact editors for editorial calendars and submission guidelines. Once published, consider purchasing reprints of the article for inexpensive, additional marketing materials.

Enlarge photographic images to use on exhibits and around the office. Keep your display images current by using your newest photographs. This creates eye-catching exhibits for your firm and raises staff awareness of current projects.

Clients are just as proud of their projects as you are. If your client has not shared the cost of your professional photography, consider giving them a framed enlargement of one of the images. This makes a nice project completion gift that they most likely will hang in a prominent place in their office and remember who gave it to them for years to come.

Maintain a photographic library. As the years go on, it becomes increasingly critical to have established a program to properly care for your photos. If you purchased the negatives for your images, you must keep these in acid-free, protective sleeves to ensure their longevity. If you bought prints only, it is important that you maintain good records to indicate who the photographer was and when the photos were taken. This is your only link to the past when you need to get a print of a 10-year-old negative still owned by the photographer. There are also a variety of software programs available to help you build and share digital media libraries. These programs provide thumbnail views of images for easy access.

Give Credit Where Credit Is Due

Photographers should be credited for their work. Even after you have paid for the photography and bought the negatives, they should be given photographic credit for the images in an appropriate manner. This does not mean your new corporate brochure needs to have the photographer's name captioned all over the place. General practice is to include the photographer's credit line, usually printed on his or her work, in at least six-point type alongside or near the photo. This helps the photographer promote his or her work and makes your firm look professional.

Bibliography

Akiko, Busch. *Photography of Architecture*. John Wiley and Sons Inc., 1997.

Gladstone, Gary. *Corporate and Location Photography (Kodak Pro Workshop Series).* Silver Pixel Press, 1998.

Harris, Michael G. *Professional Architectural Photography*. Butterworth-Heinemann, 1998.

Kopelow, Gerry. *How to Photograph Buildings & Interiors*. 2nd ed. Princeton: Princeton Architectural Press, 1997.

McGrath, Norman. *Photographing Buildings Inside and Out*. 2nd ed. Watson-Guptill Publications Inc., 1993.

Wendy Sherrill

- A graduate of the University of Michigan, Wendy Sherrill earned a bachelor's degree in English in 1991.
- Sherrill has six years of experience in marketing and public relations for Wade-Trim, a consulting engineering firm. As marketing coordinator, she assists the marketing manager in marketing, planning, public relations, corporate communications, advertising and proposal development. She also provides public involvement support for client projects. She has worked with a variety of professional photographers and is responsible for taking the majority of non-professional photographs used by Wade-Trim.
- Sherrill has been an active member of SMPS's Michigan Chapter for the past five years. She is currently serving her second year on the Programs Committee.

Acknowledgment

Special thanks to Yvonne Rizzo who authored the original chapter about photography for the first edition of *The Handbook for Marketing Professional Services.*

4.9   Using Trade Shows to Achieve Marketing Objectives

Trude Noble
Vice President and Marketing Manager
Wade-Trim

Barely cushioned by the unpadded carpet, the hard concrete floor sends stinging pains up through the balls of her feet. She quietly acknowledges that years of sitting behind a desk have softened her. Working the booth after a late dinner with clients seemed more like a physical endurance test in business attire rather than a business development opportunity.

Exhaling deeply, she stares intently at her watch. One more hour to go. The last two hours had been incredibly slow but she had enjoyed an enlightening conversation with a past client. The neutral environment of the conference helped break the ice. There appeared to be new opportunities for her firm. She also spoke with a client about an upcoming request for proposal (RFP) on a large recreation facility.

Sessions were scheduled to break in five minutes. Soon the exhibit hall would be crowded with conference attendees eager to have their cards marked by exhibitors to qualify for the drawings. Her supply of glow-in-the-dark frisbees imprinted with her company's name and brand identifier was dwindling. They were a sought-after item. The advertising shelf life was short but perceived value high. The real benefit for the conference attendee would be realized at home when the frisbee was passed into the hands of a child or the anxious jaws of a dog. The benefit to her firm was a one-minute opportunity to make a favorable impression on the potential client who was seeking their exhibit out and stretch it into a longer conversation.

This is a common scenario. Trade shows are not very glamorous and are a lot of hard work. They take stamina. Success can be hard to measure, particularly if a firm goes into the show with unrealistic expectations or without objectives. Obtaining leads should be only one of your objectives. Trade shows offer the opportunity to achieve a variety of marketing objectives. Success of your efforts depends on targeting the right shows, planning, knowing your market, spending time to develop your exhibit, taking advantage of the many networking opportunities, monitoring market trends and following up on leads.

Evaluating Trade Shows

Many associations have discovered that a good way to raise money and provide exposure for their sponsors or associate members is to host a trade show in conjunction with their conference. Exhibit halls that were once limited to national and state conferences are filtering down to regional and local levels of associations. Frequently, shows that start out as small table-top shows grow to full exhibit spaces as the number of exhibitors rises.

Trade shows should be evaluated on a yearly basis to determine whether or not they provide marketing opportunities. Just because your firm exhibited last year, doesn't mean you need to exhibit the following year. Evaluate the show objectively. Are attendees decision-makers or can they influence the decision-making process? How frequently do they use your services? Do attendees seem interested in the exhibit area or do they avoid it? Does the association promote traffic in the exhibit area? Are conference sessions held in the same building as the exhibit hall? Are half of the other exhibitors consultants, offering the same services as your firm? Would your firm stand out more if it sponsored a conference activity instead of an exhibit? Is this a conference of your peers where staff would be more effective networking as attendees? Would a hospitality suite allow you to meet your objectives better than a booth? If you exhibited last year, did you meet your marketing objectives? Why or why not?

If it is a show you have never attended, ask for a list of the previous year's exhibitors. Contact a few and ask what they thought of the show. Are they planning on exhibiting again this year? What were their marketing objectives last year and did they meet them? If you're still not sure or it's a first-time show, don't exhibit. Attend the show and spend some time in the exhibit area talking to attendees and exhibitors to see how the show is going. Make your decision to exhibit the following year based on this feedback.

Once you make the decision to exhibit, send in the exhibit contract and payment right away. Some shows sell out quickly and booths are frequently assigned on a first-come, first-served basis.

Trade Show Plan

Trade shows should be treated like any other major marketing endeavor. A plan that identifies objectives and activities to be undertaken should be developed and shared with staff. Trade show activities should be integrated into the marketing plan. Identify shows to attend, activities to undertake and speaking opportunities to pursue for the year. Specific trade show plans should then be developed for each show and used as a work plan.

The trade show plan should be given to all employees participating in conference activities at least a few days before the show. The plan should be detailed enough that any staff member could pick it up and go to the show with a clear understanding of what is expected of him or her and what will be taking place. Leave an extra copy in the booth in case questions arise.

Typically, a trade show plan addresses:

- Conference focus and market served.
- Marketing objectives.
- Market research or market trend data collection.
- Exhibit theme.
- Hospitality suite or client dinners.
- Speaking opportunities.
- Sponsorship and/or advertising.
- Competitive intelligence to be gained.

Professional associations hosting trade shows frequently select a theme for their conferences each year. It is wise to review this theme and the demographics of the typical conference attendee before selecting your exhibit theme. Review the session topics to see what the hot issues are and how they relate to your service. Sometimes, companies will select a theme that ties in with the conference theme or session topics to help the association promote its message and to tie in with issues being discussed. This can be a great conversation starter for your staff but may not differentiate your firm from the competition. Be sure to attach the official conference schedule with your plan so staff can talk intelligently to attendees about conference activities.

Identify your marketing objectives. Don't limit yourself to finding new leads. Is it important to show support for the association hosting the trade show? Do you want to introduce a new service? Do you want to learn more about legislation impacting a segment of your client base? Do you want to learn about how a specific community or company addressed a problem similar to one a client is now facing? Do you want to assess your competitors' marketing strategies firsthand? Do you want to take advantage of this opportunity for potential clients to compare you to competitors and really differentiate your firm? Do you want to conduct an informal survey of booth visitors to hear their concerns about a specific issue? Formulate objectives that are specific to the trade show and measure your success. Outline specific tasks staff needs to complete to fulfill objectives.

Projects included in your exhibit should be highlighted in the plan. Nothing is more embarrassing than not knowing where one of your projects is located or not recognizing the client when he or she visits your booth because you didn't know the project location. Include a couple of paragraphs about each project and how the clients' needs were met. The plan should also identify literature and giveaways that will be in the exhibit and strategies for distributing them. Any information you would like staff to collect from visitors should be outlined as well as staff shifts for working the exhibit.

Hospitality suite or client dinner plans and objectives should be outlined in your plan or created as a separate plan with specific objectives. Your trade show plan should also identify any sponsorships, conference program advertisement, type of competitive intelligence you would like staff to obtain and market research to conduct.

Who Is Your Market?

Knowing your market and targeting activities toward them is the key to trade show success. Why do attendees come to the show? Do they come because there are great networking opportunities to learn what their peers are doing? Or because the show is always held at a great location with lots of opportunities for sightseeing or golf? If you don't know, find out. If it is the latter, don't exhibit. Consider hosting a special event or sponsoring a part of the conference and having your staff network.

Who comes to the show? Are they decision-makers, implementers or do they influence the selection process? What are their hot buttons?

If it truly is an educational show where others come to learn about advances in the field and what their peers are doing, focus on this in your exhibit. Find something meaningful that booth visitors can walk away with that is relevant to their search. Research findings about the different ways communities are funding water and waste water improvements or their success would be more meaningful than a glow-in-the-dark frisbee in this type of environment. Establish yourself as an expert in a specific area.

Don't limit your market to attendees. Are any of the regular exhibitors clients? Or can they potentially provide referrals for your firm? Make a point of talking with them and giving them valuable information. The hosting association should also be viewed as a potential client. Introduce yourself to the staff organizing the event. They always like to connect a face with a voice on the telephone. Once you've established a relationship, they might turn to you when they need an article for their association's publication or a speaker for a seminar. Give them honest feedback on how the show is going, offer specific suggestions of how to improve something you are not happy about, and let them know when things have gone smoothly because of their behind-the-scenes work.

Consider promoting your trade show activities before the event. Direct mail can be a great way, particularly if you have a large client base attending the show. Tie the piece in with the theme of your exhibit and offer an incentive to stop by the booth. The incentive could be a report, a giveaway or a chance to win a prize. Your web site or company newsletter is another way to promote your exhibit ahead of time. Web sites offer the flexibility of instant change if you already have traffic from that market coming to your site. If you don't have a lot of traffic, promote that information on your site in hopes of enticing new site visitors. Web sites also offer the added benefit of providing a means of post-show communications and bringing potential clients back to your site after the show. If you are conducting an informal survey at the show, tell everyone you will be posting the results on your web site in two weeks.

The Exhibit

The keys to an effective exhibit are strong graphics, a concise message and talented people. Each is dependent on the other.

If you are purchasing a standard display, meet with several different vendors before you select a model. Set each one up by yourself to see how easy assembly is. Look at the number of cases required and ease of shipping them. Will they fit in a car or do you need a sports utility vehicle or van? Can the display be used as a table top and a full eight-feet by 10-feet display? Are the directions easy to follow? Is it easy to pack up again? Will it damage easily if it is not packed properly? (Don't assume staff will follow the packing instructions to the letter.) Is the display reversible? Is it easy to update the banner if you want to change the look at a later date? How do the electrical cords come together in the back? Decide what features are important enough to guide your decision-making. If you are still not sure about a display, see if the vendor will let you try it out at a show or rent it.

The size and amount of time to assemble a display should also be considered during your purchase. Some exhibit halls require the use of union labor to set up and break down displays that do not meet certain requirements. For instance, in the Detroit area, union carpenters are frequently required when the exhibit is greater than 10 feet in length or cannot be assembled by one person without the use of tools within a half hour. Associations will send these requirements out with the exhibit information. Most standard 8-feet by 10-feet displays can easily be set up by an exhibitor in the required amount of time. Set up or breakdown for simple displays, such as two adjoining 8-feet by 10-feet booths that require a carpenter, can typically be accomplished in one or two hours.

When selecting a background color for a display consider what types of photographs and graphics you will be putting on it. If you will be changing the photos frequently, be conservative in your color selection. Black, gray and neutral colors will serve as an attractive background for a variety of image types including schematics or maps. Avoid blue as a background if you will be using a lot of outdoor pictures with blue skies. (It will accentuate the variations in blue.) Company colors aren't always the best choice either, particularly if they are bright.

A display will last awhile if it is receives proper care. The fewer people handling it, the better. Take the time to pull your exhibit out at least once a year and check it thoroughly to see if it needs any repairs and if any pieces are missing. Consider sending your display back to the manufacturer for a thorough cleaning if it is looking a little battered but still has a few good years left. Recognize when an exhibit has met the end of its useful life and replace it. Sometimes you can get away with replacing the banner to push the purchase off till next year's budget. Use good judgment; a run-down display presents a run-down image.

A few large photographs are more likely to catch people's attention than a collage of smaller ones. Signs should be readable from at least eight to 12 feet away, the distance from the edge of the aisle to your display. Banners should help draw visitors into the booth. If you don't have a graphic designer on staff, work with one from the display manufacturer.

Developing a message for your exhibit that is targeted toward the show's market and consistent with your objectives is extremely important. Depending on your trade show plan, you may be able to use a particular exhibit theme at more than one show or recycle part of it. This can help reduce costs but should be exercised with care. Change for the sake of change is not necessary, but the image of a dynamic organization that is developing innovative solutions will not be created with the same exhibit that is dusted off each year at convention time. Choose your projects carefully — even if the project has won a dozen design awards, it will get stale after it has been seen for several consecutive years.

When developing a message for your exhibit, keep it simple. The exhibit should clearly demonstrate how your firm can be of service to convention attendees. Remember, they are looking for solutions to their problems — not company names and logos. Show how your service relates to their needs. Do your homework. The exhibit should demonstrate your understanding of the market. Look at every component of your exhibit to see how it can be used to help achieve your objectives. Signs and photos should relate to service(s) and explain benefits.

Consider using interactive elements that tie with your theme to attract booth visitors. Can you have a demo of a 3-D walk-through of a facility running on a computer? Think of ways to engage your visitors. People remember more when they are doing something. Interactive elements our firm has incorporated in the past include getting visitors to sign a giant partnering agreement and having the booth graphics printed in 3-D and giving visitors 3-D glasses to view it.

Literature or giveaways can also help carry your exhibit message. Use the tagline from your exhibit on the giveaway or create a special handout further expanding on the theme. Sometimes firms make the giveaway the interactive part of their display.

Just as important as the physical exhibit, is the exhibit staff. People are the most memorable part of an exhibit. Interactions with company employees give booth visitors a more realistic glimpse of the company. Because they aren't edited, proofed and mass-produced, employees truly depict the brand of a company. Use this to your advantage! A knowledgeable, trained booth staff member can differentiate your firm from the competition.

Train all staff that will participate in trade show activities once a year. If everyone is experienced, hold a meeting to brainstorm ways to improve booth performance and enhance the firm's image at the show. Review your trade show plan and budget and explain how each person can help achieve marketing objectives. Assess the previous year's performance in terms of quality of leads, cost-per-lead and competitor activities. Even seasoned marketers benefit from sharing ideas and having a refresher course on exhibit floor selling. Set up programs for experienced staff to mentor new staff. More can be learned from spending a few hours with a skilled exhibitor than hearing or reading about it.

Above all, make sure staff members are trained in communication skills. Most of us are not accustomed to daily "full body" selling; learning how to pick up on non-verbal cues is very important. Numerous studies have revealed that staff behavior is remembered most about an exhibit and that most of the information received from the conversation is non-verbal. As obvious as it sounds, using body language that demonstrates you are at the show to talk to attendees and listen to their concerns is important. It is always amazing to see the number of exhibitors eating in their booth, eagerly chatting with their exhibit neighbor, talking on a cell phone or just sitting there looking completely disinterested. Why would anyone want to stop and talk to them even if they had the best-looking exhibit at the show? Exhibit selling is not much different than retail sales; follow the same rules.

To make sure your training efforts pay off and staff remains energetic, limit booth shifts to two hours whenever possible and leave two hours off between shifts. Exhibit-floor selling is hard work, both physically and mentally.

Beyond the Exhibit

Trade shows are about networking, and the exhibit isn't the only place to do it. Frequently, there are better opportunities outside the exhibit hall.

Hosting a client dinner or hospitality suite offers the opportunity to meet with clients and potential clients in an informal setting. If you have a large number of clients attending the show, a client dinner may be more effective. The exclusivity of a client-only reception can also be beneficial. Be sure to invite clients three to four weeks ahead of time so they can plan appropriately. Client dinners can become an annual event that clients cherish over the years. They are also a great way to say thank you to your client and let them know you value their work in an environment where they are surrounded by your competitors.

Depending on past history and the number of other hospitality suites at a conference, a firm can get lost in the crowd. If convention attendees hop from room to room they may not pay attention to whose room they're in. Talk with conference organizers to find out how many other suites there will be and what days and times they will be held. Ask the hotel what type of food is being planned in other rooms so you don't have the same thing. Consider just desserts, ice cream drinks or some other theme to make your room stand out. If possible, check out the suite or room ahead of time, particularly if you have a choice of rooms. Consider how many employees are available to work the room when setting the hours. Don't have the person closing the room work the morning shift in the booth the next day.

Speaking at a session builds firm credibility with the association sponsoring the conference and attendees. Be sure to focus on the topic and not your firm. Leave a written summary of your session for attendees to take. Have copies in your booth after the session and post it on your web site.

Sponsorships are another opportunity for exposure. Does the conference need sponsors for breakfasts, lunches or breaks? Or for the keynote speakers or screens for their banquet?

Don't forget to attend conference functions outside the exhibit hall. Attend sessions (be sure to see if you need to register), lunches, receptions and banquets. Staff should be part of all the conference activities taking place, not just the exhibit hall.

Monitoring Trends and the Competition

Conventions and trade shows are a great place to find out what is happening in a particular market. Look through the convention guide and see what topics are being addressed. Attend some of the sessions so you can hear the audience feedback. What are the issues facing the market? Which ones impact the services you provide? Which ones don't impact your service but impact your client enough that they are worth learning more about? Who are the market leaders?

Attend the receptions and banquets. What are the hot topics of conversation? What are the market leaders doing and what do others think of it? Who traditionally has the best hospitality suite? Why is it the best?

Take time to conduct some informal market research. Develop a short questionnaire to identify the biggest issues facing that market segment or a wish list of what they would like to see engineers or architects provide in the future. Consider having a raffle and using the questionnaire as the entry form. Or have staff ask questions and record answers as part of their conversations.

Trade shows are one of the best places for competitive intelligence gathering because you get to see your competitors interact with their clients. You also get to see how effective they are at putting their best foot forward. What type of image are they projecting with their booth? Is it consistent with their brand? Do they feature the same projects in their booth every year? Are the projects appropriate for the venue? Is it obvious this is a new market they are trying to break into? Is this their first year exhibiting? What level of staff is working the booth and how many? Have they increased or decreased their trade show activities from the previous year? How are attendees responding to their booth strategy?

Take pictures of your competitors' booths and other booths that attract your attention. Talk to your competitors and find out how things are going. Get copies of their literature. Listen to what convention attendees are saying about competitors. Listen to any of their staff members who speak at the conference. Are competitors changing their brand? How are they positioning themselves? What are they doing to attract people to their booth? Is it working? How many people do they have attending the conference? Are they hosting a hospitality suite? Are they doing anything special with clients?

Follow-up and Evaluation

Trade shows aren't over when the exhibits are dismantled. Leads need to be followed up. Studies indicate that trade show recall drops after eight weeks and that leads should be followed up within 30 days.

Before the show is over, determine how follow-up will be conducted, who will do it and when it will be done. If there are a large number of leads, consider sending a short personal note or an e-mail stating that you are glad they stopped by the exhibit and that someone will be contacting them shortly. (Just be sure to follow up!)

Have people following up leads and document the results. For each lead, assess the probability of future work and potential dollar volume. Keep informed of the status of the work and send a memo to the file if the work is contracted. This will provide solid support for a show if it needs to be justified in the future.

Don't forget to follow up with staff while the show is still fresh in their minds. Have someone who was not involved in planning the show, conduct short telephone surveys to get their thoughts on the show. Generally, you will get more candid feedback over the phone than from a written evaluation form. Ask what they thought about the conference as a whole. Was it well-attended? What type of image did the firm project? Did clients stop by? What did they say? Which activities provided the best opportunity for networking? Were attendees aware of your sponsorship? Was the booth easy to work out of? Did attendees understand the theme? How could the booth be improved? Should your company have a booth next year? What were competitors doing? Was the hospitality room effective? Were marketing objectives met?

If you didn't meet your exhibit objectives, find out why. Was it due to improper show selection? Booth location? Booth personnel problems? Poorly designed exhibit? Poor follow-up? Low show attendance? Similarly, if you did meet your objectives, find out why. Carefully consider employee and convention attendee suggestions and don't be afraid to modify future approaches.

Additional Sources of Information

Chapman, Edward A., Jr. *Exhibit Marketing: A Success Guide for Managers.* McGraw Hill, 1995.

Friedmann, Susan A. *Exhibiting at Trade Shows.* Crisp Publications, 1992.

Levinson, Jay Conrad, Orval Ray Wilson, and Mark S. Smith. A. *Guerrilla Trade Show Selling: New Unconventional Weapons and Tactics to Meet More People, Get More Leads, and Close More Sales.* 1997.

Miller, Steve A., and William W. Mee. *How to Get the Most out of Trade Shows.* NTC Publishing Group, 1995.

Miller, Steve A., and Charmel Bowden. *Over 88 Tips and Ideas to Supercharge Your Exhibit Sales.* Hikelly Productions, 1997.

Siskind, Barry. *The Power of Exhibit Marketing.* Self-counsel Press Inc., 1997.

Weisgal, Margit B. *Show and Sell: 133 Business Building Ways to Promote Your Trade Show Exhibit.* AMACOM, 1996.

www.potentialsmag.com, *Potentials in Marketing* magazine
www.tsea.org, Trade Show Exhibitors Association

Trude Noble

- Trude Noble is vice president and marketing manager for Wade-Trim, a consulting engineering and planning firm. She oversees the firm's marketing activities including research, corporate communications, public relations and proposal support for business development. She also provides public involvement, marketing and public relations support for Wade-Trim clients. She has managed activities at local and state trade shows that Wade-Trim has participated in, as well as educational festivals for students.

- Noble has worked in the professional services industry since graduating with a bachelor's degree in marketing from Michigan State University in 1984. She has been a member of the SMPS Michigan Chapter for more than 13 years and has served as secretary and director for its board. She has also chaired the public relations committee of the American Consulting Engineers Council/Michigan.

4.10 Web Site Development

Randy Anagnostis, FSMPS
President
Anagnostis Associates Inc.

The purpose of this chapter is to explore the development and use of web sites as a valuable marketing communications tool and its potential applications regarding project management. Cost implications, design considerations, maintenance and creative applications are addressed along with helpful tips for making your web site more functional given the unique idiosyncrasies of this burgeoning new media.

Why Consider Developing a Web Site?

The phenomenal growth of the Internet in recent years has surpassed everyone's expectations. In its infancy, the Internet was primarily used for scientific research collaboration before the advent of the world wide web system allowed the general public to access this remarkable communications vehicle. Today, more than 90 million individuals and businesses have established their own web sites and the technology advances have now made it possible for even the most computer illiterate individual to establish a web presence.

As a business investment, the establishment of a web site is one of the most cost-effective marketing tools available to a firm in terms of reach and exposure to potential clients when compared to other traditional forms of advertising, communications and promotion. Perhaps even more important is the value in being perceived as a contemporary business entity simply by having a web site in today's competitive marketplace. Ten years ago, people used to ask if you had a fax machine. In just a few short years it became a standard piece of office equipment for any progressive-thinking company. Now, the questions asked are, "Do you have a web site?" or "What is your e-mail address?" These are fast becoming the standards by which consumers are assessing the validity of your firm.

A web site allows someone to gain immediate access to information about your business. Even overnight express mail delivery will delay information access by 12 to 24 hours. Access via the Internet can take place within minutes and simply accelerates the time frame in which potential business interaction can be achieved with new or existing clients. Viewed purely in terms of time management, the cost of a web site can easily be justified relative to its potential marketing and business development cost savings.

Finally, a web site is a marketing tool that is working for you 24 hours a day, seven days a week, 365 days a year. It allows individuals to learn about your firm at their own convenient time and place. It is one of the most polite forms of marketing that exists today in addition to the many other opportunities it offers, which are presented later in this chapter.

Basic Requirements for Having a Web Site

There are a few essential items necessary to consider when contemplating the establishment of a web site for your firm. First, you should have at least one computer and a modem available to be used for connecting to the Internet (or you can have as many computers connected as you desire). You will need the services of an Internet Service Provider, or ISP, which is your dial-up account for logging onto the Internet. The monthly cost of this service will depend upon the type of connection you want, ranging from basic services averaging $19.95 per month, to high-speed line connections that can run into much higher monthly fees. If you wish to have your own dedicated web address (such as, www.yourcompany.com), referred to as your URL, you will have to apply for registration of a domain name with the organization that controls this process, Network Solutions. The cost is $70 for your first two-year registration and a $35 annual renewal fee. Finally, you will need a company to host your web site, unless you intend to set up your own internal host server equipment. Outside hosting fees average $29.95 to $59.95 per month and go up in cost depending upon the size and sophistication of your particular web site and operational requirements.

With these essential items addressed, you are ready to have your web site designed and programmed for online installation. The following information provides you with a basic guideline of key components of a typical web site.

Design and Content Guidelines

Home Page

Every web site contains a starting page, referred to as your home page. This will be the first page visitors will see when they key in your web address. It should be designed to load all information and graphic images quickly — typically in less than 28 seconds or people become impatient and may leave your web site.

Similar to the design of the cover of a company brochure, your home page is the first impression of your firm, which you are offering to the general public. The design and style can reflect the image you wish to convey — from esoteric to classy to funky or traditional. Here, you may also introduce the topics of information contained within your web site — in the form of navigation buttons — to give the visitor a quick sense of what's contained in the interior pages.

Your home page should offer a good first impression of your firm.

Navigation Buttons

A properly designed web site will make it easy for visitors to continuously find their way to specific information contained on your site. The home page should serve as an index with navigation buttons that allow visitors to choose the particular areas of your web site that appear to be of most interest to them. When selecting a navigation button — which can be text or graphic images — the visitor is linked immediately to another page of your web site containing that specific information.

Throughout your web site, navigation buttons, or links, should be clearly defined to allow the visitor to move in and around your entire web site with ease. This is one of the most important elements of a good web site. You can use the most advanced forms of graphics, animation, audio, video and state-of-the-art web applications, but if your guests cannot navigate easily to the various pages of your web site, they will leave in frustration.

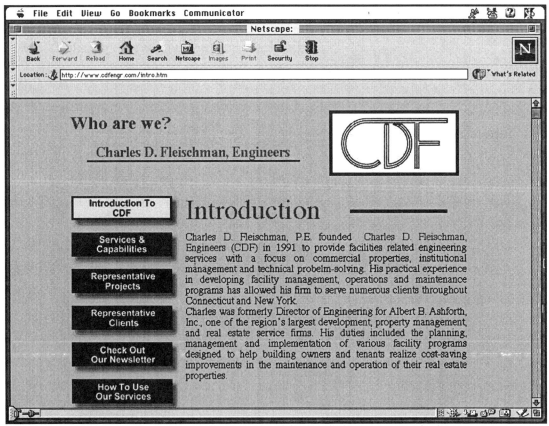

Navigation buttons should help the visitor easily browse your web site.

Text Styles, Size and Content

When designing your web site, recognize that people generally use the Internet as a means of gathering information quickly. Present key information with text that delivers a message with brevity. If you have a need for presenting lengthy information, use links from the main topics and your visitors will have the option of spending more time on your web site if they really want to delve into details. Use the example of a well-defined billboard advertisement that people drive by on the roadside in approximately three seconds — if it contains more than nine words, they probably won't have time to read the entire message. Capture people's attention and entice them to seek additional information from your web site.

Avoid using small font sizes and unusual font styles that may be difficult to see on a computer monitor. Recognize the fact that some people have 14-inch monitors while others may have 15-inch, 17-inch or 21-inch monitors. Your text —as well as graphics and images — will look different from one computer system to another, and your design must allow for these subtle nuances.

Just as you would prepare a good press release, your web site content should follow a similar concept. State your most obvious message at the beginning of the key sections of your web site and allow visitors to find details as they surf their way deeper and deeper into your site. Develop your own preliminary flow chart defining the information you wish to convey on your web site, and the design elements and navigational scheme can then be added to support the overall content of your site.

Graphics, Images, Resolution and File Sizes

Once you have determined the content of your web site, the design and style of your pages can begin to take form. You may choose to use available commercial web graphics, create your own custom graphics, incorporate scanned photos and images, or use numerous enhancements incorporating animation, audio and video applications on your site. Once again, the time it takes for an individual page to load on the visitor's screen must always be considered. Make sure that your images have been compressed to the smallest possible file sizes, which will equate to faster load time on a computer monitor. You should also recognize certain limitations of the web — a computer monitor portrays images only at 72-dpi (dots per inch) resolution. Many people make the mistake of scanning images and photographs at 300 to 1,440 dpi resolution thinking they will get a better presentation on their web site. Consequently, their file sizes become huge and load time becomes very slow. Your web site does not contain traditional printed pages — while an award-winning photograph may look glorious in a printed brochure, the web is a different medium. Visitors tend to be much more forgiving of the quality of images in exchange for quality of content and speed of information delivery.

Forms and Interactivity

The use of forms on your web site can enhance the visitor's web experience and provide a means of interacting with your firm. Without getting into the expense of real-time, online communications, forms provide a reasonable opportunity to get information from the visitor and allow the visitor to seek information from you within a reasonable time frame. A completed form is sent automatically by e-mail to you and can begin the process of communicating and connecting with the visitor beyond the time of his or her visit to your web site.

Many web sites contain guest books or similar data entry forms, which allow visitors to register their visits to your site. Developed appropriately, a guest book can be a basic marketing research tool for you. It can solicit any kind of information you wish to gather about the visitor and, conversely, can allow the visitor to request additional information about your firm, which you may wish to offer upon request. A standard guest book form will let you know who the individual is visiting your site, the company, title, address, telephone, fax, e-mail address and more. You can provide any number of items for them to select to receive information from your firm — a request for your company brochure, inclusion on your newsletter mailing list, a telephone or e-mail contact by a representative of your firm.

Perhaps you want to get creative by offering incentives for someone to complete an online form. If someone submits the form, he or she can automatically be entered into a sweepstakes drawing for a defined prize or promotional merchandise giveaway. You might want to create a trivia contest on your site, incorporating information about your services and capabilities while giving out awards and prizes to weekly entrants. Forms that create interaction with the visitor can easily be designed if you allow yourself to think beyond the basics and interject an innovative approach to their use on your web site. The possibilities are endless and simply require some creative marketing to reap better rewards from your web site investment.

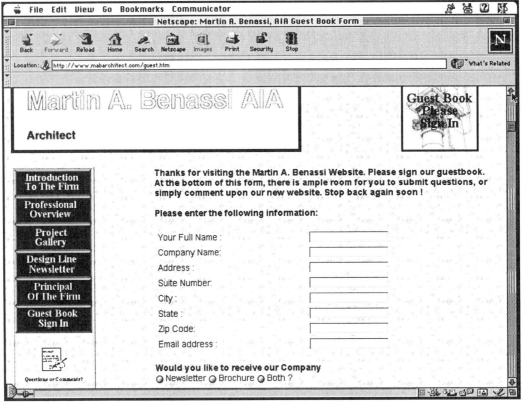

Customized forms can generate leads and information.

Ease of Contact

It is surprising to see how many web sites fail to make it easy for a visitor to contact the site owner. Small e-mail text links are often located in obscure positions on a site and force an individual to search for a way to get in touch with a firm. When designing your web site, every page should have some form of e-mail link that allows the visitor to immediately communicate with you in case he or she does not have time to go through every page of your web site to find an e-mail link.

A separate e-mail navigation button is one of the easiest ways to ensure that a visitor can quickly communicate with your firm. This link can take you to a page that contains a full e-mail directory listing of all the individuals in your offices or listings of select individuals. It is comparable to a company telephone directory but for online communication.

Since e-mail can be routed electronically any way you choose, generic e-mail addresses — such as sales@yourcompany.com, or customerservice@yourcompany.com or accounting@yourcompany.com — can offer helpful direction to visitors about where they might want to send their messages. Internally, the messages can be downloaded by one individual or separately by any number of individuals responsible for those particular functions within your organization.

Your site can also be programmed to automatically generate an immediate response to a visitor when he or she has forwarded an e-mail message to you. A page can appear that might say, "Thank you for contacting us. Your message will be reviewed promptly!" This is a simple step to let visitors know that you are attentive to their inquiries or comments and their messages have gotten through cyberspace effectively.

In addition to spontaneous e-mail contact mechanisms, be sure to prominently display traditional contact information on your site. Office locations, company addresses, telephone numbers, facsimile numbers, and key contact names may be of interest to the visitor and should be readily available unless you are trying to intentionally conceal this information from them. Whether you choose to have this on your home page, on all pages or in a separate "Contact Us" section is entirely up to you.

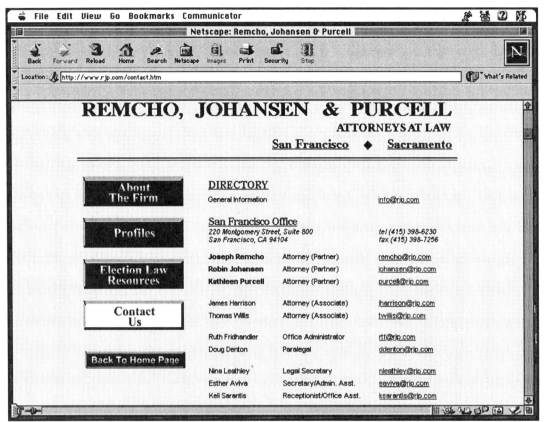

Make it easy for visitors to contact you on your web site.

Search Engines and Directories

Once you place your web site online, one of the greatest challenges facing you is letting the world know that you have a site. Building traffic to your web site is essential to realizing a return on investment for creating this communications vehicle, unless you are simply using a web site for project management purposes.

The majority of people on the Internet today rely on search engines and directories for finding sites containing topics of interest to them. There are hundreds of search engines and directories on the Internet and at least a dozen primary search engines recognized as leaders in their area of information retrieval. By typing in key words and phrases, individuals can generally locate scores of web sites matching their particular search requests.

Whoever designs your web site must be familiar with the programming requirements that assist in having these search engines and directories locate your web site when someone is seeking information that may be contained on your site. This is generally accomplished by including "meta tags" in the program language which are related to or the same as the key words that someone might use to search for the kind of information you might have to offer. While it is important to include this in your site design, it must be recognized that it has its limitations. Unfortunately, there are so many different criteria used by the search engines and directories in addition to meta tags for ranking your particular web site that it can be very difficult to count on having your site appear in the premier positions when results are displayed to the person searching for information. There are countless outsourcing firms offering assistance in placing you into search engines and directories, but their monthly and annual fees can be substantial and the results are highly questionable. While you may wish to investigate these options, your own targeted marketing efforts and use of reciprocal links may generate more positive results for using your web site as a viable marketing, communications and business development tool.

Traffic Generation

Building traffic to your web site should be a well-planned and an ongoing effort. Too many firms overlook this function and never truly realize the potential benefits their sites can offer. In dispelling the myths of relying upon search engines and directories alone for traffic generation, one must then focus on alternative means of promoting your web site.

Reciprocal Links

A reciprocal link, simply stated, is an agreement whereby you offer to put a direct link on your web site to another web site if the company, in turn, agrees to place a direct link on its web site back to yours. The more reciprocal links you establish, the higher proportionate number of individuals will be afforded an opportunity to discover your web site.

By creating reciprocal links with businesses that have some related or complementary function to your own business, the more likely the chance will be that a potential visitor may be interested in the services and capabilities that you have to offer. As an example, if you are an architectural firm, establishing reciprocal links with engineering firms, contractors, subcontractors, equipment manufacturers, existing clients, financial consultants and professional or civic associations of which you are a member can help target potential prospects. People who visit these other web sites may have an interest in your related services and capabilities. Or, if you have a specialty in designing educational facilities, perhaps you can arrange to get reciprocal links on web sites from previous educational facility clients or other educational facilities within your geographical working area. The basics of targeted marketing can be applied to your rationale in developing appropriate reciprocal links that might offer future business development opportunities in specific market segments. Since reciprocal links offer mutual benefits to both parties in terms of generating web traffic, the ease of arranging these should not be overlooked in the promotional strategies for your web site.

You may choose to set up an entire separate section of your web site that contains just listings of reciprocal links. If designed properly, it can become a valuable resource page for visitors covering any number of topics, which may be of interest to them and reflects favorably as a service you have conveniently provided to your web guest. There even exists any number of companies that, on a fee-paid basis or sometimes for free, will coordinate dissemination of your web address to other interested web site owners seeking reciprocal links for increasing their potential traffic.

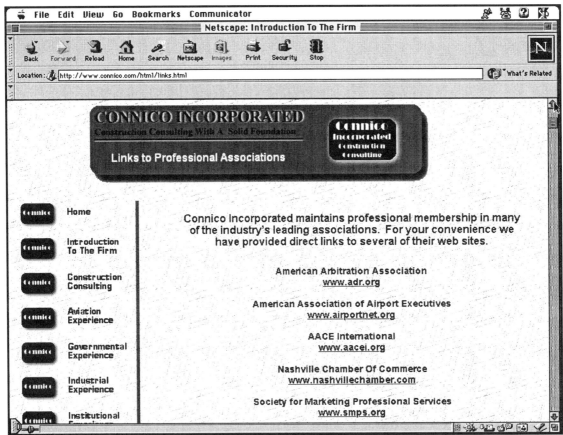

Reciprocal links can generate more traffic to your web site.

Banner Ads

While many people think of banner ads as a promotional strategy related primarily to retail businesses, they could also be used effectively to promote professional services. Many of us join professional, business or civic organizations for the purpose of networking. These same organizations quite often have web sites and may consider accepting a banner ad from your firm. It opens up another avenue for prospects to receive a communications message about your firm and the fact that it exists on the organization's site serves as a subtle form of third-party endorsement. Be prepared to offer these web site owners a similar opportunity for possibly having their banner ads on your site.

Think about clients for whom you have provided services. Perhaps they have web sites suitable for inclusion of your banner ad. Vendors, material suppliers, subcontractors, accountants, insurance agencies and others you do business with may also be potential candidates for placement of your banner ad on their sites.

Banner ads are simple to create and most web sites use a standard-size format, allowing ease of placement from one site to another. By nature of the small size of typical banner ads, your message will have to be concise and appealing. Use of the word "free" helps draw attention. Perhaps you can offer a free copy of your company newsletter or company brochure. Or you might even want to give one free hour of consultation. Be creative and your banner ads can help bring additional traffic to your web site. When possible, try to have the banner ad placed with a link that allows a visitor to click and immediately be brought to your own web site.

Once again, there are companies that, either on a fee-paid basis or for free, can arrange for placement of your banner ads on multiple sites. As a modest cost of business development, this may be worth considering.

Typical web site banner ads can also work for your firm.

Traditional and Creative Marketing

All of the traditional forms of marketing and promotion apply to the marketing of your web site. Advertising, public relations, direct mail, branding and alternative methods of business development can be used to build a public awareness of your web site presence.

Be sure to include your web site and e-mail addresses on your company business cards, stationery, fax transmittal page, invoices, brochures, newsletters and marketing collateral materials. A press release can offer your media contacts a chance to view your web site, if they so choose. Ads typically placed in publications distributed by your local chamber of commerce, civic group or community organizations should invite readers to visit your web site. If your firm participates in trade show exhibits, be sure to have promotional giveaway merchandise printed with your web site address included in addition to the standard company name, address and telephone numbers.

Add your web site address to your drawings, plans, specifications and job meeting notes. Include your web address in telephone voice message systems — people on hold may also be online and can look up your site while they are waiting to be connected to their party. Targeted direct mail programs can be one of the most cost-effective methods of persuading potential clients to visit your site. Inexpensive postcard mailings can do wonders to increasing the number of hits on your site. Simply stated, be creative and consider all avenues for distributing your web site address using traditional and creative marketing approaches.

Use creative online approaches to help promote your services.

Web Site Maintenance

Unlike a company brochure, which may have a standard shelf life of three years, your web site should be constantly maintained and updated if you are using it for more than just having a web presence. Aside from providing new content, you also want to be sure every link, form and function of your web site is always working the way it was designed. The web is not a perfect medium — a corrupted line of programming code can cause inoperative links with error messages that will chase away your visitors very quickly. If your promotional efforts are successful in getting people to your site on a regular basis, then they will want to see new and different information when they make a return visit and they will expect your site to be functioning properly.

You can establish an effective web maintenance program using your own in-house personnel or by outsourcing this service with monthly or annual web maintenance contracts. Site maintenance is a function of time and cost. Be sure to allow for this when planning your web site and when determining your annual budget beyond the basic web site design and hosting costs.

Periodic Updates

A simple approach to creating an effective web maintenance program is to break this function down into two components: content and style. Adding information about new services offered by your firm, new project assignments, photographs, staff profiles, related links and e-mail additions effectively change the content of your site. Adding new sections to your web site may be appropriate as you find more applications for using your site as a marketing communications or project management tool. Set up a schedule that will ensure updates and additions are performed regularly.

If you want to dramatically update your site, then changes affecting the style of your site can be utilized. This does not imply that these changes have to be complicated. Periodically changing the color of the background of your pages, or headlines or navigation buttons can give a fresh new look to your entire site and can be accomplished in a matter of minutes. New page layouts can be created using existing content and will effectively create a whole new look for your site without incurring much expense.

Online Services

There exist several web sites on the Internet that provide free web maintenance services. By logging onto their sites, they will provide automated checkups of your web site. This may include a check for broken links, effective use of meta tags and descriptions used by the various search engines and directories. It can analyze load times for images and graphics and evaluate related links and their ability to generate traffic to your site. A summary report is generated and sent to you via e-mail. These services can be helpful as an additional means of reviewing your site for functionality and performance.

Project Management Applications

Although a relatively small percentage of firms today are using their web sites for project management, this trend will continue to grow in the next several years for a number of reasons. A primary factor will be the time and cost benefits derived by firms within our industry and by respective clients. As with an investment in capital equipment, the return on investment to utilize the web for project management can offer significant short-term and long-term benefits for both parties. Each will have to make the investment in technology application, training and management. Once this is accomplished, the resulting benefits can have a profound impact on project profitability.

Those firms that are applying this technology management tool today are creating new standards for project management. Clients that have participated in this process will expect to have the same services available on future building projects. Consequently, online project management will become a competitive marketing advantage for the progressive building industry firm as more and more clients begin to demand this type of project delivery. This growth trend will force more and more firms to embrace online project management as it becomes a required standard in our industry.

Online Project Management Overview

The innovative approaches being used by some firms today suggest the vast potentials to be derived from online project management and its marketing benefits. Your web site can contain sections that may be accessed only by use of passwords. This prohibits the general public from viewing information that you place on select sections of your web site. You decide who gets access to this information and can develop multiple secure site sections with restricted or expanded access as you so choose.

If, for instance, you want consultants working on an assignment with you to access job meeting notes, drawings, specifications and correspondence, then you might establish a secure password just for that information on your site. Forget overnight delivery and express mail — the conveyance of information can be instantaneous. Hours after holding a job meeting, the notes can be posted online and all parties can be expected to have reviewed all information the same or next day. Drawings and specifications can be sent, modified and exchanged electronically without ever leaving your computer and it can all take place within hours.

You may have confidential information that you care to share only with your actual client and, likewise, they may want to provide you with information not to be shared with other members of the project team. A secure password can be used to limit access to satisfy this requirement. You may prepare a rendering or elevation drawing that requires client feedback, place it online, notify your client and receive their comments within minutes or hours. Using a laptop computer and a digital camera, you can transmit visual images of unexpected field conditions from a project site for viewing by your client and get comments and approvals back immediately without holding up a project.

Re-defining State-of-the-Art

Financial information, project schedules, administrative correspondence, photography, drawings, reports — all are being transmitted electronically today by firms that have ventured into this new frontier of online project management. A firm that utilizes the web effectively can establish a unique relationship with its clients and prospective clients. The related marketing benefits are substantial and go way beyond the specific benefits of online project management. Imagine an existing client, or a prospective client, viewing an online presentation of a proposed site development plan or conceptual building design — complete with animation, 3-D graphics, audio and video — without ever leaving the office. Consider the time and cost benefits you can offer to other members of your proposed project team and your prospective clients if they can embrace your technology applications. This is being done today by progressive firms and must be recognized as a technology trend that will only continue to grow. It represents a serious challenge to the way in which you currently may be conducting your business.

Summary

While one chapter can provide only an introduction to web site development, the message should appear obvious. Delaying your participation in use of this technology may be potentially damaging for your firm. Whether you choose to develop a basic web site or venture into the more sophisticated applications shaping our industry, it is a powerful medium that should be given serious consideration in your overall strategic planning. It's significance as a marketing tool should not be overlooked as you review or re-define your marketing and business development plans.

Randy Anagnostis, FSMPS

Randy Anagnostis is president of Anagnostis Associates Inc., a marketing consulting, graphic design, and web site design and development services firm established in 1986. The company specializes in providing marketing support services to firms in the building industry with clients located throughout the United States. He has designed dozens of web sites for private, public sector and non-profit organizations and has been a keynote speaker and workshop leader regarding marketing on the web for numerous national, regional and local professional organizations.

Professional accomplishments include:

- President: Anagnostis Associates Inc.; Imageweb LLC; Noteworthy Productions LLC.
- Professional certification: Fellow, Society for Marketing Professional Services.
- More than 8,000 persons have attended his marketing seminars and workshops.
- Past president: Southern New England Chapter, SMPS; the Exchange Club; North Kingstown Chamber of Commerce.
- Vice president: Professional Staff Association/National Education Association.
- Treasurer: Middlesex Community-Technical College Foundation.
- Director: Connecticut Songwriters Association; Rhode Island Chamber of Commerce Federation; Middlesex Foundation Inc.
- Chairman: Durham Economic Development Commission.
- Founder and former publisher: *The Durham Gazette Newspaper*.
- Member: Associated Builders and Contractors Inc.; BMI; Connecticut Songwriters Association; Construction Institute; Hebron Economic Development Commission; Hebron Business & Professional Association; National Academy of Songwriters; Old Saybrook Chamber of Commerce; United Way Executive Cabinet; Vermont/New Hampshire Direct Mail Association.

4.11 Awards as a Compelling Marketing Strategy

Jane Cohn, FSMPS
Principal
Jane Cohn Public Relations

How do you win an award? The answer is not a simple one. There are numerous elements to consider and steps to follow in order to prepare a submission that is worthy of a jury's serious consideration. All the necessary components will be discussed in this chapter, which I have written to guide you through the process and on your way to achieving your goal of becoming a winner. You also will learn to evaluate the value of awards to your firm and, once won, how to use them as a marketing tool.

Why Bother with Awards?

Before jumping in, it's important to assess the value to your firm of undertaking award submittals, just as you would assess any other marketing effort. Is it an activity worthy of your finite resources or would some other public relations activity serve you better? Are your projects of the caliber to win award recognition? Be ruthless in your evaluation. If the answer to the latter is yes, then ask what winning an award will achieve for you. Will it enhance your reputation and make a difference to your clients and prospective clients? Will it help your status and recognition within the profession and, if so, of what value is that? In short, does the award under consideration support your marketing goals? Is it consistent with the identity or position you hold or seek to achieve in the marketplace?

Like any other major investment, pursuing awards requires a clear understanding of what the firm wants to achieve. Award submissions should be considered as part of a firm's positioning campaign, as one of many tools, used in a conscious, deliberate and ongoing effort, to place a firm's capabilities and people in front of its targeted audiences. A positioning program comprises a variety of promotional venues, of which awards can be one.

Regardless of the position your firm seeks in the marketplace, awards that demonstrate value to clients are extremely relevant in today's business climate. In decades past, architects, engineers, planners and others involved in the building process were sought by clients to perform discrete professional functions that yielded a product. Thanks to the good work and the intelligent business planning and marketing of so many professionals in the industry, the building team is now viewed much more seriously by clients as potential allies in helping to solve corporate issues that relate to the bottom line.

Planning Is a Key to Success

If your firm decides that pursuing award competitions is consistent with its objectives, the first step is to set the goal in its proper context in the overall business plan. Without this understanding and commitment from the firm's principals, award submissions have a hard time finding their way to the list of top priorities. When push comes to shove, as it inevitably does in the typical overloaded, overstressed marketing department, proposals and other direct marketing deadlines always have a way of gobbling up the lion's share of marketing resources.

Avoid the trap of thinking an award submission is "nothing, so we'll just dash it off." Remember that "nothing is nothing" — at least nothing worth doing! Be sure that sufficient time and resources are allotted in your marketing/public relations plan so that awards submissions can receive the budget, time and attention they deserve. Far and away the largest budgetary item is photography; it's imperative to get the best you can when considering award submissions. If you're already getting the best possible photography for your projects, you're well on your way. For many firms, it is the biggest line item in their marketing/public relations budget. Others share the costs (and the glory) with other members of the building team, and when appropriate, with the client.

Photography: The Primary Consideration for Design Awards

For design awards, when it comes right down to it, the photography is nine-tenths of the battle. One editor I queried, whose magazine sponsors an annual awards program, acknowledged that the jury won't even read the text if they're not grabbed by the photography. The process is not unlike that for submitting a project for publication in the leading design publications. "The photos must be topnotch but a combination of photos and text has to be able to capture the jury's attention quickly," says Robin Lee, director of honors and awards for the American Institute of Architects (AIA), who serves as an advisor to jurors and entrants. "The jurors have to be able to quickly understand the program and what it accomplished, so the text must be succinct as well as compelling." Lee adds that "the profession of architecture is changing and clients are sophisticated and want both design and bottom line goals met. It is crucial to meet both criteria." She points out that "even large corporations with a substantial amount of capital need to demonstrate value to management, shareholders and all of their audiences."

The competition to build the grandest corporate palace ended with the '80s. Today, as corporate America is faced with increasing competition and cost-containment pressures, the focus on business-driven design approach of the last two decades is viewed as wasteful, irrelevant and politically and socially incorrect.

Something for Everyone — Awards Are a Varied Lot

Keeping the goals of an integrated marketing/communications program in mind, your selection of awards programs will reflect and support the identity you are striving to achieve for your organization. And you'll resist the impulse to pursue scattershot award programs, which have far less value. For the architecture firm seeking a high profile, there are numerous design award programs sponsored by professional associations and design publications. AIA has more than 18 awards programs at the national level alone, including co-sponsored programs with building material associations, a library association, and with various design publications and business magazines that are targeted to your clients' industries. This wide range of award-winning opportunities demonstrates the AIA's effort to encompass diversity and to recognize accomplishment for a variety of criteria and in a variety of ways.

Perhaps the most prestigious and most useful award, from a business development viewpoint, is the "Good Design is Good Business" Award co-sponsored by *Architectural Record* and *Business Week,* which was started in 1996 "to honor architectural solutions that build the bottom line," according to its sponsors. It exemplifies a growing trend in awards programs, as well as that reflected in our marketing efforts, to relate professional efforts to clients' business goals. On the value of this coveted award, Randy Brown, principal of Randy Brown Architects in Omaha, Neb., winner of the 1997 award for his firm's design for the Greater Omaha Packing Co.'s offices, says he sees direct results. Paraphrasing P.T. Barnum, Brown said, "You can have a great thing but if nobody knows about it … what good does it do you?" Brown feels that the big investment they made in time and money to prepare the award submission relative to the firm's overall budget was necessary to support their claim of "providing the highest quality design in the world that is in response to the owner's business needs." Brown says: "We do that quality of work all the time and the award brings out how good design is good for business. And, in addition, it is published in *Business Week,* with its incredible exposure to potential clients, as well as in *Architectural Record."* As a follow-up, Brown's firm mailed copies of the *Business Week* article to 250 contacts and friends and published their achievement in the local press, all of which led to more office building projects.

William McDonough, of William McDonough & Partners, Charlottesville, Va., was a winner of the 1998 "Good Design is Good Business" Award for a factory designed, with Gensler Associates, for Herman Miller Associates. Says McDonough, "Gaining the award recognition validates what we've been saying about our work. The owner points to productivity gains over 20 percent, which amounts to $10 million a year." "As a result," says McDonough, "they say the architects gave them the building as a present." McDonough's exposure in *Business Week* as a two-time winner of the "Good Design is Good Business" Award, (his participation in the design of The Gap office building also won the award) must surely have played a part in positioning him for notice by *Time* Magazine, in which he was featured as a "Hero for the Environment" in 1999.

There are, of course, additional programs on the state and local level not only in architecture but also in other disciplines. But awards are not given for design achievement alone. There are opportunities to be recognized for achievement in other aspects of building design, sponsored by a wide variety of organizations ranging from building materials associations such as steel, concrete and brick to those given by professional associations in fields such as lighting, planning and all manner of engineering disciplines.

Daisy Nappier, awards director of the American Consulting Engineering Council (ACEC), emphasized the importance of innovation in the selection of its national awards. ACEC looks for new applications of existing technologies, complexity, social and economic considerations, and meeting and exceeding the owner's expectations as criteria for its winning choices. Gay Breidinger, marketing operations director of Fishbeck, Thompson, Carr & Huber, Engineers, Scientists, and Architects, located in Ada, Mich., winner of the ACEC's 1998 Conceptor Award, said that her firm feels that the visibility obtained by an award-winning project has significant marketing value. Most of the firm's awards are won for implementing technologies that are the first of their kind, yielding increased recognition of their talent. As a result, the firm has seen an increase in new work to use the technologies employed in its award-winning projects. Furthermore, winning awards enhances its relationships with current clients and has tremendous internal value for recognition of everyone on the team. The firm employs an "atta-boy" attitude that boosts morale, pride and, hence, job satisfaction.

There are hundreds of magazines, material manufacturers, client organizations and associations for the engineering, construction and development industries that sponsor awards programs. While the need for excellent photography is especially true for design awards, as previously noted, many programs emphasize other criteria. Project management has come of age as an activity worthy of recognition by the Project Management Institute, nationally and on the state level. New Jersey offers New Good Neighbor Awards honoring corporations and their building teams for major new facilities within the state. Very likely, business associations in other states offer something similar. And don't forget to look for business-related and team-related award programs sponsored by your clients' industry publications, for example, *American School and University*'s Design Award, *Health Facilities Management*'s Vista Award and *R&D* magazine's Lab of the Year Award. Submissions for these awards and for the *Architectural Record/Business Week* require a much more substantial effort than merely recycling boilerplate information. They demand a demonstration of measurable results and team performance and often involve clients and team partners in the submission process. And what better way to demonstrate value to the jury than by involving a client in the award-submittal process, thereby demonstrating the client's satisfaction with the process and the outcome? Winners report time and again that the rewards, in marketing value, more than justify the efforts.

Getting Organized

Once you have decided to undertake award submissions you will need to get the program organized. Assistance used to be available through the availability of awards directories, of which there were a few, but, unfortunately, they have been discontinued so more of the research will be up to you. One new directory has come on the scene. (See bibliography.) To begin, you will want to go through the following steps.

- ***Identify awards programs.*** Keep a file in which you put information you clip from publications announcing award programs. If possible, begin your research well in advance of the calendar year in which you plan to launch your awards-submission program. Use the web by looking up associations and publications of interest to you to learn about their awards programs. And ask clients about awards for facility design and construction in their industries.

- ***Select appropriate awards programs.*** In deciding which award to pursue, use the same criteria you would on a request for proposal. Do your research, evaluate your chances and make an informed decision.

- ***Establish a calendar.*** Note the submission deadlines and give yourself a month to work on a submittal. Read the requirements carefully; you may need to create plans, get extra photography, obtain additional information about the project, and involve multiple parties for their participation and/or review. And remember to check the travel schedules of people involved in the process. You surely don't want to learn at the last minute that the project designer, or the client, who must approve the submittal, is away until after the due date and can't be reached!

- ***Research previous winners.*** To determine if your work is competitive, collect articles publishing winning projects for the previous year or two. Along with the entry form, awards program sponsors will supply this information if you request it. Try to get an objective opinion on whether your project stands a fair chance, in addition to the opinions of those within the firm. Ask a trusted colleague, or a consultant who has had experience with award submittals or an editor who has been involved in awards programs.

Distinguishing Your Submission from the Pack

Packaging in award submittals, as in marketing and merchandising, has an impact. Image counts. But, as Leta Griswold of J. Muller International, major bridge design consultants and winners of several ACEC Conceptor Awards, points out, "It's most important to follow guidelines and instructions to a 'T'." After that, differentiation with style and taste, within the guidelines, can have a subtle impact on the jury.

As chair of the SMPS national awards program, I had the privilege of being present at the judging for two consecutive years and I can tell you that presentation surely counts — another reason for allowing sufficient time and budgetary resources to do it right. One architect tells me that when a project that his firm had submitted for an award was rejected, he saw it for the first time and found the presentation to be unimpressive. He subsequently repackaged the same submittal with better graphics, a better binder, and a different font and type size for a comparable awards program and won.

I emphasize the importance of good, clear, concise writing, as does AIA's Lee, as mentioned earlier. She explains that the text must be compelling as well as succinct if the jurors are to quickly understand the program and the accomplishments.

Furthermore, esoteric, insider language has no place in an award submission. Architects, be careful to avoid "archi-babble" in the text. Chris Olson, former editor of *Building Design & Construction,* pointed out in a November 1993 editorial, "Designers, of course, are not the only ones to wallow in wordiness. Some developers describe their projects as 'enriching the land' or putting the land to a 'higher' use, as if building involved some kind of mystic transformation of the soil."[1] A word to the wise is sufficient. Unfortunately, Olson's caution is as relevant today as it was then. Your job is to communicate with clarity and precision.

Piggybacking with the Prime

Piggybacking, that is to say, combining efforts with other members of the project team, is an effective and time-honored tool. Consider contacting the other members of the design and construction team. You could offer your assistance with a submittal in order to gain recognition for your role in the project. Or if you are taking the lead, you might offer team members recognition, while requesting their participation. Cooperation among members of the building team on an award submittal spreads the cost, as well as the recognition, and is a strategy increasingly gaining favor. In fact, for some awards, the jurors will view it favorably. Photography, entry fees, staff time or the fee for a consultant to prepare the submission are among the costs to be shared.

Merchandising Results

Once you've won an award, don't forget to spread the word to everyone you'd like to know about it. Find out if the sponsoring organization issues a press release, and, if not, send out your own. Consider, too, sending an announcement of the award recognition to your mailing list (perhaps including a photo of the winning project) or incorporate word of your success in the company newsletter. Add the name of the award won to the project sheet of the award-winning project. Once you have won a number of awards, create an awards list to use, when appropriate, with proposals and qualifications packages. In short, if you're going to do it (and it succeeds), flaunt it!

Endnote

[1] Chris Olson, editorial, *Building Design & Construction* (Nov. 1993).

Bibliography

Cohn, Jane, and Dianne Ludman Frank. "Piggybacking is Good Business." *Architectural Record* (Feb. 1990).

Frank, Dianne Ludman, and Jane Cohn, "Who Are You?" *Contract Design* (March 1995).

PSMJ, *Best Practices*, a monthly newsletter, with an insert on awards programs.

PSMJ, *Desk Reference for Marketers*.

Jane Cohn, FSMPS

- Jane Cohn, FSMPS, associate AIA, is principal of Jane Cohn Public Relations, with offices in Sherman, Conn., and New York City. Her firm represents some of the leading architecture, engineering and construction management firms in the A/E/C industry. Her public relations programs are focused on helping clients increase market share.
- Over the years, she has received numerous awards from SMPS for public relations campaigns developed for clients (two awards won in 1993) and has submitted, and won, dozens of project awards for her clients from a wide-range of sponsoring organizations.
- She has authored and co-authored articles on public relations that have appeared in major trade publications.
- Cohn has been a speaker at national conferences for SMPS, AIA and the American Marketing Association (AMA).
- She has served on the SMPS Public Relations Committee and was chairperson for the SMPS National Awards Program in 1991, and served on the board of directors of the New York Chapter of SMPS.

Acknowledgment

The author wishes to acknowledge her collaboration with colleague Dianne Ludman Frank, with whom she co-authored articles developing the positioning and piggybacking concepts referred to in this chapter.

4.12 Newsletters That Sing

Bonnie Sloan, FSMPS
Principal
The Learning Curve

"Get black on white," advises Guy de Maupassant. But, "Don't just write words. Write music."[1]   In newsletter production, you must meet deadlines, but you also must provide value.

Newsletters have existed since 1923, when the "Kiplinger Washington Letter" was first published. It is the oldest continuous newsletter. Currently, there are tens of thousands of newsletters. The *Oxbridge Directory of Newsletters* lists more than 20,000 titles. Newsletters range from a single 8½-inches by 11-inches sheet of white paper with black type to full-color oversized tabloids on glossy paper or online interactive documents with animation. They can have any format, focus or frequency. But to qualify as a newsletter, they must be *current* and *regular*. Brochures or promotional pieces masquerading as newsletters don't qualify — they don't have news. And publications that come out only once, or at very infrequent or irregular intervals, are not really newsletters, either.

Beyond current news and regular distribution, what does a newsletter need to be successful? Actually, a whole list of qualities, such as:

- Effective planning.
- Enthusiastic people.
- Enthralling prose.
- Eye-catching pages.
- Efficient production.
- Economical printing.
- Elegant presentation.

The purpose of this chapter is to provide facts and figures, as well as tips and techniques about how to accomplish all this.

Planning

Strategic planning for your newsletter is an essential first step, just like it is with any other element of your marketing/communications plan. To get started, answer these basic questions:

- Why do we need a newsletter?
- Would some other means of communication be more appropriate?
- How does a newsletter fit in with our overall marketing plan?
- What do we want our newsletter to accomplish?
- Who do we want to reach with our newsletter?
- What do our readers want? What type of newsletter would be most beneficial to them?

When addressing these strategic questions, write your answers, be specific and gain consensus. Prepare a brief "mission statement" for your newsletter. A successful newsletter needs a clearly defined reason to exist, or it will not flourish. Developing an ongoing newsletter requires a major commitment of time and money. If you are unable to follow through on a continuing basis, it is better not to launch a newsletter. Being cautious rather than overly optimistic is of value when making this strategic commitment.

When you answer the basic questions and decide to proceed with a company newsletter, secondary questions need to be answered:

- What content should we include?
- Who do we need to commit to this project?
- Will the newsletter staff be employees, consultants or a combination?
- How frequently should we publish the newsletter?
- How much time will it take to produce an issue?
- What format should we use?
- What is our budget?

Later in the process, additional questions are:

- What other ways can we use our newsletter?
- How can we improve our newsletter?
- When is it time for redesign?
- Is it time to stop producing this newsletter?

Define Your Audience

Newsletters can be directed externally to your clients/prospective clients, internally to your staff or to both. As shown in Figure 1, the needs and interests of clients compared to staff vary significantly. Usually, it is more effective to focus your newsletter on one group or the other, or produce two separate newsletters. If your newsletter needs to address both groups, keep it professional and not overly personal. Don't list birthdays, weddings and personal items.

Depending on the size and nature of your firm, there are other possible audiences for your company newsletter(s). You may need to address stockholders, reach clients in a specific region, target a market segment or inform subsidiaries. The information presented in this chapter focuses on general company newsletters directed to clients. However, most of the tips and techniques apply to any type of newsletter.

Figure 1

Newsletters That Focus on Your Readers	
Reasons for a Client Newsletter	**Reasons for a Staff Newsletter**
• Provide valuable information. • Enhance your reputation. • Promote your services. • Provide continuous communications. • Demonstrate your capabilities. • Reward clients by featuring their projects. • Showcase company and staff awards. • Introduce new services or projects. • Increase sales with current clients.	• Educate employees about the company. • Improve internal communications. • Explain company benefits. • Promote company-sponsored events. • Provide information about new staff. • Feature employee activities. • Recognize employee achievements. • Answer employee questions. • List job openings.

Newsletter Staffing

The size, complexity and frequency of your newsletter — combined with the capabilities and available time of your in-house staff — dictate whether you can effectively produce a newsletter using in-house staff or whether you need an outside consultant.

Staff needed to produce a newsletter includes writer(s), editor(s), graphic designer(s), photographer(s), printer and administrative support/mailing house for list development and distribution. The individual who functions as the editor needs to lead the newsletter effort and have the authority to resolve conflicts and to make final decisions regarding content and layout. An advisory, editorial or expert board can be useful in setting the overall strategic direction for the newsletter and in overseeing technical quality.

The Newsletter Schedule

Newsletters imply deadlines. Unlike company brochures and some other marketing materials, news is *current*. Readers are conditioned to receiving magazines and paid subscription newsletters in a very timely (or even early) sequence. Your company newsletter needs to be as reliable in terms of delivery. Develop a well-defined schedule, provide it to all involved parties and monitor it closely. A typical schedule to produce an issue of a newsletter is shown in Figure 2 (see page 372). Many of the activities proceed simultaneously. Completion dates are not listed because tasks vary significantly depending on the size and nature of a newsletter.

Be sure to allow time for reviews by key technical experts and/or for approvals by clients. And remember, when production schedules are compressed at the end to meet the final delivery date, cost overruns occur and the risk of mistakes increases.

The Newsletter Budget

Use as much detail as practical in cost development. Estimate annual costs based on the frequency of your publication and include this commitment in your annual marketing budget.

If you use an outside designer, ask for estimates of the basic rate to design your newsletter, plus the rate for any additional charges for changes, revisions or artwork. Also, ask for estimates on messengers and phone/fax charges. Have the designer track expenses against the estimate and inform you if expenses overrun. If you have an in-house designer, you should track the individual's time as part of the marketing budget.

Significant cost items are paper and printing, so get estimates to accurately define these expenses. Get competitive bids from printers in writing. You may be able to save significantly by planning for a year of issues at one time. A sample form to request a printing estimate is shown in Figure 3 (see page 373). Note that rush charges with printers or mailing services can increase the cost of these services by 100 percent or more.

Uses for Your Newsletter

Besides distribution to your target audience, you will probably find that your newsletter is useful in other areas. When you are printing copies for your regular distribution, additional copies can be printed at minimal expense. These can be used as handouts at conferences, included in qualifications packages, sent in response to requests received at your web site and sent to magazines to provide information relating to press releases. Often the content can be used in project descriptions for proposals or as a basis for articles for magazines or journals.

Content

Content is the most important element of a newsletter. While quality paper, gorgeous design, eye-catching photography, interesting illustrations and even white space can contribute to the overall appeal of your newsletter, content is paramount. Readers want to read. They may not read the entire text, but they are interested in valuable information. Make it easy for your readers to find what they want, to understand the details and to be interested in the material. Tips for successful content development are:

- **Be honest.** Credibility of your firm is important. Be clear in project descriptions or research, exactly what the role of your firm is.
- **Be accurate.** Spend time on research, include accurate data and specific details.
- **Be creative.** In concept, content or expression; find interesting ways to present your information.
- **Be organized.** Present text in a logical, definable order that is easy for readers to follow.
- **Be current.** Understand your current marketplace, current terminology and current issues, and focus on these in your text.
- **Be special.** Try to provide content that is not available elsewhere.

In the built environment, clients and potential clients are often very knowledgeable and technically competent, so standards of reading level that might apply to the general public are not applicable. The content needs to be delivered at the appropriate level for the audience, so provide a level of language and detail that is interesting and useful.

Some ideas for the content of client newsletters are:

- Updates on industry trends.
- New technologies.
- Innovative designs.
- "How to" stories.
- Summaries — condensations of valuable information.
- Time- and money-saving examples.
- Regulatory updates/compliance information.
- New services.
- Organizational growth, new geographical areas served.
- Interesting research findings.
- Case histories.
- Staff accomplishments that establish individuals as experts.
- Company and client awards.
- Columns that feature relevant information in each issue.
- Series articles continued from issue to issue.
- Human side of your firm — improvements to the environment or quality of life.
- Pullout section, extra pages or special edition for a special topic, anniversary, etc.

Style Guide

Specify and use a style book — *The Associated Press Style Book*, *The Chicago Manual of Style* and *The Elements of Style* (Strunk & White) are good choices. Also, to promote consistency in style and presentation, it is a good idea to provide authors with a company-approved style guide for your newsletter. The tone or context needed for the newsletter may be somewhat different than the more formal tone of business letters or reports that technical staff is accustomed to producing. Reminders about organization and format are also helpful.

Authors usually prefer to work within guidelines that provide decisions already made about style and format. This enables them to concentrate on the technical material and on providing value to clients. A sample brief style guide is included as Figure 4 (see page 374). You may want to add your own list of commonly used technical terms and standard abbreviations.

Beginnings and Endings

A newsletter is really like a newspaper in the presentation of information. The typical standards apply. You need to "hook" the reader with an interesting title and first sentence. The ABCs of article titles are:

- **Active verb**
- **Brief**
- **Clever**

Make headlines meaningful, attention-getting, brief and specific. Use short words, a quote or a "how to" statement. Lead with a question, a surprising fact or statistic, or an analogy. Use opening sentences to be provocative, create excitement, make your reader care and build rapport. Be sure the lead sentence differs from the title — otherwise, one is not necessary. State the theme or purpose in the first sentence, and use topic sentences at the beginning of paragraphs. Provide information in descending order with big picture/context first, then details.

Conclude with a dramatic statement or a challenge. According to the editors of *Harvard Business Review*, "A good conclusion adds something new, but relevant to the article — a forecast, a challenge, a clinching bit of evidence, or, ideally, something to do on Monday morning."

Editing and Proofreading

Conscientious editing takes time and commitment. It can be accomplished sequentially by routing the copy to several editors in sequence or concurrently by allowing simultaneous edits by several individuals with one editor assigned to resolve differences and select the most appropriate text. The editing capabilities of most word-processing programs provide an easy method for editors to create marked up text that is readable. The following list presents tips for editing your newsletter.

- **Edit for technical accuracy.** Professional image requires current and accurate information. Be certain that knowledgeable experts have reviewed your text prior to publication. Verify facts, numbers, dates, spelling of proper names and titles.

- **Edit for order.** Do your points follow a logical sequence? Will readers understand your information?

- **Edit for author's pride.** Use short words and simple sentences. If an author is "in love with" the writing, it still may need to be changed.

Particularly in the age of desktop publishing, team projects and constant deadlines, proofreading is an important issue. Limited time and a tendency toward over-reliance on technology can cause deterioration in the quality of the final product. The projected technical and design quality of your firm, its products and services can be negatively affected by inaccurate, incomplete or sloppy text. Some tips for proofreading are:

- **Spell check plus.** Use the capabilities of your word-processing program, but don't rely on it for accuracy. Read the text as well. Then, read the text again a day later.

- **Alternate review.** Have someone previously uninvolved in the newsletter production proofread the entire text. Often, individuals too close to the project overlook errors.

- **Proofread elements.** Since errors often occur in headings, captions, etc., proofread all the headings first, then all the subheadings, then the captions, then the text.

- **Proofread backwards.** Read the text backwards. It won't make sense, but you will catch errors that you may miss when focusing on the content.

- **Proofread sideways and upside down.** Look at the text for uneven spacing, incorrect type sizes, etc. — things you may not see right side up.

- **Proofread final output.** Find any remaining errors and fix them.

Design, Layout and Printing

Figure 5 (see page 375) lists decisions that need to be made to produce a consistent design/layout. Look at a variety of other newsletters to see what appeals to you and feels right for your firm. Just as content reflects the company the newsletter represents, design and layout present a particular style or image. Be sure that this visual image is consistent with the image you want to project. A list of newsletter layout tips is included as Figure 6 (see page 376).

Some statistics about current newsletters may guide you about what works best:

- Most newsletters are four to eight pages long.

- 50 percent of newsletters are printed on white paper; another 40 percent are printed on shades of white like ecru, ivory or cream.

- The most common size is 8½ inches by 11 inches.

- Most newsletters are printed vertically on the page.

- More than 95 percent of newsletters use black type for text because it is the most readable. Some use dark blue. Green and red are infrequently used because 10 percent of men are red/green color blind and will not see these.

Designing with Text

Titles, headings, subheading, captions, sidebars and callout text are all elements on the pages of your newsletters that require graphic as well as content decisions. These textual elements call specific attention to themselves. Be sure that attention is warranted and useful in meeting your objectives.

Also, many newsletters in the built environment focus on technically complex subjects. Especially with more complicated subjects, typography needs to be simple.

Photographs, Graphics and Illustrations

Photographs, graphics and illustrations are included to visually reinforce the text. These elements can enchant and attract the reader, or can offend or distract the reader, depending on many factors. Quality, placement and the number of elements on any one page are critical to effective design. According to the Society for Newsletter Design, 72 percent of readers "enter" an article through the photos, 35 percent may not read an article without photos and 90 percent read captions on a photo even if they don't read the article.

When evaluating photographs, be certain that these fit with the text content. Use high quality photography with good subject matter, composition, action, contrast, focus and detail. Include people in your photographs — people like to look at people. Remember: Photographs are usually the most attention-getting elements on the page. Consequently, just one poor quality photograph can lessen the overall quality of your publication. Be sure to credit photographs appropriately. Typically, photo credit bylines are printed on the edge of the photograph.

Graphics, charts and figures need to be clear, simple and easy to understand. In particular, pay attention to scale. Technical staff members often want to include elaborate maps, design plans or sections, or complex diagrams that — when reduced for production in a newsletter — are unreadable. Simplify these to present only the relevant data in an attractive and understandable way.

Illustrations, similar to photographs, must be high quality, appropriate and consistent. Don't attempt to combine too many different types of graphic elements in one newsletter. For example, combining clipart (of various styles) with illustrations, charts and photographs is likely to give a very disjointed appearance. Illustrations can be useful when photographs are not available. Using only line art can provide a consistent, friendly look to a newsletter, and can be a cost-effective alternative since reproduction of photographs adds to the overall production cost.

Printing

Printing is a key element of the overall process of newsletter production, and it can significantly affect the quality of the final product. Quality control means that you recognize that each piece of paper leaving your office is a "representative" of your company.

Carefully review press proofs and work closely with your graphic designer and your printer to assure quality. At the blueline or press proof phase, it's a good idea to rethink quantity and paper quality issues, and to revisit mail house or distribution plans. When reviewing press proofs, look for:

- Trapping (registration) of all elements.
- Pictures that are not right-reading.
- Color accuracy, spot match, color in photos.
- Any errant marks or smudges.
- Any text or line art that has breaks or faded portions.
- Missing text — paragraphs or small text that might have been deleted.
- All small items like page numbers, volume number, addresses and captions.

Refer to the glossary that begins on page 377 to review common printing and design terms.

Online and Electronic Newsletters

Most of the qualities of a good newsletter apply to online newsletters as well. You still need quality writing, effective design, relevant content and current information.

One major difference is in the organization of your material. Unlike a printed newsletter where the text is presented in a linear fashion like a chain, online material is organized like a web with appropriate links to various sections and related information. Conceptual organization of the material requires knowledge of the technology, as well as consideration of the differences that readers show toward electronic as opposed to printed text. In general, your information needs to be presented more quickly and in "bite-sized" pieces. The limitations of a computer screen do not make it possible or practical to view elaborate full-page layouts at one time. Online newsletters have the potential to include sound, animation, videos and interactive items — exciting new methods not available in traditional print media.

Electronic newsletters can be distributed to clients or staff electronically, or can be posted to the company web site or intranet for viewing. The issue with an online newsletter is the potential that the audience you are trying to reach may not visit your site.

Many firms in the built environment have a "news" section on their web sites, rather than a newsletter. Primarily, firms post current press releases and information about new projects and services. A number of firms post their company newsletter or items from it on their web site, and allow viewers to request articles or to be added to the newsletter mailing list.

To see some examples of online newsletters, visit:

- **www.addarch.com**
- **www.cdm.com/pubs/CDMnews**
- **www.dprinc.com/news/current**
- **www.e-architect.com**

Newsletter Evaluations and Results

As a part of your overall publication program, obtain client or employee feedback about the effectiveness of your newsletter. Regularly send response cards with your newsletter or send a separate mailing. To obtain a higher response rate, keep evaluation forms as simple as possible with many questions that have yes/no answers or boxes to check. Use only one-page forms and put your easiest-to-answer and most important questions early in the form. The best months to send out evaluations are usually February or October, to avoid months with holidays and vacations. When readers respond to your survey, follow up with your appreciation for their time and effort. Respond to any criticisms, suggested changes or information they would like to see.

Other methods to obtain evaluations include calling representative readers, setting up a panel of readers to review your newsletter, asking in-house staff for critiques or obtaining a critique from a consultant. Measurable results include additional publicity by responding to requests for reprinting your articles or writing similar articles for relevant journals, new clients, increased market share and expansion of new services. Share the results and newsletter evaluations with management at your firm to document the return on investment of the newsletter.

Trends and Awards

It is useful to pay attention to newsletters in other fields to watch for ideas and trends. Newsletters for other service industries — for example, financial services or heath care — often cover general interest topics that may be of value for an internal publication. Newsletters from non-profit organizations, particularly museums and arts organizations, can often spur your thinking toward creative ideas or innovative graphic concepts that you can use.

Current trends in the production of newsletters include five- and seven-column grids instead of the standard three, and narrow column/wide column formats, Use of color is seen as more modern and attractive than only black and white. Newsletters are using more line art, illustrations and graduated screens. Also, experienced editors and designers are avoiding "grip and grin" photos, and taking people "out of the box" by cropping out backgrounds. All pictures don't have to be rectangular. Current computer technology makes it easy for designers to flow text around graphics and create photographs that provide interesting shapes. Large initial caps continue to be used, and end marks are used to let readers know that an article has ended. Ragged-right copy and ragged-bottom margins are prevalent.

Look at award-winning newsletters and analyze these for current techniques and for qualities that make them special. There are a number of national and international associations that focus specifically on newsletters, some of which have competitions for newsletter design/content. For example, the Newsletter Publishers Foundation has an annual competition for journalism awards (www.newsletters.org).

For businesses in the built environment, the SMPS annual awards program is an excellent source of high-quality newsletters. Visit www.smps.org to view the award-winning newsletters in the Marketing Communications Awards Program. Client comments and demonstrated results of these newsletters are proof of their value. Judges highly rated newsletters that were focused, functional and economically produced.

Madeleine Hope, marketing manager for Hazen and Sawyer, was one of the 1999 judges of the SMPS awards competition for newsletters. She commented that "… more attention was paid to the quality of design, paper stock and printing than to content. … The intent was usually to provide the reader with useful information; however, few were successful in their attempts." Another 1999 judge, Thomas Armistead, associate editor of *Engineering News-Record* wrote, "The bulk of the newsletters submitted for this competition came up short when we put ourselves in the place of their audience and asked, 'What does this newsletter offer to compensate me for investing my time to read it?'"

The "typical" industry newsletter was described as four pages, 11 inches by 17 inches folded, two to four colors, three to four columns and generally conservative in design. The 1998 and 1999 first place newsletter is produced by FMI and is the only newsletter in the competition that is not distributed free to readers. According to Armistead, "The success of FMI's newsletter challenges marketing communicators to reinvent their programs and to improve their quality. … What is important is to design and produce them (newsletters) as if they had to sell themselves, because, in fact, they do."

Ideas the judges liked were business-reply cards, perforated for tear-off and response and offsetting costs by selling copies to vendors whose names were prominently mentioned in the newsletter.

"Cars & Stripes" is an external newsletter produced by International Parking Design that won an award in 1998. This quarterly newsletter is mailed to clients and potential clients, vendors and subconsultants. It is also distributed at trade shows and conventions, and reproduced on the firm's web site (www.ipd-global.com). The objectives for the newsletter include educating clients, improving visibility, increasing trust and positioning the firm as the expert in parking design. Reader response is excellent. Readers call to ask about the next issue, and about 150 readers have returned the "Send Me More" coupons to ask for additional information. Due to requests for subscriptions, circulation grew from 1,500 in 1995 to 3,600 in 1998. The layout includes three- and four-column pages and ragged-right text. The four-page newsletter is printed in black on 100-pound Elite Velvet Dull Book white paper with a different PMS accent color for each issue. It is 11 inches by 17 inches, folded to 8 ½ inches by 11 inches. Each issue is printed at a cost of $2,329 for 8,000 copies. Articles from "Cars & Stripes" have been reprinted with permission in national industry publications.

HNTB won first place in the 1997 SMPS awards competition for an internal newsletter called "Project Management." This newsletter focused on project-management issues and was distributed to internal project teams. The objectives included becoming the primary source for information about HNTB's project-management programs and providing tools to help project teams improve performance. The newsletter grew from under 1,000 copies to close to 2,000 as staff members wanted to be added to the distribution. The eight-page newsletter is printed 11 inches by 17 inches and folded to 8 ½ inches by 11 inches. It is produced on white paper with red headlines and blue background boxes. Paragraph text is indented and justified. The newsletter was produced quarterly (2,500 copies per issue) at a cost of about $8,000 annually. The newsletter was discontinued in 1998 because it had achieved its purpose in promoting awareness and understanding of the program. A new publication called "Best Practices at Work" was created for all employees.

Conclusion

If you produce a company newsletter — internal, external or online — it always needs to complement your overall marketing plan. Newsletter production is sometimes frustrating, often difficult and always demanding. It can be expensive in terms of time, commitment, energy and costs. But, it is also an effective method of ongoing client contact in a very professional way. And it's rewarding. Newsletters can inspire, educate and inform. Newsletters can increase communication with your clients and trust in your technical capabilities. Long-term results include new projects, expanded services and increased market share.

Endnote

[1] Gary Provost, *100 Ways to Improve Your Writing*.

Bibliography

Arth, Marvin, Helen Ashmore, and Elaine Floyd. *Newsletter Editor's Handbook*, 5th Edition, Cincinnati: Writer's Digest Books, 1995.

Beach, Mark. *Editing Your Newsletter*, 4th Edition. Cincinnati: Writer's Digest Books, 1995.

Bonime, Andrew, and Ken C. Pohlmann. *Writing for New Media*. New York: John Wiley & Sons Inc., 1998.

Campbell, Alastair. *The New Graphic Designer's Handbook*. Philadelphia: Running Press, 1993.

Cohen, Sandee, and Robin Williams. *The Non-designer's Scan and Print Book*. Berkeley: Peachpit Press, 1999.

Fletcher, Penelope C., ed. *Guide to Effective Newsletter Editing and Design*. Arlington, VA: Newsletter Publishers Association, 1995.

Parker, Roger C. *Looking Good in Print*. 4th Edition. Scottsdale, AZ: Coriolis Group, 1998.

Williams, Robin. *The Non-designer's Design Book*. Berkeley: Peachpit Press, 1994.

—. *The Non-designer's Type Book*. Berkeley: Peachpit Press, 1998.

Useful Web Sites

www.ariad-ltd.com/gold.html
Newsletter that won the 1998 annual award from the Newsletter Clearing House.

www.desktoppub.miningco.com/msubnewspub.htm
Information about the newsletter industry, tips and trends.

www.managersguide.com
Information about newsletter strategies and tactics. Also offers for purchase a book titled *A Manager's Guide to Newsletters*.

www.newsletterinfo.com
Information about newsletter design.

www.newsletters.org
The Newsletter Publishers Association site with information about the International Newsletter Conference, "Hotline" (its biweekly newsletter), annual journalism awards by the Newsletter Publishers Foundation and many publications.

www.put-it-in-writing.com
Tips on producing a good newsletter, how to spot a bad one, writing and proofreading.

www.ragan.com
The Ragan Communications site features a variety of newsletters and related information.

http://pub.savvy.com
Review some of the more than 11,000 free newsletters that can be sent to you by mail.

Bonnie J. Sloan, FSMPS

- Principal of The Learning Curve in Wakefield, Mass., which provides marketing, communication and training for professional services firms.
- More than 25 years' experience in marketing for the built environment including public relations, communications, and production of newsletters and brochures.
- Speaker at AIA Build Boston, SMPS National Senior Roundtable, SMPS Boston Talking Shop and Marketing Fundamentals Programs.
- Author of technical articles published in national and international magazines.
- SMPS Boston award for outstanding professional contribution, Education Awards from Northeastern University and Boston University, listed in *International Who's Who of Entrepreneurs*.

Figure 2. Typical Production Schedule for a Newsletter Issue	
Item	Completion Date
Planning meeting to define content	_____
Research sources for graphics/photos	_____
Draft articles	_____
Revise/update distribution list	_____
Article editing	_____
Technical review by authors	_____
Client review/approvals	_____
Draft layout	_____
Reviews/changes	_____
Final layout	_____
Blue lines/press proofs	_____
Printing	_____
Distribution	_____

Figure 3. Request for Quotation for Printing

Please provide a quotation for printing the newsletter titled_____ based

on the specifications that follow. Quotations need to be received by 5:00 p.m. on _____.

Number of pages per issue:_____   Number of issues per year:_____

Quantity per issue: _____

Flat size: _____   Finished size: _____

Paper: _____

Ink: _____

Number of halftones each issue: _____

Special instructions: _____

_____

_____

Camera-ready copy to be provided. Printed copies to be delivered within five working days of receipt of camera-ready copy.

This printing contract will cover one year from date of issuance.

Quote per issue: _____

Total quote for full year: _____

Please direct your questions and send quotation to:

      Editor's Name:
      Company:
      Address:
      City, State, Zip:
      Phone:
      Fax:
      E-mail:

Authorized by Printer:_____   Date: _____

Authorized by Editor:_____   Date: _____

Figure 4. Sample Newsletter Style Guide

In this style guide, we define corporate standards for authors and editors producing materials to be included in our newsletter. The objective is to maintain a consistent image as a firm, and to improve the quality and clarity of our communications.

Client Focus

In all written communications, focus on the client's needs. Attempt to understand the client's point of view, and present information in a clear and concise manner that is easy to follow. Place information first that is critical to the client. Provide backup information or examples to support what you are telling the client. Mention any actions we are taking on the client's behalf. Focus on actions that you may want the client to take and provide the motivation for the client to act.

Organization

First consider the most appropriate way to present your information. Write one sentence stating your objective(s) before you begin to write your text. To organize your material effectively, do an outline. Choose a strong organizational pattern — sequential, cause/effect, comparison/contrast, problem/solution, process or results-then-background. Follow that pattern to develop a cohesive document. Use lists, bullets or subheadings to make complex material more understandable. Use topic sentences at the beginning of paragraphs. Think about accurate transitions for logical flow of ideas from sentence to sentence and from paragraph to paragraph.

Tense and Voice

Use present tense and active voice whenever possible. This involves the reader and makes your writing easier to understand. Active voice is more forceful and more positive. Use strong, active verbs.

Conversational Style

Always be professional and polite. Use an informal style that conveys staff is relaxed, a pleasure to work with and easy to understand. Express yourself in clear, concise language. Be specific and use concrete examples to illustrate your points. Avoid pompous language, redundancy, clichés and over-used phrases. Define abbreviations/acronyms, as appropriate. Vary your sentence length and structure to avoid boring your readers. In general, use shorter sentences and paragraphs. This makes your text easier to read and understand. Write complete sentences. Make sure each sentence has an identifiable subject. Use opening sentences that are provocative, have energy and create excitement. Use closing sentences to restate your main objective, to request action and/or to make a commitment.

Editing and Proofreading

It is policy that all written communications to clients are edited and proofread by someone other than the author. All documents will be spell-checked electronically, as well. Edit for content first or for elements that would require rewriting/reorganizing the text. Then edit for expression, word usage, grammar and punctuation. Make sure subjects agree with verbs. Use parallel construction. Keep related words together: adjectives near the nouns they modify, adverbs near the verbs they modify and dependent clauses near the words on which they depend for meaning.

Format

To facilitate review and editing, please provide your draft text in 12 pt. Times New Roman, double spaced with a 1.5-inch left margin and a 2.5-inch right margin. Clearly label tables, figures or exhibits within the text.

Figure 5. Newsletter Design/Layout Decisions	
Format	Size (trim)
	Number of pages
	Structure (grid)
	Number and size of columns
	Text justified or not
	Paragraph indentations
	Page headers and footers
Title Page	Title/newsletter name
	Logo
	Issue number
	Date
Paper	Texture
	Weight
	Color
	Coated/uncoated stock
Color	Color(s) for titles
	Color(s) for text
	Color(s) and screens for photos/illustrations
Type styles, sizes and leading	Newsletter title
	Column headings
	Article headings
	Subheadings
	Text
	Lists/bullets
	Photo/illustration captions
	Callout boxes
	Page numbers
Visuals	Photographs
	Illustrations/line art
	Tables/figures
Bulk-Mailing Stamp	

Figure 6. Newsletter Layout Tips

Important Elements

- The optical center is the prime viewing area of any page.

- The poorest viewing area is the lower-left corner.

White Space

- Some white (or blank) space is needed to make a page visually appealing. White space, especially at the bottom of a page, relaxes the reader.

- To test your page for too much dense text, place a dollar bill anyplace on the page in the same horizontal direction as the type. It should touch some graphic element, not just text.

- Shorter paragraphs increase white space and are more readable.

Boxes and Lines

- Don't place more than one item per page in a box, and limit the overall number of boxes in your newsletter.

- When using horizontal and vertical lines, be careful not to make these too thick.

Readable Text

- Maintain high contrast between type and paper.

- Serif type is easier to read than sans serif type.

- Ragged-right text is easier to read than justified copy.

- Text should be no smaller than nine-point type.

- The ideal column is no more than 45 characters wide. This is the optimum distance the human eye can travel without strain.

- Use italics and underlining sparingly.

Glossary

Bleed
A page element that extends beyond the trim marks. The bleed ensures that the image goes to the edge of the paper after trimming.

Blockout
The effect when the background is not printed in a photograph. This can be used to highlight a particular area of a cluttered photo.

Callout or pull quote
A direct quote from an article that is repeated, usually in larger type to call attention to it.

Camera ready
Artwork, copy or paste-up ready for reproduction.

Clean copy
Original copy with no errors.

Color separation
Breaking down color pages and images into the four-process separation colors (CMYK or cyan, magenta, yellow and black).

Comp
A "comprehensive" or detailed dummy showing how the finished piece will look.

Demibold
Typeface that is bolder than "regular" type, but not as heavy as a boldface type.

Direct positive copy
Copying by xerography or Photostat, reproduction of an original without using a negative.

Dirty copy
Copy that contains errors, dust, scratches or incomplete images.

Display type
Type used for headlines, subheads, etc., as opposed to text.

DPI
"Dots per inch," a method of measuring resolution when referring to printers and monitors.

Duotone
Printing a photograph or image in two colors of ink.

Fold marks
Dashed lines within the margins that indicate where the finished piece should be folded.

Generation
A reference to the number of reproductions made from an original. A first-generation image is an original, a second generation is made from the first, a third generation is made from the second, etc.

GIF
Graphics Interchange Format, a popular computer graphics format that supports bitmap information up to 356 colors.

Greeking
To indicate type by using gray tint or gibberish for the text, commonly used when preparing rough visuals.

Grid
A measuring guide for consistency. In some applications, a background pattern to which elements such as type, boxes, etc., can be locked or "snapped."

Gutter
The blank space between adjacent columns or facing pages.

Halftone
A reproduction of a photograph or other image that converts it into a series of dots. The variance in the number, size and density of the dots produces the quality of the resolution of a photograph.

Hard copy
A tangible copy of a document or image, such as paper or film.

JPEG
Graphic file format developed by Joint Photographic Experts Group. Uses compression for transmitting files over the Internet.

Kicker
A subhead printed *above* the main headline to draw attention to the headline.

Leading
The line spacing between lines of typeset copy.

LPI
Lines per inch. Refers to halftone screen resolution in printing.

Mechanical
An original document with all elements of the design in position and ready to be photographed for reproduction.

Overset copy
Final copy type that exceeds the given space requirements.

Point
Standard type size unit about 1/72 of an inch.

Proof
An intermediate stage when pages are checked for errors. A press proof is the last proof to be read before giving authorization for printing.

Recycled paper
Paper manufactured from de-inked used paper and bleached pulp.

Recyclable paper
Wastepaper or stock separated from other solid waste and designated for reuse as a raw material.

Set width
The space allowed for each character in a font. Each font has its own set width, which can be changed to increase or decrease the space between characters.

Sidebar
Short explanatory text printed alongside the main story, so that the reader understands the item is related, but separate.

Slick
Camera-ready reproduction of an illustration or a logo.

Soft copy
Copy that has not been printed (i.e., copy viewed on a computer screen).

Spot color
A color that is not built by using process color printing plates. Instead, the color is printed using an ink made exclusively for that color.

TIFF
Tagged Image File Format, a graphics format for scanned, high-resolution images.

Tracking
The adjustment of the space between the characters in text.

Tritone
Printing a photograph or image in three colors of ink.

White space
Page areas without text or pictures, often used for graphic design effect.

4.13   Creating Special Events

Barry R. Gaston
Business Development Manager
Harley Ellis

What are special events? Are they open houses or ground breakings? Are they dinners or meetings? Are they anniversaries or holidays? Are they parties or ceremonies?

Any of these situations, and many others, could be turned into special events for your organization. The recipe for making any of these situations special will require a careful sifting of your objectives, a large helping of knowledge about what stimulates your target audience and a dash of creativity. When it works, a lasting positive impression, based on the unique characteristics of your organization, will be permanently etched on the minds of your prospects.

If executed correctly, special events can cast a light on an organization's human side, personalize the organization, pull it off the printed page and out of the office building, and reveal its character and vitality. Unlike targeted direct mail campaigns, fancy brochures and other public relations staples, a creative special event can reach new prospects and old clients and engage them in a way that will put your organization in a special place on the long "bidders" list your future client maintains.

Planning a Special Event

Whether you are counting on five guests or 5,000, the secret of successful special events lies in planning. The following steps are a general road map for successful events.

1. *Define your goals.* Decide why you are planning the special event in the first place. What do you hope to realize as a result of this event? Two weeks after the event, what one thing do you want your prospects to remember about your firm? For example, you might answer, "We want our customers and prospects to remember we are the fastest growing A/E in town."

Remember that special events are only one piece of the overall public relations and marketing communication program. In fact, special events should be a standard part of your yearly public relations plan. Whatever the focus of your communications program is, that will probably lead your special events.

Of course, special event goals should be based on a careful review of your organization's concerns and marketing objectives. Does a particular market need bolstering? Will there be a new service introduced in the year ahead? If so, how should its introduction be handled? If you plan your marketing around market segments, then special events can follow. Should you offer a seminar for your clients or prospects? How about spicing up that old hospitality suite so it does more than give your prospects a free drink?

Timing is also crucial. If the event is planned to coincide with other significant happenings, its impact may be greatly increased. Thus, it is important to develop a yearly plan of special events. This also provides sufficient lead-time for the detailed planning required to execute an event properly.

2. ***Identify your audience.*** Tailor your event to suit the common interests, personal needs, age and disposition of those you invite. Determine what these people already know about you. What other means of communication have you used to approach them? What are their current impressions of your organization? Before you begin to think about the content of the program, develop an accurate list of prospects and group or individual profiles.

You may want to plan the event for some segment of your overall audience. An event targeted at a health care audience, as an example, may generate a larger benefit than trying to talk to the total list of prospects for the company. Remember each client thinks his or her business is unique and has different problems than everyone else in the world. With a segmented group it is much easier to find ways to stimulate a select set of needs or interests.

In some cases, the audience can be as select as an individual client. Remember that only 20 percent of your customers bring you 80 percent of your work. Doing something special for these folks continues to build the relationship and, in most cases, people like doing business with people they know and trust.

3. ***Develop the central concept.*** Decide what aspect of your services or specific capabilities relates most to the audience you are trying to reach. If your event satisfies some special need for your audience, you have the beginnings of a really special event. Ask yourself the question: If I were a prospect, why would I come to this event? What do I get out of the event? If your answer is, "Gosh, I don't know," then you have some more work to do.

You can plan a party and many of your existing clients may come, but what will attract the prospect that has been reluctant to give you the time of day? I know of one firm that sponsored an ice cream social as part of its annual open house. They served a large variety of ice cream — except there was no vanilla. They tied the event to the theme, "We don't do vanilla architecture." That ice cream social stimulates more interest than a bland announcement that XYZ is having an open house at its new office and it drives home a theme that positions the firm with its customers.

Remember that your firm has knowledge that your clients want. Share that knowledge. Show your customers how to improve their operations. I have known firms that are afraid to give away information to their customers. The fact is, if a customer thinks they can take your discussion and not use your services, working for them would have been a disaster anyway. The smart clients will see you as an expert and want to retain you. Over and over again, when I can give clients information that helps them do their jobs better, they keep it and refer to it, and you will get those unexpected phone calls when they need your help.

4. ***Give it the creative sparkle.*** The average American is bombarded with more than 1,800 competing advertising messages each day. Professional services firms, unfortunately, must battle with all of them for equal time. So you must find ways to capture the attention of your audience — from the invitation to the thank you.

Your prime prospects are busy people who probably receive dozens of invitations to similar events throughout the year. To catch their attention, something about your event must be *more* appealing, innovative or useful to them than what they would normally do with their time.

The difference between an event and a *special* event is that a special event employs those elements and approaches that satisfy audience needs and captures their interest. The truly *special* event presents these benefits to the audience in an unusual way. This is the point where creativity must be applied to the basic concept. Making your events stand out from your prospects' daily routine is what will deliver your company's message effectively. Part of this process is to take risks. New ideas or different approaches generate interest.

The trick is to be innovative without doing something that looks frivolous or foolish. For example, a large leading engineering firm buys a special performance of the local symphony orchestra and invites clients and prospects and their "significant others" for a classy evening. This event is not only fun, it matches the level of sophistication the large diverse firm wants to exude. On the other hand, a smaller, trendy design boutique architect recently bought out one of the opening-day showings of *Star Wars, Episode One* at a local theater and took its entire staff and clients.

Note how the vanilla architecture example mentioned earlier starts to add new dimensions and communications opportunities. The realm of possibilities for creative promotional materials is tremendous. The tie between architecture and ice cream is the creative sparkle needed to make the event memorable.

5. *Check, then double check.* You can't get through most successful special events without a checklist. This applies whether you are preparing a preliminary budget, making sure everything is arranged or writing a post-event evaluation. Start with the event itself and work backward to prepare a detailed timetable for all elements. This checklist/schedule will become the cornerstone of your planning. Make sure you list every activity and task that must be accomplished and when it has to be done. Then ask yourself, what if? By developing contingency plans and adding them to your checklist, you will eliminate a considerable amount of hassle, headaches and high blood pressure. During the execution of the event, you will have the ability to track all the little details and make sure everything comes together in the right place at the right time.

Lessons from the SMPS Awards Competitions

For several years, SMPS has held a national Marketing Communications Awards Program. I participated in several juries where clients were the judges for the competition. Each year, one of the largest categories is special event promotion. There are several lessons that can be learned by watching the judges review these materials.

- The judges see a lot of this type of promotion. They review this category very quickly. Either the pieces get their attention at first glance or they will hit the trash.
- Glitzy pieces may not help carry the message. In many cases, some very basic but elegant pieces did as well as big budget pieces.

- Innovation that is directly tied to the special event or the firm will get their attention. One geotech firm used a foam rubber rock with attached open house announcement as its invitation. Not only did it attract a lot of interest, the invitations are still on some prospects' desks.
- Let them know who you are and what you're selling. If it is hard to determine these elements, the piece will hit the old trash can.

Be careful if you do the same promotion each year. These items become stale and mechanical if you do not rethink them as a regular part of your planning. Christmas cards are a classic example. Firms send them out as a matter of routine, but fail to take into account the message about the firm these cards carry. Are you an innovative firm or do you run with the pack? How about skipping Christmas (one of the busiest and most trash mail packed times of the year) and going for Valentine's Day or the Fourth of July? Remember, you are trying to stand out from the crowd. You know, I have often wondered why no engineering firms recognize St. Patrick's Day while every engineering school I know has a big blast for the Patron Saint of Engineers.

One Final Thought

A firm's image (good or bad) is developed over time. Its image can be changed over time. One event will never tell the whole story to any group of individuals, nor will a successful format be appropriate to follow over and over again for an extended period of time. In order to develop a truly communicative marketing program, you will need to re-evaluate your prime prospects continually, redefine the communications problems, study the components of your business further and find more creative ways to tell your story to your prospects. Special events can help.

Barry R. Gaston

- Barry Gaston has more than 20 years experience in marketing and selling architectural, engineering and construction-related services.
- Most recently, he has been expanding the laboratory and research facilities practice of Harley Ellis Design nationally.
- His professional career has also involved positions with companies such as Sverdrup Corp., Hunter Engineering Co., Lloyd Baken Consultants and Washington University, all in St. Louis.
- Gaston received a bachelor's degree in mechanical engineering from Wichita State University, Wichita, Kan.
- He was a founding member of the Society for Marketing Professional Services' St. Louis Chapter, serving as president for the first two years and holding several other board positions over the years.

Part 5:
Management

5.1 Marketing Personnel: How Many Do You Need?

Amy Ostigny, CPSM

Ellen Jackson

In a perfect world, a design firm opens its doors with great fanfare — enthusiasm and anticipation spur the creative team onto greatness. They churn out a portfolio of work the envy of all competitors. The business development team, structured and staffed to fit the firm's needs like a glove, is poised to sell the firm's capabilities to appropriate market audiences.

Everyone on your staff in some way is involved in marketing your firm and products. The best return on a marketing investment comes from servicing existing clients.

Marketing in many ways is about cultivating and nurturing relationships. A positive personal relationship is crucial to repeat business. One of the basic keys to successful marketing is developing relationships — relationships with existing clients, past clients and potential clients. This requires the involvement of every member of your firm.

Generating new clients can come from all levels of the company. The enterprise thrives in this highly synergistic environment. With just the right mix of business developers and marketing professionals generating just the right amount of prospective activity and just the right talent on hand to efficiently serve clients' needs with innovative, high-quality execution, the team brings in the desired revenue, securing the firm's success and future growth and expansion.

Deal with Business Realities

Of course we don't live and work in that perfect world. So often firms are strung together with unplanned marketing structures that grow too little, too much or too late. The firm's infrastructure disintegrates. Haziness sets in along the lines of team responsibilities — the marketing team stops closing deals, second- and third-tier marketing support staff is asked to sell and business development professionals disappear in a lean quarter. Your business development efforts turn profoundly reactive — as opposed to healthy and proactive. Save for start-up operations, who has the luxury of molding a business development staff and defining responsibilities and a business plan from scratch? Move into an existing business development position and you take on the good and the bad, the "this is the way we've always done things," the backlog and the no-log and, potentially, an ill-mixed team trying to get the wrong job done.

Marketing Rx

Take heart. There's no need to settle for the status quo. Step No. 1: Find out where things went wrong, and get your team back on track. To accomplish this goal, one proven guideline is the "Closer-Doer

Model." This model lays out what design firms need in the way of a well-balanced team of marketers selling to keep creative minds busy delivering product to successfully support their businesses' respective sizes.

- **Role of the Closer:** His or her time is spent selling the firm. Has authority to sign contracts and commit resources. Is an owner/principal of the firm. Is a registered professional. Spends 100 percent of his or her time marketing and no time on projects.
- **Role of the Closer-Doer:** His or her time is divided between marketing and projects. Has authority to sign contracts and commit resources. Is an owner/principal of the firm. Is a registered professional. Spends 60 percent of his or her time marketing and 40 percent on projects.
- **Role of the Doer-Closer:** His or her time is divided between projects and marketing. Marketing focus is on existing clients. Can sign contracts in certain situations. Not an owner/principal. Fifty percent of Doer-Closers are registered. Spends 20 percent of his or her time marketing and 80 percent time on projects
- **Role of the Doer:** Project A/E, job captain, technical staff, draftsperson, etc. Not an owner/principal. Five to 10 percent is registered. One hundred percent of time is on projects. Use technical staff to convince the client that your firm understands the project issues. The firm that can demonstrate how the project will be approached to solve those issues is usually the one that will be awarded the project. Don't make the mistake of requiring all technical staff members to be involved in all aspects of marketing. To be successful in marketing efforts, you must identify each individual's strengths and channel each person's marketing participation in that direction.

Use this model, as defined below, to detect what is lacking and to identify where things are top-heavy. It may also be used to gauge requirements for future growth or anticipated downsizing.

Following, per the Closer-Doer Model, are some suggested configurations for the ideal marketing-support structure to service the specific needs of firms of all sizes.

The Closer-Doer Model
Smaller Firms
One to 24 Employees

Team definition: The principal of this firm is generally very close to clients, and the majority of the work comes from word of mouth and personal contacts. With only one or two closer-doers necessary to support a firm of this size, there is minimal need for a structured marketing department.

Recommended staffing: A principal's responsibility in marketing includes being a relationship builder with clients, a lead finder in collaboration with marketing, a proposal strategist and a presenter. Most importantly, a principal must be a cheerleader for marketing. If the principal isn't interested, there's no use going after the work. Principal in charge of the marketing effort, usually a partner, sometimes the president of the firm. The marketing principal is the chief spokesperson for the firm. This individual has the ultimate responsibility for marketing, planning, directions and budgets. In a smaller firm, this person acts as marketing director. Add a marketing coordinator. In many firms the marketing support personnel have dual roles in both marketing and clerical areas. The support staff provides typing, computer graphic design, writing/editing and public relations support for the marketing department. The marketing coordinator's focus should be on proposal production and development of marketing materials — slides, project sheets, client data base, SF254/255. Significant computer skills are a must. If there is a desire to grow the firm, this person should be capable of forward thinking — having the skills necessary to develop marketing systems capable of absorbing growth and to manage a more sophisticated level of communications.

Growing Firms
25 to 49 Employees

Team definition: This firm is beginning to bring in some larger projects and, as it approaches 49 people, the team can handle almost any size project. Two or three partners are involved in active business development, with a second tier of inside support to manage the work. Marketing needs become more sophisticated, so a two-year business and marketing plan should be developed. As public relations and sales needs increase, the marketing staff must become more diversified.

Recommended staffing: Hire a small sales team composed of a marketing manager with a marketing assistant. The marketing manager should be capable of hiring and supervising additional staff, as needed. He or she should have the ability to see the big picture, think strategically and have the maturity to represent the firm in the outside world. The marketing manager can be a decision-maker. The marketing manager is not often found in smaller firms. In larger firms, he or she will report to the marketing principal. The marketing assistant should be part-time for a company closer to 25 people, full-time with a staff count hovering near 49.

Larger Firm
50 to 99 Employees

Team definition: A firm of this size begins to require a more structured marketing effort. A principal in charge of marketing should be designated. And, if the firm is closer to 99 people, a marketing committee should be established. With as many as eight principals involved in business development, a smaller committee, charged with "go, no go" decisions, is necessary.

Recommended staffing: Your marketing department's role is to devise and direct the program to reach your firm's goals, as stated in your marketing plan. This is a team effort, and the role of building the marketing team falls to the marketing director. He or she has the responsibility of training staff members to be successful in the marketing effort so that company goals will be achieved.

So where do you find a marketing person to fit the bill? The quality of person you are able to attract to your marketing group will be directly proportional to your firm's belief in and support of that position. Remember, everyone is part of the marketing operation; no one can sustain it alone.
Evaluate what resources your company already has internally. Do you have a principal who will act as marketing director to create and lead the program?

These firms require a marketing director, marketing coordinator and marketing assistant. The marketing director will have overall responsibility for the firm's marketing effort, will report directly to the principal in charge of marketing, and be capable of strategic planning and thinking. He or she will need to be familiar with the full gamut of marketing tools — sales, public relations, proposal writing and material requirements, advertising techniques and communications. This person will definitely spend a certain percentage of time outside the office cultivating potential clients. The director typically makes the "go, no go" decisions. In the smaller firm, this is the marketing principal. He or she is responsible for planning, implementing and evaluating the marketing effort. When involving all staff members in marketing, the marketing director should evaluate each staff member to determine each person's marketing strengths and weaknesses and determine where each staff member will be most productive and effective in the overall marketing plan.

The marketing coordinator will coordinate proposals, presentations, and print media and work together with the marketing director and the marketing support staff. The coordinator maintains marketing materials. This person reports to the marketing manager, director or marketing principal, depending on the size of the firm. And the marketing assistant should be full-time if the firm has about 100 employees and part-time if the firm is closer to 50 employees.

The marketing assistant will support the marketing department with clerical work, collate proposals and qualification brochures, print presentation materials, keep current all marketing support materials and assist where needed.

Diverse Firms — Specific Market Niches
100 to 149 Employees

Team definition: A partner in charge of marketing is a must, as is a marketing committee. This firm has begun to focus on market sectors, with studios or groups dedicated to specific market niches. This firm most likely has in-house departments that have begun to market themselves independently — for example, interiors, planning, landscape, civil, telecommunications, lighting — requiring attention to consistency in pricing, promotion, production, profit strategies and expectations. If it hasn't already done so, this is also a firm discussing establishing branch or regional offices.

Regarding the principal in charge of marketing: At a minimum, one partner should be actively and completely developing business with a firm-wide, corporate focus. This partner is the firm's "goodwill ambassador," entrenched in the marketplace, whether national or international, and seen frequently — on panels, doing speaking engagements, participating in community events, publishing articles.

In addition, there should be at least three "market sector" leaders, each charged with business development for a specific market niche and held accountable for his or her segment's profit and/or losses.

Recommended staffing: You'll need a full staff with a marketing director, business-development coordinator, communications coordinator and a marketing assistant. The marketing director, working closely with the partner in charge of marketing and the marketing committee, will develop, implement and oversee the marketing, communications and business-development goals. Reporting to the director will be a business-development coordinator responsible for proposals as well as project, client, lead and data management. Also necessary at this level, reporting to the director, is a communications coordinator. Responsibilities for this person would include public relations, brochures, photography, printed project material, graphics and other similar duties. And, supporting the department would be a marketing assistant, again, part-time if this is a 100-person firm and full-time if the firm is closer to 149 employees.

Full-Service Firms
150+ Employees

Team definition: This firm is a major force in both the national and international marketplace. It has at least two partners in a full-time business development role and at least four market segment leaders. It has adequate second- and third-tier support to produce work and service the client without chiseling into marketing time. It has branch or regional operations and, if not publicly owned, probably has a diversified ownership.

Recommended staffing: A full-service firm requires a full-task marketing team: marketing director, business-development coordinator, communications coordinator and a marketing assistant. This staff is essentially the same as for a firm of 100 to 149 employees. This works because there will be additional people in the branch offices carrying out regional marketing functions.

It may be necessary, however, to add a vice president of marketing. This position will have intense strategic planning and oversight responsibilities — supervising the sales staff, developing the short- and long-term plans for the company, acting in a principal role and serving as a key decision-maker for the firm.

Don't Forget the Rules

Rule 1: Hire top down. First the chief and then the tribe. Hiring the top position first, then building a synergistic support staff is of utmost importance as you delineate marketing and business-development responsibilities among your professional staff.

Hire "closer-doers" before "doer-closers." Hire a marketing manager before a marketing assistant. You will be far more productive by getting the best top talent you can afford and then growing into the second-tier staff.

Rule 2: Stick with the plan. If the Closer-Doer Model says a firm of your size should have two to three closer-doers, two to three second- and third-tier doer-closers, a marketing manager and a marketing assistant, don't try to get by with doer-closers and a marketing assistant. It won't work.

So this isn't a perfect world, and marketing isn't a perfect science. Marketing is an investment in the future. The marketing staff members are key players in the firm's ultimate success. Proper staffing leads to a healthy, synergistic team of marketers who sell and designers who create. The Closer-Doer Model is designed to guide your organizational structure and to encourage thoughtful planning. Remaining flexible under fluctuating, ever-changing market conditions is the ultimate challenge to success — and, with some structure to guide you, this flexibility can be key to your firm's survival and growth.

Amy Ostigny, CPSM

- Amy Ostigny has more than 13 years' experience in marketing professional services.
- Ostigny currently serves as president of the Commercial Real Estate Women (CREW) of Greater Cincinnati Chapter's board of directors.
- She served two terms as president for the Society for Marketing Professional Services (SMPS), Ohio Valley Chapter.
- She is president of the Alumni Governing Board for the University of Cincinnati's College of Design, Architecture, Art & Planning.
- Ostigny serves on the Leadership Council for the Children's Hospital Medical Center of Cincinnati.
- She is an alumna of Leadership Northern Kentucky.
- She holds a bachelor's degree in design from the University of Cincinnati's College of Design, Architecture, Art & Planning.
- She received her certification as Certified Professional Services Marketer (CPSM) from the SMPS.
- She is a lecturer and published author.

Acknowledgment

Special thanks to Ellen Jackson who authored the original chapter on marketing personnel for the first edition of *The Handbook for Marketing Professional Services.*

5.2   Staff Development: Creating Rainmakers

Ford Harding
President
Harding & Co.

Managers of professional firms know the problem. They encourage their people to become rainmakers, but after a few limp efforts to bring in business, most give up. Those who run the firm are likely to conclude that rainmakers are born and not made. They, too, give up, give up on their efforts to teach people to make rain. Earlier in our lives, the founders of our firm all faced situations when giving up was not an option. Survival meant bringing in business and helping others learn how to do it. Those experiences lead us to study why many professionals are so quick to give up their efforts to bring in business and what to do about it.

Curiously, few are defeated by the market, which would reward them if they kept at selling. They just stop trying. Why? Certainly not because they are fools or wimps. To the contrary, most are smart people and tough enough to push themselves and others to the limit to satisfy a client. Nor is it because they are hopelessly unskilled. A few may be, but others who have solid interpersonal skills and may even have received sales training give up just as quickly. Why? If we can figure that out, we may be able to do something very hard to do; we may be able to *create* rainmakers.

The Valley of Death

My firm's research shows that giving up usually results from a misfit between the way professionals manage projects and the way sales grow. Most professionals see the relationship between hours worked on a project and results as linear (see Figure 1). Three hours of effort should produce three hours of results. Young professionals learn early to work hard and so avoid a conversation with a project manager that begins, "You've spent a week on this, and I don't see a week's worth of result."

Figure 1

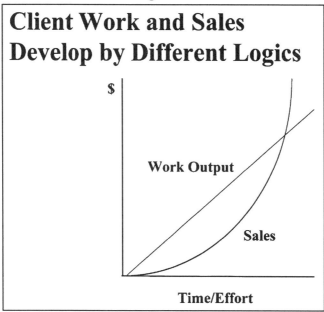

Client Work and Sales Develop by Different Logics

Source: Harding & Co.

When a professional begins to develop business, he or she approaches the effort with the same mentality: an hour's effort should produce an hour of result. But client development doesn't work that way. Instead, it grows much the way a steady annual investment grows at a fixed interest rate. At first there is little, if any, result from the time spent. Later, small results may come, but they seem minuscule and a scant return on all the effort invested. During this period, seasoned project managers who aspire to be rainmakers may even see their performance decline in other areas. They may, for example, manage fewer projects because they are diverting time to client development. This deeply discouraging period is the "Valley of Death" from which few professionals emerge as rainmakers. Most rededicate themselves to those activities in which they perceive they get a higher return on the time they invest, e.g., project work.

Firm management often contributes to this problem by pressuring professionals to bring in business when there is an urgent need, but tolerating inattention to business development when times are good. This reinforces the impression that business-development efforts are expected to bring in work quickly, and that results will come even if effort is turned on and off periodically. That simply isn't the way it works.

Somehow, true rainmakers have learned that client development requires long-term and continuous effort. Kenneth Diehl of Smith Seckman Read Inc. in Nashville, Tenn., remembers being told early in his career that it takes one to three years to develop a relationship that will bring in business. Over the years he has found this to be true. Norman Kurtz, founder of Flack + Kurtz of New York, describes an even longer development cycle that many rainmakers have benefited from. He says, "In your 20s, 30s and 40s you have to develop a lot of relationships with people you work with. Some will make it big and some won't, but by the time you are older, some can give you work."

He offered this example: "There was a guy in here earlier today who had been with a large architectural firm. I had worked on a project with him in 1980. He was laid off there many years ago, and I tried to help him get another job. We had lunch and talked. Now he turns up at a client who has a problem and so he comes to me. The relationship is already there, and it's based on respect and confidence."

The Sales Success Cycle

The few professionals who persist at client development, as these two rainmakers did, learn that success grows geometrically. A slow start is natural and is often followed by small success that leads to sudden and substantial sales growth. Our challenge is to get professionals through the Valley of Death to the stage where success feeds itself. Once there, professionals enter the Sales Success Cycle shown in Figure 2. Success builds self-confidence, which gives them the self-motivation to work through the many small setbacks inevitable in selling until they succeed again. Once in the cycle, few ever leave it.

Figure 2

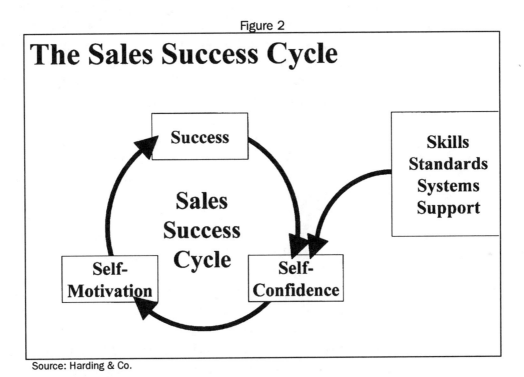

Source: Harding & Co.

Professionals can enter the cycle at any point. Our database of rainmakers has examples of people entering at each of the three points on the cycle. A few have early, lucky success that convinces them they can bring in business. Shortly after taking her first job, one of the people we interviewed went to a party at a neighbor's. There she met the head of a local college who hired her firm. After that, she just kept selling.

Others seem to have always enjoyed the self-confidence that carries them through the early stages of client development when results are slim. As Ron Schmidt, founder of the New Jersey architectural firm of Ronald Schmidt & Associates, says, "I've been influenced by positive-thinking people all my life. Marketing is about attitude. When you read books about great salespeople, it's all about attitude. They never give up. You have to put the fear aside and go ahead."

Still others enter the cycle because they are suddenly motivated to do so. One civil engineer told us this story: "I started my own firm when one client at the firm I had been working for told me he would give me all his business. A week later he died. I had a wife, kids and a mortgage. That's how I became a marketer."

How You Can Help

The management of a professional firm must help its people enter the Sales Success Cycle at one of these three points. We recommend a four-part intervention process that gives professionals *skills, standards, systems* and *support*.

Skills: Your professionals will need skills to succeed at selling. Above all else, they need good questioning skills. Most have a mistaken belief that selling equals talking. They feel that they must tell a prospective client about past projects and about the firm's ability to solve problems. Left to their own devices, many will talk themselves right out of winning a project. Sales training will help build better habits. If your people are likely to give presentations, training in that area is also valuable. This is where most firms begin and end their efforts to create rainmakers.

But skills training alone will not see your people through; the slow rate at which business first develops doesn't result from an absence of skills. It is a natural phenomenon that the accomplished project manager understands neither logically nor emotionally. Here are some additional tools you can use to help your aspiring rainmakers through the Valley of Death.

Standards: The sense of failure that professionals in the Valley of Death feel results from applying project management standards to client development where they cause great harm. So, for example, it is so unusual to call an active client six times and not receive a return call that it would be reasonable for a project manager to feel concerned should this occur. But if you call a former client to whom you haven't spoken for several years, it can take many calls to get through. These are different situations requiring different reactions. When developing business there are many such small judgments that will be in error if they are made on the basis of standards developed managing projects. Cumulatively, they will discourage an aspiring rainmaker and increase the chances that he or she will give up.

There are several things you can do to recalibrate professionals' expectations, including:

- Emphasize building relationships that will foster new business throughout a career rather than focusing on sales now. Professionals are often reluctant to make calls because they believe that the people they know won't react favorably to a sales call. Usually, they're right. As Leonard Koven, a founder of Atkinson Koven Feinberg LLP of New York, says, "If you want people to call you, call them first. I don't just call to get business. I call people when there is no project at stake, just to say hello, see how things are going and talk about friends we have in common." Develop good relationships with buyers and people who will give you referrals and work will follow.

- Help your aspiring rainmakers develop the appropriate discipline. Specific disciplines include meeting new people, making calls and having meetings with people they already know. A true rainmaker will make a minimum of 25 calls a week to develop relationships and pursue business. This number is far out of reach of most of your people; many will find it difficult to draw up a list of 25 people to call even once. In such cases, they need to meet more people. There are opportunities all around them on the projects they work. There are owners, developers, engineers and architects, real estate brokers and others.

- At one firm we know, young professionals are expected to collect five new business cards a month. This will add roughly 50 people to their contact lists each year, of whom five are likely to be keepers. The professionals are then asked to make periodic calls to the people whose cards they have collected. By the time a professional has been with the firm for five years, he or she will have relationships with 25 true players in the marketplace and additional relationships with others who may be helpful.

Systems: Our interviews with more than 100 rainmakers show that virtually all maintain the call and meeting discipline required to bring in business by working a system. The system dictates what they need to do at any given time and holds their feet to the fire. Give most professionals 15 minutes to do some marketing and most will use up the time just figuring out what to do. Give 15 minutes to a rainmaker and he or she will know just what to do because the system dictates what calls need to be made or letters written.

The exact nature of the systems varies from rainmaker to rainmaker, but all work a system. A system is a dynamically linked set of processes. A generic diagram of a rain-making system is shown in Figure 3. Boxes represent processes and arrows the linkages between processes. Both are important.

Figure 3

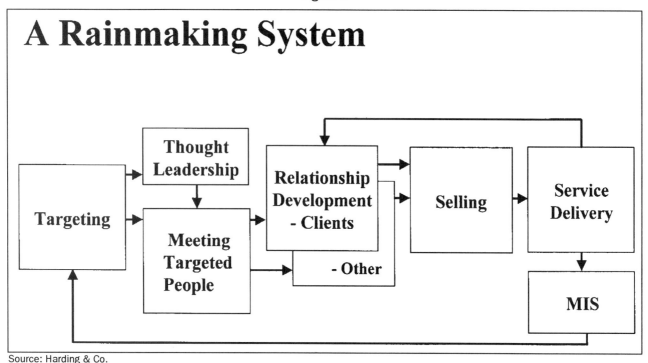

A Rainmaking System

Source: Harding & Co.

Usually the processes for meeting people and developing relationships drive the rest of the system. Elements in these processes often include:

- Call and meeting quotas. Rainmakers are always on the phone and out meeting people because they understand the most basic rule of selling; you will never sell anything unless you talk to people.

- Contact tracking, the development of which has been greatly eased by the emergence of contact management software.

- Processes for meeting new people to add to the contact base. Examples include actively participating in professional associations, running seminars, working for charities and participating in formal networking groups.

Judy Nitsch, founder of Judith Nitsch Engineering Inc. of Boston, built her system around working with professional associations. This is how she describes her approach to business development:

"I have built much of my business through relationships developed by working with colleagues in professional organizations. I have been a member of the Society for Marketing Professional Services, the Boston Society of Civil Engineers, American Consulting Engineers Council and New England Women in Real Estate. I picked these organizations because the members include prospective clients and other worthwhile contacts.

"When I join a group, I volunteer to work in it actively. That way, I get to work with the other members. It is good to get to know them as people, and they are more likely to give or refer work to you if they have seen you in action in an association. If you are competent at volunteer work, they know you will be conscientious as a paid consultant.

"I always try to have association meetings in our offices to show that my firm is real and substantial. We make sure that our offices look good for those meetings. People who come say, "I didn't know you had so many people," and "You have better computers than we have." That makes an impression, and as a result, it helps some of them become clients. Association work gives me the chance to meet people, it helps me get to know them, and it helps structure my marketing efforts so that I stay in touch and stay visible."

Every rainmaker has a different system, but each has one. Helping each of your would-be rainmakers develop a system that works for him or her is a key part of the staff development effort.

At a firm level, you also need to make sure that your compensation system is aligned to the client development behaviors you want to encourage. During the first year that aspiring rainmakers work at client development, cash incentives may not be appropriate, but there are other things you can do, including providing them a modest budget for client development or praising actions that will lead to work later.

Management should also make sure that the marketing organization runs smoothly in support of the professionals' client-development efforts. The professionals need to be able to get out letters and other marketing documents efficiently. They need to be able to invite their contacts to firm marketing events.

Support: Compared to project management, client development is an emotional roller coaster. The uncertainty of turning an initial contact into a client can give a professional a feeling of complete loss of control, and professionals, like most people, like to feel in control of their own fates. Cheering them when they win and helping them see loss as simply a necessary step to winning that same client at some future time are critical management responsibilities. More subtly, a principal showing interest and enthusiasm for the project manager's client-development efforts week in and week out — even when the principal is busy and distracted by other things — will contribute to the manager's success. With some people, good-natured nagging may also help.

Emotional support is a critical part of the mentoring required to create rainmakers. This support is particularly important while professionals are in the Valley of Death and see little return on their marketing efforts. Many of the rainmakers in the survey commented on how important support was to their success. Both A. Eugene Kohn, founder of Kohn Pedersen Fox Associates PC, and Tom Bathgate, one of the owners of PWI Engineering, remember the support they received from the architect, Vincent Kling, a highly dramatic and successful rainmaker, early in their careers.

Much hinges on the development of rainmakers: your success in the next downturn; the sustainability of your profits when an aging rainmaker retires; and your ability to build new practices and open new offices. In some cases, the very survival of the firm is contingent on the rainmaker's success. We all need to pay more attention to helping aspiring rainmakers cross the Valley of Death.

Ford Harding

- Ford Harding is author of *Creating Rainmakers: The Manager's Guide to Training Professionals to Attract New Clients* (Adams Media, 1998) and *Rain Making: The Professional's Guide to Attracting New Clients* (Adams Media, 1994).
- Based in Maplewood, N.J., his firm, Harding & Co., consults to professional firms on marketing and sales with a focus on helping professionals make the transition from managing and doing client work to selling it.
- Harding has consulted to professional firms in 12 countries.
- He speaks frequently on the marketing of professional services to such groups as the Society for Marketing Professional Services, American Consulting Engineers Council, ASFE and many others.
- Prior to founding Harding & Co., Harding served as director of marketing at a large architectural firm. He is an alumnus of Harvard and Northwestern University's J. L. Kellogg Graduate School of Management.

Acknowledgment

Special thanks to Lou Marines who authored the original chapter about staff development for the first edition of *The Handbook for Marketing Professional Services.*

5.3 Balancing Marketing and Operations

Jean R. Valence, FSMPS
Vice President
Blackridge Ltd.

Balance between marketing and operations. What does that mean?

On one side of the scale is the fact that marketing is anathema to most architects and engineers. It represents overhead. It costs even more in time than in hard cash. It requires inordinate amounts of smiling. And if anyone actually wanted anything to do with marketing, he or she wouldn't have gone to engineering or architectural school in the first place. On the other side of the scale is the fact that without marketing, technical professionals would starve. And in most firms the people who rise to the top are those with marketing skills. This is balance?

For purposes of discussion, we are better thinking in terms of coexistence that eventually evolves into synergy. We'll first consider ways that marketing people can encourage operations and technical staff to contribute their skills to the marketing effort. And then we'll look at ways that marketing professionals can help address management and operational issues.

Inspiring Operations and Technical Staff

Anyone who has been in the design and construction arena for very long has powerfully experienced the ramifications of at least one economic downturn. Although every new generation includes people who cannot really understand why the firm invests so much effort on marketing when there is too much work for current staff to handle, the great majority of staff support marketing and want business development to be taken seriously. Preferably by someone else.

Converting marketing observers into contributors requires a commitment to quality client service, a clear marketing plan, a variety of definable marketing activities and a program for relentless reinforcement. Staff members' willingness to contribute, and their ability to do so effectively, is directly proportionate to the degree to which their needs are met. Staff members need at least six things:

- Awareness of mission
- Information
- Skills
- Achievable goals
- Reinforcement
- Recognition

Awareness of mission. Staff members want to know where the firm is going and how it plans to get there, first in terms of product and quality, and then in terms of marketing. A page in the employee handbook, which they receive during orientation, promptly lose and then recover five minutes prior to departure, is not a powerful medium for presenting "big picture" goals.

Information. Staff want to know about billings, profitability, investments in technology and information systems, and recruitment plans. They want data about projects, and they want to capture knowledge gleaned on projects so it can be used to benefit future projects. They want this information to substantiate the firm's mission. In short, they want to feel as if they are integrally part of the firm that wants their help in developing business.

Skills. As John Kemper tactfully pointed out in this chapter originally: "Everyone is well aware that operations personnel are typically technically oriented and don't have the communications skills necessary to be effective in marketing. Firms must work to develop their technical staff into better communicators." If we ask them to support marketing, operations staff expect support. We need to provide training programs in networking, public speaking, correspondence, and proposal writing to introduce concepts and demonstrate the firm's internal marketing processes. We need to address e-mail and telephone protocols, as well as professionalism, confidentiality, attire and other sensitive matters.

Achievable goals. Telling staff to become active in professional associations, to react more effectively to opportunities for cross-selling, to provide project data quickly, and generally to get their marketing act together isn't helpful. Giving them direction is. Once our support systems, marketing information systems and training programs are in place, we must assign tasks and set deadlines.

Reinforcement. We must reinforce staff learning through active coaching and mentoring programs, marketing meetings, business development debriefs, as well as through internal media. We must present the project-delivery process as a marketing activity, linking client maintenance and constituent networking opportunities to the firm's mission and marketing plan.

> *Bringing it all together.* In preparation for its gala celebration of the firm's inclusion on the *Inc.* 500, Judith Nitsch Engineering Inc., a Boston civil engineering and surveying firm, closed its doors for three hours one morning and sent its entire office, including field crews, to be trained in "Painless Mingling." The program was designed expressly for JNEI so that staff would feel well-prepared for the quasi-socializing that typically reduces brilliant engineers to speechlessness. Everyone role-played and practiced. They received checklists and guidelines that suggested conversation-starters; reviewed specific, likely-to-be-asked questions; and learned skills that would not only help them the night of the gala, but also enhance their day-to-day interaction with clients and team members.
>
> According to Nitsch, "I knew my senior staff would be comfortable in a cocktail setting with clients. Our more junior staff and our field and CADD employees, however, would be uncomfortable — I knew they'd want to do a good job, but they don't get the opportunity to meet clients and to know what really is appropriate to say and do." Their training consultant suggested developing a list of questions that staff would likely have to field at the gala, and during the training session staff developed succinct, and accurate, answers to queries like "How did you make the *Inc.* 500?" "What's your backlog?"

"What's it like to work for a woman?" The day after JNEI's party, one field surveyor thanked Nitsch for the training, saying, "I was asked every single question on the list and I felt great knowing I could answer them appropriately."

Was training technical and administrative employees worth the investment? JNEI's estimate is that the hard costs for the session (trainer's fee, venue and food) plus the lost billings (three hours for all employees) probably equaled half the cost of the party itself. "However," says Nitsch, "clients were so impressed with our staff that the cost was incidental to the value received."

Technical and operations staff members appreciate efforts to ease their anxiety in marketing situations and are quick to see application of marketing techniques to the performance of their own jobs.

Recognition. Professionals are inspired by accomplishment and encouraged by praise. They require consistent, frequent feedback. They are motivated by the ability to grow professionally. One milestone on everyone's career path within the firm must be marketing.

Other chapters in this handbook offer guidelines and approaches to training and team building. Because professionals in our industries care deeply about producing quality work and are motivated by feedback on their performance to this end, we will look more closely at the performance-review process as a tool for spreading marketing commitment throughout the firm.

Reinforcing a Sense of Marketing Urgency: Performance Reviews

We need everyone in our firm to support and enhance the firm's marketing effort. All staff should be articulate about the firm's services and markets, and knowledgeable of new commissions. In addition, they must embrace the firm's core values, culture and distinguishing personality, which serve as our competitive edge in the marketplace.

Marketing Measures for the Entire Firm

When it comes to making a choice, technical staff will invariably focus on billable time rather than overhead, and administrative employees will channel their energies toward doing the work they were hired to do. One of the best ways to create a sense of urgency about our firm's universal marketing imperative is to ensure that the annual performance-review process reflects marketing criteria in every job description. At a minimum, generic criteria should include:

- Communication skills.
- Business etiquette.
- Sensitivity to client service.
- Ability to communicate the firm's services, general history and structure.
- Attendance at in-house marketing presentations and major project reviews.
- Demonstration of work values compatible with the firm's culture.

Communicating Criteria for Advancement

In most firms, expectations for marketing contributions increase as technical staff rises through the ranks. Barton Malow Co. is a $725 million design and construction-management company headquartered in Southfield, Mich. Aspiring project managers (PM) there are expected to complete a two-year rotation in business development, and all projects include an allocation of non-billable time to accommodate the marketing responsibilities of PMs and project superintendents. At Flansburgh Associates Inc., a 35-year old Boston architectural practice that has doubled in the last five years, the marketing imperative is clearly reflected in performance-review criteria for anyone who aspires to senior management. The evaluation form describes four management skill clusters (project management, professional development, project profitability and marketing effectiveness). Specific marketing activities are spelled out (see Figure 1).

Figure 1
Marketing Criteria

MARKETING EFFECTIVENESS	Performance					
	NA	1	2	3	4	5
New business initiatives						
Client maintenance						
Marketing group participation						
Participation in professional client associations						
Presentation and interviewing skills						
Proposal writing ability						
Form D completeness and accuracy						
Level of marketing effort						
Effectiveness of marketing effort						
Ability to represent the firm						
	1 = Unsatisfactory; 5 = Outstanding					

If you want to be a leader in this firm, you need to join client associations, contribute to new business development and client relationship-building, hone your presentation and communications skills, and religiously provide all data on completed projects to the marketing department via "Form D."

Assessing Marketing at the Top: Equal Expectations

At senior positions, firms typically raise the bar for marketing contributions. The relative importance of principal marketing performance, as compared to other operations responsibilities, tells us a lot about a firm's culture, as does the process for analyzing and rewarding principal achievement.

Among the most formulaic approaches we have seen is a two-phase model that first measures employees' job performance in a typical annual review process, and then assesses their contribution to each of four practice imperatives (see Figure 2). The former is used to determine salary, the second to establish individual bonuses.

For the bonus phase, the imperatives are defined as individual job performance, billability, contribution to firm operations and new business development. Imperatives are weighted, and bonuses distributed accordingly. The bonus formula reveals expectations for new business development for anyone serving in a project management or principal role. In this firm, business-development professionals fall into the "Project Manager" category, rather than "Department Manager," for bonus allocation.

Figure 2
Performance Areas

Performance Areas				
	Individual Job Performance	**New Business Development**	**Billability**	**Operations**
Principals/Executives	1/4	1/4	1/4	1/4
Department Managers	1/3		1/3	1/3
Project Managers	1/3	1/3	1/3	
Technical Support	1/2		1/2	
Administrative Support	1			

If we focus just on the senior staff level, then the relative weight of marketing in this firm's culture, specifically new business development, is powerful, valued at one-third of a project manager's contribution and one-quarter of a principal's. In other words, for a principal to receive full bonus, he or she must meet goals in all four imperatives (see Figure 3).

Figure 3
Principle Bonus Circle

Accommodating Individual Goals at the Top

In contrast, at Einhorne Yaffe Prescott, a 450-person architectural and engineering firm headquartered in Albany, N.Y., senior staff members' contributions are seen as skill sets, and reviewed in terms of individual performance rather than weighted by seniority or role. President Steve Einhorne explains, "We need so many different kinds of people with different skill sets to accomplish EYP's long-term goals, that our performance reviews and promotions must be individual-based."

EYP's principals and associates are evaluated in marketing terms, as well as in project/client management skills, technical skills, people skills and leadership. "We would not expect, or even want, people at the senior level to perform equally well in all areas. But everyone does need to be aware of, sensitive to, and supportive of all of these skill sets. By reviewing the performance of senior staff in each area, we increase their buy-in to the importance of each," states Einhorne.

At EYP, marketing is one of five cultural attributes that senior staff are expected to support actively and to demonstrate as individually appropriate (see Figure 4).

Figure 4
Skill Set Bubbles

A senior staff member's achievements in each set reflect personal and corporate goals established on an individual basis each year. In terms of marketing expectations, accomplishments can be cited in such areas as client feedback, client maintenance, relationship-building and new business development. The relative body of achievement in one skill set versus another is irrelevant. EYP actively encourages senior staff members to pursue their individual talents and interests.

No matter what the process is for evaluating individual performance in marketing and business development, it must be clear and measurable, and it must reflect the firm's values and strategic plan, even as it accommodates individual skills and goals. (See sidebar "Managing Business Development Fervor.")

Managing Business Development Fervor

As a firm grows, it can become vulnerable to each office's goal to serve a client's every need without interference. "No one is going to know this client better than we" is an acceptable attitude for the firm to adopt, and a counterproductive one for an individual studio or office to assume to the exclusion of its internal siblings. How can we avoid internal business development competition? Here's a start.

- Provide a substantive corporate marketing program that channels information, materials and services toward studios/offices and that reinforces the firm's full capabilities and track record.
- Assume that corporate marketing will invariably give more than it gets from individual profit centers.
- Support marketing and project cooperation through a relentlessly current data base that is useful and accessible to all staff.
- Demonstrate hands-on investment by corporate marketing in the success of local marketing initiatives. Go there to help work, not just to wield nickel-plated shovels.
- Encourage face-to-face exchange between offices, relying on e-mail and voice mail for time-sensitive information, rather than for creative thought, solution-generating or investigation.
- Participate in the design of the firm's professional development program, ensuring that the firm's cultural attributes and mission are reinforced in all programs, and that the corporate mission drives future leaders.
- Structure a senior bonus program that rewards cross-selling, strategic client development and support of corporate initiatives. Revise reward programs that incite internal competition and pit studio against studio, office against office.

Making the Time

Now that we have technical and administrative staff identifying goals and defining marketing tasks, all we need to do is give them the time to achieve them. For most technical staff, marketing efforts are woven into the project-delivery process. During project kickoff meetings, project managers spell out client issues related to service expectations, communication processes and relationship milestones. Close-out processes require final marketing information reports. Client debriefings address perceptions about the firm's technical performance and project-related administrative functions, such as invoicing procedures, voice mail system and information systems.

Operationally, marketing can also be invisible. Corporate processes, systems and formats should reflect universal sensitivity to marketing, so that staff support the effort unconsciously. Employee attitude surveys can reveal staff's awareness of, active involvement in, and responsibility for the marketing culture (see Figure 5).

Figure 5
Sample Questions from an Employee Attitude Survey

1	2	3	4	5	**Proposals and presentations receive appropriate attention from senior staff.**
1	2	3	4	5	**The first time I hear about a project is when we start work.**
1	2	3	4	5	**Marketing is a part of my day-to-day activity.**
1	2	3	4	5	**I am encouraged to take initiative in the performance of my job.**

1 = Strongly agree; 5 = strongly disagree.

Management's expectations for staff contribution to marketing is often most evident in the degree to which staff members understand how to assign marketing efforts on their timecards. Every employee should be informed of the number of hours he or she is expected to charge to specific sales activities and to general communications or marketing support. Employees must understand when their participation is to be assigned to marketing or to professional development or to client service. Staff deployment plans should reflect such assignments, and staffing projections should anticipate appropriate commitments. When marketing hours go unreported, not only is the integrity of the marketing budget at risk, but chances are the accurate allocation of billable hours to projects is also vulnerable.

Enriching Operations Through Marketing Expertise

We have been looking at how operations and technical staff contribute to the firm's marketing effectiveness; now we consider ways marketing should apply their skills to management and operational issues. Design and construction firms seldom enjoy deep administrative or marketing support, whether times are good or bad. Technical switch hitters increase their value to the firm in their ability to perform more roles and to tackle a greater variety of assignments, and so can marketers.

Marketing professionals, particularly those whose backgrounds do not include architectural or engineering degrees, learn about the business of design and construction so that we can understand the range of experiences that affect a client's attraction to, and satisfaction with, our firm. Business development requires that we understand the project-delivery process. Strategic marketing demands our attention to everything else.

Human Resources

An unofficial role filled by the marketer frequently is that of "corporate shrink," whose communication skills, ability to read people and desire to be useful attract people with issues. For most marketers, however, an interest in staff satisfaction is purposeful, fueled by the desire to keep good people and maintain quality of products and services, and flamed by frustration when any client fails to award us the next project.

Recruitment of top technical staff, particularly in a competitive environment, requires an astute marketing approach. Senior marketer Tim Barrick, vice president and principal of Ratio Architects Inc. in

Indianapolis, assisted in developing the firm's recruitment plan. As a task force member, Barrick reviewed the hiring plan in terms of Ratio's marketing plan and helped design a scholarship program aimed at recruiting young talent. He led research into potential institutions and created supporting media expressly attractive to young graduates.

Kate M. Brannelly, principal and treasurer of Flansburgh Associates Inc., spearheaded critical human resource initiatives long before she became a principal. She began by designing an orientation program for new employees and then directed an effort to develop a comprehensive employee handbook, updating and creating policies to address deficiencies. Brannelly's efforts to improve the experience of new employees encouraged her to investigate frustrations that current employees experienced. Before long, the firm had job descriptions for senior technical staff, as well as for administrative and operations personnel, and was adopting an integrated system for performance evaluation. "In all of these cases," Brannelly emphasizes, "I was filling a serious gap in Flansburgh's practices and responding to a compelling need. Otherwise I would not have invested time away from marketing."

Project Delivery

Not surprisingly, star marketers command respect among operations and technical staff long before they become principal candidates, some by contributing billable services to projects. Brannelly is not an architect, but shortly after joining Flansburgh she extended her marketing expertise to the development of a new service to attract public sector clients. As a way to maintain the firm's leadership position in the hot New England school market, Brannelly sold, and then filled, the role of community relations manager, helping municipalities to educate voters about issues affecting their school projects and to muster local support at the polls.

Similarly, Sheryl Maibach, FSMPS, Barton Malow's vice president of marketing, evolved from providing bond issue campaign management services on the construction manager's public sector projects, to stepping into the project executive role at the clients' request. She and her marketing staff now regularly contribute to projects through client satisfaction management, project web site development, owner progress reporting newsletters and project community outreach programs. As Maibach points out, "Understanding firm operations is essential for marketers. How can we sell benefits, if we don't understand the process and the value our services bring to a client? First-hand project experience helps me do a better job coaching young marketing managers, and I have a stronger voice at the executive table with other company officers."

Troubleshooting

Sometimes marketing attributes of tenacity, targeting and talk combine to solve critical operational issues.

In 1989 Mike Savage was a new marketer at Jerry Kovacs & Associates Inc., a Los Angeles geotechnical engineering firm. The Southern California economy was shaky and everyone was on reduced wages when Savage learned about the situation in accounts receivable. "People weren't paying, and it was money out of our pockets, and" he admits, "I took it personally." Determining that the firm would benefit more at that moment from collecting money already earned than from chasing new work, Savage volunteered to pursue some overdue accounts.

One potential bad debt problem was a developer. "I realized that my first step was to get him to take my call in the first place," explains Savage. "Basically I was selling people on the idea that they should pay us." In an effective approach that Savage points out both tapped and fed his ability to communicate with clients, he addressed the developer, and others like him, with tact and respect, demonstrated compassion for the client's situation and proposed a solution, often a simple payment schedule. Savage was successfully conducting relationship marketing in the trenches, and sometimes in court.

Shaping the Practice

Once in a while exceptional marketers earn the opportunity to make exceptional contributions to their firms. Sylvia Wheeler is senior vice president of Boston-based Haley & Aldrich Inc., a national provider of underground engineering and environmental services. Initially attracted to the firm by its commitment to applying strategic thinking to everyday management, Sylvia contributed to the firm's direction-setting by helping key leaders "listen to the marketplace, understand it and make a match with their own motivations."

Wheeler participates in operational activities in support of training, performance review systems, operational restructuring, and merger/acquisitions assessment and implementation, observing that "each of these roles has been more or less directly tied to the core function of strategic positioning — making needed operational changes to meet our long-term strategic plan."

More recently, as part of H&A's re-engineering activities, Wheeler has contributed to a particularly powerful initiative. Spearheading a new Coaching for Performance program, she and her team have crafted a system and supporting processes to stimulate individual excellence through coaching techniques and team support. "In a mature firm, leadership is always shared," explains Wheeler. "Strong leaders at the top are still part of a legacy that has been sustained by their predecessors." That view, and her strategic marketing perspective, pervades H&A's emerging team-based culture.

Contribution Versus Cost

The attitude that contributors like Barrick, Brannelly, Maibach, Savage and Wheeler apply to other areas of professional practice is often as powerful as their professional skills. Non-technical marketers who effectively extend their reach share common attributes. They are energized by "the chase," by substantial challenge. And they are accustomed to targeted and efficient pursuit. They want to examine an issue, identify an effective solution, craft necessary systems, and donate the finished product to the appropriate managers for implementation and fine-tuning. Their priority is to enrich the practice, enhance client satisfaction and increase employee retention.

Marketers' ability to communicate, organize and work to self-imposed deadlines often help map a path through operational jungles. Sensitivity to image and the ability to make a convincing case, particularly in other people's terms, also benefit corporate causes.

The primary risk inherent in applying marketing skills to operational matters is potential depletion of marketing resources. Our challenge is to extend the marketing contribution, rather than to deplete it.

Before allowing ourselves to be lured into other business roles, marketers must ensure that our primary value to the firm is not undercut. (See sidebar "Reality Check.")

Reality Check

Does it really make sense for you, as a marketing professional, to rise to this particular extra-marketing challenge? Each individual affirmative response brings you closer to a resounding "Yes!"

1. Is this an *ad hoc* assignment that I can complete within a reasonable time frame?
2. Is this a project that will require my initial involvement, but be able to be shared with, or delegated to, someone else for maintenance?
3. Is this assignment critical to either client satisfaction or employee satisfaction?
4. Will the successful completion of the assignment enhance the firm's effectiveness in developing or maintaining clients?
5. Can I meet all of my marketing responsibilities at the same time I am tackling this assignment?
6. Can I ensure that my involvement will not unduly burden someone else in the firm?
7. Is this activity in the firm's best interest rather than in my own?
8. Am I willing to undertake this assignment without expectation of a raise, additional staff or praise?
9. Is my involvement fully endorsed by the person currently responsible for this business practice?

Summary

In a professional services firm, marketing and operations exist in synergy. Administrative and technical employees are encouraged to contribute their skills to the marketing effort, and marketing professionals channel some of their skills to address management issues.

In order to earn the attention and involvement of technical and administrative staff in marketing efforts, the firm must evidence a commitment to quality client service, a clear marketing plan, a variety of definable marketing activities and a program for relentless reinforcement. Staff members' willingness to contribute, and their ability to do so effectively, is directly proportionate to the degree to which their needs are met. Staff members need to be aware of the firm's mission. They need access to relevant information. They must be trained in applicable skills. Achievable goals must be set to measure staff members' effectiveness. Staff's performance must be reinforced along the way and recognized upon successful completion of assignments.

One way to set goals and recognize performance is to build them into the annual performance-review process, increasing expectations to reflect career paths. Generic criteria pertaining to all employees might address communication skills, sensitivity to client service, attendance at marketing functions, as well as compatibility with the firm's values. As staff aspire to leadership positions, expectations for marketing contribution increase, often opening the door to more substantial roles with heightened recognition and financial rewards.

Time must be earmarked for the performance of marketing functions by administrative and technical staff. The project-delivery process offers substantial opportunity for people to contribute to client maintenance effectively and economically. Corporate management processes, systems and formats should also reflect universal sensitivity to marketing. Employees' timecards must reflect their efforts in specific sales activities, general communications and/or marketing support. Staffing budgets should reflect the extent of the firm's marketing imperative.

Just as technical and administrative employees increase their value to the firm by contributing to marketing, so do marketers provide greater service to the firm by lending a hand to operations and administration. Human resource and project-delivery initiatives benefit greatly from the communications and organizational skills of marketing professionals. An individual's unique abilities can be mustered to address such *ad hoc* problems as receivables or such powerful opportunities as strategic re-engineering. As long as peak marketing performance is maintained, marketing staff members can share their skills with other business areas to the benefit of all.

Jean R. Valence, FSMPS

- Jean R. Valence, FSMPS, is vice president of Blackridge, Ltd., management and marketing consultants in Wellesley, Mass.
- Former principal of Drummey Rosane Anderson Inc., architects and planners in Newton Centre, Mass.
- One of the first marketing professionals in the United States to achieve principal status without benefit of technical training or family connection.
- Was principal-in-charge of private sector projects and responsible for DRA's marketing and business development program, interior design services and project profitability oversight.
- Joined Blackridge in 1992. Assists design firm owners and builders in ownership and management transition planning, staff development programming and business development effectiveness.
- Spearheads Blackridge's survey services, which benchmark client satisfaction, market position and employee attitudes.
- Former SMPS national treasurer and regional director, a founder and past president of the Boston chapter, and inaugural recipient of SMPS Boston's *Professional Achievement Award*.
- Served on many SMPS juries, including the national Marketing Achievement Award and the Fellows Recognition Program.
- Member of the board of directors of the Boston Architectural Center, a frequent speaker at AIA conventions and a national contributor to the AIA Continuing Education System.

Acknowledgment

Special thanks to John E. Kemper who authored the original chapter about balancing marketing and operations for the first edition of *The Handbook for Marketing Professional Services*.

5.4 Internal Marketing: Keeping Your Firm Motivated

Randle Pollock, FSMPS
Regional Director
Carlson

The most enduring, successful firms in the design and construction industry share at least five traits:

1. They retain the majority of their existing clients — serving them on many projects over many years.
2. They implement effective strategies to capture new clients and develop new sources of revenue.
3. They know how to deliver profitable work.
4. They plan their work and work their plans.
5. They market "internally" — to their employees — because they know that their valued "internal clients" are vital to their future.

Indeed, internal marketing has emerged as a key quality of truly great firms. To them, internal marketing is smart business. They integrate it into the culture of the firm. They do not subscribe to the silly, old-fashioned notion that only principals or marketers have the responsibility to secure work that feeds the firm.

Still, for all the thousands of firms in the American design and construction industry, internal marketing is among the least practiced activities, the one most overlooked, the one usually eclipsed by the obsessive, feverish pursuit of new clients and the servicing of existing ones. But internal marketing, not unlike outer space, represents the last frontier for professional services firms. Having perfected their client capture strategies, having figured out how to keep clients satisfied, the greatest firms of the new millennium will be defined by those that market internally — and make it an art. They will focus time and resources on such "internal markets" as the technical staff, executives and senior managers, and non-technical support staff as well.

What Is Internal Marketing?

As defined in *Principles of Marketing*, internal marketing is what service firms do to train and motivate client-contact employees and support staff to work as a team to provide client satisfaction.[1]

In short, internal marketing focuses on the people *inside* a firm. It fosters training and motivation of employees — principally those with client contact, but support employees as well. It requires leadership, direction, planning and constant attention. Its sole focus is inside a firm, toward the people who perform the work. It is as central to a firm's survival as is external marketing, which is focused on the people *outside* a firm — clients, prospects, referral sources, consultants, vendors and suppliers.

Why Do It?

There are at least three salient reasons to market internally.

One is trite, but all too true: We are what we sell. In professional services firms especially, marketing is truly everyone's business. It shapes what the firm is and what it will be. Marketing distinguishes professional services firms — those providing accounting, architecture, construction, construction management, engineering, graphic design, interior design, landscape architecture, law, program management and search/recruiting services — from every other type of business.

At Gensler, the international design firm, for example, every one of its 1,800 employees is considered part of the firm's "marketing organization." Says the firm's founder, chairman and CEO, M. Arthur Gensler Jr., FAIA, RIBA: "Our marketing organization is comprised of the 1,800 people in our firm, and it includes everyone from administrative assistants to partners. ... Everyone at Gensler carries a business card and is expected to help us find and service customers through their contacts, friends, and relationships. It is the responsibility of all to nurture clients. We have to do it."

Perhaps the chief reason marketing is everybody's business, believes Charles B. Thomsen, FAIA, author of *Managing Brainpower* and chairman of 3D/International, "is that our reputation is our most valuable asset. And everybody in the company contributes to that reputation."

Another reason to market internally is to retain good employees. They are increasingly hard to find in the highly skilled technical and professional fields of the design and construction industry. Evidence shows that shortages of skilled talent are projected for many decades. The cost of finding and training new employees is increasing. The loss of corporate "memory" and the associated disruptions when people leave one firm to join another are daunting.

These signs and others combine to incentivize firms to develop ways to do everything they can to retain existing employees, who expect a lot from their jobs today. Beyond improved compensation and benefits, they want to improve or expand their skills. They want a career road map, a compelling future, enabling them to prosper and do stimulating work. They desire a sense of belonging and contributing to a team, to a firm that rewards and recognizes their efforts.

"We found out a long time ago," says Harvey K. Hammond Jr., P.E., chairman and CEO of HNTB, "that people in our industry want to be successful, they want to enjoy what they're doing, and given direction, they'll do it."

To retain employees in the 21st century, firms will need to do much more to enhance their appeal. Of all that can be done, one activity they can do is internal marketing. Not only does it offer a high return on investment, it makes good sense.

A third reason to market internally is that having an external focus alone, no matter how targeted or creative it may be, is not enough to survive in today's marketplace. Marketing must be central to the firm's culture, rather than merely something that is done exclusively by firm principals or the marketing staff. According to a study by the International Association of Business Communicators Research Foundation, such a culture must be truly participative, with two-way communication systems that allow information to flow down and up. Marketing is a continuous process, a constant effort that focuses externally on clients and internally on the people with client contact and those who support them.

Let's look now at what can be done and who should be involved in internal marketing.

Marketers Are the Catalysts

Leading the effort to develop internal markets are marketing professionals, their various roles outlined in detail in SMPS's *Career Ladder Guide for Professional Service Marketers.* These roles range from marketing principals, directors and managers to marketing coordinators, assistants and specialists. External business developers, as well as the corporate communications or public relations staff, may also contribute to the internal marketing program.

While the focus of their roles will vary from internal to external markets, marketers — whatever their specific responsibility — function primarily as catalysts. They make things happen. They generate results. They orchestrate the effort to secure external as well as internal clients. They lead the efforts to train and motivate their in-house colleagues to work as a team.

Marketers play many positions on a firm's marketing team, alternating as coaches, quarterbacks, cheerleaders or support. Their responsibilities can range just as widely. As William L. Peel Jr., chief administrative officer of the Metro National Corp. real-estate company and a former design firm executive, puts it: "Marketers get their strokes from the firm's collective successes. They build other people's reputations in support of the firm's overall strategic goals. Rarely in the limelight, they focus the spotlights and flip all the switches."

Marketers are catalysts in developing both external and internal markets. Three typical internal markets include:

- Technical staff.
- Executive and senior managers.
- Non-technical support staff.

Implementation Strategies

Technical Staff (Discipline Leaders to Junior Staff)

The pre-eminent internal market in a professional services firm is composed of the technical project staff, involving those who actually perform the work and charge as much as 100 percent of their time to a client's project. Since the majority of work is (or should be) derived from past or existing clients — an estimated 70 to 90 percent, in fact — a firm's fortunes rise or fall on the quality of its technical staff.

Technical staff members play an essential marketing function that is the underpinning of a successful firm. Once a client has been contracted and its project work begins, technical staff members have the most direct, frequent and continuous exposure to clients. Of all staff, technical staff members carry the biggest responsibility for furthering the firm's business. Good work must be delivered. Clients must be satisfied and expectations met. As intermediary between client and firm, the technical staff members must deliver outstanding service that will maintain business and engender future project opportunities with clients confident about the firm's work.

At Harely Ellis, architects, engineers and planners in Southfield, Mich., for example, the firm's associates are required to report on a chapter from SMPS's *The Handbook for Marketing Professional Services* or other publications at monthly meetings in order to create an awareness among technical staff that "marketing is everybody's job." R. Craig Rutherford, the firm's marketing director, explains that this also "acknowledges that they are expected to participate, and gives them an active role."

In truth, technical staff people function as "client account managers," responsible for maintaining and advancing valuable client relationships. This is their most important role. Since the firm is now part of a client's life cycle, it is up to the technical staff member to maintain the life cycle and minimize (if not eliminate) future competition.

Client account managers, says veteran public relations consultant Joan Capelin, FMP, PRSA, of Capelin Communications, "understand what will make a client happy but, even more significantly, what a client's worse fears are."

She encourages internal marketing that is expressly tailored to technical staff on a project team. Writing in *DesignIntelligence*, she recommends that specific information be shared with project staff, such as:

- The project's mission, so far as the client is concerned.
- The reason the job was sought.
- The reason the assignment came to the firm.
- What was promised to the clients, and why?
- What definition of success pertains?
- Whether a public project has special requirements.[2]

More generally, internal marketing focuses on the technical staff by providing special training, information and motivation in specific areas that need improvement. Those areas may include:

- Presentations.
- Verbal communications.
- Non-verbal communications such as posture and gestures.
- Technical or proposal writing.
- Negotiating or conflict resolution.
- Project initiation and maintenance.
- Client contact.
- Leadership development.

- Motivation.
- Time management.
- Team building.
- Listening.
- Personal image and attire.

Executives and Senior Management (Principals, Owners, Senior Officers)

An equally important internal market comprises the firm's executives and senior managers, the group ultimately responsible for hiring, firing, building and maintaining business. Whether they make the initial cold call, close a deal at the culmination of the client capture effort, negotiate the contract or go on to participate in the execution of the project, they are crucial targets of internal marketing.

Here's why: They set the tone. They lead by doing. They set strategy and lead in the implementation phase, hopefully in an atmosphere of mutual trust and respect. They empower others to realize their dreams and ambitions. Personifying the firm's values and credibility, executive and senior managers foster a corporate culture that is strong and creative enough for internal marketing to take root and thrive. They nurture an environment in which everyone wants to contribute to its success.

There is one essential condition to any successful internal marketing initiative, however. It is that without a top firm executive who demonstrates that it is a priority, internal marketing is doomed to failure.

W. Bruce Lea III, corporate marketing director for Gilbane Building Co. and a former SMPS national president, agrees: "If the top executive is not involved, if they do not demonstrate that participation in marketing and business development is a prerequisite for both advancement in the firm and better compensation, and if they don't make sales and marketing the first agenda item on any meeting of principals, no matter what you do, you will get a short-term result that will eventually stall and fail — much like pushing a rope.

"The marketer's job is to provide the tools, training and internal communication for all that's being accomplished. Its the CEO's job to provide the motivation — through behavior and policy, as well as words — for the long term."

James J. Moynihan, AIA, the president and CEO of Heery International, a group of professional practices specializing in architecture, engineering, construction management and program management, based in Atlanta, Ga., is one who practices what he preaches. He actively participates in "Heery University," an ongoing training program, involving both local and regional staff from the firm's 30 offices as well as other executives.

The point is that without the right leadership, internal marketing will not succeed. With the right leadership, with executive buy-in and support, it will flourish and take root deep in the culture of a firm.

Internal marketing focuses on executives and senior managers by engaging them to ensure that current work yields future work, and that the full resources of the firm are positioned to work effectively on behalf of its external markets. Those areas typically include:

- Closing strategies.
- Leadership development.
- Negotiating or conflict resolution.
- Contracts and legal administration.
- Effective communications.
- Consensus building.
- Motivation.
- Time management.

Non-technical Support Staff (Administrative, Clerical, Resources Personnel)

A third key internal market in professional services firms is the non-technical support staff — those who *support* the firm's work (the administrative, clerical, financial and human resources groups) and typically do not charge their time to a client's project. They play a critical, necessary function that varies in impact from role to role as shown in the following examples.

- The receptionist has the first crucial contact with clients, prospects and visitors.
- The project secretary facilitates communication between the project team and clients.
- The human resources representative works for the team's overall well-being.
- And, the office manager keeps everything running smoothly.

Non-technical support staff members contribute to a firm's future by keeping the executives and technical professionals they support satisfied, and by ensuring a smooth operation. Non-technical support staff people also can contribute to a firm's success through direct and indirect exposure to clients, vendors, referral sources, prospects and visitors.

Van Dijk Pace Westlake Architects, a 100-person firm with offices in Cleveland, Ohio, and Phoenix, Ariz., for example, holds bi-weekly, all-staff meetings at which key projects are reviewed and discussed. This has proven to be a good way to keep everyone "in the loop," and educates all levels of staff about the firm's efforts on many fronts.

Internal marketing focuses on non-technical staff by providing special training, information and motivation in specific areas that need improvement. Those areas may include:

- Performance and productivity.
- Computer operations.
- Database development and management.
- Telephone etiquette.
- Interpersonal communications.
- Working as a team.
- Health and safety.
- Vendor/supplier relationships.
- Benefits management.
- Personal image and attire.

Some Great Internal Marketing Techniques

The best firms in the design and construction industry execute some kind of an internal marketing program. Each one does it differently, in its own way and at its own pace. They do it because they believe in it. They know the benefits. They have observed the positive advantages it brings to each employee and thus to the firm as a whole. In such firms, internal marketing has helped mobilize a collective team effort to grow the business of the firm.

Below are other highlights of how some notable firms keep their staff motivated, trained, informed, recognized and rewarded through some exceptional internal marketing efforts.

DPR Construction, a large general contractor with 11 offices, headquartered in Redwood City, Calif.:

- Provides 120 hours of "training events" every year for each employee.
- Hires training directors for each of its 11 regional offices.
- Operates a "Continuous Improvement Program" that functions as a laboratory, involving people who have an idea of how to do something in a better way, that studies a process, develops an implementation plan and follows through on execution.

Gensler, an international architecture, interiors and planning firm with 1,800 employees and 13 offices, headquartered in San Francisco, Calif.:

- Incentivizes employees by awarding bonuses twice a year. One is generally based on individual performance, the other on the performance of the specific office and the overall firm. To personalize the occasion, a letter accompanies each bonus check from Art Gensler and/or a meeting with the office's managing principal.
- Conducts weekly conference calls among all offices.
- Produces an Internet newsletter every two weeks.
- Sends a monthly newsletter to all employees.
- Publishes an annual report for clients that are also sent to employees at their homes.

G2 Architecture (now Mulvanny G2), a 25-person architecture firm in Seattle, Wash.:

- Sponsors an annual "Soaring Eagle Award" program — with a cash award of $10,000 recognizing one employee who most closely reflects the firm's values.
- Hands out bonuses ranging from 20 to 100 percent of salary.
- Closes the firm the week between Christmas and New Year's.
- Blasts the musical theme for *Miami Vice* through the office every time a new project is won.

Hart Crowser Inc., environmental and geotechnical engineers with 10 offices, based in Seattle, WA:

- Publishes an internal monthly e-mail newsletter titled "Wins & Wows" that recaps project wins and the strategies that won them.
- Announces all big project wins "real time" via e-mail to everyone in the entire firm.
- Conducts internal seminars called "Hart Crowser Marketing 101" that educates staff about marketing and builds credibility for the marketing staff.

- Holds numerous contests that reward staff for good marketing practices, such as soliciting and obtaining letters of recommendation from clients. Those who succeed in obtaining letters are rewarded with "HC Bucks" (akin to Monopoly money), that can be used in the "HC Store" to purchase items like baseball or symphony tickets, movie passes or dinner for two.

Hellmuth, Obata & Kassabaum (HOK), an A/E with 24 offices worldwide, based in St. Louis, MO:

- Empowers employees to "bring his or her best, and the best in the firm, to each client," according to president and CEO Jerry Sincoff, FAIA.

HNTB Inc., an architecture, planning and engineering company with 45 offices, based in Kansas City, MO:

- Individualizes a "career development planning process" for each employee that is tied to the firm's overall strategic plan.
- Conducts an ongoing training program called "common denominators for success" that emphasizes best practices, so everyone in the firm will know what they are.

Van Dijk Pace Westlake Architects, a 100-person firm with offices in Cleveland, OH, and Phoenix, AZ:

- Publishes a weekly newsletter that posts each new commission and key initiatives in business development.

Action Items to M.O.T.I.V.A.T.E. Your Firm

1. **M**obilize teams or groups to identify specific ways they will participate in marketing programs. Monitor efforts. Provide leadership, direction. Identify rewards.
2. **O**rchestrate training programs for those needing improvement or skill development.
3. **T**ell about the firm's success, and which individuals helped, over and over and over again. There's no such thing as too much recognition.
4. **I**nform everyone of the firm's overall marketing plan and objectives, and their individual roles in achieving them. Set goals for the firm, the department or division, and individual staff members.
5. **V**erbalize praise publicly and give recognition often.
6. **A**cknowledge staff accomplishments for outstanding performance. Reward those who meet extraordinary goals.
7. **T**ake time to celebrate! Make an occasion of winning a project. Ring the bells; blast the music! Have fun with your colleagues. Spread the glory and share the riches.
8. **E**mpower employees to take risks, make mistakes, act independently, help obtain work, develop solid client relationships and contribute to the success of the firm.

Summary

Internal marketing focuses on the people *inside* a firm. A continuous, participative process, it fosters training and motivation of employees — principally those with client contact, but support employees as well. It requires leadership, direction, planning and constant focus. Its sole focus is inside a firm, targeted to the people who perform the work — mobilizing their energies and motivating their pursuit of shared goals — and shared rewards.

Endnotes

[1] Philip Kotler and Gary Armstrong, *Principles of Marketing*, 5th ed. (Englewood Cliffs, N.J.: Prentice Hall, 1991).

[2] Joan Capelin, "Internal Marketing," *DesignIntelligence*. (Reston, VA: Design Futures Council, June 16, 1997): 1-4.

Bibliography

Capelin, Joan. "Internal Marketing" *DesignIntelligence*. Reston, Va.: Design Futures Council (June 16, 1997): 1-4.

Career Ladder Guide for Professional Services Marketers. Alexandria, VA: Society for Marketing Professional Services, 1991.

Connor, Richard A., Jr., and Jeffrey P. Davidson. *Marketing Your Consulting and Professional Services*. New York: John Wiley & Sons, 1985.

"Excellence in Public Relations and Communications." International Association of Business Communicators Research Foundation, unpublished, quoted in *Carlson Voyager,* Pace Communications, Inc., Greensboro, N.C. (May-June 1993): 30-31.

"Flying with Eagles," interview series with firm executives published in the SMPS *Marketer*. Society for Marketing Professional Services, Alexandria, VA. April 1998, Dec. 1998, Feb. 1999, April 1999, Aug. 1999.

Kotler, Philip, and Gary Armstrong. *Principles of Marketing*. 5th ed. Englewood Cliffs, N.J.: Prentice Hall, 1991.

Thomsen, Charles B. *Managing Brainpower*. Washington, D.C.: American Institute of Architects Press, 1989.

For more on the subject of employee motivation and morale building, check out these web sites:

www.meaningatwork.com — by Tom Terez, a human relations consultant who spent two years studying employee morale through focus groups, interviews and other research. He gives 22 keys to help companies boost morale and producivity.

www.nelson-motivation.com — by Bob Nelson, a motivation consultant who writes widely on the subject of motivation and is the author of "1001 Ways to Reward Employees and 1001 Ways to Energize Employees."

www.workforceonline.com/research — *Workforce* magazine, which focuses on everything from motivational techniques to case histories.

Randle Pollock, FSMPS

Randle Pollock, FSMPS, is a regional director for Carlson, the leading single-source provider of consulting, design and implementation services for mission-critical facilities, with 11 offices nationwide. He has more than 20 years' experience in marketing and business development for some of the largest and most prestigious firms in the design and construction industry.

A former director on the National SMPS Board and past president of SMPS Houston, he gained a graduate degree and early training in architecture. Since 1998, he has been editor of the SMPS *Marketer*.

Certified an SMPS Fellow, he can be reached by telephone at 972-250-3972 or by e-mail at **rpollock@carlsonsolutions.com**.

5.5 Measuring Marketing Success

John Coyne, FSMPS, APR
President
Coyne Associates, Marketing and Public Relations Consultants

There is more to measuring the success of a firm's marketing effort than just looking at the numbers. Equally important is to:

- regularly gauge the attitude of management and staff toward the marketing program and their participation in the program
- evaluate the degree that the marketing program leads and guides the firm toward desired goals
- measure the efforts of staff people fixed with marketing responsibility—both management and business responsibilities

Following are some questions to ask and some ideas to consider when you are measuring how well your firm's marketing program is working. We'll look at key intangible factors that impact the marketing effort.

PART I: Evaluating the Program

A. What does our marketing program include?

The first order of business is to determine if you and your associates have the same understanding of what marketing is. There are basically eight ingredients to marketing (see Figure 1 on the next page):

1. planning
2. market research
3. strategy setting
4. selling
5. public relations
6. sales tools
7. advertising
8. monitoring or evaluation.

Marketing, a term often misunderstood, is not just sales. Sales is one function of marketing. If an A/E/C firm truly understands the marketing function, then it will recognize that the eight steps from planning through evaluation make up a program. The first three set directions for the firm and are necessary to make the selling efforts meaningful. The strategy step brings together the planning and research efforts to form the marketing plan. Any selling that follows is then according to the plan. The support functions of public relations, sales tools (brochures, proposals, and so on), and advertising then become more effective because of the direction established. The final element of marketing (evaluation or monitoring) is an important ongoing management function. Does your firm's program include all or just some of these elements?

Figure 1
The Eight Steps to Marketing

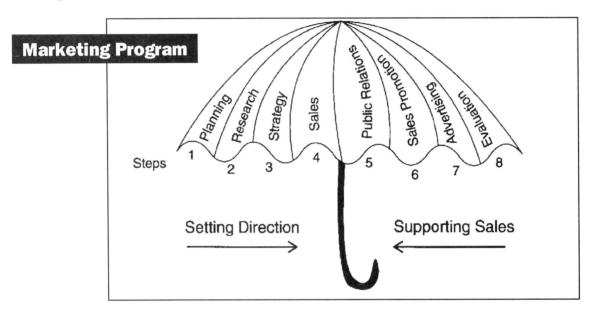

B. *Has marketing been adopted by our firm as a near-term, stop-gap measure or is it considered a positive, long-term, integral part of the firm's operation?*

If by chance your firm's marketing is not going well, then it's important to ask this question. By all means, avoid fingerpointing inside the firm. It's too easy to fault management for failure of the marketing program, just as it is too easy to blame the marketing people for falling short of goals. When evaluating your effort, look at the obvious things such as sales figures, number of leads, effectiveness of presentation (interviews or brochures), but also consider deeper questions. Determine if the following are operating inside your firm.

1. Do you measure on a continuing basis what the principals expect from your marketing program? Are their desires written down?
2. Has your firm made a commitment to have marketing be a serious, all-out, continuing discipline, recognizing that it takes time and constant work to develop an effective program--that it takes time to find and qualify leads for new work?
3. Is your principal-in-charge-of-marketing or the marketing director doing the defined job? Is this person keeping management and staff informed on prospects and how the firm is doing in getting new work?

C. *Are we achieving the desired level of firm growth? Are our marketing goals and strategies being met?*

The answers to these questions directly influence whether your marketing program is highly aggressive or low key, far flung or localized, centralized or decentralized, expensive or low-cost, and so on. For example, if your firm's goal is to double in size and billings or volume in five years, then the program to lead the way for such growth will likely be high powered and the marketing principal/director to head it will most likely be very knowledgeable and experienced in marketing. On the other hand, if your firm desires to hold to present size (staff and billings) and operate in existing territory, then (depending on the economy and competition) your existing program and staff may be adequate. You need to continually assess firm position against marketing plan.

D. Are our expectations of marketing reasonable?

A common downfall of A/E/C firms is to expect dramatic increases in new work right after they hire marketing directors and business development people. Going hand-in-hand with this is the fallacy of looking at the marketing director as a one-man/woman band, the "super salesperson" who is going to bring in all the work. In fact, it takes time to put an effective marketing program in place--and it takes time to instill a "we" attitude within the firm for getting new work where management, designated staff, and marketing people are involved in a team selling effort. For a new marketing program or marketing director to show significant results, it can take one to one-and-a-half years.

I caution A/E/C firm management: When new marketing programs or marketing directors are in the works, be wary of changing directors or willy-nilly changing a well-thought-out marketing program at about the six- to eight-month mark of implementation. I call this time frame the "patience factor" that frequently tests firm management. How does your firm stack up on expectations?

E. How have we positioned the marketing function within the firm?

Marketing should be positioned in importance along with production and finance. However, all too often, marketing programs and people have to take a back seat to these functions. Certainly architects and engineers need to design and bill their work and contractors need to build and bill their work to make money and profits. Let's not forget that you have to get (sell) the work to design or build it.

Management personnel who are too production-oriented often do not adequately support the marketing effort — e.g., they are not available to help sell when needed — and do not have a proper regard for the marketing function or its people. Firms that realize they need a balance of three elements to be successful — good production, financial systems, and marketing — are generally successful and know why they are successful. These also are the firms that, because they appreciate the value of the marketing program, create career opportunities for their contributing marketing people as well as for their technical personnel. Has your firm properly positioned marketing inside the firm? Do you have a good balance of disciplines?

PART II: Measuring Progress

Coming to grips with how the firm's marketing is doing requires an objective look at specific measurable topics. This evaluation starts inside the firm and is termed an internal marketing audit.

This audit tells us what we're doing right and wrong, and how well we're doing against strategic plan, sales, and market/project type mix goals. The audit most often is conducted:

1. when beginning the process of developing a new or updated marketing plan
2. when new management or principals are appointed
3. when there is serious concern about the effectiveness of the marketing effort.

The key benefit of the audit is that it helps us gather known, not assumed, data about our firm's marketing to make informed decisions which form the basis of marketing strategy.

The internal marketing audit takes the form of 10 steps whereby a series of questions are asked of your firm's management and staff. Here are some of the questions to ask and areas to study.

Step 1. *Determine fees sold for the past two fiscal years.* Net contract fees or revenue actually placed under contract and authorized *after payouts to consultants or subcontractors.* Do not confuse this with gross billings.

Step 2. *Determine fees earned (for contractors — net margin) for the past two fiscal years.* If you can't get two years get one. It is important to deal with real, not guessed, firm numbers. Then compare fees earned (same as net billings) against "fees earned per technical" using design or construction industry standards to gauge levels, pricing of services, and profit yield.

Step 3. *Determine net backlog for two fiscal years.* Net backlog equals fees or potential revenue ready to be earned, unencumbered by projects on hold or receivables. At the beginning of these two years, was backlog rising, even, or was our firm working off but not replacing backlog?

Step 4. *Analyze fees sold, fees earned, and backlog for two years (information gathered thus far in Steps 1, 2 and 3).* Did fees earned outdistance fees sold or vice versa? How dependent was the firm on specific project types and public- or private-sector market segments?

Step 5. *Determine from net backlog weeks/months of work.* Do not confuse this with production scheduling. You want to assess the level of backlog starting with the past two years to see if the firm generally had 6, 8, 12 or whatever months of work. Again, this tells you how long the firm could figuratively operate (comfort level) if no new work came in. Was this a healthy level or a thin, near-term level? How thin or narrow the level will help dictate how aggressive your marketing program should be.

Step 6. *Analyze the past client list and project new client penetration.* Which clients represent true repeat business and how much? Group on a map geographic clusters of clients. Where are they? How far do you have to go to get to clients? What cost and time are involved to get to them? Look at the frequency of client contact. Consider degree of provincialism or territory (past and future). Evaluate selection process and buying influence by project/market type (past and contemplated).

Step 7. *Review the quality and credibility of firm services.* Is the quality level of services high, slipping, and so on in the eyes of client and staff? Is the firm creatively and technologically "with it"? Is the firm's fee range competitive and realistic? If the firm is to diversify services, are you credible in new fields?

Step 8. *Evaluate the current and recent sales effort.* How many jobs on an average are you selling (number of leads)? What's your success ratio by project type, geography, and size? How many presentations/interviews/proposals did you generate last year? What's the success rate? Which individuals within the firm were most involved in marketing and most successful in sales effort (jobs sold, average number of leads, proposals, interviews, complete qualifying data gathered, most cooperative, team players)? What is your marketing leadership level? Is marketing management leading or following, alert, aggressive, informed? Does your marketing management keep you informed, research new fields, develop strategy, and so on?

Step 9. *Analyze public relations/brochure/proposal support to marketing.* Are the desired firm image and follow-through consistent and timely? Are materials effective/competitive? What's needed? Can you standardize? What do you spend on promotional materials and proposals as a percentage of sales cost? What is the success rate for the firm and compared to the industry? What adjustments are needed? What public relations, advertising, newsletter mix is required?

Step 10. *Review the marketing/communications budget for the past two fiscal years.* Are you spending enough or not enough in the right places? Does the budget include enough factors —time of staff, salaries, benefits, public relations media and promotion materials, travel, telephone, office space and expense for marketing, marketing membership/seminars — all costs related to marketing and public relations?

It costs most A/E/C firms a significant amount of money to market services just as it costs other businesses to sell products or services. Therefore, it's best to face up to, and manage, this cost. Frequently, A/E/C firms fail to count all of what should be counted as marketing, therefore they undershoot what's needed or professional egos come into play. For example, "It only costs us 5 percent, 3 percent, 2 percent of fees because we're so good clients beat a path to our door." Ergo, we don't have to spend much on marketing. Usually, they are spending and don't know it. They are paying for hidden costs such as unrecorded principal and staff time. I suggest as a guideline that you compare the total costs of your marketing budget (counting everything noted earlier) against the following:

Number of staff	Percent of firm net billings/margin
0-20	20-25%
25-75	15-18%
75-150	10-12%
Over 200	7-9%

Construction marketing budgets average two to three percent below these levels.

Summary

We have covered a number of subject areas that need to be assessed internally: Questions must be raised and answers received in order to measure marketing success. This process is key to assessing and improving the marketing effort. Regularly practiced, this process helps to:

- verify findings within the firm
- foster informed decisions on sales goals, marketing mix, and marketing strategy
- raise the credibility of the marketing discipline within the firm
- promote a management/staff "we" attitude toward the need to market as a team.

Bibliography

Coyne, John. "How to Effectively Put Your Marketing Program to Work," *SMPS News* (October 1985).

— . "Marketing Plans," *A/E Marketing Journal* (August 1986).

— . "Sales and Marketing Are Not the Same," *Civil Engineering News* (December 1994).

— . "The Marketing Audit—A Key Step to Evaluating Your Marketing Program." Speech at 1993 SMPS Region III Conference; St. Louis, MO, April 1993.

John Coyne, FSMPS, APR

John Coyne is president of Coyne Associates, a nationally-recognized marketing and public relations consulting firm specializing in assisting architects, engineers, and contractor/developer firms. Prior to forming his firm in 1975, he served as vice president of marketing and public relations for Ellerbe Architects/Engineers/Planners (pre-Ellerbe Becket), during which time the firm grew from Number 23 to Number 9 on *Engineering News Record*'s list of architecture/engineering firms. Coyne is a charter member of SMPS, an accredited counselor of the Public Relations Society of America, and a frequent speaker on professional services marketing at national conferences and chapters of SMPS, AIA, ACEC, AGC, NECA, and ASPE. He is also a frequent author and served five years as the marketing columnist for the University of Wisconsin's quarterly *Building Newsletter*.

5.6   Financial Information for Marketers

Dennis A. Paoletti, CPSM, FAIA
President
Paoletti Associates Inc.

Introduction

Just a few years ago, marketers had little interest or desire in knowing much about the financial side of a firm's business. Marketing was typically seen as a separate, independent discipline from business. A good marketer could turn up leads, research potential clients and help bring in (sometimes single-handedly) new business. The Society for Marketing Professional Services (SMPS) reworded its purpose to recognize that marketing involved more than just bringing in new business. It introduced the concept that the marketer should be aware of business and finance by bringing in projects that are profitable.

Why should a marketer be concerned with whether or not a potential project will be profitable? Isn't this the job of the technical staff, project managers and principals? At the outset, it may seem like marketing and finance are two distinct and separate disciplines, but in fact they are not. In well-run, cohesive and profitable firms, marketing and finance should be inseparable. Producing a profitable project may be heavily dependent on how good a project the marketer uncovers; how financially solid the client is (check the Dun & Bradstreet rating); how real the project is (does it have funding?); and is the client willing to pay a reasonable fee in a timely manner for services rendered (check with other firms that have worked for the client)? The marketer can be instrumental in helping to answer these questions.

Although it is possible for an excellent marketer to climb the corporate ladder to become a principal, that person becomes a lot more valuable to a firm, and has many more options for personal growth, if he or she understands the business and finance side of a firm.

Review of financial information should be approached with a common-sense attitude. Financial information should be clear and understandable. Do not be afraid to ask questions regarding financial statements. A question often leads to a healthy discussion and leaves you better informed.

Let's take a look at some basic business concepts and financial information that could be valuable to any marketer.

For some, the thought of reading and/or understanding financial statements may seem as complicated as understanding the detailed inner working of a personal computer or an automobile. Think of it this way: We probably all drive automobiles and operate computers. We can have varying levels of knowledge about how they operate and the principles behind them. As a marketer, you too can and should understand the basics of business and finance. The level of personal understanding you undertake is up to you.

Reasons for marketers to expand their knowledge of financial principles are:

- *International work.* As we expand toward a global economy, there will be emerging opportunities that require a successful marketer to feel comfortable, not only in the business aspects of a local or regional economy, but also in dealing with foreign businesses for which currency, operations and business approaches are different from what he or she is used to.

- *Company resource.* A marketer can be a more valuable resource to a firm's principals and management team if he or she can direct responsibility for the firm's profitability.

- *Personal growth and advancement.* Showing direct financial results (profitability) from one's activities is a strong motivator when one's performance is evaluated and when opportunities arise for advancement in a firm.

- *Training and education.* Learning financial business principles can help to prevent burnout by expanding one's perspective and developing new levels of interest, knowledge and talent.

- *Increased success.* The more understanding a marketer has of the firm's financial condition, for example, backlog, history of trends and paying clients, the more effective he or she will be in assessing which projects and clients to pursue. Without this kind of information a marketer might continue to market an area that has historically been unprofitable for the firm.

Marketers have some unique talents and personality traits that enable them to function and perform well in the business/financial community, without having to be a "bean counter." First of all, they know what's happening in the business world. In researching leads and potential business opportunities they can uncover new trends. They have the potential to meet and talk with lots of business people and know how to ask questions. By the time a marketer passes a potential client to the proposal writers and technical staff, they probably know more about that prospective company than anyone else. The marketer could stay more involved with the client during the duration of a project. Remember, in a professional services organization, people really buy people — not firms or services. There are a number of logical and beneficial tasks that marketers can perform to stay in touch with the client, and to help ensure that a project is satisfactory and profitable, which brings out the next unique characteristic of marketers — their people skills. Keeping in contact with the client seems only natural for the marketer who made the original contact. Maintaining client relations is the maintenance that leads to the next project.

Project Management

Most marketing philosophy assumes that the technical staff is responsible for a project once it's in the office. This is a situation, however, where the potential profits from a project can evaporate. Marketers can be very helpful during this time. They should re-emerge — not disappear. It would be beneficial for a marketer to know a few simple facts and critical issues about a project.

- What is the basic scope of the project?
- What is the anticipated value of the contract?
- What type of contract is it?
- What are the key schedule/performance dates?
- Who are the key players for the client and your firm?

An occasional friendly call from the marketer to the client emphasizes the firm's sincere interest in maintaining client contact. This contact determines if the client is happy with the firm's service. Some carefully asked questions such as "How are we doing?" or "Is everything going OK with the project?" will probably quickly uncover any aspect of the project that needs attention. The information a client transmits to a marketer (assumed to be remote from the daily personalities involved in the project) could be very valuable to the project team and the firm's management.

Client relations need to be sold in-house and should be a team effort initiated by the marketer. The project manager should understand how the marketer can help keep the client happy and the project profitable.

Business Management

This is the area where most people would expect to discuss financial information. Financial information, however, is really only one part of an overall business continuum that should include marketing, business strategy, project management and accounting.

A firm's financial statement describes the financial condition of the company, including its profit or loss information. Before getting involved in the details of financial statements, there are a few rules of thumb in the form of ratios that are used by most professional services firms to get a quick picture of certain business parameters. Our industry has compiled statistics using these ratios, which are relatively easy and straightforward to understand. Marketers should grasp the concepts associated with these ratios.

Charge Multiplier

The ratio of an employer's bill-out rate to its payroll rate is the charge multiplier. If someone is charged out at $70 per hour and paid a salary of $20 per hour, the charge multiplier is 3.5. It is not uncommon to leverage various charge multipliers in a firm, using lower multipliers for higher-paid staff (principals) and higher multipliers for lower-paid staff (production staff). A typical average rule of thumb for a charge multiplier is 3.0.

Net Multiplier

The net multiplier is the ratio of net revenues (generated by in-house labor only, without reimbursable expenses) to total direct labor (raw labor salary only, without any fringe benefits). If a firm's net revenues are $2.8 million and its total direct labor expense charged to projects is $800,000, the net multiplier would be 3.50. This multiplier is what the firm actually achieved and is a measure of efficiency.

Overhead Multiplier

The overhead multiplier is the ratio of overhead costs (operating expenses not assigned to projects, including indirect salaries) to total direct labor. If a firm's overhead costs are $1.28 million and its total direct labor is $800,000, the ratio would be 1.60 or 160 percent. This number can vary significantly depending on many factors particular to the firm. Values in the range of 125 to 175 percent, however, are common in the building services industry.

Staff Utilization Ratio

The staff utilization ratio is the ratio of a firm's total direct labor to its total labor (all salaries including fringe benefits). This factor depicts how chargeable the company is and is related to the net effective multiplier. If a firm's direct labor is $800,00 and its total labor is $1.23 million, the ratio would be 65 percent. The industry standard is somewhere in the range of 60 to 65 percent.

Current Ratio

The current ratio is the ratio of the firm's current assets (for example, cash, accounts receivable, unbilled services, notes receivable, prepaid expenses) to its current liabilities (for example, accounts payable, advanced billings in excess of revenue, short-term notes payable, payroll, payroll taxes). If a firm has current assets of $1.04 million and current liabilities of $300,000, the ratio is 3.47. Current assets should exceed current liabilities by a ratio of at least 2-to-1.

Net-Profit Ratio

The net-profit ratio is the ratio of net profit (income minus expenses) to net revenues. Depending on how one's firm is structured, the net-profit ratio or percentage can vary depending on one's definition of revenue. It can be based on net (before) or total (after) revenues. Pass-through items such as consultants and other reimbursable expenses, distribution of profit, bonus and other discretionary items may be included or excluded. A firm's profit can vary — but let's all agree — it should be a positive number.

Accounts Receivable Collections

The average receivable collections is the average number of days it takes to collect from clients for services (from the date of billing to the date of collection). First it is necessary to determine the average day's sales by dividing 365 (days in a year) into the annual total revenues; then divide the average accounts receivable by the average day's sales. Sixty to 65 days is common in our industry for accounts-receivable collections. This descriptor affects cash flow. The longer it takes to collect moneys due from invoices, the more interest a firm must pay to cover the moneys it had to borrow to pay for the work already performed.

Financial Statements

Financial statements generally include a balance sheet and a profit/loss or revenue/expense statement. In compiling these documents, there is a considerable amount of variation, but mostly in relative details.

There is a "generally accepted accounting principle" (GAAP) approach that outlines the procedure and format for preparing accounting information. Taken in its most basic form, marketers should realize that for A/E/C firms, income (or revenue) is generated almost exclusively by charging time to projects and collecting payments for the fees generated. Expenses include all costs a firm expends in the process of doing business. Some costs are reimbursed by a client/project. Profit (i.e., revenues minus expense) can be distributed by firm management as it sees fit. Bigger project budgets (or bigger proposals) don't necessarily mean more profit, especially if the projects are not managed properly. Any means by which expenses can be reduced could have a positive impact on bottom-line profitability. Look for significant over or under amounts for income or expense categories, and request clarification.

International Projects

When considering the pursuit of international assignments, marketers should be aware of the political and economic risks of working on, and making profit on, such projects. The temptation is great to take on work overseas as many firms become "global" in their vision and strategy. However, from the financial perspective, overseas work can represent a very different set of guidelines, rules and legal requirements.

It is obvious that foreign countries have different currencies. What needs to be realized is that the exchange rate for each country's currency can fluctuate greatly and frequently. Likewise, political risks can include general turmoil and changes of government (also on short notice). A marketer could keep abreast of a country's financial and/or economic stability via some basic research on the Internet, the U.S. Department of Commerce, or a number of magazines, newspapers, etc. (e.g., the *Financial Times*, the *Economist*). The U.S. Department of Commerce maintains extensive data bases of every foreign country. This information is available for free most often, and accessible via designated university or Department of Commerce computer networks.

Contracts and legal documents for work overseas can be very complicated — and difficult to enforce. This is an area for experts in the legal profession. Consult an adviser.

How and when will moneys transfer should be realized. Obtaining retainers and letters of credit via home banks is desirable before starting any work. Invoicing and payment schedules should be clearly worked out and agreed upon in writing though, in foreign countries, this will not guarantee payment. Legal recourse is not in your favor. Networking with other firms that may have had experience working in countries may prove to be invaluable.

The potential impact on the profitability and survival of the firm in a global environment may be dependent on the clarity and understanding a marketer may bring to the firm.

Tracking Backlog

Backlog is defined as the work (revenue) logged that has yet to be completed. Backlog can be tracked via client type, when the work needs to be performed and/or by dollars. Barring any unforeseen difficulty, a firm should be able to count on the revenue from this backlog in its long-term financial planning. It also will help to determine the potential human-resource requirements to perform the forthcoming work. A firm can use backlog to help plan for its future.

Decisions regarding potential growth can be supported by the amount of work a firm can be confident it has on the books. Tracking backlog should be done in conjunction with accounting, marketing and project-management staff. Work with accounting in compiling the financial information, the numbers, the forms and the charts. Develop meaningful data that can be tracked easily and presented. Number of proposals written, number of successful projects, priority and percent of proposals and projects is of value, as is the market sectors the work is coming from. Number of projects from new vs. existing or former clients is informative to track. It is a well-known fact that it costs less to market existing clients than it does to find new clients.

Work with project managers and principals to let them know what you are tracking and why. Make sure your co-workers are all heading in the same direction; and get their support and assistance. Your job will become easier as your associates work with you in tracking backlog.

Conclusion

A careful review each month of the financial statement of activity, in conjunction with a review of the program activities, should enable a marketer to know what's going on financially. By doing this, and by asking questions about anything not understood, a marketer can feel confident that he or she is contributing to the financial success of the firm.

Marketers can be extremely valuable personnel in professional services firms and can find their way to principal and management positions. Basic knowledge of business and accounting principals can help achieve career goals. Once involved in some of the business aspects of a firm's operations, marketers will clearly learn how comfortable they are dealing with the issues, personalities and nuances of the firm's operations. Understanding and helping to implement financial information in a firm can be beneficial to everyone: the marketer who will grow professionally, the technical staff who will appreciate the assistance of the marketer, and the firm's management who will realize a positive contribution to the firm's health and stability.

Using much of the financial information noted above, and the business knowledge the marketer has gained throughout his or her career, a marketer can be an asset to a firm, beyond chasing leads and bringing in work.

Bibliography

Dixon, Robert L. *The McGraw-Hill Thirty-Six Hour Accounting Course.* New York: McGraw-Hill, Inc. *Management of Accounting Practice Handbook,* American Institute of Certified Public Accountants.

Dennis A. Paoletti, CPSM, FAIA

- Dennis Paoletti is president and principal consultant in acoustics and audiovisual systems of Paoletti Associates Inc. in San Francisco.
- He directs his firm's overall strategic planning and marketing activities.
- Paoletti has served the SMPS organization as San Francisco Chapter secretary and president; and two terms as Pacific Northwest regional director and national board member.
- He is a Fellow of the American Institute of Architects.

5.7 Value Pricing: Don't Wait for Tomorrow!

Thomas E. Smith Jr., AICP, FSMPS
President
BonTerra Consulting

Profit margins in the A/E/C industry have traditionally been very low. While the value of design to the quality of urban life appears evident, the design sector has profited little from its efforts. In the 1998 *PSMJ Resources* survey of the financial performance of U.S. design firms, the median value of profit, before profit and distributions and taxes, was 8.9 percent of gross revenues. *PSMJ*'s 1990 survey yielded similar results, showing a 7.3 percent median value. [1,2] In comparison to the 10-year (1988-1998) total investor return of 17.6 percent achieved by the Fortune 500, profitability of the design industry, on the whole, lags behind.[3] The diversity of clientele, firm size, services offered and geographic location, however, suggest other factors are driving the profitability of our industry. Value pricing is an important solution to the profit pinch.

Value Pricing Defined

Value pricing, in its simplest form, is setting the price of a service based on its value to the client. In comparison to cost-based pricing, which focuses on how many hours (costs) it will take to complete an assignment, value-pricing techniques require more sophisticated pricing strategies.   Lump-sum, percentage-of-construction-cost and unit-pricing (for example, per sheet) contracts are examples of value pricing. Time and materials or hourly rate fees are examples of cost-based pricing.

Data from the *PSMJ Resources* Financial Performance reports suggest that cost-based pricing is a major culprit in the design industry's low profitability. Other service firms are beginning to use value pricing to improve their bottom lines. As competition increases and profits are squeezed further, the design industry needs to look harder at value-pricing techniques for survival. But don't jump on the value-pricing bandwagon without first ensuring that principals and project managers are trained in basic strategies that will facilitate successful implementation of this technique.

What Is Value?

Value can be an elusive idea; what is valuable to one client may not be to another. Factors that have typically provided value opportunities for design firms include: unusually shortened project schedules, use of rare or unique building materials, public controversy, complex agency regulatory and permitting processes, and also more subjective factors such as quality design, world-class building, use of emerging technologies or capturing market opportunities.

Marketers and the project managers of design firms must be constantly seeking ways to turn value opportunities into financial rewards. One element of value that all firms address each day is customer service. If you are creating value for the client in your technical work, but not meeting production schedules or not returning the client's calls on a timely basis, you are missing value opportunities. The proliferation of e-mail and the opening of the Internet have raised client expectations manyfold. Clients are demanding faster design (without loss of quality) and accelerated service delivery. The firms that will prosper in this environment have an excellent opportunity to use value pricing with their clients.

The widespread use of computers and the web in the design industry are also changing the rules for service delivery. The relationship with the client is becoming more important than ever; increased client communication is critical in such a fast-track environment. Peppers and Rogers, in *Enterprise One to One*, describe a process of relationship building with clients that can generate not only high levels of client loyalty, but also insulate firms from competition. This opportunity is realized through a dialogue they describe as "The Learning Relationship":

"A Learning Relationship between a customer and an enterprise gets smarter and smarter with every individual interaction, defining in ever more detail the customer's own individual needs and tastes. ...

"A Learning Relationship ensures that it is always in the customer's self-interest to remain with the firm that has developed the relationship to begin with ... making loyalty more convenient for the customer than nonloyalty." [4]

Relationship building can therefore provide another mechanism for firms to provide value and increase profitability.

Strategic Factors

To successfully implement a value-pricing program, you must first evaluate several factors intrinsic to your business. Consider the following factors described below to maximize your value-pricing benefits.

Client needs. Understanding the client's objectives and services requirements is only one part of the relationship. Communication techniques preferred by the client must also be clearly understood. Does the client use e-mail to communicate regularly with associates and consultants? If so, regular e-mail from the project manager describing project status, issues that require resolution, schedule adjustments, etc., will probably be expected. If the client is techno-phobic, telephone calls or meetings will be necessary. Don't make assumptions about communications — ask!

Value profile. Many clients in the private sector are familiar with value concepts and therefore will be receptive to them. Others are not (particularly those in the public sector) and will need to be educated on the benefits for all involved. You must understand the services the client needs and the value the client is likely to receive from your firm's services before entering into a contractual agreement. For example, if the service saves weeks or even months of governmental processing delays, a substantial value condition exists that can be captured by a knowledgeable firm. Or, if a design will save construction time and reduce costs over a more traditional approach, the savings represent value created by design or management talent that should be compensated accordingly.

Consider the strength of the client relationship in determining which value-pricing technique to use. If you have used the same contract type (for example, cost plus fixed fee) for the past 10 years and the client has steadfastly refused to alter any of its contractual provisions, then value-oriented contracts are probably not possible. This same client may consider, however, a lump-sum contract for certain tasks. Propose only those techniques that have the highest potential for acceptance.

Competition. If the services you provide in a particular area are also available from many other firms and your client typically conducts competitive selection for services, then your value-pricing options are more restricted than in situations where your services are either rare or unique. In less competitive markets, pricing that achieves "what the market will bear" is an effective, time-honored value-pricing technique. If you are in a competitive market, however, don't despair. There are ways (see techniques list below) to create value-pricing opportunities.

Staffing selection. We are all different. This reality can create value opportunities in almost every client situation. The client whose project must be completed in three weeks should be assigned to a staff team that is highly motivated to meet deadlines. The client who wants a world-class design should receive the attention of your most talented designer. Closely matching client needs with your firm's capabilities can position you to capture maximum value from each assignment.

Value-Pricing Techniques

Many tools are available to help you move toward value pricing in your firm. An exhaustive listing is available from *PSMJ Resources*[5] and in Ronald J. Baker's book *The Professional's Guide to Value Pricing*.[6] A summary of several of the more easily implemented techniques are described below.

Change contract form. Ironically, the most readily available tool for value pricing is typically the least used in the design industry: the lump-sum contract. There are risks inherent in this type of contract for firms that do not have adequate financial data on the costs for producing various assignments. Without knowledge of what it costs to complete a task or series of tasks, any pricing will be hit or miss, with corresponding impacts on profitability. Another important factor is a mutual understanding between the A/E/C and the client on the specific services being provided, described in a definitive scope of services. However, when properly used, the lump-sum contract can result in much higher profits than cost-based pricing.

Define unique services. Niche-marketing principles can be used to create increased value. When a firm provides a service that is in high demand relative to supply, substantial value opportunities exist. How can an architect or civil engineer involved in a general practice achieve the benefits of niche marketing? One way might be to ask clients how your services could be modified to create more value for them. An example is developing techniques for faster completion of working drawings.

Stop sooner. Continuing to strive for design perfection has killed more than one potential profitable project. Even time and materials contracts have limits usually established to maintain financial control. Most of the critical elements of a task are completed in the early stages of the project time line; subsequent efforts usually provide only refinements, not major rework. Initiating a design review when

50 percent of the budget is expended can ensure that only necessary refinements are completed, saving value and time that is often wasted.

Develop faster techniques. As the saying goes, "time is money." If you can provide a service equivalent to your competition in a shorter time frame, you have created value for the client. It is surprising how few design firms take advantage of this simple rule. To do this consistently requires staff commitment, efficient support systems and proactive project management. Administrative assistants who can assist project managers in providing faster responses to clients, organize meetings, and prepare and distribute timely communications can create value far in excess of their salaries.

Increase client loyalty. How many of your clients also use your competitors? Customer loyalty creates many opportunities for providing value. Loyalty often takes the form of repeat business that does not involve competitive bidding. Marketing costs are therefore reduced, increasing profitability. Review your client list and identify those clients with whom you would like to develop a "Learning Relationship." Assign project managers who communicate well to those clients; train them in the principles of "one-to-one marketing" and watch your profits increase.

Cut your client list. Not all clients have the same value. Some have more challenging projects, generate more profits or are simply more fun! However, you must proceed carefully in pursuing this approach. Start by identifying the "nightmare" clients and vowing not to work with them again. Then prioritize the remaining clients into high, medium and low value potential. Be sure that the firm's key resources are applied to the high-value clients and that minimal resources are provided to those with low value. Further guidance on this subject is available from the Peppers and Rogers Group electronic newsletter at http://www.1to1.com.

Now or Never!

The time to improve your firm's profitability is now — especially when the economy is on the upswing. While competition ebbs and flows with economic cycles, not all firms are affected similarly. Did you ever wonder why your competitor across town is hiring (or laying off) staff when you are not?

To ensure that your value-pricing efforts are beneficial, a systematic approach is needed to guide and evaluate your actions. A written plan is the best way to document your intentions. Without one, you will never really know if the techniques you used achieved the desired results. As noted by Clare Ross in the *Professional Services Management Association* (PSMA) document entitled, "Value Marketing":

> "... receiving value-based compensation from your clients requires a rethinking of existing marketing approaches. Marketing planning ... is the essential first step in developing a process for value marketing in the design firm." [7]

A key element of this type of marketing is demonstrating to clients, through specific project examples, how your firm creates value in the provision of services. To do this requires the use of terms that clients associate with value. Typically these terms should reference: dollars saved in design, construction, or operations and maintenance activities; time saved in receiving agency approvals, completing construction or achieving targeted occupancy rates; and reduced time and costs of legal defense.

Orient your marketing plan to emphasize client types that are receptive to value messages. Be prepared to provide specific project examples and client testimonials that validate your examples. Train all project managers in effective ways to communicate value techniques in their discussions with clients. Monitor results and adjust your message to achieve the goals you have set for value pricing.

Be creative. Take some calculated risks. Using a lump-sum contract pricing scheme might actually give you a competitive edge. At a minimum, the client will perceive a benefit in knowing exactly how much it will pay for a specific service. If you play your cards correctly, your clients will be happier, and you will have more financial rewards for your efforts.

Endnotes

[1] "Financial Performance in Design Firms, 18th Annual," *PSMJ Resources Inc.* 1998: 25.

[2] "Financial Statistics Survey," *Professional Services Management Journal* 1990: 20.

[3] "Total Return to Investors: 10 Years," *Fortune 500: The Medians*
    www.pathfinder.com/fortune/fortune500/medians6.html.

[4] Don Peppers, and Martha Rogers, Ph.D., *Enterprise One to One: Tools for Competing in the Interactive Age*. (New York: Doubleday, 1999) 13-16.

[5] Frank A. Stasiowski, *Value Pricing for the Design Firm* (John Wiley & Sons, 1993).

[6] Ronald J. Baker, *The Professional's Guide to Value Pricing* (New York: Harcourt Brace Professional Publications, 1999).

[7] Clare Ross, *Value Marketing: Eliminating Fee Bidding & Getting More Clients*, Professional Services Management Association, Focus Group Report (1991).

Bibliography

Baker, Ronald J. *The Professional's Guide to Value Pricing.* 1999.

Financial Performance in Design Firms, 18th Annual Survey and Report. PSMJ Resources Inc. 1998.

Financial Statistics Survey. Professional Services Management Journal. 1990.

Peppers, Don, and Martha Rogers, Ph.D. *Enterprise One to One: Tools for Competing in the Interactive Age.* 1999.

Peppers and Rogers Group. *Inside1to1.* Web newsletter at http://www.1to1.com.

Practice Management Associates, Ltd. *Value Pricing, Negotiating and Contracting.* Seminar Notebook. 1990.

Ross, Clare. *Value Marketing: Eliminating Fee Bidding & Getting More Clients*, Professional Services Management Association, Focus Group Report, 1991.

Stasiowski, Frank A. *Value Pricing for the Design Firm.* 1993.

—. *Value Pricing.* PSMJ Resources. Executive Briefing Series Audio Cassette. 1990.

"Total Return to Investors: 10 Years." *Fortune 500, The Medians* (April 1999) as reported at http://www.pathfinder.com/fortune/fortune500/medians6.html.

Thomas E. Smith Jr., AICP, FSMPS

- Thomas Smith is president of BonTerra Consulting, a woman-owned small business environmental planning and natural resources management firm based in California. The firm specializes in impact assessment and biological resources studies and habitat restoration services for controversial projects for both public and private sector clients.
- As a founder of the company, Smith has been responsible for new business development and marketing since its inception in 1996.
- He has been a practicing environmental planner and program manager for 25 years and has been marketing professional services for more than 20 years.
- He is currently serving on the SMPS National Certification Committee. He was the SMPS Region 6 (Pacific South) director in 1993-1994 and served as the SMPS National Publications Committee chair from 1990-1993.

5.8 Marketing Factors to Consider Prior to an Acquisition, Merger or Ownership Transition

Brian J. Lewis, P.E.
Principal
The Brian J. Lewis Co.

"Change is not made without inconvenience, even from worse to better."

— **Richard Hooker, 1554-1600**

"The body of Benjamin Franklin, Printer (like the cover of an old book, its contents torn out and stripped of its lettering and gilding), lies here, food for worms; but the work shall not be lost, for it will (as he believed) appear once more in a new and more elegant edition, revised and corrected by the Author."

— Epitaph on Himself (composed in 1728)
Benjamin Franklin, 1706-1790

Potential firm buyers or the likely dominant party in the merger of two firms (there rarely is a merger between two equals, in fact a merger is often a euphemism for a sale by the seller) generally have concluded their strategic goals cannot be met by continued internally generated (organic) growth and that market growth can be met best by acquisition or merger.

Thus, before any acquisition or merger action is initiated, firm principals need to evaluate the consequences of their actions in relation to the firm's marketing. The motivations of sellers and buyers are not necessarily complementary, and without advance preparation, the acquirer may learn too late that the acquisition has not been "made without inconvenience."

Buyers' and sellers' motivations and their impacts on marketing include the following:

Buyer's Motivations	Seller's Motivations
• Grow by acquisition instead of organically. • Enter new territory/markets. • Acquire new disciplines/capabilities. • Acquire additional staff. • Gain entry to seller's national clients in the buyer's region. • Gain entry into new, growing markets to replace diminishing old markets. • Opportunity for staff growth. • Failure to address adequately a past mistake; has "poisoned the well" with prospects.	• Release of equity. • Tired of "fighting the battle." • Lack of qualified staff to follow seller as leader/seller/entrepreneur. • Retaining or adding key staff. • Old market(s) shrinking; inability to adjust to need for new clients/markets. • Inability or unwillingness to meet new client or market requirements.

Buyer's Marketing Considerations	Seller's Marketing Considerations
• Need to understand the culture of the acquired firm and its markets. • Learn territorial/market idiosyncrasies. • Need to understand marketing requirements of new disciplines; train staff in same. • Understand acquired clients and their needs. • Learn how to serve new markets with different requirements from established clients. • Ensure next generation is trained in marketing.	• Diminution of firm's ability to finance non-revenue activities. • Loss of old, established contacts. • Failure to keep abreast of clients' new generational needs. • Loss of client contacts as "skinners" (those accustomed to "doing" the technical work) take over from "hunters" (those accustomed to stalking the client and "bringing home the bacon" for others to handle the specifics of the project). • Revenues diminish in mature markets and are not replaced by revenues from emerging markets. • Loss of marketplace credibility. Need to learn the "new game."

Three Common Models for Acquisitions/Mergers

Acquisitions/mergers may take several forms, each of which has different marketing implications. From the marketing viewpoint, three basic unions generally occur. (See Figure 1 on the next page.)

End-to-End

Two firms without technical disciplines and client types in common join in an end-to-end union, hoping that each can sell the other's capabilities as its own. Well managed, the potential for gain may be the greatest, but an in-depth evaluation of the seller's marketing activities is warranted to ensure the buyer can evolve a viable game plan to take over and, particularly, replace those departing as a consequence of the sale.

Particular attention must be paid to determine if the two units are truly end-to-end or whether there is a gap between them. If the latter, how will the gap be bridged?

Marketing considerations could include style, market and generational differences between the two firms' staffs and clients. Particular emphasis will be needed on staff training within each unit to minimize client migration to other service providers.

Overlapping

Although there is some overlapping of both client types and disciplines, each firm has a unique client and work area. The buyer needs to ensure it can comfortably address the needs of clients not previously served. This is particularly true for clients retained by the seller due to old political or generational friendships. If the departing seller has been a business "rainmaker," the buyer must determine if other staff can step in and perform the same function, and if not, how will new business acquisition be addressed?

It will be important to assess whether there is simply a market overlap or whether client types within those markets also overlap. For example, luxury cars and minivans are both in the automotive market but the buyers' needs and sales pitch to which each responds are quite different. Again, staff training will be essential to maximize old client retention and new client capture. However, in some situations training alone may not be sufficient, it may be that new staff will need to be brought on board to address changing firm goals and to fill staffing gaps that may become apparent as the merger, acquisition or union unfolds.

Parallel or Side by Side

Two firms with similar disciplines, types of clients and maybe territory, join together to effect greater market spread or penetration. Because they probably have so much in common, there should be few marketing wrinkles the buyer needs to learn. Primary attention will need to be directed to bringing about smooth client transfers from the seller to the buyer.

Particular attention should be paid to ensuring matches between individual client representatives' styles and the new service provider's representatives' styles. It is a version of "there are horses for courses."

Figure 1
Types of Design Firms Acquisitions/Mergers

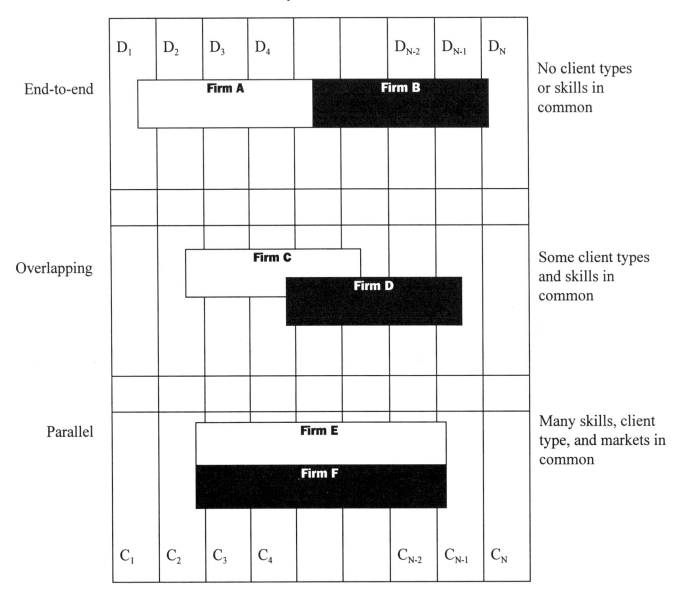

Disciplines or skills

Types of clients or markets

What About Marketing? Key Questions to Ask

Questions that should be asked and answered dispassionately before committing to a purchase/merger are listed below.

Who has handled the seller's marketing and selling? This question is particularly essential when the departing seller is an entrepreneurial founder and/or chief rainmaker. Has the seller had long-established links with client representatives that may be difficult to replicate? This may be compounded when a client is in the course of its own generational change of leadership.

The buyer should draw up a list of key or major seller clients and be able to place the name of one of its own appropriately matched client representatives against each name (without adverse impact on its current clients) and indicate what available resources can be furnished to ensure acquired client retention. Unless the buyer devises a viable marketing game plan to address this question, revenues may fall.

Are the clients personally committed to the seller? If some clients have a personal relationship with the seller, will they transfer that relationship to the buyer or will they use the seller's departure as an opportunity to transfer their business to another firm that has been courting them for a long time? This concern is particularly germane where the client ties may be generational in nature and where the client could well use a "changing of the guard" in each organization as reason for switching service providers.

Could the seller be impacted adversely by the loss of one or two key clients? Examination of a list of clients constituting 80 percent of the seller's revenues should be made. It might indicate that loss of one or two key clients due to the sale/merger would be very detrimental. Evaluate this likelihood. Do 80 percent of the revenues come from 20 percent of the clients? Can you devise a viable strategy to prevent key client loss?

By selling to a larger firm will the seller lose a small business or minority set-aside position? If the seller has been able to capture some governmental business through small business set-aside programs, will union with the buyer preclude such project capture due to overall larger firm size? Continuing the seller's firm as a wholly owned subsidiary may not solve the problem.

This question may be compounded if the seller is a minority firm and the buyer is not. While a minority firm may truthfully claim that it has progressed technically and professionally to the point where it can acquire work on its own capability merits, the reality may be that a selection "tie-breaker" used by some clients is a desire to involve minority-owned firms on their projects.

Will common clients continue to use both firms? Where both buyer and seller have clients in common, will those clients continue the same volume of business with the successor firm? Or might some say, in effect, "In the interest of spreading our work around several firms, we will not be able to maintain the volumes you both received independently." Can you live with the worst-case scenario?

Is the seller running out of markets or unable to attract needed staff? Running out of markets, not being able to hire needed staff, or inability or unwillingness of existing staff to learn or adapt to current marketing techniques is often a motivation for selling, but can they be overcome by the buyer? The buyer may be able to add technical staff, but what is needed to address a declining market?

Does the seller have ghosts in the closet the buyer can exorcize? If the buyer has suspicions the seller has not revealed all past ghosts or skeletons, an image survey may reveal some and enable the buyer to determine if a rehabilitation can be effected. Is there a viable and economical strategy for turning lemons into lemonade?

Should the seller refuse to acquiesce with conduct of an image survey that should be a serious reason for the buyer to pause and reassess its acquisition posture. The buyer should be able to convince the seller that an image survey can be designed to not highlight the seller in the minds of interviewees but merely position the firm as one of a group of firms being assessed. If the seller still demurs, that may be a reason to call off the union.

Are the two firms' cultures compatible, thereby allowing easy meshing of marketing approaches? The largest single reason for failure of acquisitions and mergers is incompatibility of cultures. For example, one firm may be market-driven and the other client-driven. Early comparison of the two firms' cultures will enable the buyer to determine if its marketing approach can be implanted successfully into the seller's organization. If the seller relies on interpersonal relationships for sales, what is the long-term prospect for those relationships? If the buyer uses a multi-faceted, orchestrated sales approach with a marketing/sales staff handing off to service providers, how or will the seller's staff adapt to the new (to them) approach? Can or will seller staff redundancies be expected, voluntarily or involuntarily? If so, what will be their impacts and costs?

Does the seller occupy a niche in the market that would suffer in a broad-based clientele firm? Or vice versa? If one of the parties in the proposed union serves a niche market and the other works with a broad variety of services would the marketplace strength of the niche firm be affected adversely by becoming part of a supermarket of services? Would they lose their unique selling proposition?

Can the seller survive a head office/branch office relationship? If the seller has existed as an autonomous firm and now is to become a branch office, how will key staff react to being directed from afar? Conversely, does the buyer's staff need training in how to relate to a branch office? Will training be needed by both sides?

Does the seller have conflicting, ongoing joint venture or prime/sub relationships that would have to be addressed? The seller may have joint venture or prime/sub relationships with other service providers that might have a conflict with similar relationships held by the buyer. How might these be addressed? Should any of these arrangements be eliminated from the buy/sell/merge transaction by, for example, disposition to a third party?

Are there areas of ongoing competition between the two organizations that should be addressed and/or eliminated? There may be current or potential future job opportunities where the two parties are in real or potential competition. Should these be allowed to proceed unaltered until after the sale/merger is completed or would both parties be served better by some modification of their respective arrangements forthrightly?

Are there marketing technology incompatibilities? Do the two parties have technological, system, software or other incompatibilities that will need to be addressed? What would be the time frame and cost?

Can the buyer allocate adequate resources to bring the seller's marketing into line without adversely impacting ongoing marketing activities? Considerable effort will be needed to integrate the seller's marketing with the buyer's. This effort should be analyzed in advance to determine if it can be effected without prejudicing ongoing marketing activities. Can the activities be conducted in a timely fashion?

Steps for a Smoother Transition

Necessary steps that will require investing marketing staff hours and financial resources include, but are not limited to, the following:

1. Analyze the seller's marketing organization by answering the questions listed above.
2. Conduct an image study, if warranted.
3. Prepare a marketing integration game plan.
4. Budget for, and later prepare, new marketing materials, letterhead, business cards, announcements of the union, open houses, publicity, news articles and so on.
5. Introduce the buyer's staff to the seller's staff to effect client hand-off, where needed, and ensure client continuity.
6. Update the seller's strategic plan to reflect the marketing impact of the union and to incorporate the acquired unit into the plan.
7. Arrange appropriate marketing training for both the buyer's and seller's staff to maximize downstream gain from the union.
8. Determine if there is a probable lack-of-fit with any of the acquired staff that cannot be addressed by appropriate training and may necessitate redundancies. How will the impact of such redundancies be addressed? At what cost?

Clearly, marketing concerns can be a major driver in a buyer's decision to initiate and proceed with an acquisition. Once potential acquisition target firms have been identified, rigorous attention to the questions addressed previously will minimize the "inconvenience of change." Indeed, we may remember the words of Thomas Carlyle that "Today is not yesterday … change, indeed is painful, yet ever needful." Proactively managed, change can be enjoyable and worthwhile.

T. Boone Pickens, a corporate raider who enriched himself and his stockholders with many unsolicited corporate acquisitions, opined, "I have always believed that it's important to show a new look periodically. Predictability can lead to failure."

Bibliography

Baron, Paul B. "When You Buy or Sell a Company." Meriden, CT: The Center for Business Information Inc., 1986.

Cooper, David G. *Architectural and Engineering Salesmanship.* New York: John Wiley & Sons, 1978.

Coxe, Weld. *Marketing Architectural and Engineering Services*, 2nd ed. New York: Van Nostrand Reinhold, 1983.

Coxe, Weld, and Brian J. Lewis, et al. *Success Strategies for Design Professionals.* New York: McGraw-Hill, 1987.

Gilmore, Thomas North. "Making a Leadership Change." San Francisco: Jossey-Bass, 1988.

Lewis, Brian J. "The Business of Consulting Engineering." American Consulting Engineers Council, 1998.

—. "A New Model for Successful Management of Engineering Design Firms — SuperPositioning." *Engineering Management International* 5 (1988): 31-44.

—. "The Globalization of Consulting Engineers." *Engineering Management Journal* 4 (1992).

—. "Consulting Engineers Must Adapt Practice to a New Global Market." *American Consulting Engineer* 4 (1993): 33-36.

Maister, David H. "True Professionalism." New York: The Free Press, 1997.

—. "Managing the Professional Service Firm." New York: The Free Press, 1993.

PSMJ. "The Complete Guide to Ownership Transition." Newton, MA: PSMJ Resources, Inc., 1996.

Scanlon, Brian. *Marketing of Engineering Services.* London: Thomas Telford, 1988.

Weingardt, Richard. "Forks in the Road." Denver: Palamar Publishing, 1998.

Brian J. Lewis, P.E.

- Brian J. Lewis has acted as a management and marketing consultant to firms in the built and natural environments since 1980.
- His prior experience includes 26 years in consulting engineering, including founding a 60-person firm and acting as marketing vice president and president of a 550-person environmental firm.
- His experience with firm acquisitions commenced in the 1960s when he acquired two engineering firms to gain geographical market expansion for his consulting engineering firm in Bellevue, Wash. Subsequently, he oversaw two acquisitions while associated with a large environmental consulting firm.
- He now specializes and consults on aspects of firm acquisitions and mergers for clients in the United States, United Kingdom, Germany and Australasia.
- His activities have included acting as a consultant to the Treasury of the Government of New Zealand on aspects of privatization and sale of a government-owned, 1,200-person, engineering/architecture firm and a civil engineering construction firm.
- He is the author of *The Business of Consulting Engineering*, American Consulting Engineers Council (1998), and co-author of *Success Strategies for Design Professionals* (New York: McGraw-Hill, 1987).
- He acts as associate editor of "The Forum" section of ASCE's bi-monthly *Journal of Management in Engineering*.
- He has written, published and lectured on the marketing of professional services in the United States, United Kingdom and New Zealand.
- Lewis earned a bachelor's degree in civil engineering from the University of Durham, United Kingdom, and a master's degree in engineering from U.C.L.A. He also holds a post-graduate certificate in public health engineering from King's College, Newcastle-upon-Tyne, United Kingdom.
- He joined SMPS in its founding year, and is a fellow of the American Society of Civil Engineers and of the Institute of Transportation Engineers. He is a member of the American Council of Consulting Engineers.
- In spring 1999 he merged The Brian J. Lewis Co. with FMI Corp. and now practices from its Denver, Colo., office.
- Lewis is a Registered Professional Civil Engineer in 11 states, and is a Registered Professional Traffic Engineer in California.

5.9 Contracts

Dennis B. Schultz, Esq.
Richard T. Hewlett, Esq.
Shareholders
Butzel Long P.C.

Overview

Agreements involving design professionals in the construction industry range from the simple to the complex. Generally the size and scope of the project, as well as the range of services to be performed by the design professional, dictate the type and complexity of the professional services contract. The design professional should strive to reach an agreement that clearly defines: (1) Its responsibilities on the project; (2) The responsibilities of the party with whom it is contracting; (3) The specific scope of its work; (4) Its compensation for services, including additional services, and whether reimbursable expenses will be recovered; (5) The time period in which the work should be performed; and, (6) Under what conditions the relationship may be terminated. Likewise, in any agreement, the design professional should attempt to balance the risks inherent in providing its services on the project with its obligations under the agreement. In other words, only agree to be responsible for the things that you can control. Finally, the design professional should strive to enter into agreements that are clear, concise and unambiguous, so as to attempt to avoid disputes at a later date concerning the language of its agreement.

This chapter is intended to provide a general overview of contract formation principles, various contract forms that are used by design professionals on construction projects and discuss specific contract provisions that are often used in contracts.

Contract Formation

What is a contract? A contract is an exchange of promises between two or more parties that creates a legal obligation between them. For example, one party agrees to provide a certain service; the other party agrees to pay a certain amount for that service.

Offer: An "offer" occurs when a party offers to perform a service or provide a good in exchange for certain consideration, or a party offers to pay a certain amount in exchange for receiving a service or a good. An offer that is limited as to the length of time it will remain open for acceptance is called a "firm offer."

Acceptance: A party "accepts" an offer when it agrees to provide a service or exchange certain consideration for the service. A party may accept an offer by simply engaging in the performance of the service that is requested. A response to an offer that varies the terms of the offer is deemed to be a counter-proposal or counter-offer and is not an acceptance of the offer. (It is then up to the original offerer to decide whether it wants to accept the counter-offer on the same terms as proposed or make its own counter-offer.)

Consideration: Consideration is defined to be the "value" that is exchanged between the parties to a contract. It can consist of promises, services, goods and/or money.

The Different Forms of Contracts

Oral Contracts

An oral contract is a contract based on spoken words and is formed when parties exchange verbal promises between each other. One advantage to an oral contract is that it is more easily reached and may be simpler to create than a written contract. A disadvantage to an oral contract is that it is, or may be, harder to prove its exact terms in the event of a dispute. Another disadvantage to an oral contract is that it is often subject to different interpretations by the parties.

Written Contracts

A written contract is created by an exchange of written promises between two or more parties. Examples of written contracts are described below.

Letter of Intent. A letter of intent generally describes what form of agreement the parties intend to enter as well as the material terms of their agreement. A letter of intent may itself be a binding agreement between parties.

Letter Agreements. There are occasions when a design professional will simply have an agreement in the form of a letter with its client. Letter agreements are enforceable as a contract, just as a more formal written agreement. In any letter agreement, at a minimum, the following items should be specified in detail:

- Scope of work to be performed.
- Time in which the work is to be performed.
- Terms and conditions in which payment will be made.

Standard Form Contract. There are a series of standard contracts that are often used by design professionals that have been issued by the American Institute of Architects (AIA). The AIA contract documents attempt to provide uniformity and consistency on a wide range of issues pertaining to various services, depending on the type of relationship between the design professional and its client. The AIA documents that are generally used in the owner/design professional relationship are:

- AIA Document B141 Standard Form of Agreement between the Owner and the Architect in multi-part format (also see Construction Manager edition B141-CM).
- AIA Document A201 General Conditions of the Contract for Construction (which is a supplement to the Standard Form of Agreement).

- AIA Document B151 Abbreviated Standard Form of Agreement between Owner and Architect.
- AIA Document B161 Owner/Architect for Designated Services.
- AIA Document B171 for Interior Design Services.
- AIA Document B727 for Owner/Architect for Special Services.
- AIA Document B901 for Design/Build Services.

Customized Contracts. In addition to the variety of standard agreements provided by the AIA, or other construction or design associations, design professionals may elect to use a customized contract. Generally, customized contracts incorporate many provisions of the standard AIA form agreements, but include various revisions to those documents that reflect a project's specific requirements and allocate risks appropriately. When using customized contracts, the design professional should be aware of provisions that purport to change the standard of practice in the industry and change the responsibilities between the design professional and client so as to place an undue burden or risk on the design professional. It is not unusual for the owner to require the use of the owner's customized contract. Beware, from a risk-management standpoint, these contracts must be carefully reviewed. The design professional may find that there are clauses contained within the contract that are simply not worth the risk. One example of a possible "deal breaker," may be the owner's insistence that the design professional comply with "all published guidelines."

The purposes of a contract are:

- To appropriately allocate the risk between parties.
- To avoid ambiguity in connection with the material obligations and responsibilities between the parties.
- To establish time lines and compensation.

Important Contract Provisions

Scope of the Work to Be Performed

One of the most critical items in any agreement made by the design professional is to identify in specific terms the scope of work to be performed. The more detailed the description of the scope of services, the better chance the design professional has of avoiding disputes concerning its services down the road. This rings particularly true with respect to changes in scope made by the owner or others to the project during the course of the design professional's work. If the design professional has a detailed scope of work prepared, supported by estimates showing what it anticipated doing, then it will have greater leverage in obtaining additional fees for performing work that it can show is beyond the original scope.

The Design Professional's Obligations

Related to the scope of work definition is the detail concerning the identification of the obligations of the design professional under the agreement. The design professional should carefully review all of the obligations it intends to perform during the course of a project and make sure they are accurately reflected in the context of its agreement. There are numerous responsibilities that can be associated with the design professional's services on any given project. Some examples are:

- Will consultants be required to perform some of the work, and if so, how will they be used?
- During what time period will the professional services be performed?
- What is the standard of care to be used to measure the design professional's services?
- Whether the owner or others will use a designated representative(s)?
- The handling of client information and whether it is deemed confidential?
- The design professional's obligation to review and abide by laws, codes and regulations that concern the project.
- The development and completion of drawings, specifications and other documents, including those in electronic form, and the issue of copyright protection for its work product.
- Whether project administration services will be provided and, if so, the scope and nature of those services, and the corresponding compensation?
- The design professional's obligation to provide preliminary evaluations and planning services with respect to the cost of the project and budget.

Responsibilities of the Owner

Every design professional contract should identify with specificity the obligations that the owner, or person with whom the design professional is contracting, has to the design professional. These obligations should also be defined as to the time periods in which the owner or client will complete the obligations. The design professional should also consider including a provision concerning when additional compensation is due, should the owner deviate from its obligations. Typical owner responsibilities include:

- Providing full information regarding requirements for the project, including a detailed description of the program objectives, scheduling, space requirements and relationships.
- An overall budget for the project including the construction costs.
- Evidence of the owner's financial stability.
- Whether the owner has designated a representative authorized to act on the owner's behalf.
- Providing detailed information that the owner may have in its possession concerning physical characteristics of the project site and other drawings concerning existing portions of the project to the design professional.
- Identifying whether other consultants will be involved on the project.
- Providing all legal accounting and insurance counseling services as may be necessary.
- Providing prompt written notice to the architect if the owner believes any fault or defect in the project exists or there is a non-conformity in the contract documents.

Construction Cost of the Work

Generally the written agreement should include a definition of what constitutes the "construction cost" of the work. This is particularly important if the design professional's fee is based on a percentage of the cost of the project. The agreement should identify exactly what categories of cost constitute the "cost of the work" and how the fee will be calculated.

Use of Architect's Drawings, Specifications and Other Documents

The design professional should confirm that its drawings, specifications and other documents, including those in electronic form, are to be used solely for the project at issue. The architect and its consultants should be identified as the authors and owners of the documents and retain all rights including copyrights to those documents. The issue of whether the design professional grants a non-exclusive license to reproduce the documents to the owner, may be considered.

Alternate Dispute Resolution

The design professional should consider whether it wants to include alternate dispute resolution procedures in its agreement. The primary mechanisms are mandatory, non-binding mediation and arbitration administered by the American Arbitration Association (AAA) pursuant to the Construction Industry Arbitration Rules of the AAA. The typical provisions follow.

Mediation generally involves any dispute between the parties and provides that any dispute between the parties shall be submitted to mediation as a condition precedent to an arbitration or legal proceeding. What is mediation? A procedure in which the parties submit their dispute, including the details of their positions, to an independent, third-party mediator. The mediator then discusses the dispute with the parties, including the mediator's view of the strengths and weaknesses of each party's position. The mediator then helps the parties attempt to reach a settlement of their dispute. The parties are generally obligated to demand mediation pursuant to the construction industry mediation rules of the AAA. The parties may agree to have a private mediation outside of the AAA rules as well. Generally the procedure is required to be completed within 30 to 60 days. In the event the parties do not resolve their dispute through the mediation process, then, typically, the parties proceed to arbitration (or litigation, if otherwise agreed).

Arbitration Agreements. In order to have a binding arbitration agreement, the parties must, in writing, agree to submit any claim or dispute to arbitration. Generally the parties agree to submit the arbitration to the AAA per the Construction Industry Arbitration Rules. Many design professionals have developed their own set of arbitration provisions that address such issues as the number and qualifications of the arbitrators; the types and amounts of claims that may be arbitrated; and the procedure itself, including whether discovery is permitted, whether the rules of evidence apply, whether it is an AAA or private arbitration and whether the award is appealable. The decision of the arbitrator(s) is binding on the parties, and the arbitration takes the place of a lawsuit. An important feature of arbitration is that it is a private proceeding.

Waiver of Consequential Damages

Consequential damages are those damages that are not directly caused by the breach, but may result from it. The new 1997 AIA documents contemplate the parties' waiving claims for consequential damages against each other. The waiver of consequential damages should be clear and specify the kinds of consequential damages that are considered to be waived, including home office overhead, loss profits and the like.

Termination of the Services

The design professional should insist that the agreement clearly defines under what circumstances the owner/client or the design professional may terminate the services. Particularly important is whether the services may be terminated at will (i.e., for convenience) and, if so, what compensation shall be due to the design professional under that circumstance. In addition, notice requirements should be included in the agreement, indicating as to what notice should be given prior to termination.

The agreement may also contain provisions as to what constitutes termination for cause. Those matters should be specifically identified, and, again, language should be included as to what constitutes the basis for a "for cause" termination.

Conclusion

This article has presented a brief survey of contract principles applicable to contracts between design professionals and their clients. It should be clear that a properly prepared contract is critical to the avoidance of disputes and in identifying the rights and obligations of the parties to the transaction. It should be equally clear that obtaining legal advice from a knowledgeable attorney is also extremely important to assuring that a contract is properly prepared.

Dennis B. Schultz, Esq.

- Dennis B. Schultz is a shareholder practicing in Butzel Long's Detroit office. He is an honors graduate of Wayne State University and a *cum laude* graduate of the Detroit College of Law at Michigan State University, where he was an editor-in-chief of the *Detroit College of Law Review.* Prior to beginning his legal career, he spent more than 10 years in construction contracting and real estate development.
- Schultz has represented owners, general contractors, construction managers and subcontractors in negotiating and drafting contract documents and negotiated settlements of claims on a variety of construction projects, including design, product and system performance, contractor performance and numerous contract disputes.
- He has served as lead counsel in the litigation of claims on major construction projects, including public and private projects such as office complexes, waste water treatment plants, industrial processing facilities, manufacturing facilities, automobile manufacturing plants and major health care projects. His experience includes numerous arbitrations of disputes and litigation in the state and federal courts of Michigan, Ohio, Pennsylvania, New Jersey, Illinois, Colorado and Washington, D.C. Disputes have involved amounts ranging from $100,000 to $35 million.
- Schultz serves as administrator of Butzel Long's business litigation practice. He is a member of the American Bar Association and the State Bar of Michigan, of which he is a member of the Construction Law, Alternative Dispute Resolution, Real Estate and Litigation sections.

Richard T. Hewlett, Esq.

- Richard T. Hewlett is a shareholder in Butzel Long's Detroit office, primarily practicing in the areas of business and commercial litigation, dispute resolution, sports law, construction law and professional liability matters involving attorneys, accountants and architects. He is a graduate of the University of Michigan and the Detroit College of Law at Michigan State University.
- Hewlett has concentrated his practice on the prosecution and defense of a variety of business matters, professional negligence and liability claims, and commercial, business and construction disputes. He also has extensive experience in advising clients on contract matters as well as drafting and negotiating construction and business contracts. Hewlett has been involved in numerous shareholder disputes in closely held companies, partnership disputes and matters involving non-competition agreements and confidentiality clauses.
- He is active in the State Bar of Michigan Litigation Section. He also speaks at the Federal Bar Association's New Lawyer Seminar on basic state court practice twice a year. He is a member of the State Bar of Michigan, the American Bar Association and the Metropolitan Detroit Bar Association.

Acknowledgment

Special thanks to Steven H. Rosenfeld, AIA, who authored the original chapter about contracts for the first edition of *The Handbook for Marketing Professional Services.*

5.10 Key Areas of Potential Marketing Liability

J. Michael Huget, Esq.
Butzel Long P.C.

The emergence of the information age has focused more awareness on property rights in intangible works. This new era is one of both risk and reward for those engaged in marketing. While there is an ever-increasing risk of liability for using another's intellectual property, there are also significant opportunities to profit from the exploitation of intellectual property, so long as the appropriate measures are taken to protect such information.

The Fundamentals of Intellectual Property Protection

What "intellectual property" has as a common thread is that it involves property originating with ideas. The phrase "intellectual property" typically refers to patents, trademarks, copyrights and trade secrets. In addition, marketers must be mindful of individual rights analogous to "intellectual property" — namely, an individual's right to control the use of his or her name, image and likeness. Although each form of intellectual property is distinct, and has a separate body of governing law, there is overlap. Often there can be several types of intellectual property protection relating to a single product. For example, consider a pharmaceutical product: conceivably, there could be a patent on the formula, a trademark on the name (e.g., "CLARATIN"), and a copyright on the advertising materials (brochures, etc.) that feature the product.

Patents

A patent is a federally granted monopoly that provides the owner with the exclusive right to make, use or sell the patented invention for a period of 20 years. A patent can be obtained on any invention that is novel, non-obvious and useful. Because a patent is a government-sanctioned monopoly, an applicant is put to a demanding examination process with the U.S. Patent and Trademark Office. Once a patent is obtained, however, the owner possesses a potentially significant competitive advantage that can be commercially exploited.

Trade Secrets

A trade secret may consist of any formula, pattern, device or compilation of information used in one's business, which gives the owner of the information a competitive advantage over competitors that do not possess the information. Unlike a patent, there is no formal governmental recognition of information as a "trade secret" unless a trade secret owner is required to enforce its rights in court. Trade secrets can remain protectable so long as the information is maintained in confidence, and not publicly disclosed. Great care must therefore be taken to maintain secrecy. For example, access to the information should be restricted to those who need to have it, and secrecy agreements should be signed with all those who will have access to the information.

Compared with a patent, a wider variety of information can be considered a trade secret. For example, under the appropriate circumstances, customer lists can be considered a trade secret. However, protecting trade secrets is more difficult because of the lack of an official government imprimatur (except as may be acquired through litigation) that the information is a "trade secret."

Copyrights

Like a patent, a copyright is a federally granted monopoly. A copyright provides its owner with the exclusive right to reproduce, distribute, publicly perform or display, or create derivative works from original works of authorship. Copyrights differ significantly from patents in that copyrights protect only the expression of a particular idea, and not the underlying idea itself.

One of the most common misconceptions about copyrights pertains to creation and ownership. A copyright arises upon creation of a work, and not the registration of that work with the Library of Congress. Absent a writing expressly transferring ownership of a copyright, or a "work for hire" arrangement, the copyright is owned by the creator. Thus, when an advertiser hires an advertising agency to create advertising materials, the materials are owned by the agency and not the advertiser unless there is a specific writing that transfers ownership. In turn, any independent contractor hired by the advertising agency owns whatever work he or she created absent an agreement to the contrary. As such, it is critically important for any person or entity hiring another person to create works covered by the Copyright Act to make sure ownership issues are properly addressed.

This issue is even more critical because of the significant range of works covered by the Copyright Act, including musical works (including accompanying words), literary works, dramatic works, pictorial, graphic and sculptural works, motion pictures and other audiovisual works, sound recordings and architectural works. The threshold requirement to obtain a copyright is that such works must be original and fixed in a tangible form. Thus, any form of advertising and marketing material is subject to the copyright laws, but the ideas underlying such material cannot be protected.

Although not absolutely necessary, it is advisable to mark in a prominent place all works with the copyright symbol ("©") along with the year of creation. For example:

© 1999 Butzel Long

or

Copyright 1999 Butzel Long

However, the failure to include a notice will not cause a loss of the copyright.

Trademarks

A trademark is a name, symbol or device that identifies goods or services. Although most commonly thought of as words or symbols, trademarks can also include smells and sounds. Although there is a federal registration system, obtaining a federally registered trademark (denoted by the "®" symbol) is not necessary to be entitled to trademark protection. The common law also protects trademarks, so long as the trademark owner can prove that members of the relevant consuming public associate the mark with his or her goods or services.

Examples of well-known trademarks include COCA-COLA® and CITIBANK®. A trademark does not give the owner the right to prohibit another from making and selling soft drinks or operating a financial institution, but it does give the trademark owner the right to prohibit another from, for example, naming the soft drink "CLEO COLA" or the bank "CITY BANK."

Service marks are similar to trademarks except that rather than being fixed to a particular product they are associated with a particular service.

Right to Publicity

Well-known people also have a right to control the use of their name, image and likeness, and to prevent others from using their name, image or likeness for advertising purposes. For example, placing the picture of a well-known athlete on a poster promoting a brand of beer would not be permitted absent the athlete's consent. "Image" or "likeness" has also been broadly defined. In a recent well-publicized case, singer Bette Midler successfully sued an advertising agency that hired one of her former backup singers to imitate Midler's voice for a television commercial.

Avoiding Intellectual Property Problems

In all likelihood, there is some sort of intellectual property protection available for almost any sort of creative output. Accordingly, care must be taken to account for all potential intellectual property ownership rights when using materials from other sources.

Copyrights

Because of their pervasiveness, copyrights tend to be the most problematic. For example, photographs may not be borrowed from other sources without first determining whether there is a copyright in that photograph. One of the great fallacies of the Internet era is the widespread belief that because something is available on the Internet, it is presumptively free for others to copy and use. The Internet, however, is fundamentally not any different from any other medium in which expressive works are made available. Simply because a library makes books publicly available free of charge does mean that the reader is free to make copies or otherwise exploit a book from the library for personal gain; likewise, simply because a picture or other content is made available on the Internet does not mean that someone viewing that content is free to download the information and incorporate that into his or her own work.

As such, before incorporating work obtained from another source, it is important to determine the owner of the work. If that cannot be determined, and if the work itself does not contain a license permitting the use contemplated, then there is a risk in using the work.

Another less obvious risk arises from using works created by vendors or independent contractors. As stated earlier, absent an express agreement conveying copyright interests from the independent contractor, the hiring party does not acquire the underlying rights to any intellectual property that was created, even though the hiring party paid for the work. At most, all that has been obtained is a non-exclusive license to use the work for certain purposes. Thus, if a photographer is hired for the purposes of taking a series of photographs to be used in a certain proposal, the hiring party only has a limited license to use those works, and its rights may be limited. There has been significant litigation in the past few years regarding a publisher's right to take previously published articles written by freelance writers and photographers, and to republish those articles as part of an Internet site. Without an express assignment or license of the works at issue to the publishers for all purposes, they have been unable to convince courts that they should have unlimited republication rights. Thus, the most prudent course of action is to require that all independent contractors, freelancers or vendors assign their rights to any copyrightable subject matter to the entity that paid for the work.

Trademarks

Trademarks of another company can be used in marketing materials so long as it is apparent from the usage that no representations are being made that the trademark owner is sponsoring, or is affiliated with, the products or services offered. For example, if a Microsoft software program is referred to, care must be taken not to suggest or imply that Microsoft approves, is affiliated with or in any way sponsors the usage.

If a new product or service is being developed, it is important to determine, before adopting a trademark, whether someone else is using a similar name to identify a product. If a name is adopted that is likely to be confused with another trademark, a court can order such use to cease, and force the destruction of any materials incorporating the infringing name. In addition, in the appropriate circumstances, damages can be awarded for an infringing use.

A trademark is likely to be confused with another trademark if, among other things:

- The marks are similar in sound and or appearance.
- The goods or services to which the marks are applied are related.
- There has been actual confusion between the marks.
- The marketing channels in which the marks are used are similar.

Although there is typically no confusion if the same mark is used for unrelated products (e.g., "Cadillac" for automobiles and for coffee), the Federal Trademark Act (known as the "Lanham Act") was amended a few years ago to provide additional protection for strong and famous marks. Thus, a party is at risk adopting any famous mark (e.g., KODAK) even though the proposed use is for wholly unrelated goods or services.

Other Potential Liability Problems

Liability problems can also be created by making false representations of fact concerning a competitor's goods or services, or regarding one's own goods or services. These problems most often arise when criticizing a competitor's product characteristics or making insupportable statements regarding one's own products.

With respect to statements regarding one's own goods or services, it is important to distinguish between false statements of fact and statements of opinion. Generally, a statement is considered to be a statement of fact, and not opinion, when it can be independently verified (e.g., "Ford is the number one selling car company in the world"). A statement of opinion, also known as "puffery," is more difficult to objectively quantify (e.g., "Ford makes the best cars in the world"). Similarly, making comparative statements concerning a company can create liability problems if statements of fact are made that cannot be verified (e.g., "Ford trucks outsold GM trucks last year") as opposed to comparative statements of opinion (e.g., "Ford trucks are better than GM trucks").

It is also important not to misrepresent the qualifications or attributes of those who are proposing to perform services in proposals. If the qualifications are overstated, and the work performed is inadequate to the point where it causes damage to business or property, the misrepresented qualifications may be used as a basis to impose liability under any number of legal theories, including negligence and fraud.

J. Michael Huget, Esq.

- J. Michael Huget is a shareholder practicing in Butzel Long's Ann Arbor office.
- He is a graduate of the University of Michigan (bachelor's degree, 1982) and the Detroit College of Law (*cum laude*, 1986) where he received the prestigious Edward Rakow Award.
- Huget concentrates his business litigation practice in advertising matters, commercial disputes, trademark and trade secret claims, patent and unfair competition litigation, and contract claims.
- He is an active member of the International Trademark Association Publications Committee.

Acknowledgment

Special thanks to Mary Jane Augustine, Esq., and James E. Frankel, Esq., who authored the original chapter about potential liability in marketing for the first edition of *The Handbook for Marketing Professional Services*.

A

B

C

D